MEDIATION ADVOCACY

Second Edition

John W. Cooley

National Institute for Trial Advocacy

Reproduction Permission
National Institute for Trial Advocacy
Notre Dame Law School
Notre Dame, Indiana 46556
(800) 225-6482   Fax (574) 271-8375
E-mail: nita.1@nd.edu
Web site: www.nita.org

Cooley, John W., *Mediation Advocacy 2d ed.*, (NITA, 2002).

ISBN 1-55681-780-0

Library of Congress Cataloging-in-Publication Data

Cooley, John W., 1943-
    Mediation advocacy / John W. Cooley.--2nd ed.
        p. cm.
    Includes bibliographical references and index.
    ISBN 1-55781-780-0
        1. Mediation--United States. I. Title.

KF9084 .C57 2002
347.73'9--dc21

                            2002071867

MEDIATION ADVOCACY

ABOUT THE AUTHOR

John W. Cooley is a former United States magistrate, assistant United States attorney, senior staff attorney for the United States Court of Appeals for the Seventh Circuit, and a partner in a Chicago law firm. He is a past chairman of the Chicago Bar Association's Arbitration and ADR Committee, a past president of the Chicago Chapter of the Society of Professionals in Dispute Resolution (SPIDR), and the past secretary of the International SPIDR organization, now called the Association for Conflict Resolution.

In private practice in the Chicago area, he currently serves on the judicial panel of Judicial Dispute Resolution, Inc. (JDR) as a mediator, arbitrator, facilitator, and consultant in the design of dispute resolution systems for governments and corporations. Additionally, he has served as a Special Master for federal judges and as an arbitrator and mediator in a wide variety of complex, multimillion dollar antitrust, personal injury, healthcare, medical malpractice, commercial, manufacturing, employment, insurance, banking, communications, and construction disputes, both domestic and international in character. He has conducted ADR training in major United States law firms and multi-day mediation and arbitration training programs for lawyers in Brazil. He is a Fellow of the American Bar Foundation, the International Academy of Mediators, and the Chartered Institute of Arbitrators, London, England.

An adjunct professor of law at Northwestern University School of Law, he teaches a course in negotiation and mediation. In addition, he is the principal designer and instructor of a new mediation advocacy cybercourse that was developed by Northern Illinois University in cooperation with the American Bar Association's Section of Dispute Resolution. He is the author of this NITA book and its earlier (1996) edition; *Arbitration Advocacy* (NITA, 1997 coauthored by Northwestern University Law Professor Steven Lubet); *The Arbitrator's Handbook* (NITA, 1998); *The Mediator's Handbook* (NITA, 2000); *Callaghan's Appellate Advocacy Manual* (Clark Boardman Callaghan, 1989); and more than fifty articles on litigation, judicial, and ADR topics.

Mr. Cooley, a Vietnam War veteran, is a graduate of the United States Military Academy at West Point and the University of Notre Dame Law School, where he received a year of his legal training in international and comparative law at the law school's Centre for Legal Studies in London, England.

To Maria, John, Christina, Mom, and Apple Pie

TABLE OF CONTENTS

Chapter Eight

Effective Advocacy in Cybermediation **231**

PREFACE

THE EVER-EXPANDING ROLE OF THE LAWYER AS ARCHITECT

In the late 1980s, when I was juggling the launch of a solo law practice and writing my first book, the *Appellate Advocacy Manual* (Clark Boardman Callaghan, 1989), I experienced an important revelation that the lawyer's role is very closely akin to that of an architect. For years I had spoken and taught about the lawyer being an artist, a scientist, a problem designer, and a problem solver, but it was not until I put pen to paper back then that I really began to intimately understand the essence of those separate lawyering functions and how they intermeshed and complemented one another.

In creating *Mediation Advocacy* and in cocreating its companion book, *Arbitration Advocacy*, I have had the unique opportunity to view in detail the lawyer's role as an advocate in alternative dispute resolution (ADR) from the inside out and have come away from the experience even more convinced of the relevance of the architect analog. What is now clearer to me than ever, and what may be equally clear to those of you who routinely practice in ADR, is that we are moving into an age where a premium is being placed on a lawyer's creative ability to design *processes* for resolving disputes, in addition to the traditional tasks of designing *problems* and *solutions*. It is not enough anymore for an advocate to design wonderfully elegant legal problems and solutions and take them to court for adjudication. Clients are now beginning to expect, and sometimes demand, that their lawyers select or design streamlined, cost-efficient mechanisms for processing the raw materials of arcane legal problems and legal solutions into practical, serviceable, economically appealing end products in the form of early mutual-gain settlements or limited-risk private adjudications. It is the architect in every advocate that can make this happen. It is the architect in us that can shape the process appropriately to satisfy the often unique needs of the dispute and the disputants.

I have written this book using what I call a "pracademic" approach—taking care to create throughout a judicious blend of practice and theory. I have also written with several separate audiences in mind. First, I have written for *ADR practitioners*—advocates representing clients who have either opted, or who have been mandated, to resolve their disputes by means of an ADR process. Organized into eight chapters and an appendix of mediation forms and rules, the book provides a full range of features geared to assist mediation advocates in representing their clients competently and efficiently. Chapter 1 introduces uninitiated advocates to the two principal ADR processes—mediation and arbitration—and provides basic information regarding the nature of the two processes and their relative advantages and disadvantages in relation to the court adjudication process. Chapters 2 through 6 provide useful information and practice tips for advocates regarding every stage of representation in the mediation process. Each of these chapters includes a checklist to ensure that the advocate does not forget to take key actions at critical stages of the mediation process. Chapter 7 addresses the hybrid ADR processes (mini-trial, summary jury trial, etc.) and provides descriptions of successful applications of certain hybrids. Chapter 8, a new chapter in this second edition, addresses the topic of effective advocacy in cybermediation. The appendices contain sample mediation forms and rules, and a list of ADR providers organized geographically together with a list of nonprofit organizations that study and promote the use of ADR.

Next, I have written for the *organizers of and participants in continuing legal education (CLE) programs* around the country. The step-by-step approach, analyses of critical process issues, and the succinct presentations of useful information in chart form, make this book an ideal teaching tool for mediation seminars.

A third audience for this publication comprises the teachers and students of *law school courses* on mediation advocacy. At this writing, very few, if any, textbooks provide detailed "hands-on" instruction to law students on effective representation of clients in mediation. This book seeks to fill that gap in ADR literature for law school instruction.

Finally, ADR *neutrals*—mediators and arbitrators—may find this book quite useful. In particular, Chapter 5 on effective advocacy in mediation sessions may provide mediators insight into how the advocates appearing before them can function most effectively in presenting information and in bringing a dispute to closure.

In conclusion, I would like to make a few observations about the style and architecture of this book. At my editor's good suggestion, I have made every effort to use a personable and personalized writing style, as if I were having a face-to-face conversation with you. I hope you find this style friendly and engaging, as intended. Beginning in chapter 3, you will encounter what some of you will believe is rather unusual for a law-related publication. You will discover that I have liberally scattered anecdotes—some funny, some not; some about famous people; some about ordinary people—throughout the various sections discussing advocacy. I have done this for several reasons. First, anecdotes can enliven and invigorate instructional passages that would otherwise be hortatory and didactic. Second, anecdotes are considered to be the "origin of all teaching," assisting readers not only in understanding the teaching points being made, but also in remembering when and how to apply the teaching points later in practice. Third, CLE and law school instructors can use the anecdotes as teaching devices in ADR advocacy seminars and courses. Additionally, advocates can use them (particularly the ones appearing in chapter 4) to explain to their clients the do's and don'ts of client conduct during mediation sessions and arbitration hearings.

Regarding the use of anecdotes, Abraham Lincoln once said: "They say I tell a great many stories; I reckon I do, but I have found in the course of a long experience that . . . people . . . are more easily informed through the medium of a broad illustration than in any other way, and as to what the hypercritical few may think, I don't care." I suppose if we follow the lead of the great communicator Abe Lincoln, we will be in pretty good company.

ACKNOWLEDGMENTS

I welcome the opportunity to thank the people who, over the years, have played significant roles in shaping my experience in the field of alternative dispute resolution, culminating in the development of this book.

Particularly, I want to thank Senior Circuit Judge Thomas E. Fairchild, United States Court of Appeals for the Seventh Circuit, and Circuit Executive Collins Fitzpatrick, who in the late 1970s gave me what I now realize was an opportunity of a lifetime to chair a court-sponsored subcommittee to study possible alternatives to litigation in the federal court system. It was in that role that I was able to educate myself about the mediation and arbitration processes and about the courts and organizations around the country that—even at that early period—were administering the use of court-annexed and private dispute resolution.

It was also during that subcommittee work that I came in contact with Richard A. Salem, who was then regional director of the United States Justice Department's Community Relations Service. He was actively engaged in mediating the Nazi-Skokie conflict in Chicago, and he had previously participated in the mediation of the Kent State war protest matter and the Wounded Knee incident in the early 1970s. Dick willingly shared his vast knowledge of mediation with me and soon we codesigned and cotaught at Loyola University of Chicago School of Law, one of the first law school ADR courses ever offered in the country. We taught this course for several semesters together, and even though I was a teacher, I profited immensely from Dick's insights and inspiration concerning effective mediation methods and techniques. I am grateful to Dick for his selfless sharing of his accumulated skills and experience.

I also wish to thank Loyola University of Chicago School of Law, its faculty, and particularly its dean, Nina Appel, who had the courage in those very early years of the ADR movement to allow Dick and me to experiment with an innovative ADR course and, to her great credit, to encourage students to participate in it. Acknowledging the Loyola connection would not be complete without recognizing three other persons—I extend special thanks to Dr. Paul Lisnek, former assistant dean at the law school, and a nationally recognized author, teacher, and practitioner in ADR, communications skills, and jury consulting. We have had great fun teaching seminars together, blending communications theory and practical experience in interesting, dynamic, and provocative ways. I look forward to our future teaching teamwork. I also wish to acknowledge Professor Jamie Carey, the director of the law school's trial practice program, for the support and encouragement he has given me over the years in my quest to bring more practical skills courses into the law school. Finally, I acknowledge Ted Donner, a former student of mine, who has recently become my teacher, having published a treatise on negotiation and ADR that I have read with great interest.

Similarly, I thank Stephen B. Goldberg, Jeanne Brett, and Max Bazerman for my many years of involvement in the Dispute Resolution Colloquium sponsored by the Kellogg Graduate School of Management, Northwestern University. I have benefitted greatly from those spirited exchanges of interdisciplinary viewpoints between and among experts on dispute resolution from all over the country. I also wish to especially acknowledge Professor Lynn Cohn, who supervises the ADR program at Northwestern University Law School where I teach. She is a brilliant teacher and a valued professional colleague.

I am very pleased to acknowledge with gratitude the insights about mediation advocacy that Dr. Petronio Muniz, President of Instituto Arbiter, Recife Brazil, shared with me over the years. Similarly, I appreciate the insights that architect Keila Porto of Recife has shared with me about the relationships between the mediator and architect functions. In addition, I wish to acknowledge that some of the material contained in this second edition was inspired by my work with Professor James Alfini and lawyer-mediator Eric Galton in designing what we believe to be the first mediation advocacy cybercourse, which at this writing is accessible for enrollment through the American Bar Association.

These acknowledgments would not be complete without mention of the persons who were responsible for my initially becoming involved with the National Institute for Trial Advocacy (NITA) as a faculty member: Thomas Geraghty, associate dean and professor of law at Northwestern University School of Law, and Mark Schoenfield, commercial litigator, author, and NITA instructor. I am very grateful to them for that opportunity and to NITA, particularly John Maciejczyk, for inviting me to author the original *Mediation Advocacy* and for gently and wisely shepherding its publication. Last, but not least, I wish to thank Barbara Van Holsbeke for supervising this second edition to publication and for quietly attending to details and painlessly dealing with imperfections I could not see.

Chapter One

GENERAL DESCRIPTION OF MEDIATION IN THE ADR CONTEXT

"The plaintiff and defendant in an action at law, are like two men ducking their heads in a bucket, and daring each other to remain longest under water."

— *Samuel Johnson*

In the last decade of the twentieth century, the legal profession has experienced vast changes. Not insignificant among them is a growing interest among advocates in the use of alternatives to traditional court litigation to resolve their clients' disputes more efficiently and economically, with less risk and better results. In the days of Samuel Johnson, as suggested by the opening quotation, no alternatives to the traditional judicial process existed. Lawyers took their cases to court and subjected themselves to a seemingly interminable, self-torturing ordeal, with the worst-case potential of double asphyxiation. Fortunately for today's advocates, alternatives now exist. We can learn about and apply new and innovative methods for resolving disputes when the court process does not appear to provide the best procedural alternative to satisfy our clients' emotional, economic, and psychological needs and interests.

Among the many dispute resolution alternatives available to us today, the most prominent are mediation and arbitration. Although this book focuses principally on mediation, it is instructive to view it initially in the context of other dispute resolution processes, particularly arbitration. A companion NITA book, *Arbitration Advocacy*, provides in-depth treatment of the arbitration process and the art and science of arbitration advocacy. This chapter will discuss several topics necessary to developing a working knowledge of both processes. We will define mediation and arbitration and view them in the context of other dispute resolution mechanisms, consider the differences between the two processes, compare the relative advantages and disadvantages of court litigation, arbitration, and mediation, and gain an understanding of the distinctions between mandatory and voluntary mediation and arbitration. In addition, we will become familiar with the three basic steps to initiating alternative dispute resolution—choosing which process to

1

use, persuading opposing counsel to participate, and selecting the appropriate provider of dispute resolution services.

1.1 OVERVIEW OF THE PROCESSES

Mediation and arbitration are two principal processes in a broad spectrum of means for resolving disputes, collectively called alternative dispute resolution, or ADR.[1] Mediation may be defined as a process in which a disinterested third party (or *neutral*) assists the disputants in reaching a voluntary settlement of their differences through an agreement that defines their future behavior. The essential ingredients of classical mediation are (1) its voluntariness—a party can reject the process or its outcomes without repercussions—and (2) the mediator's neutrality, or total lack of interest in the outcome. Arbitration, on the other hand, may be defined as a process in which one or more neutrals render a decision after hearing arguments and reviewing evidence. The essential distinction between the two processes lies in *who* makes the resolution decision for the parties. In mediation, the parties participate in a joint decision-making process and make the decision themselves. In arbitration, the parties relinquish their decision-making right to the neutral who makes a decision for them. By preagreement, the decision of the neutral is either binding or nonbinding. If binding, the decision is final, and the winning party may enforce it against the losing party. If nonbinding, the decision is advisory in aid of settlement.

It may be helpful to view the two processes in the context of the ADR spectrum as shown on the following page.

---

1.   See generally, Stephen B. Goldberg, Frank E. A. Sander, and Nancy H. Rogers, *Dispute Resolution: Negotiation, Mediation, and Other Processes*, 2d ed. (Little, Brown and Co., 1992); Leonard L. Riskin and James E. Westbrook, *Dispute Resolution and Lawyers* (West Publishing Co., 1987). See also, Eric Galton, *Representing Clients in Mediation* (Texas Lawyer Press 1994); Christopher W. Moore, *The Mediation Process: Practical Strategies for Resolving Conflict* (Jossey-Bass Publishers, 1986); Dwight Golann, *Mediating Legal Disputes: Effective Strategies for Lawyers and Mediators* (Little, Brown 1996); Robert H. Mnookin, *Beyond Winning: Negotiating to Create Value in Deals and Disputes*, (Harvard University Press 2000); James J. Alfini, Sharon B. Press, Jean Sternlight, Joseph B. Stulberg, *Mediation Theory and Practice*, (Lexis Publishing 2001); Edward Brunet and Charles B. Craver, *Alternative Dispute Resolution: The Advocate's Perspective* (LexisNexis 2001).

ALTERNATIVE DISPUTE RESOLUTION SPECTRUM

LEAST FORMAL ↑ ↓ MOST FORMAL	NEGOTIATION CONCILIATION FACILITATION MEDIATION MED-ARB ARBITRATION COURT-ANNEXED HYBRIDS COURT ADJUDICATION

The ADR spectrum may be viewed graphically as extending from the least formal process on the top of the above chart—pure negotiation—to the most formal process on the bottom—court adjudication. Pure negotiation, which is familiar to all advocates, is the only process in the spectrum in which the parties and counsel engage without the assistance of a neutral. Many times, however, it serves as an ancillary dispute resolution mechanism to other processes in the spectrum. Moving down on the chart, in conciliation the neutral's goal is to assist in reducing tensions, clarifying issues, and getting the parties to communicate. In essence, it is the process of "getting the parties to the table" and inducing their active involvement in solving their problem. In facilitation a neutral functions as a process expert to facilitate communication and to help design the process structure for resolving the dispute. Ordinarily a facilitator deals only with procedures and does not become involved in the substance of the dispute.

Mediation and arbitration, already defined, combine in the process called med-arb. In med-arb, by preagreement of the parties, the neutral first conducts a mediation to settle the entire dispute or part of it, after which the neutral arbitrates any unresolved issues. The same neutral may perform the role of mediator and arbitrator, or different neutrals may serve in those roles. Court-annexed or mandatory arbitration is a form of nonbinding arbitration administered by court systems. Hybrid processes are specially designed to meet the procedural needs of particular kinds of disputes. Hybrids that have, in recent years, become recognized methods of ADR include the mini-trial, summary jury trial, simulated juries, and expert panels. Chapter 7 describes these and other hybrid processes. The most formal and final of the dispute resolution processes is, of course, court adjudication. It is always a viable alternative to the other ADR processes, and in some instances it may be the most advantageous alternative to best protect and serve your client's interests.

1.2   IMPORTANT DIFFERENCES BETWEEN MEDIATION AND ARBITRATION

As previously noted, the most basic difference between arbitration and mediation is that arbitration involves a decision by the intervening third party, or neutral, after an evidentiary hearing, while mediation does not. Another way to distinguish mediation and arbitration is to compare the neutral's mental functions under each process. In arbitration the neutral uses primarily "left brain" or "rational" mental processes—analytical, mathematical, logical, technical, administrative; in mediation the neutral employs mostly "right brain" or "creative" mental processes—conceptual, intuitive, artistic, holistic, symbolic, emotional. Further, an arbitrator deals largely with the objective, whereas a mediator deals primarily with the subjective. The arbitrator is typically a passive participant whose role is to determine right or wrong; the mediator, by contrast, is generally an active participant who attempts to move the parties to reconciliation and agreement, regardless of who or what is right or wrong.

Because the role of the mediator involves instinctive reactions, intuition, keen interpersonal skills, and sensitivity to subtle psychological and behavioral indicators, in addition to the application of logic and rational thinking, some people find it much more difficult to perform effectively than the role of the arbitrator.

Besides the distinctions outlined above, the two processes also differ in that they are typically employed to resolve two different types of disputes. Parties generally use mediation where they reasonably believe they will be able to reach an agreement with the assistance of a disinterested third party. Mediation is also used when parties will have an ongoing relationship after resolution of the conflict. On the other hand, parties generally use arbitration under two conditions: no reasonable likelihood of a negotiated settlement exists, and the relationship between the parties will not continue after they have resolved the dispute. If parties use the two processes in sequence, mediation occurs first, and if it is unsuccessful, the parties resort to arbitration. Viewed in terms of the judicial process, arbitration is comparable to a trial, and mediation is akin to a judicial settlement conference.

Although mediation and arbitration differ substantially, they both have the underlying structure of a decision-making process. The chart on the next page depicts the interrelationship of their various stages; the stages of mediation are discussed in more detail in section 2.1.

STAGES OF MEDIATION AND ARBITRATION

MEDIATION PROCESS	ARBITRATION PROCESS
Initiation	Initiation
Preparation	Preparation
Introduction	Prehearing Conference
Problem Statement Problem Clarification	Hearing
Generation & Evaluation of Alternatives Selection of Alternatives	Decision Making
Agreement	Award

1.3 RELATIVE ADVANTAGES AND DISADVANTAGES OF MEDIATION, ARBITRATION, AND COURT ADJUDICATION

Most trial advocates are well aware of the advantages and disadvantages of litigation culminating in a court adjudication. They are not always as knowledgeable, however, as to the advantages and disadvantages of arbitration and mediation and how to assess them in relation to court adjudication. This section seeks to clarify the relative advantages and disadvantages of these three processes by analyzing them in terms of the nature of the forum, the nature of the procedures, and cost.

1.3.1 Relative advantages of the processes

With regard to the nature of the forum, court adjudication of course occurs in a public forum where judges are randomly assigned cases that they are responsible to supervise and decide and for which decisions they are held accountable. Both mediation and arbitration are nonpublic, a trait advantageous to resolving certain types of disputes where the parties desire privacy of the proceedings and of the outcome. Further, in both private mediation and arbitration, by mutual agreement the parties select qualified neutrals, who sometimes have specific expertise relevant to the dispute. Also, in arbitration, but more so in mediation, the parties usually have significant control over the resolution process. Representation by counsel is advisable but not necessary in some instances.

As to the nature of the procedures, in the court adjudication process, the procedures are highly structured and institutionalized, typified by detailed rules and numerous compliance mechanisms. Rules of evidence enhance the reliability of proof of claims and defenses. Court adjudication yields results that are appealable and ultimately final and binding and enforceable, making absolute closure a real possibility. In disputes not requiring these types of stringent procedures, mediation and arbitration offer certain measurable advantages. Arbitration, while having some of the evidential and procedural regularity of court adjudication, is conducted in a less formal and less rigorous setting, thereby enhancing the potential for a more expeditious resolution. Applying legal and equitable norms and creating remedies often tailor-made to the situation, arbitrators issue decisions as awards that can be enforced through the judicial process, bringing finality to the conflict.

Some disputes are best resolved in settings having few, if any, procedural restraints. With respect to those disputes, the mediation process offers several advantages. With minimal procedural requirements, mediation provides an unlimited opportunity for the parties to exercise flexibility in communicating their underlying concerns and priorities regarding the dispute. It can educate the parties about potential alternative solutions, empower them to improve and strengthen their relationship in future interactions, and stimulate them to explore and to reach creative solutions affording mutual gain and a high rate of compliance.

As to the cost of the process, court adjudication is publicly funded—tax dollars pay the cost of the judges' services and other court administrative services. In mediation and arbitration, the parties usually share the neutrals' fees and certain administrative costs. Depending on the nature of a particular dispute, however, the fees and costs associated with private mediation and arbitration processes are normally much less than those associated with a case that traverses the course of the court adjudication process.

1.3.2   Relative disadvantages of the processes

Each of the three processes also has disadvantages. With respect to the nature of the forum, the proceedings of the complex court adjudication process routinely mystify parties, who usually need to be represented by legal counsel. Moreover, a judge randomly assigned to hear a particular case may not have the necessary substantive or technical expertise to fully appreciate the intricacies of legal counsel's arguments.

Also, the crush of court caseloads sometimes results in substantial delay in processing individual cases. Parties often find that the court adjudicative process significantly disrupts their personal lives over long periods of time and ultimately produces a result that leaves them even more polarized than they were when they commenced the process.

Arbitration and mediation similarly have forum disadvantages. Private arbitration lacks quality control since the arbitrators are independently selected in individual cases and are not generally accountable to any supervisory authority. In mediation the neutrals have little power or authority over the parties and certainly no power to impose unwanted outcomes on them. Consequently, one or more parties can significantly influence settlements in some situations by the power they possess and exercise behind the scenes. Moreover, in mediation there is no application or development of public standards.

As to procedural disadvantages of the court adjudication process, a limited range of possible remedies exists, and because of the rigidity of the procedural structure, compromise is difficult. Arbitration, a process becoming increasingly encumbered by "legalization," has its own drawbacks, which include the lack of public norms, the lack of binding precedent, insufficient opportunity for full discovery, relaxed rules of evidence, usually no written reasons for decisions, no uniformity of decisions, and usually no opportunity for appeal. Similarly, mediation has several procedural disadvantages: no real due process safeguards exist, participation by the parties cannot be compelled by subpoena or otherwise, access to information may be severely constricted, and outcomes need not be principled. Closure to mediated outcomes is weak in the sense that they are nonbinding and unenforceable, except as provided by relevant contract law.

Finally, as to costs, the public substantially funds the administration of the court adjudication process. In many situations, however, it can be extremely expensive to use because the cumbersome discovery process and delays sometimes cause huge investments in attorneys' time and therefore increased attorneys' fees. Some complex arbitration hearings can spread over weeks and months, costing the parties much more than they had initially projected. Unsuccessful preadjudication or prearbitration mediations can also add somewhat to the overall cost of securing closure of a dispute.

For your convenience and quick reference, the charts that follow present the advantages and disadvantages of the three processes.

ADVANTAGES OF THE PROCESSES

COURT ADJUDICATION	ARBITRATION	MEDIATION
Public forum	Privacy	Privacy
Neutrals are accountable	Parties control forum	Parties control forum
Already institutionalized	Expertise	Parties select neutrals
Rules of evidence	Parties select neutrals	Reflects concerns and priorities and disputes
Announces and applies public norms		
Precedent	Written procedures	Flexible
Deterrence	Expeditious	Process educates disputants
Uniformity	Choice of applicable norms	Addresses underlying problem
Independence		
Decision appealable	Tailors remedy to situation	Often results in creative solutions
Binding/closure	Enforceability	High rate of compliance
Enforceability		
Publicly funded	Relatively inexpensive	Relatively inexpensive

DISADVANTAGES OF THE PROCESSES

COURT ADJUDICATION	ARBITRATION	MEDIATION
No control over selection of judges	Lack of quality control	Neutrals have no power to impose settlement
Lack of special substantive or technical expertise	Neutrals unaccountable	No power to compel participation
Requires lawyers	Becoming increasingly encumbered by "legalization"	Limited access to information
Mystifying		
Delay	Relaxed rules of evidence	No due process safeguards
Time consuming	Limited or no discovery	Powerful party can influence outcome
	No public norms	Weak closure
Polarizes, disruptive		Not binding
	No precedent	
Compromise difficult		Lacks enforceability
	No uniformity	
Limited range of remedies		No application/ development of public standards
	Usually no written reasons for decision	
Expensive		Outcome need not be principled
	Usually no appeal	

1.4 MANDATORY VERSUS VOLUNTARY MEDIATION AND ARBITRATION

Traditionally, mediation and arbitration have been voluntary in the sense that the parties agree, either before or after the dispute arises, to submit such dispute to one or both resolution methods. However, in recent years there has been an increasing trend toward the creation of statutes and court rules providing for mandatory (also called court-annexed) mediation and arbitration both as a means of easing the backlog of cases and as an attempt to reduce the amount of time and money the parties spend to resolve their disputes. The rules governing these programs vary significantly from jurisdiction to jurisdiction, and you should take care to apprise yourself of the specific requirements of the jurisdiction in which you are representing a client. For example, with respect to mandatory mediation, in some jurisdictions the courts send all cases of a particular type to mediation as a prerequisite to litigating in the system. Some rules permit defendants to waive the mediation requirement, others do not. In some jurisdictions, the mediations are facilitative; in others, evaluative. (See section 2.2.) In some states, judges can independently determine whether a case should be submitted to one of any number of ADR processes for treatment, and in others, rules require neutrals to report back to judges on settlement progress. Some mandatory ADR programs require the parties to share the cost of the neutral, while others appoint the neutrals and pay them a nominal session fee. Some mandatory arbitration programs impose penalties, in the form of court costs and fees, on parties who reject the mandatory arbitration award, go to trial, and fare worse than they did in the arbitration proceeding.

Many people criticize these programs for their coercive nature, pressuring parties who are sometimes unrepresented into forgoing substantial due process rights they would otherwise enjoy in the traditional trial proceeding. However, because a growing number of courts consider early settlement of cases to be in the parties' and the court's best interests, the courts are likely to expand rather than shrink their employment of mandatory mediation and arbitration.

1.5 INITIATING THE PROCESSES

How you initiate the mediation and arbitration processes will depend on the particular circumstances. If you are proceeding in a court that has a mandatory ADR program, the court will notify you of the date that it has scheduled your case for a mediation conference or an arbitration hearing, as appropriate. If the dispute in which your client is involved arises out of a contract and the contract contains a mediation and/or arbitration clause, then the terms of that clause determine the steps to initiate the appropriate ADR process. If the contract clause contains no specific guidance, or if the dispute is not based in contract, then you will have wide latitude in initiating the appropriate ADR process. But you must negotiate several hurdles before you can accomplish initiation: you must (1) tentatively decide which process would be most appropriate for your dispute, (2) convince opposing counsel that the process you are suggesting is the appropriate one, and (3) with your opposing counsel, jointly decide on the provider of neutral services that you will engage.

1.5.1 Choosing between mediation and arbitration

Assuming you have narrowed your options to mediation and arbitration for use in resolving your dispute, you should consider several important criteria in choosing between them. Section 2.5 discusses additional criteria. If the parties to the dispute will have future dealings with each other and it is desirable for them to preserve a continuing relationship, mediation is indicated. On the other hand, if the parties do not need or desire to have future dealings, or if they have repeatedly acted in bad faith and have become hostile toward each other over a long period of time, arbitration, providing a decision on past events, may be the better choice. If one party is considerably more powerful than the other, the party with less power may benefit from the fairness-determining aspects of arbitration. If one or more parties need to avoid a win-lose decision—a published opinion, for example, which may concretize undesirable rights and/or duties into the future—mediation is the favored choice. Large corporate clients, for example, that are engaged as defendants in a high volume of low-dollar disputes, where there is also a premium on speed of decision, privacy, and closure, may be well advised to opt for arbitration over mediation. If, in a particular dispute, your client has no clear legal entitlement, you are probably better advised to use mediation so that you can concentrate on favorable facts in the process or end the process at any point you think appropriate. A case having multiple parties and/or multiple issues may be better suited for mediation than arbitration because a greater opportunity for beneficial trade-offs exists in such a facilitated bargaining process. If a fair resolution of the dispute requires that certain witnesses be compelled to be present, then you clearly should choose arbitration over mediation. The chart that follows organizes and highlights some of these important criteria you should consider when choosing between mediation and arbitration.

IMPORTANT CRITERIA FOR SELECTING BETWEEN
MEDIATION AND ARBITRATION

MEDIATION	ARBITRATION
Desire to preserve continuing relations	Need to offset power imbalance
Emphasis on future dealings	Need for decision on past events
Need to avoid win-lose decision	High volume of disputes
Disputants desire total control of process	Need to compel participation
Dispute has multiple parties and issues	Premium on speed and privacy
Absence of clear legal entitlement	Premium on closure

1.5.2   Persuading opposing counsel to participate

After you have tentatively selected mediation or arbitration and have convinced yourself of the wisdom of your choice, you must then convince your opposing counsel that your choice of process is a reasonable one. This is not always easy. Lawyers who have never used or been involved in a mediation, for example, are reluctant to use it for the first time. This is just human nature. If they have never experienced it, they feel unknowledgeable and therefore uncomfortable about recommending it to their clients. What if their clients ask questions about the process? Those lawyers will inevitably be embarrassed when unable to provide their clients with an explanation. Or worse yet, they may provide information that is incomplete, inaccurate, or derogatory of the mediation process altogether.

If confronted with the situation of an opposing counsel who is uneducated in ADR, you might try the following. Agree to meet with him to explain your experiences with mediation, for example, and answer any questions he may have. Or, offer to provide a videotape of a mediation of the type of dispute in which you are engaged. Many videotapes available through law school libraries and other sources are quite instructive on the process and the dialogue one may experience during the ordinary course of a mediation. Viewing the video may be enough to quell counsel's jitters. Another option may be even better: you can contact the dispute resolution organization that you propose to engage to administer the mediation and have one of its case managers give your opposing counsel a call. Case managers spend a great deal of their time persuading opposing parties in cases to use ADR, and they are frequently quite successful.

1.5.3 Selecting the appropriate type of neutral services

Currently many sole practitioners and even law firms offer ADR services. You can obtain background information on these lawyer-providers from ADR directories available in most law school libraries. In addition, by one estimate nearly 400 nonprofit and for-profit organizations across the United States specialize in providing ADR services.

For your convenience, a list of various dispute resolution organizations appears in appendix K.

Chapter Two

PRELIMINARY PREMEDIATION CONSIDERATIONS

*If you come at me with your fists doubled, I think I
can promise you that mine will double as fast as
yours; but if you come to me and say, "Let us sit down
and take counsel together;"... we will presently find
that we are not so far apart after all....*
— *Woodrow Wilson*

The legal profession is expanding the use of consensual methods of resolving disputes, of sitting down and taking counsel together. Mediation, a process in which a third party assists in building consensus, is the centerpiece of these methods. Although an adjudication by a neutral third party, either a judge or an arbitrator, is the only viable option for resolving some disputes, advocates are beginning to appreciate the many other types of situations in which a mediated solution may be more desirable and beneficial than adjudication in ending conflict. This chapter addresses specific considerations that you should take into account when initiating the use of mediation in a particular case. We will explore the stages of the mediation process, the differences between facilitative and evaluative mediation, variations in the application of the mediation process to different areas of law, the primary and secondary reasons for using mediation, and considerations in selecting cases for mediation and in choosing the appropriate mediator.

2.1   STAGES OF THE MEDIATION PROCESS

Classical mediation consists of eight stages: (1) initiation, (2) preparation, (3) introduction, (4) problem statement, (5) problem clarification, (6) generation and evaluation of alternative(s), (7) selection of alternative(s), and (8) agreement.

In a typical mediation, stages 4, 5, 6, and 7 sometimes overlap or are repeated before the parties reach a consensus on all issues and conclude a final agreement.

Initiation. As noted in section 1.5, mediation may be initiated in two principal ways: the parties submit the dispute to a public or private dispute resolution organization or to a private neutral; or, alternatively, a court order or rule in a court-annexed mediation program refers the matter to mediation.

Preparation. Counsel for parties to a dispute in mediation prepare by becoming well informed on the circumstances underlying the dispute and the needs and interests of their clients, the legal claims or defenses of each side and their relative strengths and weaknesses, and the specific remedies or results they seek. Mediators prepare by becoming knowledgeable about the parties and the characteristics of the dispute, including the following, where possible:

- The balance of power between or among the parties.
- The primary sources of pressure exerted on the parties.
- The pressures motivating the parties toward agreement, as well as those hindering agreement.
- The economics of the industry or particular company or entity involved.
- Existing political and/or personal conflicts within and between the parties.
- The extent of settlement authority of each of the parties.

Introduction. In the introduction stage, the mediator explains the nature and format of the mediation process to counsel and their clients. During these few minutes the mediator assesses the participants' attitudes about mediation and their readiness to commit to the process, and she encourages their active engagement in it. At this point the mediator first establishes her credibility, integrity, and neutrality in an effort to gain the parties' acceptance. The mediator also establishes control of the process, determines the issues in dispute and the positions of the parties, initiates the agreement-forging process, and encourages the parties to continue direct negotiations.

Unlike a judge in a settlement conference or an arbitrator who wields the clout of a decision, a mediator typically does not command the parties' immediate trust and respect. Rather, the mediator earns them through a carefully orchestrated and delicately executed ritual of rapport building.

The content of the mediator's opening remarks is, in most cases, critical to establishing the necessary rapport with the parties and the respectability of the mediator and the mediation process. Opening remarks focus on the following: identifying the mediator and the parties; explaining the procedures to be followed, including caucusing—an ex parte conference between a mediator and a party; describing the goals of the process while emphasizing the continued decision-making responsibility of the parties; and reinforcing the confidentiality and integrity of the process.

Finally, the mediator must assess the parties' capacity to participate in the process. If either party has severe emotional, drinking, drug, or health problems, the mediator may decide to postpone the session. Further, if the parties are overly hostile and verbally abusive, the mediator must attempt to calm them, by preliminary caucusing if necessary.

Problem statement. In this stage, the parties begin to openly discuss their dispute either by stating their respective positions and discussing each issue as it is raised or by first identifying the issues and reserving a detailed discussion of the positions until they have identified all the issues. As a general rule, the complaining party tells his "story" first. This may be the first time the opposing party has heard the whole basis for the complaint. The mediator's task at this point is to listen actively and empathically, taking notes if necessary and using positive listening techniques such as restatement, echo, and nonverbal responses.

The mediator also:

- Asks open- and closed-ended questions at the appropriate time and in a neutral fashion.
- Hones in on important "signals" that the parties send through their behavior and body movements.
- Calms a party, as necessary.
- Clarifies the narration by asking pointed questions.
- Objectively summarizes the first party's story and diffuses tensions by omitting disparaging comments from the summary.
- Ascertains whether the second party comprehends the first party's story.
- Thanks the first party for his contribution.

This process is then repeated with the second party.

Problem clarification. In the clarification stage, the mediator isolates the genuine underlying issues in dispute. The parties to a dispute often intentionally distort the core issues. The mediator penetrates this fog of distortion through separate caucuses in which the mediator asks direct, probing questions to draw out information that one party would not disclose in the presence of the other party. In a later joint session, the mediator summarizes areas of agreement and disagreement, being mindful not to reveal matters that the parties shared with the mediator in confidence. The mediator then assists the parties in grouping and prioritizing issues and demands.

Generation and evaluation of alternatives. Assuming the parties successfully complete the previous stage, the mediator next calls into play two fundamental principles of effective mediation: creating doubt in the parties' minds about the validity and strength of their positions on issues, and suggesting alternative approaches that may stimulate agreement. To accomplish these tasks, the mediator directs the parties to separately brainstorm to produce alternatives or options, discusses the viability of each option, encourages the parties by commenting on the probability of success, suggests alternatives not raised by the parties, and then repeats the process. In this stage, the mediator sometimes suggests new options not considered by the parties, presenting them in such a way that the parties can comfortably accept or reject them.

Selection of alternatives. The mediator may compliment the parties on their progress and use humor, when appropriate, to relieve tensions, assist the parties in eliminating unworkable options, and help the parties determine which of the remaining workable solutions will produce the best results. The main goal of this stage is to get the parties to decide on an outcome. To achieve that end, the mediator may need to encourage them to compromise on some of the smaller points.

Agreement. Before bringing the mediation to a close, the mediator summarizes and clarifies the terms of the agreement reached and obtains the assent of each party to those terms, sets a follow-up date, if necessary, and congratulates the parties on their reasonableness. The mediator usually does not become involved in drafting a settlement agreement. This task is left to the parties or their legal representatives.

2.2 FACILITATIVE VERSUS EVALUATIVE MEDIATION

An initial question you should ask yourself when selecting a mediator is whether you want a facilitative mediation, an evaluative one, or a combination of both. In a facilitative mediation, the mediator neither offers an opinion on the value of the case nor recommends how it should be settled. Rather, the facilitative mediator assists the parties and their counsel, through information interchange and creativity, to reach their own joint decision on a reasonable settlement or solution. The evaluative mediator, on the other hand, is hired by the parties to give an opinion or recommendation on settlement value or some other solution. In a combined facilitative-evaluative mediation, the mediator first attempts to achieve a resolution facilitatively, and if that is unsuccessful, the mediator, near the close of the final session, offers an opinion on how the case should settle. Some mediators are primarily facilitative, others are primarily evaluative, and others provide either type of mediation (or a combination) by request of the parties or their counsel. It is very important that you and the mediator both know which type of mediation you desire. The type of mediation will probably influence the way you prepare for it. Also, being very clear about the type of mediation will minimize the chance that you will be disappointed in the results.

Depending on individual style, the mediator may assume a variety of roles and functions to assist parties in resolving disputes, even during the course of a single mediation. Examples of these roles and functions include the following:

- **Opener of communication channels** who initiates communication or facilitates better communication if the parties are already talking.

- **Legitimizer** who helps all parties recognize the right of others to be involved in negotiations.

- **Process facilitator** who provides a procedure and formally chairs the negotiation session.

- **Trainer** who educates novice, unskilled, or unprepared negotiators in the bargaining process.

- **Resource expander** who provides procedural assistance to the parties and links them to outside experts and resources, such as lawyers, technical experts, decision makers, or additional goods for exchange, that may enable them to enlarge acceptable settlement options.

- **Problem explorer** who enables people in dispute to examine a problem from a variety of viewpoints, assists in defining basic issues and interests, and looks for mutually satisfactory options.

- **Scapegoat** who may take some of the responsibility or blame for an unpopular decision that the parties are nevertheless willing to accept. This enables them to maintain their integrity and, when appropriate, gain the support of their constituents.

- **Agent of reality** who helps build a reasonable and implementable settlement and questions and challenges parties who have extreme and unrealistic goals.

- **Leader** who takes the initiative to move the negotiations forward by procedural or substantive suggestions.[1]

---

1. Moore, id. at 18.

The facilitative mediator can comfortably assume any of these nine roles. The evaluative mediator may employ some of these roles but normally concentrates on the leader and agent of reality roles. He usually takes charge of the process, and the parties and counsel wield much less control than in a facilitative mediation. Some evaluative mediators are more facilitative, others are more aggressive. Highly aggressive evaluative mediators, also referred to as "bashers," can be dominating, coercive, and heavy-handed, and they often attempt to foist their opinions on parties and counsel through their hubris and use of belittling tactics. If a basher is unsuccessful in resolving the dispute, it often polarizes the parties and adversely affects their future ability to negotiate a settlement. This is why, as pointed out in section 2.7, counsel and their clients must take great care in selecting a mediator suitable for the dispute situation. The differences between facilitative and evaluative models of mediation are discussed in more detail below.

Classical facilitative mediation. Generally speaking, the facilitative mediator assumes that the parties are intelligent, able to work together, and able to understand their situations better than either their counsel or the mediator.[2] As mentioned above, the facilitative mediator does not give his opinion, either because he feels an opinion might impair his neutral function or he feels he does not have, nor will ever have, enough information to provide an informed opinion. A mediator using the facilitative model will normally have either a narrow or broad focus—that is, he will define problems narrowly or broadly. The facilitative-narrow mediator helps parties become realistic about their dispute situations by asking questions about the strengths and weaknesses of their cases, the best, worst, and most likely outcomes of litigation, and the consequences—including costs—of a decision not to settle the case. The facilitative-broad mediator helps parties define, understand, and resolve problems they bring to the table. But, in addition, he allows them to design or define new problems that have solutions that better accommodate their respective underlying needs, concerns, values, and interests. In a broad facilitative mediation, the parties' legal arguments occupy a lesser position than in a narrow facilitative mediation, and sometimes no role at all.

Transformative mediation. In recent years, a highly facilitative, nondirective model of mediation has emerged that is quite useful in disputes involving parties whose relationships need to be repaired and/or maintained.[3] Called transformative mediation, it is considered by some

---

2. See Leonard L. Riskin, "Mediator Orientations, Strategies and Techniques," *Commercial Contract Disputes*, appendix B, CPR Institute for Dispute Resolution (1994).
3. See Robert A. Baruch Bush and Joseph P. Folger, *The Promise of Mediation*, (Jossey-Bass Publishers, 1994).

experts to be on the outer fringes of classical facilitative mediation because its process roots extend from a nonintrusive style of psychotherapy. This model of mediation is effective, for example, in family and employment dispute situations. It has limited value where disputes need an expedited resolution, where there was never a pre-existing relationship between the parties, or where a continuing relationship between or among the parties is neither desirable or possible. Total reconciliation of disputing parties is an admirable goal, but often it is an elusive one that becomes impractical and financially costly to pursue because of the parties' available time and the parties' individual needs simply to get on with their lives. In a transformative mediation, the mediator's goal is to facilitate empowerment and recognition, to support full deliberation and informed decision-making by the parties, to enhance the parties' decision-making, perspective-taking, and communication.

It is important to note that in transformative mediation, a final agreement is not necessarily a primary goal of the mediation process. Most proponents and practitioners of this model of mediation subscribe to the view that increased clarity and understanding by the parties are the true goals of the process and serve as valuable accomplishments in themselves. The parties are in near-total, if not complete, control of the process, deciding what the ground rules should be as they move through it. Movement through the process is kept "transparent" so that parties can make clear decisions on process direction, pace, and stage.

The transformative mediator offers procedural or substantive suggestions provisionally and tentatively based on cues given by the parties. These suggestions are phrased with multiple alternatives and offered only after first acquiring the parties' own suggestions. The mediator views the rejection of his or her suggestions as the parties' exercise of empowerment, and he or she welcomes such rejection as their inherent process right. Parties' violations of ground rules are considered by all participants as opportunities for empowerment and/or recognition and are met by the mediator's invitation to reopen discussion of ground rules as an important issue in the resolution process. The parties may choose to use or not use caucusing. At the end of the session the parties, with the facilitation of the mediator, prepare a document that records all accomplishments of the session and noting all decisions regarding process, content, and recognition throughout the session.

The evaluative model. In contrast with the style of the facilitative mediator, the evaluative mediator is hired by the parties to give his or her opinion or recommendation as to settlement value or other solution.

Unlike the facilitative mediator, the evaluative mediator assumes that the parties want and need the mediator to provide direction as to how and why the case should settle a certain way or for a certain amount of money. In the evaluative model, the mediator further assumes that the mediator is qualified to provide such direction on the basis of his experience, training, objectivity, and other qualities. A mediator using the evaluative model will normally have either a narrow or broad focus when defining problems. The evaluative-narrow mediator studies relevant pleadings and briefs and helps the parties understand the strengths and weaknesses of their positions and the likely outcome at trial—not predominantly through a questioning technique as used by the facilitative-narrow mediator—but rather through verbally communicating specific proposals to the parties and urging acceptance of them as being the best solutions for the parties in the circumstances of their dispute. The solutions are usually compromise-based and involve prediction of court or agency decisions based on the mediator's assessments. Like the evaluative-narrow mediator, the evaluative-broad mediator studies pertinent documents and recommends settlement solutions emphasizing their needs and interests over the relative merit of their legal positions. The evaluative-broad mediator considers herself to be in the best position to know what is good for the parties whether that be a monetary settlement, a non-monetary settlement or a combination of the two.

The combined model. As mentioned earlier in this section, in a combined facilitative-evaluative mediation, the mediator normally first attempts to achieve a resolution facilitatively, and if that is unsuccessful, the mediator, near the close of the final session, offers an opinion as to how the case should settle. Use of this model is quite effective in many dispute situations because it allows the parties to first attempt to develop their own settlement ideas and proposals. If the parties are successful, the settlement may be more satisfactory and durable than a third-party's suggested compromise solution. If the parties are unsuccessful, then they can look to the neutral's proposal to help them measure what is fair for the situation.

Some mediators use an evaluative style first, and if that is unsuccessful, they revert to a more facilitative style. The weakness of this evaluative-first model is that the mediator, once she gives her opinion as to a settlement, loses her neutrality and perhaps her credibility as well. If a party believes that the mediator's assessment is substantially inaccurate, the party may lose complete confidence in the mediator's ability to assist the parties in reaching a more collaborative solution.

2.3 PROCESS DIFFERENCES DEPENDING ON THE AREA OF SUBSTANTIVE LAW, THE NATURE OF THE PARTIES, AND THE TYPE OF DISPUTE

You should be aware that the mediation process, and thus your experiences in mediation, may vary depending on the area of substantive law involved, the nature of the parties, and the type of dispute. Some of these variations are discussed in relation to labor, construction, family law, and insurance claim mediations.[4]

For example, private sector labor mediation tends to reflect the competitive and positional nature of traditional union-management collective bargaining. In labor disputes, a mediator will typically spend considerable time caucusing with the parties. The parties themselves will also spend substantial time caucusing separately without the mediator present. Mediation may continue for several days. On the union side, power struggles may be ongoing between the union representatives or between the representatives and their constituents. These disunifying conditions are sometimes present on the management side also, but to a lesser extent. Clearly identifying the true underlying needs and interests of the parties can be a great challenge for the mediator and can result in a protracted, tedious, issue-by-issue analysis in caucuses and joint sessions. These disputes invariably involve both monetary and nonmonetary issues, so that once the mediator successfully assists the parties in clearly identifying, qualifying, and prioritizing them, the parties can resolve their dispute through a process of issue trade-offs and packaging.

In the construction industry, the parties are often practical people, accustomed to the give-and-take compromising characteristic of the mediation process. General contractors, subcontractors, materials suppliers, and property owners and developers are in the business of negotiating deals. They bring this wealth of negotiating experience to the mediation setting, which can be either helpful or detrimental to the success of a mediation, depending on whether they choose to employ competitive or cooperative tactics. On their face, construction disputes usually involve only money, but subsurface, many other agendas may be operating. Other construction contracts may be under negotiation by these same disputants; some of the parties may be worried that their reputation in the construction community depends on the outcome of the mediation; one of the subcontractors may be on the brink of bankruptcy, and mediation may be its last resort to restore cash flow; a general contractor may need money to satisfy ongoing payroll obligations

---

4. For additional information on variations in mediation, see Bette J. Roth, Randall W. Wulff, and Charles A. Cooper, *The Alternative Dispute Resolution Practice Guide* (Lawyers Cooperative Publishing, 1993).

or to pay suppliers for materials and equipment in another job; or a nervous owner may be worried about depleting construction loan funds. All of these subliminal concerns usually combine to enhance prospects of a mediated resolution. Unusual aspects of construction mediations are that they sometimes involve site inspections by the mediator and occasionally involve conducting mediation at the construction site while construction is ongoing.

Family law mediation, though not therapy, has characteristics akin to it in that the mediator tries to keep the divorcing or divorced parties focused on the future and encourages them to move through various emotional stages toward a mutually beneficial resolution for themselves and any affected children. Actually, psychological issues are so prevalent in family law disputes that some lawyers co-mediate such disputes with a psychologist. The mediator emphasizes the need for respectful communication, attempting to offset any power imbalance between the parties by affording them the ability to participate equally in the communication process. Customarily, attorneys meet with their respective clients prior to the mediation to discuss goals, agendas, and strategies, but they usually do not attend the mediation sessions with their clients. Common exceptions are sessions in which the parties will discuss legal issues, and the concluding session when the parties work out the final terms of the settlement agreement. Family mediators caucus less with the parties than do mediators in other settings. Some family mediators, sensitive to trust issues existing between the parties, as a matter of practice never caucus separately with the parties.

In the mediation of personal injury and property damage insurance claims, liability and damages are generally the only two issues, and the parties are, in many instances, unlikely to have a continuing relationship after the mediation. Credibility is usually a critical issue in these disputes, and therefore it is crucial that at least the complaining party be present at the mediation session. It is common for insurance companies to send a claims adjuster unaccompanied by counsel to the mediation session. Typically the adjusters have very limited settlement authority but can obtain more by telephoning their supervisor. Multiple caucusing is the primary technique mediators use to forge agreement on a reasonable settlement figure. If the parties do not reach settlement by the end of the mediation session, mediators often attempt to expedite settlement by offering an opinion on the value of the case. Insurance claims that do not settle during the mediation itself normally settle shortly afterwards as a result of continuing negotiation by the parties' representatives, sometimes assisted by periodic telephone follow-up by the mediator.

2.4 PRIMARY AND SECONDARY REASONS FOR USING MEDIATION

Normally the primary reason for using mediation is to resolve the entire dispute existing between the parties. But do not immediately reject an opportunity for mediation just because you feel that it cannot succeed in settling the entire dispute. As explained below, you might want to schedule a mediation in a particular case for many other reasons, apart from achieving complete resolution.

2.4.1 Resolve part, if not all, of the case

Sometimes settlement negotiations stall because the parties have assumed entrenched positions on one or more aspects of a dispute. If they can obtain assistance to get past these hurdles, then a settlement is likely to fall into place. For example, in some personal injury cases, parties can agree that the plaintiff probably will be able to establish liability at trial, but they disagree strongly on the amount of damages a jury might award or on a reasonable settlement figure for the case. Disagreement often centers on several issues, including whether the plaintiff was overtreated medically to unreasonably augment the amount of special damages, whether the treating physician's prognosis is unreasonably exaggerated in plaintiff's favor, whether plaintiff's work and recreational activities are limited to the extent contended, and whether plaintiff could have returned to work earlier, thus minimizing the damage claim. In such instances, an evaluative mediation involving several reality-testing caucus sessions could help the parties reach consensus on a reasonable settlement range or settlement figure. If the mediation does not completely resolve the case, the parties may have a clearer idea of the strengths and weaknesses of their positions on the individual damage issues and will be better equipped to negotiate a settlement of those issues within a short period after the mediation.

In other situations, parties may agree on the amount of damages to which a plaintiff would be entitled if the plaintiff were to prevail at trial. Their consensus on the damage amount may be based on the liquidated damage provision of a contract or a specific damage amount provided by statute, or the like. Nonetheless, they may differ strenuously on whether plaintiff breached the terms of the contract, thereby giving rise to a claim for the liquidated damages. In these circumstances, a facilitative mediation could help the parties consider the probability of prevailing on the liability aspects and the risks, in terms of delay, expense, and business detriment, of continuing on the judicial track through trial and an inevitable appeal.

It is not uncommon that large business disputes have multiple aspects, some of which are clearer than others on liability. Often parties would rather reach a settlement on the concessionable aspects before trial so they can avoid having these matters come before a jury, perhaps prejudicing the jury against them on the whole case. Mediation can be useful in helping the parties perceive and weed out those aspects of the case with the goal of streamlining the courtroom presentations and optimizing the amount of trial time spent on the highly contested issues in the case.

2.4.2   Narrow or focus issues in the case

Occasionally you will encounter an opponent who, as a litigation power play, has loaded the Complaint or Counterclaim with every theory of recovery imaginable. Sometimes several of these claims are based on allegations that, in your opinion, could never be proved. As to some of the other claims, even if they could be proved, they would not, in your view, state a claim for relief under the applicable law. Still other claims have vague allegations that require a more definite statement before you can effectively defend against them. Filing the necessary motions, including motions to dismiss and for a more definite statement, would be very time consuming and expensive. A decision on the several motions might take months or even more than a year. Requesting a pretrial conference with the judge or magistrate assigned the case to discuss these pleading issues would be the logical first step. But if that option is not available, then an alternative is to arrange a mediation conference, perhaps with a former judge whose judgment both lawyers respect, to discuss the state of the pleadings with the goal of narrowing or focusing the issues in the case to a number and scope that are reasonable and humanly manageable. Opposing counsel might welcome such an opportunity, particularly if he knows he has overpled and exaggerated the scope of his case and that someone other than the trial judge assigned the case will be scrutinizing his draftsmanship.

2.4.3   Test a theory of claim or defense

If you are representing a plaintiff with several legal theories supporting a claim for damages and one is rather novel or unconventional, you may consider testing its potential in mediation conducted by a former judge before actually presenting the novel claim in front of a jury. The same is true if you are representing a defendant with a novel defense. No matter how legally sound you and your law partners may think your novel claim or defense is, there is no substitute for obtaining a neutral's evaluation of its merit and of the reaction it might evoke from a jury. Even if the mediation confirms your initial feelings about the merit of your novel claim or defense, you will have wasted no time, because the knowledge you have gained will enhance your confidence in future settlement negotiations with your opposing counsel. More important, you will no doubt gain new insights into your claim or defense from the mediation experience that will ultimately aid you in presenting it more effectively at trial.

2.4.4 Evaluate your case as you move through discovery

Prosecuting or defending a civil case in the judicial system is like painting a realistic scene or sculpting a human figure from clay. Lawyers design their claims and defenses from a vast amount of available ideas and information that must be identified and selected for relevancy and reliability and then pieced together to make a convincing statement of what it purports to represent. When the plaintiff's lawyer prepares a Complaint or a defense lawyer prepares an Answer, neither is certain that this initial sketch or roughed-in sculpture will persist through the artistic process of discovery and become the final product of their artistic-scientific efforts—the case they present to the jury.[5] New ideas, new information, new insights may alter the artist-scientist's initial plan.

Thus in a complicated case involving numerous factual issues the complexion of a case may change substantially perhaps several times during the course of discovery. For instance, a deposition or a request for documents may turn up information that makes one or more of the parties seriously consider the settlement options as an alternative to continued expensive discovery process. Continuing discovery could precipitate uncovering even more information harmful to that party's position, or it could result in the unearthing of neutralizing information. The risk of going forward, however, can be substantial. In such situations, it sometimes is much easier for the lawyer with the stronger position to recommend mediation. You should stay alert for such mediated evaluation opportunities. If you are the lawyer whose position is weakened by discovery, and you feel awkward initiating settlement discussions, you might consider contacting a dispute resolution organization whose administrative staff member could make the initial contact.

2.4.5 See how the opposing party would impress a jury as a witness

If you are representing a client in a potentially settleable case involving the credibility of the parties, and you estimate that deposition of the opposing party will take one or two days of your time and correspondingly be an undue financial burden on your client, you may consider suggesting a mediation conference to your opposing counsel with the understanding that both parties will attend and present their

---

5.   John W. Cooley, *Appellate Advocacy Manual* (Clark Boardman Callaghan, 1989), sec. 1:05 D and E.

respective stories. In this situation, settlement becomes the secondary reason for the mediation. In a one- or two-hour mediation conference, you will be able to determine how the opposing party would impress a jury and to evaluate the relative credibility of the parties. The question you will be answering for yourself in this brief session is not so much who is actually telling the truth, but rather which of the parties can best convince a jury that she is telling the truth. At the end of that session, if you have not settled the case, you and your client will be much better prepared to decide whether to engage in further settlement negotiations or to invest the time and money in taking the opposing party's deposition and continuing with other discovery.

2.4.6 Get an independent assessment of your own client as a convincing witness

In your practice you probably have been confronted with clients who have a highly exaggerated idea of the strength of their position and the value of their case. They developed these ideas from watching television, from settlement stories their friends told them, or from articles they read in newspapers or magazines. If you cannot convince your client that the case is not worth what he thinks it is, you may consider arranging for a mediation conference. In such a situation, it is helpful to have a former judge as the mediator. At the mediation, your client will have the opportunity to explain to an unbiased third party the basis of his claim and why he believes it is worth the figure he demands. In a caucus, the experienced former judge will be able to test the reality of these figures by pointing out deficiencies in your client's proposed testimony and other evidence and comparing them with the type of evidence required to obtain high jury awards or high settlements in other cases in her experience. Your client will then realize that if he cannot convince the former judge of what he believes his case is worth, he probably will not be able to convince a jury either. Your prior advice to your client will be affirmed by the mediator, and your client will be more inclined to be realistic about the true jury or settlement value of his case. He may even be willing to reach a settlement during the course of the mediation.

2.4.7 Obtain early discovery in a small case so that it settles early

As more fully discussed in subsection 2.5.4, there is nothing unscrupulous about a lawyer discovering information through mediation that will assist in proper assessment of the relative merit of the parties' positions and the settlement value of a case. Most of the favorable and unfavorable information concerning either side's case will eventually surface in the discovery and trial process, so usually no real advantage accrues to either side by delayed disclosure. In many cases filed in court, too little is at stake to warrant the expense of using ordinary discovery procedures to prepare for trial. Early mediation of these types of cases provides a cost-saving method of discovery and enhances the potential for early settlement.

2.4.8   Work out a procedural schedule in a complex case

In complex cases with multiple parties, witnesses, claims, counter-claims, cross-claims, etc., the scheduling of discovery can be a major problem. The egos of lawyers, parties, and witnesses can combine to form a witches' brew of dissension and discord. Disagreements can arise over very mundane topics, such as when, where, and how to take a deposition, the order of taking discovery, whose claims have priority in discovery, who can be present at depositions, when parties should produce the reports of experts, and a host of other scheduling considerations. Although these disagreements may seem innocuous to the ordinary observer, they can provoke caustic communication among counsel that results in further lack of cooperation and even outright hostility. These repetitious discovery battles overburden the judge assigned such a case, result in unjustifiable and excessive litigation, and distract counsel from their real discovery objectives. One method of short-circuiting this kind of potentially explosive, progress-debilitating situation is to arrange for a mediation in which the parties can work out a master schedule, taking into account the interests of all the affected individuals.

2.4.9   Resolve discovery disputes

In the ordinary, noncomplex case, discovery disputes arise that sometimes impede advocates from pursuing their discovery objectives efficiently. You can, of course, file motions to compel discovery or to protect documents from disclosure, etc., but these motions and related legal memoranda can be very expensive to research, prepare, and file, and perhaps more important, even after they are on file it may take months before a judge functioning in a busy court can issue a ruling on them. If the discovery is crucial to the case, case preparation often ceases pending the ruling. Advocates facing this type of situation commonly engage the services of a mediator to help resolve the disagreements. In a one- or two-hour conference, a mediator can often lead the parties to find ways to settle their differences on the basis of the pleadings and related discussion, without the need for detailed motions and memoranda. The mediator can also be engaged to be available in person or by telephone should future discovery disputes arise.

2.4.10 Use a mediator as the communicator of a creative proposal

Creative lawyers are often frustrated litigators. They are able to generate numerous ideas for settling cases, but they are not always sure that their ideas are suitable for practical application. Even when practicality is not an issue, they are reluctant to share the ideas with opposing counsel for fear of being ridiculed or being thought of as some sort of crackpot or oddball. Creative lawyers now have a solution to their dilemma—a mediator. In caucus, the mediator can serve as a sounding board for creative ideas, testing them, perhaps improving them, and even suggesting additional ones. Then the mediator can lend legitimacy and credibility to the ideas by presenting them to opposing counsel in a separate caucus. The instantaneous shock that opposing counsel would ordinarily experience when exposed to a new idea, a new proposal, or a new perspective on the same situation is tempered by the context of the exposure—the mediator's neutrality, impartiality, and levelheadedness. Because the new idea seems to have originated with the mediator, the opposing counsel is more apt to try to see its relevance as a solution or an element of a solution. Opposing counsel may even come up with a corollary idea that can be combined to form an acceptable overall resolution.

2.4.11 Use a mediator to disclose favorable "bombshell" information

In discovery, advocates sometimes withhold extremely favorable information, hoping to spring it on their opponent at trial and achieve a gloriously stunning victory. These advocates justify the nondisclosure of such "bombshell" information on the basis that the opponent did not specifically request it in discovery. There comes a point in pretrial preparation, however, when advocates realize that the bombshell information may be as beneficial in settlement discussions as it would be before a jury. A large settlement would negate the necessity for a protracted, expensive jury trial. Moreover, if they wait until the middle of the trial to disclose the existence of the evidence, they run the risk that the trial judge may exclude the evidence as unfair surprise, and consequently it would be of absolutely no value to their case. Thus, disclosing the existence of the information to opposing counsel in pretrial negotiations seems to be the more prudent course of action. But at that point the nondisclosing advocates face a dilemma. It may be very awkward for the nondisclosing advocates to disclose a critical piece of information after opposing counsel have invested two years of their time and their client's money in discovering the case. Opposing counsel may take a differing view of the legitimacy of the nondisclosure and may believe that their discovery requests covered the production of the information.

They may seek an order excluding the evidence from trial or an order for sanctions, or both. Again, the solution for the nondisclosing advocates may be to arrange for a mediation conference. Disclosing the bombshell information through the mediator in the context of settling the entire case would probably take the edge off opposing counsel's angry feelings. They could more rationally evaluate the possible detriment to their case with the assistance of the calm, insightful, thoughtful input of the mediator. Settlement could result, but if it did not, the lawyers would probably be able to continue litigating in a civil manner.

2.4.12 Use a mediator to filter and diffuse harmful information

No case is perfect, some cases are less perfect than others, and a few are downright difficult to prosecute or defend because of adverse information that develops out of your investigation. Consider the situation where you are defending a small clothing manufacturing company against a terminated employee's claim of age discrimination. You are near the close of discovery in the case, and your principal defense is that the employee was terminated along with several other employees as part of a downsizing and corporate restructuring. Long ago in the court proceeding, the employee's counsel requested copies of the documents in her personnel file and you produced them. Yesterday the company's chief executive officer (CEO) notified you that he had more documents related to the employee's file that had been "misplaced." Reading through those documents you run across a handwritten note from the CEO to the personnel director in which the CEO, referring to the plaintiff employee, wrote, "She still does a fine job, but the old gray mare ain't what she used to be." After you recover from the shock of what this document may do to your case, you immediately call the CEO, who informs you that the note must be read in the context of his other conversations with the personnel director and that it was all a joke. He explains that the employee used the oldest sewing machine in the plant for all the years she was employed with the company. The gray clunker of a machine is so antiquated that everyone in the plant refers to it as "the old gray mare." The company had tried many times to provide the employee with new upgraded equipment, but she had refused, stating that she was comfortable using the old equipment and that she was still as productive using it as the other workers were using "those new-fangled gadgets." You believe this explanation, but that does not solve the problem of the double meaning of the note and how you might disclose this information to opposing counsel. You would rather not do it during a pretrial conference with the judge in your case, because you may not have sufficient time to explain how all this came about and why you did not produce the document sooner. Whatever your explanation, the judge may think less of your case—and maybe less of you also. Perhaps your best alternative would be to arrange a mediation in which you and your CEO client could first explain your dilemma to the mediator in caucus and then you both could strategize with her as to the best procedure for disclosing it to opposing counsel. You may decide to do it in a joint session, perhaps in conjunction with a preparatory caucus conducted by the mediator with opposing counsel. Assuming that the mediator finds the CEO's explanation plausible, the mediator would probably be a helpful ally in your efforts to filter and diffuse information potentially very harmful to your case.

2.4.13 Determine possible trade-offs in a multiparty case

In cases involving multiple parties, it is often impossible for the parties locked in litigation to examine their own true interests and the interests of their adversaries and to discover overlapping interests, opportunities for joint gain, or areas of minimal-loss compromise. Normally settlements in these cases occur only when the court takes an active role in encouraging and facilitating settlement or when counsel for one of the parties assumes the intermediary role and takes the responsibility of exploring avenues for settlement. Sometimes neither the court nor counsel wish to assume this mediative role. Such circumstances are ideal for a mediator's involvement. A mediator can first meet privately with each of the parties and their counsel and facilitate the introspective interest-identifying process. After gathering this information and analyzing it, the mediator will have a full grasp of the true interests and needs of the parties and will be able to perceive potential opportunities for trade-offs and compromises that can be presented to all the parties in a joint session. Then, working with the parties in separate caucuses after the joint session, the mediator will determine the parties' respective thoughts about which trade-offs and compromises are desirable and which ones are undesirable. Through further joint sessions and caucuses they will refine the solution. If the solution is not fully satisfactory to all the parties, this process may result in fewer parties and fewer claims remaining in the case for judicial resolution.

2.4.14 Determine who the parties in interest are in a multiparty case

In a multiparty case, it is very difficult sometimes to determine, except through a protracted, tedious discovery process, all the parties in interest in the litigation. This is particularly true in complex construction litigation involving numerous players including owners, general contractors, subcontractors, suppliers, manufacturers, etc. For example, in a case where a plaintiff initially sues three defendants, the situation may lend itself to a mediation conference soon after the filing of the Complaint to quickly identify additional parties and discuss how these parties can be brought into the dispute resolution process—be it court litigation or continued mediation. The initial mediation conference may spark a chain reaction resulting in a common interest in trying to achieve an early settlement of the case. Unsued parties who are contacted regarding the pending litigation may be willing to participate in efforts to resolve their part of the dispute instead of being dragged into what they perceive as someone else's battle, guaranteed to subject them to costly litigation.

2.4.15 Use a mediator to reach a bracket for high-low arbitration

Recently it has become a common practice for advocates to use mediation as a prelude to high-low arbitration. In high-low arbitration, explained in more detail in section 7.1, parties proceed to arbitration after having established a last-demand, last-offer bracket through negotiation. By preagreement, they submit the case to an arbitrator, who is not informed of the bracket figures. If the arbitrator's decision falls outside the bracket, the award will be the closest endpoint of the bracket. If the decision falls within the bracket, the decision figure will coincide with the award in the case. The idea is to limit each party's risk in having a third party decide the damage award. Sometimes the parties are unable, through conventional negotiation, to move from high-demand, low-offer starting points, thus leaving an extremely large gap to close. Mediation can assist in closing this gap; if it is not successful in fully closing the gap, it can narrow the gap, making high-low arbitration a realistic dispute-ending alternative for the parties.

2.5 SELECTING CASES FOR MEDIATION

2.5.1 When should mediation be considered for a particular dispute?

Advocates often ask, when should mediation be considered? When is it most effective? The stock answer is that it should be considered as soon as the conflict arises and after traditional negotiation attempts fail. That answer is helpful to some extent, but you should not initiate mediation instantly in many situations, and in certain circumstances, you should not initiate it at all. For example, you should not consider mediation or use it at the inception of a dispute where an emergency situation requires a court order to prevent dissipation or sequestering of corporate assets, or where persons or property are likely to suffer other kinds of irreparable harm without court protection. Other typical situations in which early mediation may be counterindicated include the following: all the real parties in interest need to be formally served; one or more of the parties has everything to gain and nothing to lose by delay; and a party has a rigid view of his legal rights and seeks revenge. Sometimes negotiation of a conflict may be perceived as violating public policy or the public interest, as in the case of environmental or antitrust cases. If early mediation occurs in these situations, the appropriate federal, state, and local governmental agencies often intervene to represent and protect the public interest.

Notwithstanding these counterindications, you should consistently consider using mediation at specific junctures of the judicial process: just before a lawsuit is filed; after the Answer is filed; after the judge rules on dispositive motions such as denying motions to dismiss or for summary judgment; prior to the initiation of expensive discovery; after completion of discovery and prior to the initiation of intensive trial preparation; immediately prior to trial; and after judgment and prior to or just after the time a notice of appeal is filed. As explained in section 2.4, at each of these junctures there may be different reasons for engaging the services of a mediator—some tactical, strategic, and competitive, and others, resolution-oriented and collaborative.

2.5.2 Favorable situational indications for mediation

No one can reasonably deny that early settlements of disputes guarantee benefits for the disputants and other affected individuals. A fair settlement that is reached quickly spares clients—and sometimes their families, business colleagues, and friends—the stresses, delays, inconveniences, and expenses of litigation. Moreover, the result that is achieved is more apt to advance the intangible interests of the disputants, such as the need for respect and cooperation. It is common knowledge that 95 percent or more of all court cases eventually settle; many times the parties do not conclude the settlement until the eve of trial. Many cases could settle earlier if the advocates could accurately perceive when a case is ripe for the involvement of a mediator. This task is not always simple, but the following considerations can help you determine mediation ripeness.

If the parties desire a prompt settlement but have reached deadlock, mediation is indicated, particularly if they have shared sufficient information (or could share it in mediation) or sufficient discovery has occurred, and the parties are willing to participate in a half- or full-day session to see if they can make any settlement progress. Parties who must maintain a business or a family relationship during and after resolution of a conflict and want to minimize the cost of litigation usually have a substantial interest in an early settlement of their differences. Thus, in a contract dispute between a manufacturer and distributor who are engaged in an ongoing business or in a child custody dispute where the parties need to work out the terms and conditions of a visitation schedule, a skillful mediator can help the parties identify their underlying interests and can efficiently guide the parties and their counsel past positional bargaining and assist them to see opportunities for mutual gain. In the case of a business contract, early mediation allows the parties, if they desire, to renegotiate a whole new agreement—to transform the dispute from a destructive conflict situation into the joint negotiation of a new transaction that satisfies all interests involved. Such a nonmonetary remedy, subscribed to by both parties, is rarely available through court adjudication. Besides, a court adjudication may establish a precedent that would be harmful to one or more of the disputants in other existing business contracts or contracts under negotiation with other firms.

Multiple-party, multiple-issue disputes are particularly conducive to resolution through mediation because they offer advantageous opportunities for complex trade-offs through negotiation. Many companies facing the prospect of being sued are now resorting to presuit mediation to minimize adverse publicity that a lawsuit might generate and to keep the settlement results confidential to avoid encouraging lawsuits by other individuals or companies.

2.5.3 Unfavorable situational indications for mediation

Despite the many advantages of mediation, it is not necessarily appropriate in every situation. For instance, if one party to the mediation lacks relevant knowledge, has little or no power in relation to the other disputant, and is unrepresented by counsel, mediation is not a preferred resolution process. The situation would place the mediator in the very awkward stance of trying to be neutral yet trying to bring the unequal knowledge/power condition into equilibrium by offering advice, legal or otherwise, to the less powerful party and by being overbearing with the more powerful party. Such conduct would most probably violate the mediator's code of ethics. Thrust into such a situation, any professional mediator would suggest that the less powerful party obtain legal counsel and would withdraw as mediator if the party did not do so. Such disputes are best resolved in an adjudicative setting, where procedures guaranteeing due process can offset power imbalances. An exception to the rule that power imbalances generally negate the effectiveness of mediators occurs in family law mediation. Usually a well-trained and experienced mediator can achieve at least temporary relational equilibrium between the parties by dealing directly with the emotional and psychological aspects of the relationship and by suggesting strategies and techniques for enhancing their interpersonal communication—at least for the purpose of resolving their current conflicts.

Other situations not conducive to mediation include those where the disputants have a history of bad-faith negotiations. Parties who have refused to deal forthrightly with each other will probably not be forthright with the mediator either. Such parties typically make settlement offers through the mediator and later withdraw them or make them more onerous to gain negotiation leverage. They often deny that events occurred when they actually did occur or assert that events occurred when they did not. Such circumstances make the mediator's function difficult to perform and sometimes render the mediator totally ineffectual. Agreements reached through deception and pretense rarely endure, and therefore time spent by the parties in mediation is often wasted. Bad-faith negotiations normally occur where parties are emotionally volatile, where anger has turned to hatred, and where at least one party wants to punish the other. Business or financial deals turning sour and marriages going on the rocks are two spawning grounds for bad-faith dealing. In some of these disputes, because of limited financial means of the parties, mediation often appears to be the only affordable process for resolving the dispute. However, if you are representing a client in this type of situation, you are probably well advised to convince opposing counsel to arbitrate the matter as cost-consciously as possible, so that a neutral third party can independently assess and fairly determine the credibility of the parties.

Situations in which a party seeks to establish legal precedent or a judgment with preclusive effect, as in major cases testing constitutional rights or the legality of a new statute, are not ordinarily suited for resolution through mediation. Similarly, situations in which insufficient information has been developed to evaluate a settlement proposal are not generally suitable for mediation, unless the parties recess the mediation while they gather additional information. Finally, mediation is not normally suitable where one party is threatening to press criminal charges or where parallel criminal charges are actually pending. First, it is professionally improper for a lawyer to threaten criminal action against an opposing party to gain an advantage in a civil lawsuit. Second, a mediator who would communicate such threats or use them to achieve a settlement in a civil case would, to a virtual certainty, be deemed to have acted unethically. Third, a civil case in which the government is unrepresented that is mediated to settlement while parallel criminal charges are pending could give rise to the unsavory perception that the criminal case, and thus the public interest, has been compromised during the mediation process.

2.5.4   Invalid reasons for not using mediation

Advocates unfamiliar with or inexperienced in the use of mediation sometimes advance several reasons for not using mediation: (1) suggesting the use of a mediator to your opponent is a sign of weakness, (2) mediation is merely a ploy by one party to discover the other side's case, and (3) mediation will not work because the case involves complex legal issues or strong emotions. These are generally invalid reasons for not using mediation.

Lawyers who have used mediation successfully know how beneficial it can be for their clients. They know that regardless of whether their case is strong, weak, or close, it is a sign of strength and wise advocacy—not a sign of weakness—to suggest mediation. In all likelihood, the case will settle shortly before trial anyway after extensive pretrial preparation. They know the mediation process has the capacity to cut through quickly to the inevitable truths at the heart of a dispute and to obviate the lengthy pretrial litigation. But even if a particular case does not seem amenable to a pretrial settlement, suggesting mediation early in the process is not a sign of weakness but rather of prudence. For example, if you go to trial with a weak case, you will probably lose at trial, but if your case survives the trial, you will undoubtedly lose on appeal. If you go to trial with a strong case, you will probably win at trial, and if you do not, you will probably be a winner in the appellate court. It does not make much sense to go to trial in a close case. If you win or lose there, it is usually a toss-up as to what will occur on appeal. Thus the prudent lawyer knows that if she has a strong case before a jury and an appellate court, it will be strong in mediation; if it is weak, it will be weak in mediation; if close, it will lend itself to a compromise resolution in mediation. Continued litigation simply delays the inevitable. In the current state of the profession, where the use of mediation is expanding by almost geometric proportions, a lawyer's inability to perceive timely opportunities for mediation is a sign of weakness, or at the very least, a sign of indifference or of a lack of professional growth. Advocates who say that mediation is merely a ploy to discover the other side's case forget that the purpose of the litigation process is to do just that—to allow the parties to discover the other side's information in anticipation of the parties' presentation of discovered information to a jury or judge, preliminary to a decision. Thus if discovery is an essential part of the litigation process, why shouldn't the discovery that occurs informally in the mediation process foster rather than impede the litigator's purposes? With more court systems today requiring *voluntary* disclosure of information by parties in the discovery phase of litigation, the "discovery ploy" reason for not using mediation is no longer meaningful or convincing.

Finally, the position that a case is too complex or the parties too emotionally charged for mediation is no longer tenable. Today, parties are
submitting cases that are extremely complicated, legally and technically, to skilled mediators in increasing numbers with highly satisfactory, expense-saving results. Mediation has, by and large, proven itself
to be a far superior process to court adjudication and arbitration in finding mutually agreeable solutions to emotion-packed conflict. Adjudication tends to exacerbate and prolong angry feelings; mediation has the
capacity to end them.

2.6 INDICATOR GUIDE FOR SELECTING CASES FOR MEDIATION

2.6.1 Favorable indicators

The guide below collects some situational indicators favorable to a
mediated settlement of a dispute.[6] The presence of only one of these indicators (and the absence of any unfavorable indicators) may be sufficient to trigger scheduling of a mediation.

FAVORABLE INDICATORS FOR MEDIATION

- The parties and counsel are agreeable to participating in the
  mediation process and desire a prompt settlement.
- The parties will have to maintain a direct or indirect relationship
  after resolution of a dispute.
- Sufficient discovery has occurred to make settlement discussions
  meaningful.
- The parties desire to minimize litigation costs.
- In addition to or instead of damages, the parties desire a remedy
  that is nonmonetary or one that the court cannot provide.
- The parties wish to avoid establishing a judicial precedent or a
  judgment that may have a preclusive effect.
- The parties or their lawyers have difficulty initiating negotia-
  tions with the other side, lack adequate negotiation skills, or are
  deadlocked in negotiations.
- The parties have differing appraisals of the facts of a case.
- Resolution requires complex trade-offs.
- The parties want the matter settled confidentially.

6.   These indicators are adapted from John W. Cooley, "Merging of Minds and
Microcomputers: The Coming of Age of Computer-Aided Mediation of Court Cases," in
Systematic Analysis in Dispute Resolution, ed. Stuart S. Nagel and Miriam K. Mills
(Quorum Books, 1991), 86. See also, Nancy H. Rogers and Richard A. Salem, *A
Student's Guide to Mediation and the Law* (Matthew Bender, 1987), 41–51.

2.6.2   Unfavorable indicators

The guide below collects some of the situational indicators unfavorable to the use of mediation.[7] The presence of one of these indicators could be a sufficient basis to decline using mediation to resolve a particular dispute.

UNFAVORABLE INDICATORS FOR MEDIATION

- A party cannot effectively represent its best interests and will not be represented by counsel at the mediation sessions.
- The parties have a history of acting in bad faith in negotiations.
- A party seeks to establish legal precedent or a judgment with preclusive effect.
- Significant parties are unwilling to mediate.
- The parties are engaged in a dispute directly affecting public interest, and the government is not represented.
- A party is threatening to press criminal charges.
- One or more parties stand to gain from a strategy of delay.
- A party needs more formal discovery to obtain necessary information before settlement can be achieved.
- The parties have rigid assessments of the law applicable in the case and desire the court to decide who is right and who is wrong, legally.
- A third party neutral needs to make an immediate decision to protect the interests of a disputant or of the public.

2.7   CHOOSING THE APPROPRIATE MEDIATOR

When choosing a mediator for a particular dispute, you should be sure that the person selected is properly trained and/or experienced in mediation; possesses the requisite personal traits, such as honesty, trustworthiness, patience, flexibility, and creativity; and is able to satisfy the parties' practical needs for availability and affordability.[8]

Many lawyers believe that to be effective in mediating a specific case, a mediator must have extensive experience in the particular area of substantive law and with fact patterns as close as possible to the one in the case being suggested for mediation. Actually, if facilitative

---

7.   These indicators have been adapted from information in Cooley, id. at 87; Rogers and Salem, id. at 51–58.

8.   See generally, Ted A. Donner and Brian L. Crowe, *Attorney's Practice Guide to Negotiations*, 2d ed. (Clark Boardman Callaghan, 1995), sec. 22:07.

mediation is desired, such focused experience is not always necessary. In fact, extensive experience as a litigator in a particular field of substantive law may serve to bias the mediator and prevent him from seeing potential creative solutions that a mediator fresh to the field might perceive.

Far and away, the most basic quality of a good mediator is the ability to remain neutral. The mediator must have no stake whatsoever in the outcome of the mediation and must be able to remain objective while assisting the parties in bringing about a settlement that satisfies their respective needs.

The effective mediator is able to see the many connections between and among the disputants and others. She must be sensitive to the emotional needs of all the parties, including their expectations of respect, equality, security, and myriad other nonmaterial interests that may exist in a given case. Additionally, a good mediator is able to listen effectively. Listening may well be the mediator's most important dispute-resolving tool. By listening well, the mediator is able to discover the underlying emotional, psychological, and value orientations that may hold the keys to resolving more quantifiable issues. By listening effectively, the mediator is able to gain a clear understanding of the parties' interests and difficulties from their perspective and is able to convey that understanding back to the parties. This is something that the parties are often unable to do for themselves, unassisted.

The effective mediator also knows how to facilitate communication between the parties. Sometimes one of the parties' shyness or inability to articulate a position causes the failure of communication. A good mediator is able to take steps to ensure that all viewpoints, including those of the shy and reticent, are put on the table with equal clarity. A mediator must also be skilled in asking probing and important, but nonthreatening, questions. This technique can be very effective in apprising one side of the other side's concerns, while encouraging the parties to reexamine and articulate their respective views, an exercise that is useful in sparking reality awareness in the minds of the parties.

In summary, when selecting a facilitative mediator, you should consider candidates who are unquestionably neutral and who are skilled in moving parties from competitive negotiation to cooperative problem solving while encouraging interaction between them. Former judges normally are good candidates to serve as evaluative mediators, but some attorneys can perform such service equally well. The best advice for you to follow in selecting any mediator for any purpose is to inquire of other lawyers who have experienced mediations conducted by your mediator candidates.

2.8 DRAFTING/REVIEWING THE MEDIATION AGREEMENT; REVIEWING APPLICABLE MEDIATION RULES AND STATUTES

As an advocate, you may be engaged to represent a client who is a party to a dispute where the parties, at the time of contracting, preagreed in writing to submit any dispute arising out of the contract to mediation. Thus, you will need to carefully review the mediation clause of such a contract to determine whether its terms might alter the way you approach the mediation, the way you prepare your case or client for the mediation, and the way you conduct yourself at the mediation itself. In other situations, you may also be asked to draft a future-dispute mediation clause or a present-dispute mediation agreement. Sample mediation clauses and a mediation agreement appear in Appendices F and G, respectively.

A typical future-dispute mediation clause provides that before either party sues the other, each shall, in good faith, attempt to have the dispute resolved through the assistance of a mutually agreed upon mediator, who shall be given a period of time, a fixed number of hours or days, in which to attempt a solution. Some such clauses require that if mediation proves unsuccessful, the parties must submit the dispute to arbitration after the mediation period has expired. Also, you should know that some future-dispute mediation clauses are quite elaborate, consisting of all the considerations to be taken into account when a dispute is mediated. The elaborate future-dispute mediation clause and a present-dispute mediation agreement is likely to contain provisions regarding the following topics:

- Role of the mediator.
- Nature of the process (facilitative/evaluative).
- Exchange of information (what and when).
- Information to be provided to the mediator.
- Requirement of settlement authority.
- Requirement to participate in good faith.
- Confidentiality requirements.
- Ground rules regarding caucusing.
- Procedure upon party's withdrawal from mediation.
- Procedures and requirements for paying fees and expenses.

Before you draft any future-dispute mediation clause or present-dispute mediation agreement, you should carefully review the applicable mediation rules and statutes of the jurisdiction in which the dispute will likely be mediated. Many states have statutes and many court systems have rules in place that govern the conduct of mediations within their jurisdictions. It is predictable that such rules and statutes will proliferate in the future. February, 2002 marked the culmination of five years of work by the National Conference of Commissioners on Uniform State Laws and the American Bar Association Section of Dispute Resolution to win the organization's approval of a Uniform Mediation Act (UMA). (See appendix M). As finally approved, the Act included three central provisions beyond the definitions and principles of construction and scope of the Act. The centerpiece of the Act is a privilege that permits the parties, mediator, and nonparty participants to prevent the use of mediation communications in legal proceedings that take place after the mediation. The Act further bars mediator disclosures to courts, administrative agencies, and other government entities, and it also provides parties with a right of accompaniment, including counsel, which is particularly important in mediations that are compelled. Now that the Act is finally approved, State legislatures, in future years, will be considering whether to adopt the UMA, or perhaps variations of it.

2.9   DESIGNING THE ADR PROCESS IN COMPLEX CASES

As was mentioned in the preface to this book, as an advocate, you will be increasingly called upon by clients to design *processes* for resolving disputes. Some of the disputes requiring dispute resolution process ideas may be extremely complex. In this section we will walk through a design process yielding alternative process designs for a typical complex, multiparty dispute.

Assume that a client has asked you to prepare alternative designs for a dispute resolution mechanism to resolve a complex litigation dispute involving at least two court cases. The dispute has multiple parties and primarily involves intellectual property ("IP" or "Liability") and insurance coverage ("Coverage") issues. You are told that the IP and Coverage issues overlap in the sense that some of the evidence and legal arguments relating to one may also be relevant to the other. The plaintiff in the case is an advertising company and the defendants are a major fast food chain and two of its parent companies ("Corporate Defendants") and three insurance companies ("Insurers"). The parties have already experienced an evaluative mediation that has been unsuccessful in resolving the dispute.

You should first be aware that cases involving Liability and Coverage issues are very complicated to litigate in the court system. In a typical tort suit of this kind, plaintiff files suit against an insured defendant. The insurer files a declaratory judgment action against the insured defendant alleging noncoverage of the claim. There are two possible judicial alternatives. The court can allow the declaratory judgment action to proceed, which may result in resolving the coverage issue before the conclusion of the underlying tort suit. Or, the court can stay the declaratory judgment action until the tort suit is resolved. The coverage question will thus linger unresolved during the pendency of the underlying lawsuit. Appeals taken in either of these proceedings can dash any hope of speedy resolution of the overall case. But most importantly, there are usually major problems with allowing the Coverage case to proceed. Positions taken by an insurer in the Coverage case may seriously harm the insured defendant vis-a-vis the plaintiff in the tort case. For example, in the declaratory judgment proceeding, the insurer may try to prove that the insured caused the intentional injury. The insurer's evidence may seriously undermine the insured in the tort suit, even if the insured is being represented by independent counsel in the tort suit. If the insured were forced to argue in the Coverage proceeding that he acted only, or at most, "negligently," the insured may seriously weaken his position in the tort suit that he was not negligent at all. To resolve these problems caused predominantly by the highly structured and public nature of court litigation, some experts have recommended the design and use of more flexible and dispute-tailored processes. Concurrent mediation is one such process.[9] "Concurrent mediation" does not mean that all of the issues between and among all the parties are mediated simultaneously. Rather, the term means that the Liability and Coverage issues are privately mediated to resolution in a systematic and orderly fashion, without leaving one or the other issue for court adjudication.

Clients sometimes require lawyers to hastily suggest alternative process designs based upon extremely limited information about the parties and the configuration and substance of the respective claims and defenses. Since "form generally follows function," you might want to tell your client, in the present exercise, that you may need to modify some of your design proposals when you receive more specific information about the parties, claims, and defenses. Even on the sparse information provided above regarding the presented case, however, there are several potential process designs suitable for consideration. They include: (1) classic co-mediation; (2) classic mini-trial procedure; (3) modified mini-trial procedure; (4) any of these three mechanisms with a blind bidding enhancement. Before proceeding with this exercise, you may want to review chapter 7, which describes these pertinent hybrid processes in considerable detail.

9. See generally, Ellen S. Pryor and Will Pryor, "Concurrent Mediation of Liability and Insurance Coverage Disputes," 4 *Conn. Ins. L. J.* 485 (1997–98).

Classic co-mediation. As explained more thoroughly in section 7.4, an ADR hybrid that has gained widened use over the past few years is co-mediation. Simply defined, co-mediation is a process in which more than one person serves as a mediator. It involves the concepts of team mediation and interdisciplinary problem solving, and it can be tailored to the needs of a particular dispute. Multiple mediators are commonly used in complex disputes where there are multiple parties, sometimes on each side of the case, and an intricate configuration of claims, cross-claims, and counter-claims. Typically, one mediator is designated as the lead mediator. That mediator is the chief strategist, coordinating the mediation activities of the other mediators and serving as an advisor and clearing house of information for them. With respect to the presented case and configuration of parties and claims, the co-mediation process takes this format:

- Parties enter into a mediation agreement naming at least two neutrals as co-mediators.
- One mediator ("Coverage mediator") is assigned to Coverage parties; caucuses with each party privately; and then continues caucusing or brings Coverage parties together for a joint session. The Coverage mediator's goal is to help the insurers (and insured as appropriate) to reach a consensus on their percentage of contribution to a settlement, perhaps involving creative, mutual gain elements.
- Second mediator ("Liability mediator") is assigned to Liability Parties; caucuses with each party privately; and then continues caucusing or brings parties together for a joint session. The Liability mediator's goal is to help the parties reach a fair settlement value of the underlying IP and related claims, perhaps involving creative, mutual gain elements.
- The Coverage mediator and the Liability mediator will caucus at appropriate intervals and will control the sequence of the caucusing and joint sessions.
- This process is estimated to take three days, though, because of caucusing, the individual parties will not be engaged in it continuously.

Classic mini-trial procedure. As more thoroughly explained in section 7.6, *infra*, the mini-trial, as apparent from its name, is an abbreviated trial or hearing. This method of dispute resolution is a relatively new approach. Its principal advantage is that the mini-trial involves high-level corporate representatives in the dispute resolution process. It is best suited to large disputes and complex litigation. Cases involving breaches of complex contracts, particularly if there are complex technical issues; patents cases; antitrust cases; major construction cases; and products liability cases may be most appropriate for mini-trial resolution.

The mini-trial agreement specifies who will comprise the panel for the mini-trial. This panel normally consists of three people: a business executive from each side and a third party neutral. The third party neutral is instrumental in insuring that the resolution process stays on course. The business executives appointed to the panel must have the full authority to negotiate a settlement. Without that power, the hearing may be for naught. Also, it is advisable that an executive deeply involved with the case not be designated as a panel member. No panel member should be asked to pass judgment on a superior, or a person who reports directly to them, in the ordinary course of the party's business.

Before the mini-trial hearing, the parties to the mini-trial exchange brief position summaries (and document and witness lists if evidence is to be presented at the hearing). After an abbreviated period (usually a few hours or a day) of argument and/or presentation of evidence (as the parties elect), negotiation commences. The success of the entire process rests on this period of negotiation. In order to insure its success, the mini-trial agreement sets up its parameters in a way most conducive to achieving settlement. The negotiation normally extends into several sessions. Normally, the two business executives meet on by themselves or with the third party neutral. In the event that negotiations break down completely, the mini-trial agreement normally provides for a mandatory period of time to elapse before the decision is made to resume the original litigation. A "cool-down" period often allows the parties an opportunity to re-think their reasons for entering mini-trial negotiations in the first place, and often generates new settlement ideas.

With respect to the presented case and configuration of parties and claims, the classic mini-trial alternative could involve a format comprised of two sequential mini-trials:

- Parties enter into a mini-trial agreement naming two neutrals—one neutral (Coverage neutral) for the Coverage mini-trial and one neutral for the Liability mini-trial); The two neutrals would be former judges.

- The Coverage neutral chairs the Coverage panel which is additionally comprised of high-level representatives of the insured and the insurers.

- Insured's and insurers' lawyers present abbreviated cases to Coverage panel.

- After conclusion of cases, Coverage neutral meets with other panel members and seeks to help them reach a consensus on their percentage of contribution to a settlement, perhaps involving creative, mutual gain elements.

- If parties are unable to negotiate percentages, they can preagree to accept the recommendation of the Coverage neutral as a last resort or can preagree to some other finally determinative method. In either event, the role of the Coverage neutral in the process ends.

- It is estimated that this portion of the process will last one and one-half days.

- The second or Liability phase of the process begins.

- The Coverage neutral agrees not to disclose anything that occurred in the Coverage mini-trial to the Liability neutral.

- The Liability neutral chairs the Liability panel which is additionally comprised of high-level representatives of the plaintiff and the insured defendant.

- Plaintiff's and insured's lawyers present abbreviated cases to liability panel.

- After conclusion of cases, Liability neutral meets with other panel members and seeks to help them reach a consensus on the underlying IP and related claims, perhaps involving creative, mutual gain elements.

- If parties are unable to negotiate percentages, they can preagree to accept the recommendation of the Liability neutral as a last resort or can preagree to some other finally determinative method.

- It is estimated that this portion of the process will last one and one-half days.

Modified mini-trial procedure. The modified mini-trial procedure would provide for a technical advisor to each of the Coverage neutral and the Liability neutral described immediately above. The technical advisor for the Coverage neutral would be a lawyer skilled and experienced in insurance coverage law; the technical advisor for the Liability neutral would be a lawyer skilled and experienced in IP law. There would also be a third neutral called the Process neutral who would observe both the Coverage and the Liability mini-trial proceedings, and intervene in them as explained below. The mini-trial procedure described immediately above would be modified as follows:

- After the conclusion of the Coverage mini-trial, the Coverage neutral and his/her technical advisor would confer with each other. The Coverage neutral alone would come to a decision as to the contribution percentages of the insurers (and the insured as the case may be), write it on a piece of paper, and place the paper in a sealed envelope. The roles of the Coverage neutral and his/her technical advisor would at that point end.

- The Process neutral (who does not know the decision of the Coverage neutral) meets with other panel members and seeks to help them reach a consensus on their percentage of contribution to a settlement, perhaps involving creative mutual gain elements.

- If parties are unable to negotiate percentages with the assistance of the Process neutral, they open the sealed envelope containing the decision of the Coverage neutral, and by preagreement are bound by it.

- This same procedure is replicated in the Liability mini-trial with the Process neutral intervening as mediator after the Liability neutral puts his/her decision in a sealed envelope.

- If parties are unable to reach a settlement with the assistance of the Process neutral, they open the sealed envelope containing the decision of the Liability neutral, and by preagreement are bound by it.

Blind bidding enhancement. A blind bidding enhancement can be used in conjunction with any of the above alternative designs. This procedure is frequently used to help parties reach a settlement on the damage aspects of a case, and has been successfully employed in the past to settle multi-million dollar claims. This procedure is most commonly used when the parties reach a bracket in negotiation or mediation but are unable to close the gap through the use of ordinary negotiation techniques. In this procedure, as a last resort, each party confidentially submits a bid to the mediator. For the plaintiff, the bid represents the lowest figure that the plaintiff will accept to settle the case; for the defendant, the bid represents the highest figure the defendant will pay to settle the case. Only the mediator knows both (or all) the figures submitted. By preagreement, the parties decide what they will do depending on the outcome. For example, they can preagree that if they are X dollars apart, the mediator will disclose the numbers and they will split the difference. They can also preagree that if they are only Y dollars apart, the mediator will not disclose the actual figures, but they will continue mediating (or negotiating). Finally they can also agree that if they are more than Z dollars apart, the mediator will not disclose the figures, and they will proceed to trial. This procedure encourages the parties to submit realistic bids in order to avoid the substantial risks and expense of proceeding to trial.

Location of settlement meetings. The place you suggest for holding the ADR proceeding may be as important as the ADR process you suggest. For complex multi-party cases, you should seriously consider recommending that a nontraditional, less-structured location than law firms be used for the final phase (or all) of the settlement meetings. The idea would be to choose a place that has an informal, comfortable, corporate retreat-like atmosphere. Research has shown that the choice of setting often can have a favorable influence on the success of dispute resolution discussions.

Creo pie chart tool and blind trust method. Mediator Robert A. Creo has experimented with specially tailored ADR processes which have proven to be very successful in facilitating the resolution of complex, multiparty, multi-issue disputes. These processes are called the Creo Pie Chart Tool and the Creo Blind Trust Method. A detailed description of how these settlement techniques have been applied in actual cases may be found in CPR Institute for Dispute Resolution's *Alternatives*, Volume 18, No. 5, May 2000, page 1 (Creo Pie Chart Tool) and in Volume 17, No. 8, September 1999, page 1 (Creo Blind Trust Method).

Chapter Three

PREPARING THE CASE FOR MEDIATION

*"I don't know that there are any shortcuts to doing
a good job."*
— *Justice Sandra Day O'Connor*

If problem solving is viewed as the primary mission of lawyering, it is not difficult to see how a lawyer can play an important role in the mediation process. Long before a dispute arises, for example, you can advise your clients about the benefits of mediation and encourage them to insert a mediation clause into any contracts they enter into. A typical mediation clause, examples of which appear in appendix F, provides that before either party sues the other, each will, in good faith, attempt to resolve the dispute through the assistance of a mutually agreed upon mediator, who will be given a period of time, a fixed number of hours or days, in which to attempt a solution. Some clauses require that if mediation proves unsuccessful, the parties must submit the dispute to arbitration after the mediation period has expired.

In general, once a dispute has been submitted to mediation, your problem-solving role continues. You can help guide your client through the intricacies of the process, advise her concerning the legal aspects of the dispute, predict the probable outcome of the dispute in the adversarial arena, advise your client when a settlement offer is reasonable and worthy of serious consideration, and if a settlement is reached, ensure that the written settlement agreement meets your client's current needs and contains appropriate language to protect her against future problems that she may not have perceived or considered.

Effective advocacy in mediation has four discrete aspects: (1) preparing the case for mediation, (2) preparing the client for mediation, (3) advocacy during the mediation session, and (4) mediation-related advocacy after the mediation session. As a practical matter, the first and second aspects consist of many of the same steps you take in systematically planning for a negotiation: gathering and organizing information; analyzing timing issues; identifying issues, goals, and the parties' underlying interests; assessing strengths and weaknesses; setting the opening position and bottom line for your client; estimating the other party's bottom line and opening position; considering win-win outcomes and possible concessions and trade-offs; planning

49

appropriate strategies and tactics; and determining presentation format, agenda, and communication issues.[1] In preparing for the mediation, however, you will need to take some additional steps, including counseling the client on the nature of the mediation process, on the role of the mediator, and on the role of the client at the mediation conference. Forms to assist you in preparing your case for mediation are contained in appendix B-1 (analysis of your own case and strategies) and appendix B-2 (analysis of the other party's case and strategies).

In this chapter we will explore the first aspect of mediation advocacy—preparing the case for mediation. Shortcuts to performing this task exist, but as Justice O'Connor implies in the opening quotation, if you use the shortcuts, you may be doing less than a good job. The suggestions that follow will aid you in doing a good, and possibly an excellent, job of case preparation.

3.1   REVIEWING THE CASE FILE

A common complaint of mediators is that advocates come to mediations only partially prepared, and sometimes fully unprepared.

Excuses for lack of preparation range from "I'm just filling in for my law partner who's on trial," to "I thought this mediation was scheduled for next week until my client called yesterday afternoon and reminded me about it." These kinds of remarks offer little solace to an opposing counsel who has diligently prepared for the mediation and whose client is paying for half the expenses associated with it. Settlements are rarely reached in mediations in which one of the lawyers is not prepared. The prepared lawyer, resentful and believing that opposing counsel is not taking the mediation seriously, is reluctant to share information; and the unprepared counsel, unconfident and defensive, is disinclined to share much information for fear of saying something inaccurate that he will live to regret down the road. Such mediations typically result in a total waste of time for all persons involved, including and perhaps most important, the clients. Thus, to ensure that the mediation experience is as fruitful as possible, all lawyers need to come to the conference fully prepared. For cases in litigation, that preparation begins, simply enough, with a thorough and careful review of the case file.

The amount of time devoted to a review of the case file will, of course, depend on the nature and complexity of the case. Cases with multiple parties, multiple pleadings, and extensive discovery might require a day or more of file review, whereas smaller cases may require as little as

---

1. See Mark K. Schoenfield and Rick M. Schoenfield, *The McGraw-Hill 36-Hour Negotiating Course* (McGraw-Hill, Inc., 1991), 273. See also, Thomas F. Guernsey, *A Practical Guide to Negotiation* (National Institute for Trial Advocacy, 1996), chap. 4.

an hour. The amount of time you spend will also be a function of your familiarity with the file. If you are responsible for the file and appear in court often regarding it, you may be very familiar with it and will need less time than normal for preparation. If, on the other hand, the case has languished awhile on the court docket or the file is one for which your law partner has primary responsibility, you may have to spend a considerable amount of time—even in a small case—to bring yourself up to speed.

It is best to begin by reviewing the pleadings in chronological order. Be especially attentive to the separate claims of the parties and related relief requested, any counterclaims or other types of claims and relief requested, types of motions filed and the orders and opinions entered with respect to them, the nature and status of pending undecided motions, the status of the overall discovery, the discovery closure date, if any, and the latest order setting the case for trial, if any.

Next, review important documents in the case and transcripts of depositions, or important excerpts of them, noting the pages where the testimony and related exhibits are strongly supportive and strongly unsupportive of your legal positions in the case. Try to be as honest with yourself as you can in doing this. Remember, the mediation conference is not an oral argument where you are expected to present only your strongest legal positions. In the mediation conference you and your client will invariably be asked to evaluate realistically the relative strengths and weaknesses of your case and of your opponent's case. Your honest appraisal of all the available evidence in the case file during your preconference preparation will significantly aid your ability to realistically evaluate the case.

Finally, carefully read the correspondence in the case file. Make sure you know the sequence of any prior demands and offers to settle the case. Above all, be sure to find out what the last demand and last offer were. Also take care to read any communications from your client providing instructions or limitations on your negotiating authority. If there is any case precedent that you believe absolutely forecloses a claim, defense, or theory of damages of your opponent or renders their merit highly suspect, you would do well to read those cases. Realize, however, that in the typical mediation conference the parties spend very little time, if any, discussing case law.

When you have completed all this, make copies of the documents that you think will be helpful in arriving at a fair settlement of your case at the mediation conference.

3.2 ENSURING YOU HAVE ALL PERTINENT INFORMATION

Aside from unprepared counsel and uncommitted parties, the third leading cause of unsuccessful or ineffectual mediations is the absence of needed information. Thus, when you are reviewing the case file in preparation for a mediation, be especially careful to note any information that is not in the file that may be helpful to all concerned in the conference session. Then make every effort to locate the missing information and bring it with you. Depending on the importance of the missing information, you may decide to postpone the conference until you can acquire it.

In personal injury cases, for example, parties sometimes have to scuttle mediations midsession because of the unavailability of a recent report from a treating or consulting physician. In other situations, photographs of the vehicles or of the victim's injuries snapped shortly after the collision are misfiled in the lawyer's office and can be of no help to the mediator. Police reports available but never requested by counsel, and depositions taken but never ordered transcribed, are often important case elements whose absence at the mediation significantly inhibits an advocate from making a well-organized and cogent case presentation. Existing but absent medical lien information can cause mediations to recess unnecessarily while claims adjusters scurry to have their office colleagues locate the paperwork and fax it to them at the conference. Adjusters' well-intentioned and good-faith suggestions of structured settlements play out as hollow, unhelpful rhetoric without preplanning and workup of illustrative annuity schedules. No shortage of important missing information exists in other types of mediated cases: absent patient waivers of liability in medical malpractice cases that the lawyer asks the mediator to accept "on faith"; missing, critical work order changes in construction cases; "temporarily misplaced" bills marked "paid" in child support and custody disputes; the forgotten original of the business contract showing the signatures of all parties and the date executed. These are but a few examples of missing information that render a mediator less effective, and in some instances, totally ineffective. You should take the same kind of care in collecting necessary documentation for a mediation as you do in preparing for trial. No competent lawyer would present a case to a jury or judge in a court of law with a critical document missing. The same rule holds true for a mediation.

3.3 CONSIDERING ANY TIME CONSTRAINTS

The well-known expression, "good things happen to those who wait," has special significance in the settlement arena. The lawyer who is willing to be patient and wait until time constraints caused by natural or unexpected events force the opponent to accept less or pay more is often able to obtain quite favorable settlement results for his client. However, considerable risk is associated with this philosophy put into practice. The awaited events may never occur, or they may be imperceptible if they do occur. Patience can be power in litigation, but it also can carry with it some undesirable parasites—excessive expense and elevated anxiety. The prudent advocate knows that she does not necessarily have to wait for the favorable time-constraining situations to occur. She can create them. And she can do it through mediation. In scheduling the mediation, you should consider the time-constraining influences that could affect all parties, both from a broad perspective and a narrow one. Consider the situation, for example, where a new five-star hotel that will have its grand opening in a couple of weeks has not paid a uniform manufacturing company for the hotel's uniforms. The hotel, part of a well-known national chain, contends that many of the delivered uniforms were of inferior quality, and it wants the uniform manufacturer to replace them at no charge. The manufacturer refuses, contending that the uniforms met the written specifications, and the parties deadlock. Assume you represent the manufacturer. You have spoken to your client and opposing counsel, and all agree that the matter should be mediated. When do you want to try to schedule the mediation—before or after the grand opening? If it is compatible with your schedule, you should try very hard to set it before the grand opening. In that way you will garner for your client the additional leverage of threatening to file a lawsuit if the mediation is unsuccessful. Undoubtedly the hotel chain will stage a press conference in the local community on the day the new hotel opens. The last thing the hotel wants is the adverse publicity from a contemporaneous lawsuit filed by your client. If your client employs unions, you may also be able to raise the specter of a sympathy protest by some of the unionized hotel workers. From the broad perspective, setting up these kinds of time-critical issues greatly enhances the prospect of achieving a mediated settlement prior to the hotel's opening.

From a narrower perspective, you can use time-constraining influences to gain an advantage during the course of the mediation itself. If you wish to employ competitive tactics in the mediation, you can announce at the beginning of the session that you have another important meeting you must attend in two hours and you are hopeful that a settlement will be concluded by then. You are not lying. You intentionally planned the second meeting so that the mediation would have a precise ending time. After saying that, you let everyone know, politely but firmly, that your client intends to immediately file a lawsuit if a solution to the problem is not reached that day. As the mediation proceeds, you continue to courteously remind your opposing counsel and the mediator of your need to leave at a definite time. Do not worry about offending the mediator with your repeated reminder of time constraints. Experienced mediators know that their best allies in settling disputes are time limitations. Miracles can happen in the last few minutes of a mediation session.

3.4   IDENTIFYING THE PARTIES' UNDERLYING NEEDS AND INTERESTS

You should keep in mind that preparing for a mediation is much like preparing for a negotiation. Many of the same preparation principles apply.[2] Chief among them is identifying *all* parties' needs and interests. To do this effectively, you must understand the differences between legal issues, negotiation issues, legal positions, negotiating positions, the parties' needs, and the parties' interests.

Teachers of mediation advocacy commonly exhort their students to be as well prepared for a mediation as they would be for a trial on the merits. That advice is sound, but it does not go far enough. In fact, the mediation advocate must be more prepared than the trial advocate. In addition to being very familiar with all the pertinent evidence and well versed on the relevant legal positions, the mediation advocate must have a clear understanding of what is actually negotiable. That is, he must be aware of his client's and the opposing parties' needs and interests so that he can take appropriate negotiating positions at various points throughout the mediation process. To understand the scope of the mediation advocate's preparation, you need some definitions. As a vehicle to help clearly convey these definitions we will use a comparison between the "adjudication game" and the "mediation game."

3.4.1   The adjudication game

In their most basic sense, legal positions are offensive and defensive formations in a game called adjudication. They are derived from legal issues, which in turn are derived from legal theories. Simply defined, a legal position is a statement of a claim or defense that is supported by

---

2.   See generally, Guernsey, id. at chap. 4; Schoenfield and Schoenfield, id. at 269–329; Paul M. Lisnek, *A Lawyer's Guide to Effective Negotiation and Mediation* (West Publishing Co., 1993), chap. 2; Donald G. Gifford, *Legal Negotiation: Theory and Applications* (West Publishing Co., 1989), 45–72; Charles B. Craver, *Effective Legal Negotiation and Settlement*, 2d ed. (The Michie Co., 1993), 47–68.

evidence and by legal authority (constitution, case precedent, statute, etc.), a subset of game rules. Several legal theories and hence several legal authorities may support a single legal position. Another player may admit that a particular claim is valid or may contend that it is invalid by advancing a defense. Legal positions consisting of claims and corresponding defenses are adjudicated, that is, a disinterested player holds them to be valid or invalid (right or wrong). According to the adjudication game rules, a claim must actually pass three validity tests, two provisional and one final, to entitle the claimant to win—to have a right to a remedy. The first and second provisional validity tests are applied to a claim without reference to any corresponding defense. For a claim to survive the first provisional validity test, the subset of game rules must provide a basis for the legal position—that is, an authorized claim must be stated. For a claim to survive the second provisional validity test, sufficient evidence as defined by another subset of game rules must support the claim. If a claim survives these two validity tests, then the claim is tested against its corresponding defense and the associated evidence and legal authorities. If a claim is ultimately held more valid (both on the evidence and on the legal authority) than the corresponding defense, then, as stated above, the player who advanced the claim is the winner of the game and is entitled to a reward—a remedy defined by legal authority. If the adjudicator holds that the claim is less valid than the defense, the player who advanced the defense is the winner of the game, and the claimant is not entitled to a remedy. That is a simplified description of the adjudication game. As you can see, the adjudication game is highly structured, procedurally intricate, mystifying, and at times stultifying.

3.4.2 The mediation game

The mediation game is different. During the course of the mediation game, the adjudication game, if played at all, is normally played hypothetically and only in the minds of the mediation game players. Actual adjudication moves are made only in the rare situation of tandem mediation and adjudication games. The essence of the mediation game is simultaneous negotiation games—the mediator-player negotiates with the party-players (and counsel) together and at times separately, and the party-players sometimes negotiate directly with each other. Those negotiation game players follow sets of rules that are entirely different from the adjudication game rules. Under the mediation game rules, legal positions of the party-players are secondary and sometimes irrelevant. If addressed at all, the legal position of the party-players are discussed in terms of their potential validity, normally a subject of broad speculation. In contrast to the adjudication game, in the mediation game the party-players are concerned with their negotiating positions, not their legal positions. Negotiating positions are defined by the party-players' negotiation issues, which in turn are shaped by the players' underlying needs and interests or their conscious or unconscious hopes and fears relating to the protection of those needs and interests.

Whereas legal positions rarely change, negotiating positions may change at any time. Your overall goal in the mediation game is not, as in the adjudication game, to have the legal positions of your player declared valid or invalid by a disinterested player. Rather, your overall goal is to have an agreement that ratifies as many of your player's ultimate negotiating positions as possible—to satisfy as many of that player's needs and interests as possible. To do that, you often must also perceive ways to satisfy the opposing player's needs and interests. Thus, in preparing for the mediation game, you must have as clear an understanding as possible of the specific needs and interests of all the party-players, potentially giving rise to their negotiating positions. You must also understand what resources may be available to satisfy the specific needs and interests of the parties. The obvious question then becomes, what are needs and interests?

Basic needs are the most powerful human interests, and they fall generally into five categories: economic, emotional, psychological, physical, and social.[3] Basic needs are underlying interests, some compatible, some overlapping, some conflicting. Even where the parties perceive their needs to be purely economic and seek a wholly monetary (distributive) solution, often their underlying interests are compatible and overlapping when identified and expressed *in terms of value* instead of dollars. These interests reflect desires or concerns of the parties and form the basis of their negotiating positions. Even in tort cases, traditionally considered to have only purely monetary solutions, the parties may share compatible or overlapping interests: amount in controversy, cost of recovery, time of payment, exchange rate, method of payment (annuity, etc.), identity of payees, payment in kind, payment in services, payment in real estate, and tax or tariff considerations.

3.4.3 Techniques for identifying needs and interests

Although, as a mediation advocate, you have prepared your case properly by analyzing the needs and interests of all the parties, you may find during the course of the mediation that your opposing advocate has

3. Professor Abraham Maslow of Brandeis University, in his book entitled *Motivation and Personality* (New York: Harper & Row, Publishers, 1954), identified seven categories of needs as basic factors in human behavior: physiological, safety and security, love and belonging, esteem, self-actualization, to know and understand, and aesthetic. These seven factors can be condensed to the five needs as presented above. See Gerard I. Nierenberg, *Fundamentals of Negotiating* (Hawthorn/Dutton, 1973), 82–83. See also Roger Fisher and William Ury, *Getting to Yes: Negotiating Agreement Without Giving In*, 2d. ed. (Penguin Books, 1991), 48.

not done so. In fact his negotiating positions may be inspired by his client's unfounded fears or unrealistic hopes, instead of actual concerns or desires, and therefore are unreflective of the client's true needs and interests. What do you do? How do you determine the opposing party's true needs and interests? Roger Fisher and William Ury in their landmark book on negotiation, *Getting to Yes*,[4] offer these suggestions:

- Ask why. Put yourself in your opposing advocate's shoes and ask why she would be taking a particular negotiating position. What could be the desires, concerns, fears, hopes behind it? Or ask the opposing advocate why, either directly or indirectly through the mediator.

- Ask why not. Again, put yourself in opposing advocate's shoes and ask why she has not embraced your negotiating position. What desires, concerns, fears, hopes are precluding it? Are they legitimate? If not, what can you do or say to help the opposing side see that they are not legitimate. If they are legitimate, what can you do to modify your negotiating position so that the opposing party's needs and interests can be better satisfied? Realize that the mediator can help you determine answers to these questions through caucuses with the opposing party and the opposing advocate.

Another way to identify your own client's interests and to anticipate the interests of the opposing party is to engage your imagination. Resources available to satisfy those interests can be similarly identified. The table that follows provides a useful survey of possible interests and interest-satisfying resources of parties in any dispute or transaction situation.[5] The interests may relate to different needs of the parties and may actually be overlapping or compatible in achieving an integrative solution (nonmonetary or combined monetary and nonmonetary) in both personal and corporate disputes. Your premediation analysis should include both interests and resources related specifically to the dispute and, equally as important, general interests and resources unrelated to the dispute. Through your imagination you can expand the universe of possible interests and resources geometrically.

---

4.   Fisher and Ury, id. at 44–55.
5.   See John W. Cooley, "Descartes' Analytic Method and the Art of Geometric Imagineering in Negotiation and Mediation," *Valparaiso University Law Review* 28 (1993): 114.

INTEREST-RESOURCE TABLE

Time	Words	Secrecy
Place	Apology	Release
Quantity	Control	Reinstatement
Quality	Persons	Assurances
Size	Nature	Procedure
Context	Structure	Opportunity
Distance	Types	Guarantee
Responsibility	Volume	Publicity
Rate	Proportion	Security
Space	Exchange	Share

For example, when preparing the case for mediation, consider the items in the above table metaphorically—in the broadest sense possible. Thus, if you are preparing for the mediation of a business dispute, "volume" could refer to tripling a marketing effort (i.e., turning up the volume of the corporate message), decreasing the amount of production output, or increasing the amount of storage space in a warehouse. "Rate" could refer to frequency of occurrence, or a commission or discount, or an evaluation of products, services, or performance, and so on.

3.4.4 Applying the techniques—an example

The following example demonstrates how you might use these techniques when preparing for a mediation. Assume you are preparing for mediation in which you represent a supplier of computer parts ("Supplier") in a dispute with a company that manufactures computers ("Manufacturer"). You have filed a lawsuit on behalf of the Supplier alleging that the Supplier entered into a contract to sell 100 gross of connector cables to the Manufacturer for $200,000 plus shipping costs. You asserted in your Complaint that the Supplier shipped the parts to the Manufacturer by a common carrier and that the shipment was lost in transit. You alleged that the instant the Supplier put the shipment into the hands of the common carrier, the risk of loss transferred to the Manufacturer. You seek damages on behalf of the Supplier in the amount of $200,000 plus shipping costs and interest. The Manufacturer filed an Answer contending that there was a verbal agreement that the Supplier would insure the shipment, that the Supplier had made a prior shipment to the Manufacturer and had insured it, and that the Supplier's claim therefore was without merit. In a Counterclaim, the Manufacturer asserted that the Supplier breached the contract by not supplying the goods on time and consequently forced the Manufacturer to purchase cover goods at a cost of $60,000 over the original contract price. The Manufacturer further alleged that the Supplier's failure to deliver the goods caused the Manufacturer to lose a contract with a major retail computer store chain and caused the Manufacturer to incur damages of $180,000. The Supplier replied to the Manufacturer's Counterclaim by alleging that the verbal contract regarding the shipping was illegal and unenforceable, but that, even if it were enforceable, the Manufacturer failed to mitigate its damages. Pretrial discovery has been completed. The parties have agreed to submit the dispute to mediation for resolution.

The charts that follow show how you might analyze the parties' respective legal positions; needs, interests, and resources; and potential negotiating positions prior to the mediation. The charts represent only a partial analysis. Notice that the concept of "value" in the parties' perceptions may take different forms. Also note that the potential negotiating positions of the parties range from competitive to very cooperative. Some of the needs, interests, and resources have been developed using the interest-resource table, on the preceding page.

SUPPLIER

LEGAL POSITIONS	NEEDS AND INTERESTS AND RESOURCES FOR SATISFYING THEM	POTENTIAL NEGOTIATION POSITIONS
Claims Breach of Contract Uniform Commercial Code *Remedies* Compensatory damages Shipping costs Intoroot on unpaid bills *Reply to Counterclaim* Supplier's employee was not an authorized agent and could not bind supplier to any agreement to insure shipment. Manufacturer failed to mitigate damages.	*Dispute-Specific Interests* To be made whole for lost shipment. Avoid paying damages *Possible Resources* Manufacturer pays. Common carrier's insurance, if any. New contracts with Manufacturer paying premium price. Manufacturer introduces Supplier to its retail outlets (possible parts supply contracts). *General Interests* 1. Supplier needs to updated computer equipment. *Possible Resource* Manufacturer supplies microcomputers at cost. 2. Supplier needs to expand plant. *Possible Resource* Manufacturer has vacant plant for sale or rent.	*Competitive:* Manufacturer pays damages in one lump sum. Manufacturer pays damages in twenty-four monthly installments. Manufacturer pays large part of damages. *Mildly Cooperative:* Manufacturer pays premium on each connector cable under new contracts until damages repaid. Suggest bringing common carrier's representative into the mediation *Moderately Cooperative:* Supplier purchases computer equipment from Manufacturer at cost. *Very Cooperative:* Supplier buys or rents plant from Manufacturer.

MANUFACTURER

LEGAL POSITIONS	ANTICIPATED NEEDS AND INTERESTS AND POTENTIAL RESOURCES FOR SATISFYING THEM	POTENTIAL NEGOTIATING POSITIONS
Defense Verbal agreement between Supplier's and Manufacturer's agents to insure shipment is legal and enforceable. *Counterclaim* Manufacturer forced to purchase cover goods. Failure to deliver caused Manufacturer to lose a contract. *Remedies* Damages for having to purchase cover goods. Damages for lost profits.	*Dispute-Specific Interests* · Avoid paying damages to Supplier. Require Supplier to make Manufacturer whole for cover goods and lost business. *Possible Resources* Make Supplier pay damages. Determine whether common carrier has insurance or will otherwise contribute to settlement. Supplier supplies cables at no cost. New contracts with Supplier at per-item discounted price. *General Interests* Manufacturer may acquire Supplier or purchase stock. Manufacturer may adapt Supplier's successful quality-control procedures. Manufacturer may want settlement confidentiality. *Possible Resources* Worth discussing.	*Competitive:* Manufacturer pays Supplier nothing. Supplier pays all damages. Supplier provides Manufacturer with connector cables at no cost. Supplier pays large part of Manufacturer's damages. *Moderately Cooperative:* Suggest common carrier be brought into mediation. Suggest new contracts with Supplier at discounted price. Explore possibility of settlement confidentiality agreement. *Very Cooperative:* Explore acquisition of Supplier or purchase of part of stock. Explore information and temporary personnel exchange to implement total quality-management program in Manufacturer's plants.

If you analyze both parties' legal positions, needs, interests, re-sources, and potential negotiating positions in this manner, you will be fully prepared for the negotiating aspects of the mediation conference. You may also be prepared to suggest to the opposing party through the mediator creative yet realistic options for settlement that he may never have considered.

3.5   DETERMINING THE OVERALL GOAL, PLAN, AND THEME FOR YOUR CASE

After you have completed the analysis described in section 3.4, you are ready to tentatively determine the overall goal, plan, and theme for your case.[6] Keep in mind that mediation sessions are usually short, some lasting only one or two hours and few lasting more than six or seven hours. Your objective when preparing a case for mediation should be to design a case presentation that is succinct, pithy, and focused. The case presentation at least should have the following elements:

- **A Goal**—an articulated tentative settlement range, and/or an analysis of the needs and resources associated with a nonmonetary solution, and or an integration of the two.

- **A Plan**—an assignment of roles to be played in the mediation by the client, the lawyer, and by any other participants.

- **A Theme**—a distillation of the dispute into one or more key strategic themes that will capsulize the position of the party and the thrust of the negotiations.

3.5.1   Selecting a goal

At least six categories of goals may be selected by the parties during the course of a mediation: aggressive, competitive, cooperative, self-centered, defensive, and combinations.[7] The parties' negotiation goals may change during the course of a mediation because they generally track the tactics that the advocates believe are effective at any particular point in the mediation. These changing goals are not the subject of this discussion; rather, this subsection concerns your overall goal as an advocate—your predominant strategic goal in settling the dispute.

In disputes where a claimant is seeking monetary relief only, the goal ordinarily should be an articulated tentative settlement range, reflecting a high aspirational value at the extreme end in the direction of the client's interest. You should have in mind a reasoned basis for

---

6.   This section is an adaptation of a discussion published by this author in Donner and Crowe, supra at secs. 22:11–22:13.

7.   Schoenfield and Schoenfield, supra at 16–28.

selecting this settlement range. In disputes where claimant is seeking nonmonetary relief only, your goal should be the development of several creative suggestions for evaluating and satisfying the parties' nonmonetary interests through a needs/resources analysis. In disputes where claimant is seeking both monetary and nonmonetary relief, your goal should be a combination of the two previously described processes plus an analysis of integrating the parties' monetary and nonmonetary interests through assignment of monetary values to nonmonetary needs and resources to satisfy those needs.

In a typical personal injury case, for example, where the relief sought is purely monetary, regardless of which side you represent, you should analyze the case procedurally and substantively for its strengths and weaknesses. Review jury verdict reports to determine high and low verdicts in recently tried similar cases. Try to evaluate your case as realistically as possible. If it is possible that a jury could return a verdict of zero damages, you, as plaintiff's lawyer, should not be blind to this potential. Take that potential seriously into account in establishing the settlement range goal. Conversely, if it is possible that a sympathetic jury could award the plaintiff more than a million dollars in a particular case, you, as defendant's lawyer, should not suppress this possibility in your settlement range analysis.

3.5.2 Designing a plan

The plan for the mediation presentation should be flexible. A mediation session is not as structured as the trial process, where lawyers usually know at all stages who is entitled to ask questions or to speak. By contrast, the setting in mediation is normally quite informal, the ebb and flow of discussion being influenced by a variety of factors including the personalities of the parties and their counsel and the style of the mediator. Take this fact into account when designing your plan for mediation. Knowing the characteristics of the typical mediation session and having a solid plan of action in steering a course through the natural spontaneity of mediation can greatly assist you in controlling premediation nervousness and apprehension.

In a typical personal injury mediation, your plan of action should include at least the following:

- A succinct opening statement regarding the accident and the injuries and the nature of any settlement demands or offers made up to the present time.
- If representing a plaintiff, a typed summary of damages for the mediator and opposing counsel concisely listing the special damages (medical, property damage, lost wages, etc.).

- If representing a defendant, a separate typed summary reflecting the items of special damages that the defendant contests (e.g., inflated medical or repair bills, unverified work absences, etc.).
- A booklet of documentary evidence logically organized with a table of contents and tabs if possible, including medical records, medical experts' reports, police reports, crucial portions of deposition transcripts, insurance policies, etc.
- Demonstrative evidence in the booklet, including photographs of the accident scene, diagrams, blow-up charts, transparencies, and so on, which can quickly give the mediator the "big picture" as to what occurred from your point of view.
- An analysis of your opponent's legal and negotiating positions and responses to them.
- A determination of the appropriate nature and amount of your client's or other persons' verbal participation in the mediation session.

3.5.3   Developing a theme

Just as the development of a good trial plan includes the creation of a theme of the case, designing a good mediation plan requires the generation of a theme or themes that capture the interest of the mediator. Some examples of themes that might be appropriate in a personal injury case are the following:[8]

From the plaintiff's point of view:

Major theme—the defendant made a sudden turn directly in front of the plaintiff, who never had a chance to avoid the collision.

Minor theme—plaintiff was thrown sixty feet from her motorcycle and slammed into some thick bushes.

Minor theme—plaintiff had permanent head injuries, a broken knee, and was not able to graduate with her college class. Her medical expenses were in excess of $300,000.00.

From the defendant's point of view:

Major theme—the plaintiff was driving 20 miles per hour over the speed limit, and the defendant had no opportunity to see her.

Minor theme—motorcycles are inherently dangerous, and motorcyclists should slow down at busy intersections.

Minor theme—the law required plaintiff to wear a helmet, and she was not complying with the law at the time of the accident.

---

8.   See George P. Haldeman, *Alternative Dispute Resolution in Personal Injury Cases* (Clark Boardman Callaghan, 1993), sec. 5.4.

Minor theme—the plaintiff was flunking out of college at the time of the accident and would not have graduated with her class anyway. Her head injuries, though serious, are not permanent.

As is evident from the above example, mediation themes focus on points of disagreement between the parties. They foster the advocates' concentration on presenting evidence and arguments to the mediator— and to each other—that go to the very essence of the dispute. And most important, they provide the mediator with information she can use to facilitate a realistic and reasonable settlement. Good mediation preparation includes not only developing your own themes, but also anticipating likely counterthemes of your opponent and preparing replies to them. To be effective, your themes should be realistic, consistent, and supported by the facts and law pertinent to your case.

3.6 SELECTING DOCUMENTS FOR PRESENTATION TO THE MEDIATOR

Reviewing the case file as discussed in section 3.1 will undoubtedly refresh your memory about important aspects of your case. Noting critical documents as you peruse the file will prepare you for the next step in preparing your case for mediation—selecting particular documents you wish to use in your premediation submission, if required, and those you wish to use during your opening statement or during one or more of the caucuses.

In large cases, the premediation submission may consist of a position statement of ten to fifteen pages or more accompanied by a binder of documents, appropriately indexed and tabbed. Small cases sometimes have no premediation submission at all; advocates present documents only at the mediation session itself. In both large and small cases, mediators are usually interested in documents falling into six categories: (1) defining the rights and duties of the parties by agreement or by law; (2) confirming the occurrence or nonoccurrence of pertinent events; (3) confirming the type of conduct engaged in or not engaged in by the parties; (4) including language that may be interpreted as admissions of wrongdoing, knowledge, or lack of knowledge; (5) verifying the nature and extent of damage, loss, or injury; (6) explaining or confirming the potential for trade-offs and win-win or integrative solutions. Depending of course on the nature of the dispute, examples of documents in category 1 include a business contract or relevant portions of one, a residential or commercial lease, an employee manual, a warranty, a release, a will, a trust, an operator's manual, an ordinance, a court rule, a statute, a court opinion, etc. Examples of category 2 include a police or security guard report, receipts, telephone records, hospital reports, sign-in registers, construction change orders, and the like. Category 3 includes eyewitness statements, excerpts from deposition transcripts, monthly (securities or bank) account statements, videotape, letters, notes, and other types of correspondence. Admissions of the type described in category 4 might appear in correspondence between the parties, deposition transcripts, statements given to police, application forms, performance evaluations, releases, and the like. Photographs, X-rays, doctors' reports, estimates, time sheets, attendance records, accountants' reports, billing statements, work logs, etc., are category 5 documents. Documents that might help describe a creative settlement proposal, as defined by category 6, include a sketch, an organizational diagram, a modified work schedule, a flow chart, a model, a benefits manual, an annuity schedule, a catalog, etc. Many of the types of documents falling into category 6 have to be prepared especially for the mediation.

The important point to remember about documents is not only that they are helpful in making your presentation to the mediator (and the opposing party, who may be seeing them for the first time), but also—and perhaps of even greater significance—that they will be helpful to the mediator in discussing the merit of your claim or defense in caucuses with the other side. Also, for strategic purposes, you may decide to stagger the disclosure of certain documents, disclosing them to the mediator in caucus at critical times to gain leverage in the ongoing negotiation. This technique, wisely employed, often quickly turns the tide in favor of settlement.

3.7   DECIDING THE FORMAT OF THE PRESENTATION

Lawyers who mediate regularly know that every dispute is different, and some are quite unusual. In fact, that is what makes the mediator's job extremely interesting. Disputes have common aspects, but those little twists, those quirks, those human elements always give them a unique shape. Because disputes differ, they often require different methods—different formats—for description and presentation. As an advocate, you should be attuned to this phenomenon and take it into account when preparing your case for mediation.

When considering the format for your presentation, you should keep in mind that every dispute has two principal aspects: the substance or subject matter of the conflict and the relationship between the parties. Mediators recognize the importance of keeping these aspects separate and of analyzing them individually. That is why some mediators, as a matter of practice, conduct premediation conferences with the lawyers either in person or by telephone, separately or together. In those conferences they try to gain a better understanding of the nature of the conflict and the attendant emotions of the parties that may inhibit resolution. They are also seeking your ideas, your suggestions, and your insights on ways to facilitate resolution.

For example, if your client is embroiled in a bitter business dispute with a business partner, and the mediator you have selected has not scheduled a premediation caucus, you probably need to do some mediation format planning. You might call the mediator and suggest that she meet with each side separately before the joint conference. The purpose of these preliminary caucuses is to allow the parties an opportunity to vent their anger privately to a third party to avoid the possibility of having angry exchanges disrupt the initial joint session or terminate it altogether. Also, such preliminary caucusing permits the mediator to help the angry parties separate their emotions from the substance of the dispute and to begin thinking rationally about possible solutions. Sometimes parties have kept their feelings of anger or hurt pent up for months or even years waiting to tell their side of the story to a willing listener. The mediator fills this role. Once these feelings are released in caucus, the parties are better able to come to the table with the mediator at a joint session and participate more objectively in the problem-solving process. There may be some angry flare-ups during the joint session, but the mediator, having established a trust relationship with the parties in the preliminary caucuses, should be able to bring the outbursts under control quickly.

In disputes where the parties' emotions are not particularly a problem, you may still want to obtain the mediator's approval for counsel to submit premediation position statements, confidentially or with copies served on opponents, or you may suggest that the mediator conduct a telephone conference call with the lawyers. In your planning you should also take into account format issues relating to the mediation conference itself. You should ensure that there will be adequate break-out facilities for the mediator to use in caucusing. Multiparty cases may need several rooms for this purpose so that the parties themselves can meet separately and the mediator can shuttle between them. With respect to the format of your opening statement, consider how you wish to communicate your client's story to the mediator and to the other side. You need to determine if you will use visual or audio aids in your presentation and to make arrangements for the necessary equipment. You also need to consider the sequence in which you will present documents and which documents you will withhold for presentation in the caucus.

The format you choose for your story will have a direct impact on its persuasive value. Only rarely do unplanned formats succeed in any kind of presentation. One such rare instance occurred during World War II when General Dwight D. Eisenhower, accompanied by a major general, was paying a visit to front-line troops. It was a rainy day, and the mud was ankle deep. Eisenhower addressed the men from a makeshift platform, then, as he got off, slipped and sprawled in the mud. The GIs howled with glee. The major general, embarrassed by his troops' reaction, helped Ike to his feet and apologized for the behavior of his men. "It's all right," Eisenhower said. "That fall probably helped their morale more than the speech!"[9]

3.8 DETERMINING WHAT INFORMATION SHOULD BE KEPT CONFIDENTIAL

In any mediation in which parties are represented by counsel, several layers of confidentiality may operate simultaneously. At one level, lawyer-client communications are confidential by virtue of the attorney-client privilege, and at another, the lawyer's investigative materials and mental impressions, etc., are shielded from disclosure by the doctrine of work product immunity. At yet another level, mediators owe a duty to the parties and the lawyers not to disclose to anyone information communicated to them in confidence, and unless otherwise agreed, the parties, their counsel, and the mediator alike owe a duty to each other not to disclose information developed in the settlement conference to anyone not directly related to the dispute. Other kinds of information, though not in fact confidential, must be treated as confidential because they relate to a strategy or tactic to be used in litigation or at trial, either enhancing or detracting from the merit of a party's claim or defense.

An example of confidential information in this last category is a judgment of conviction for a crime. Of course the document itself, being a public record, has no inherent entitlement to confidential treatment. However, the *fact* that a certified copy of such judgment is in the hands of either a plaintiff or defense lawyer—without the knowledge of the other side—is confidential in that it might afford a significant tactical advantage to the holder of the information, if for no other reason than for its impeachment value. Thus, when you are preparing for mediation, you must mentally sort through the available information and make at least some decisions on what information is currently confidential; what information should stay confidential vis-à-vis the mediator, the opposing counsel, or both; and what confidential information you may disclose, to whom, under what circumstances, and in what manner.

Many times, information you deem confidential can be disclosed to the mediator in confidence, and although the mediator may not disclose such information to the other side, the mediator's knowledge of it may aid him in proposing settlement solutions. For example, suppose you

---

9. Anecdote adapted from Jacob M. Braude, *Lifetime Speaker's Encyclopedia*, vol. 1 (Prentice-Hall Inc., 1962), 495.

represent a computer software firm in a dispute with a real estate management company over the terms of a commercial lease. From your reading of the lease, the management company was to pay for certain remodeling of the space before your client moved in but failed to do so. The management company maintains that the same provision, properly interpreted, required your client to give the management company written notice of its desire to have the space renovated thirty days before the parties were to finally negotiate the lease fee. In that way the management company would augment the monthly lease fee to reflect the amortized cost of the renovations. Both parties agree that the lease provision on this point is somewhat vague and capable of several interpretations.

Your client has told you that several commercial tenants with whom your client does business in the building have had the same problem with the management company, and that in each instance the management company, in separate confidential agreements, has reduced the monthly rent considerably. Your client does not want you to disclose his knowledge of these facts to the management company because he does not want his customers in the building "to get into trouble with the landlord for breaching their confidentiality agreement." With your client's permission, you could inform the mediator of this situation in a caucus. Then, in a separate caucus with the management company and its lawyer, the mediator—without disclosing any specific names of tenants—could inquire whether the management company had ever had any prior problems with its commercial tenants over the proper interpretation of the lease's renovation provision. Regardless of how the management company answers that question, the mediator could ultimately propose a reduction of the monthly lease fee for the computer software firm as a solution to the present dispute. Knowing that eventually it might have to disclose in litigation the lease concessions made to other similarly situated tenants, the management company may indeed agree to the solution proposed by the mediator.

3.9 DETERMINING WHETHER A PREMEDIATION MEETING OR CAUCUS WOULD BE HELPFUL

You can often enhance the efficiency of the mediation process and the ultimate quality of the mediated settlement by scheduling premediation meetings or by caucusing privately with the mediator. Your premediation meeting with your client or clients is an essential prerequisite to the success of the mediation, even if it is held only shortly before the mediation begins. In that meeting, apart from learning your client's desires regarding settlement and determining any limitations on your settlement authority, you can prepare your client for the mediation experience by explaining the stages of the mediation process and the roles of the mediator, the lawyers, and the clients.

Depending on the dispute and the particular stakes involved, other types of premediation meetings may be appropriate. For example, you may want to arrange a premediation meeting or telephone conference with opposing counsel to discuss any possible changes in their last settlement position that might precipitate a settlement without the necessity of mediation. Such a meeting or conference may signal a need for another meeting involving the clients, perhaps leading to a negotiated settlement. Even if a determination is made to proceed with the mediation, undoubtedly the advocates will be more fully informed of the issues, positions, goals, and interests of the parties and consequently better prepared to advise their clients during the mediation. For some advocates such a meeting helps them refine the types of strategies and tactics that will best serve their clients in the mediation itself.

You may also consider scheduling a meeting with opposing counsel and the mediator. The purposes of such a meeting are to explore possible areas of emphasis for the mediation, to determine what other parties, if any, should be invited to participate in the mediation, to determine what premediation materials may be helpful to the mediator, and in a complex case, to determine the agenda, format, and logistics of the mediation. Such a meeting may also explore the lawyers' views on the possibility of mutual gain in the dispute, which the parties are not yet psychologically capable of considering. Another purpose, particularly in a multiparty dispute, is to discuss the benefits of the mediator having premediation caucuses with each party.

Finally, you may consider having a premediation caucus with the mediator, either alone or with your client. This of course requires the approval of the mediator and opposing counsel. A premediation caucus may be helpful in the following situations:

- There are several parties and premediation caucusing with each one would reduce the parties' and their counsel's wait-time at the mediation conference.

- Your client is very angry and he or she needs to be calmed before any discussion in a mediation session can be fruitful.

- You need to apprise the mediator of technical, legal, or highly confidential information, which if done in a caucus at the mediation, would take a great deal of time and be an imposition on the opposing parties and their counsel.

- You desire to get the reaction of the mediator to several unusual proposals for settlement and to plan with the mediator how to best present such proposals at the mediation.

- You want the mediator to meet one or more persons who have information relevant to the dispute, but who will not be present for the mediation itself.

3.10 KNOWING THE STATUS OF THE LITIGATION AND NEGOTIATIONS

When mediating a court-filed case, a mediator is very interested in knowing the status of the pending litigation and of any prior negotiations between the parties. As to the status of litigation, of particular interest to the mediator is the status of the discovery in the case—whether the parties have been deposed, whether expert reports are available together with the experts' depositions, whether disputes exist over critical documents, the nature of the discovery remaining to be done, and the date, if any, set for discovery cutoff and/or for trial. This procedural and substantive information can provide the mediator with valuable tools to use in caucuses with the parties and their counsel to encourage settlement. For example, if a party or an expert witness has made a damaging admission in a deposition, the mediator can use this information in a caucus to assist the affected party to evaluate his case realistically. In some situations, if the parties need to take more discovery to pin down certain facts before settlement is possible, and discovery is not closed, then the mediator can suggest that the mediation be continued until that discovery may be taken. In other situations, where the parties do not want to spend any more money on the case, the mediator can use the suggestion of more discovery as a catalyst for the parties to reach a speedy resolution. Similarly, if the case is scheduled for trial in a short time, the mediator can draw attention to the expense, inconvenience, and stress of final trial preparation, the ordeal of the trial itself, and the prospect of going through a protracted appellate proceeding—even if the party is successful in the trial court. Because so much of this type of information is useful grist for the mediator, you should be well versed on what has taken place previously in discovery and the current status of the litigation.

Equally important to the mediator is the status of the negotiations. Advocates commonly come to mediations either with no knowledge of prior demands or offers of settlement or with only vague knowledge that has to be confirmed by a time-consuming search through the correspondence folder or worse yet, a call to the lawyer originally responsible for the case to verify the opponent's representation regarding the last demand and offer. Such interruptions can cause unnecessary delay and expense. The mediator of course needs information about the status of the negotiations so that she does not waste time replowing already

71

plowed ground and she needs the information prior to convening the first caucus. A new mediator learns quickly that if the parties do not agree upfront on the amounts of the last demand and last offer, the mediator may spend as much as an hour or more caucusing before communicating an offer from one side to the other only to hear the receiving side cry "foul," since the offer is much less than what was already on the table months before. The fouled party normally capitalizes on such an event by accusing the opponent of bad-faith bargaining, setting up a condition of doubt and distrust that might take the mediator some time to bring back into equilibrium. These problems are of course compounded when several parties are involved in the litigation, where several negotiation sessions have taken place in the past, where new counsel have come into the case, or where a combination of these circumstances exists. One way to avoid such problems is to read the correspondence file carefully before coming to the mediation and to telephone the opposing counsel to confirm the status of the negotiations. You may be able to resolve discrepancies in memories prior to the mediation. If that is impossible, at least you and opposing counsel will have reached a consensus on an appropriate starting point for the negotiations at the mediation.

3.11 KNOWING THE LIMITS OF SETTLEMENT AUTHORITY

Ordinarily, mediators expect that all advocates participating in a mediation will bring with them persons who have full authority to settle the case. Thus, in preparing for mediation you need to make your client aware of this requirement and to ensure that the person who accompanies you to the mediation has such authority. That is good advice in principle, but compliance by parties is not always practicable, particularly when the client is a corporation. Sometimes senior-level decision makers are called out of the country on business, or business emergencies arise that demand their immediate attention on the day of a scheduled mediation. If the person who is to accompany you is a midlevel decision maker for one of your corporate clients, it behooves you to ask him about the extent of his settlement authority and to verify it with the appropriate senior-level decision makers, at least by telephone. It can be very embarrassing for an advocate to reach a settlement in a case, only to later find out that she had no authority to do so. Because of this potential for embarrassment, and indeed the potential for malpractice, some advocates prefer to have the limits of their settlement authority spelled out in writing before they attend a mediation session. If the authority is given orally, some advocates will confirm their understanding of the limits of their authority by letter or fax. Many advocates arrange to have their senior-level decision makers available by telephone during the course of the mediation if those executives are not able to be present in person.

Mediation of disputes involving multiple issues can raise special problems for advocates. Situations of multiple issues increase the incidence of misunderstanding of settlement authority limits on individual issues. Busy corporate executives or general counsel of corporations do not always have a grasp of all the aspects of a particular piece of litigation that the lawyer who deals with it day-to-day has. Thus, when you obtain settlement authority from a client, you should briefly summarize all the issues involved in the case so that your client does not mistakenly extend to you more authority than he wishes you to have. How you settle the present case may impact negatively on a settlement or a litigating strategy your client is taking in another case or group of cases in another locality. Being specific with your client about individual issues can also have the effect of expanding the limits of your settlement authority. For example, assume your client is a supplier of parts to a large manufacturer. Reminding your client of the defective parts issue in the present case may spark interest to settle other pending claims against this manufacturer regarding other parts as a "package deal."

When representing multiple parties in a mediation, you need to proceed very cautiously. You must be absolutely certain that you have no actual conflict of interest in representing the parties jointly, that you have fully advised the clients of any potential conflict, and that your clients have consented to the joint representation in writing. Also, when you are representing multiple parties, it is imperative that you either meet personally with or have a telephone conference with your clients before a mediation to achieve consensus on the limits of your overall settlement authority or to determine the limits that individual clients may set. It is most important that each client knows what the other client expects to receive in settlement. If you hesitate to have such a discussion with your multiple clients for fear of derailing perceived settlement opportunities, you should take it as a strong sign that you cannot represent the interests of all the parties effectively and that another lawyer should be brought in to represent one or more parties with divergent views on settlement.

3.12 DETERMINING A REASONABLE SETTLEMENT RANGE, OPENING POSITIONS, AND BOTTOM LINES

In a case involving money damages, if you are plaintiff's counsel you probably have some idea of what a jury would award your client if you won. If you are defendant's counsel, you realize that if you won before a jury, your client would pay nothing. But the jury value of your case, based on either side winning, is not what is at issue in a mediation. What is at issue is the reasonable settlement value of your case *at the time of the mediation* without proceeding forward in litigation. The reasonable settlement value of any case depends on a variety of factors, including the risks of discovering new information, of losing the advantage of evidence through death of witnesses or unintentional destruction or loss of documents, of changing case precedent on liability or damages, of full or partial uncollectibility of a judgment, and of increased expense due to expansion of litigation. Thus, when you prepare for a mediation, you are not primarily concerned with what a jury would award your victorious client after all the evidence is in. Rather, your paramount concern is what your case is worth today, considering all the favorable and adverse risks of going forward. You must realistically evaluate the present strengths and weaknesses of your case based on current information and determine, as accurately as you can, the probabilities of winning and losing. After that evaluation you will be able to determine what your client's opening position at the mediation should be and at least an initial impression of what your bottom line will be—the point beyond which there is decidedly more potential benefit from going forward with the litigation than settling at the figure proposed.

In personal injury cases, there are crude "rules of thumb" for determining the settlement values of cases which insurance claims adjusters customarily avoid. Nonetheless, whether or not these "rules of thumb" are actually verbalized in a particular negotiation or mediation, they are often applied tacitly when a party or the mediator suggests a settlement figure. In a case not involving permanent injury, the most common rule of thumb is three times the alleged special damages. Special damages normally consist of hospital bills, doctor bills, other medical bills, lost wages, and the like. Thus, in a personal injury case where the plaintiff has nonpermanent injuries and special damages totaling $5,000, applying a factor of three would yield a settlement figure of $15,000. Practically speaking this would break down into $5,000 to reimburse the client for medical expenses and lost wages, $5,000 to the plaintiff for pain, suffering, and inconvenience, and $5,000 as the lawyer's fee. In cases involving permanent but not incapacitating pain or disability, the factor may increase to five, and for permanent disability interfering with or precluding gainful employment of the plaintiff, the factor may increase to ten or more. Insurance adjusters normally do not include an amount for lost wages in the special damage calculation, but instead add it to the figure resulting after the multiplier is applied.

Apart from this simple technique for roughly measuring the reasonable settlement value of a personal injury case, several more complicated methods exist including decision-tree analysis and computer-aided evaluation.[10] However, one reasonably simple method, more accurate than the rule of thumb technique, involves the use of a fair settlement value (FSV) formula.[11] The FSV formula is also adaptable to cases other than those involving personal injury. Determining the fair settlement value is a prerequisite to determining the reasonable settlement range and the opening positions and bottom lines.

The elements of the formula are as follows:

PAV — The probable average verdict

PPV — The probability of a plaintiff's verdict

UV — The uncollectible portion of the verdict

PC — The plaintiff's cost in obtaining the verdict

DC — The defendant's estimated cost of defense

I — The value of other intangible factors

FSV — The fair settlement value

Algebraically the formula may be expressed as follows:
$$FSV = (PAV \times PPV) - UV - PC + DC \pm I$$

The following considerations determine a value for the individual elements of the formula.

- **PAV** assumes a situation where liability can be proved and you can determine its value by reviewing the jury verdict reports in your jurisdiction for the type of injury the plaintiff sustained. In some jurisdictions this information is available through periodical publications, subscription computer disks, or a computer on-line service. If it is not available, you will have to insert amounts for incurred special damages; estimates of expenses for future medical care, including surgery and rehabilitation; property damage; and realistic estimates for related intangible damages (pain and suffering, disfigurement, loss of consortium, etc.).

---

10. For a discussion of decision-tree analysis, see Marc B. Victor, "Litigation Risk Analysis and ADR," in *Donovan Leisure Newton & Irvine ADR Practice Book* (Wiley Law Publications, 1990), 307–32. For information about the use of decision-aiding software, see Nagel and Mills, *Systematic Analysis in Dispute Resolution*. See also section 5.7.2, *infra*.

11. See Robert L. Simmons, *Winning Before Trial: How to Prepare Cases for the Best Settlement or Trial Result* (Executive Reports Corporation, 1974), 708–15; see also Gerald R. Williams, *Legal Negotiation and Settlement* (West Publishing Co., 1983), 115–19.

- **PPV** takes into account the strengths and weaknesses of plaintiff's case on both law and facts, considered independently. For example, if you represent the plaintiff and believe all the legal instructions the judge will give to the jury will be favorable to your case, then your probability of winning a verdict on the law is 100 percent or 1.0. If you estimate that only 90 percent of the instructions will be favorable, then the probability is .90, and so on. This analysis also takes into account the risk of modification of any pertinent case law prior to final judgment.

  As to the facts, if you believe a jury will find for you on 85 percent of the critical facts, then your probability of winning a verdict on the facts is .85. This determination includes an evaluation of the relative credibility of witnesses, of whether critical items of evidence (yours and/or the other side's) will be admitted into evidence at trial, and of the relative reliability of both sides' documentary and other evidence. The combined probability for these two independent events—the judge determining the instructions and the jury determining the facts and applying the law as the judge instructs—is the product of the two probabilities. Thus, if your probability on the law is .90 and your probability on the facts is .85, the combined probability of a plaintiff's verdict is .90 × .85, or 76 percent.

- **UV** is present in cases where some parties are uninsured, underinsured, or, for some other reason, are partially or fully judgment proof.

- **PC** includes court costs, discovery expenses, fees for expert witnesses, model construction costs, etc. (Include attorney fees and expenses if attorney is not on a contingent fee.)

- **DC** includes a percentage of costs defendant saves by not having to go to trial.

- **I** encompasses factors that may be considered by the jury in a particular case in determining a higher or lower award of damages such as the skill or experience of counsel, the reputation of the corporation(s), the ability of the parties to elicit the jury's sympathy, and the nature of the illegal conduct.

Now consider a hypothetical example and apply the formula to determine a fair settlement value. Assume that you represent a plaintiff in a case against a small construction company and the driver of one of its pickup trucks. The driver of the pickup truck struck your client while she was crossing the street late one afternoon and caused her serious injuries. Your client sustained a compound fracture of her right leg that left a lengthy scar, a serious knee injury requiring surgery, and bruises and contusions over much of her body. The accident left her toes without feeling, which has precluded her from engaging in many of her favorite recreational activities including dancing, ice skating, and skiing. She also frequently experiences severe pain in her knees, especially if she stands for long periods of time. This has caused some problems for her in her job as a customer service representative for a local bank. Your expert testified in his deposition that the feeling will never come back to her toes and that she will experience pain in her knee probably for the rest of her life. Defendants' expert testified that the feeling in her toes will return and the knee pain will all but vanish in five years with the appropriate exercise and rehabilitative treatment.

In deposition your client testified that she was crossing the street at the intersection, with a "walk" signal, and within the lines of the cross-walk when she was struck by the defendant driver. The driver testified that she stepped off the curb and ran in front of his truck fifty feet in front of the intersection while he had a green light. Witness testimony was mixed. One witness supported your client's version of what occurred, whereas two witnesses placed her outside of the crosswalk but additionally said that the truck had a red light. A few depositions remain to be taken in the case. One witness to be deposed is a bartender who was with the defendant driver a few minutes before the accident occurred. He apparently will testify that the driver had a couple beers but was not drunk when he left the bar. Another complicating factor is the issue of whether the driver was acting in the course of his employer's business at the time of the accident. Because of the lateness of the day and the driver's activities immediately before the accident, it is possible that the jury could find that the driver was off duty when the accident occurred. This could pose a potential problem for your case, since the driver's personal insurance policy has limits of $150,000.

The values for the individual terms of the FSV formula might be computed as follows:

- **PAV = $350,000.** You have surveyed your online jury verdict information for cases in which plaintiffs sustained similar injuries and have determined the average to be $350,000.

- **PPV = .64.** You estimate that the probability is 85 percent that the trial judge will give the jury instructions on the law favorable to your case. This includes the consideration that the judge will give an instruction on contributory negligence. You further believe that the probability that the jury will find in favor of your client's version of the facts is 75 percent. Thus the combined probability of a verdict in your favor on the law and the facts is .85 x .75, or .64 (rounded).

- **UV = O.** You have reviewed the pertinent case law, and you are convinced that the jury will find that the driver was acting within the scope of his employment. Thus, in your opinion, the company can be held responsible, and no portion of the judgment will be uncollectible.

- **PC = $40,000.** You have already spent $20,000 in case preparation, largely because of the several experts you have hired to review the case. At least three experts will testify at trial. You believe that to take the case through the remainder of discovery and trial will cause the expenses to double.

- **DC = $60,000.** You are not exactly sure what the defendant's total costs will be. Based on your experience, you believe that a reasonable estimate for the total future defense expense would be $90,000. You believe defendant would be willing to put up to two-thirds of that figure ($60,000) toward settlement.

- **I = $25,000 in favor of defendants.** As for the intangible consid erations, from the driver's deposition you know that he comes across rather brash and indignant. Also, the jury is not going to like the fact that the driver was drinking before the accident. You believe that this will potentially boost a jury verdict $25,000 in your client's favor. Other considerations may tend to reduce the jury verdict. Your client's yuppie attitude tends to make her testimony seem condescending. Her starchy, stiff-upper-lip style may put off some jurors and make her complaints about frequent severe pain less believable. You have told her about this problem, but to no avail. Also, the company has a very favorable reputation in the community. It annually spends tens of thousands of dollars sponsoring programs for handicapped children, a telethon, and the Special Olympics. You estimate that these considerations may have the effect of reducing the potential jury verdict by $50,000. The combination of the favorable and unfavorable intangible considerations may be estimated to have a $25,000 negative effect on the jury verdict.

Substituting these figures into the FSV equation yields the following estimate of a fair settlement value for the case:

FSV = (PAV x PPV) - UV - PC + DC ± I
FSV = ($350,000 x .64) - 0 - 40,000 + 60,000 - $25,000
FSV = $224,000 - $5,000
FSV = $219,000

Although the formula yields an estimated fair settlement value of $219,000, the analysis does not end here. You must realize that the FSV is based on estimates—reasoned estimates—but estimates nevertheless. Obviously the parties' estimate of the probability of verdict (PPV) can have a great impact on the FSV figure. It is very important that, as plaintiff's counsel, you not be overly optimistic in estimating the strength of your case on the law and facts. It is equally important that the defense counsel use great care to avoid underestimating the PPV estimate. In short, the FSV is only as accurate and useful as the lawyers are objective in arriving at their estimated component values. When deriving the FSV, advocates should "think like a mediator," attempting at all times to be objective and reasonable.

It must be emphasized that no one figure represents the number at which a case must settle. More helpful is the concept of reasonable settlement range. You may determine this by establishing a bracket whose endpoints are 10 percent on either side of an objectively estimated fair settlement value. Thus, in the example presented above, the reasonable settlement range would be roughly between $200,000 and $240,000. This bracket establishes the premediation, estimated "bottom lines" for the plaintiff and defendant. The plaintiff would not be expected to accept less than $200,000 and the defendant would not be expected to pay more than $240,000. These bottom lines, of course, might be modified as the parties develop information during the course of the mediation.

From this bracket of reasonable settlement range, plaintiff's and defendant's opening positions can be selected. For example, plaintiff's counsel might select an opening position of three or more times the upper end of the bracket, or $720,000. Defense counsel might choose an opening position of one-third or less of the lower end of the bracket, or $65,000. Of course, defense counsel's opening position might be different depending on what figures he or she inserts in the FSV formula.

With respect to the FSV formula itself, even if you think that certain terms should be added to it or deleted from it, or that other values should have been used in the present analysis in computing the FSV, the important point of this exercise is that you should use some objective, systematic method of valuing a case and of determining the opening and bottom line positions. In that way you will be better able to advise your clients on what they should expect in a mediated settlement and what strategies and tactics you need to satisfy those expectations and to reach your settlement goals.

3.13 CONSIDERING THE POTENTIAL FOR CREATIVE SOLUTIONS

In many dispute situations, opportunities for creative solutions are overlooked, either because the advocates are not aware of creative thinking techniques or have simply not taken the time or put forth the necessary effort to think creatively. Win-win, optimal, and even superoptimal solutions are almost always present and waiting to be discovered in dispute situations where the parties have both monetary and nonmonetary interests. As pointed out in section 3.4, such solutions also may be possible in what appear on the surface to be disputes purely involving money. You should always be on the lookout for these opportunities to best serve your client's interests through maximizing the parties' mutual gain. A discussion of some of the creative techniques for discovering these beneficial opportunities follows. Applications of some of these techniques are further discussed in section 5.6.

In *Lateral Thinking: Creativity Step by Step*,[12] Dr. Edward de Bono presents several techniques for stimulating creativity. According to Dr. de Bono, lateral thinking is closely related to insight, creativity, and humor. Whereas vertical (logical) thinking is concerned with proving or developing concept patterns, lateral thinking is concerned with restructuring such patterns (insight) and stimulating new ones (creativity). Usually, the mind has alternative ways of arranging available information, and it can suddenly "switch over" to another arrangement. According to Dr. de Bono, when the sudden switch over is temporary, it gives rise to humor; if the sudden switch over is permanent, it gives rise to insight.[13]

Lateral thinking is a process of effecting switch overs of arrangements of information to achieve restructuring of the information and the stimulation of new ideas. It enhances the effectiveness of vertical thinking by challenging the arrogance and the cliché-pattern thinking associated with logic. Both vertical and lateral thinking are essential to effective problem solving. As Dr. de Bono has observed:

> The differences between lateral and vertical thinking are very fundamental. The processes are quite distinct. It is not a matter of one process being more effective than the other for both are necessary. It is a matter of realizing the differences in order to use both effectively.
>
> With vertical thinking one uses information for its own sake in order to move forward to a solution.

---

12. Edward de Bono, *Later Thinking: Creativity Step By Step* (Harper & Row Publishers, 1990).

13. Ibid., 35–36. See also John W. Cooley, "Mediation and Joke Design: Resolving the Incogruities," *Journal of Dispute Resolution* 1992 (1992): 281. See generally Julian Gresser, *Piloting through Chaos: Wise Leadership: Effective Negotiation for the 21st Century* (Five Rings Press, 1995).

> With lateral thinking one uses information not for its own sake but provocatively in order to bring about repatterning.[14]

In his book Dr. de Bono describes the following lateral thinking techniques: (1) generation of alternatives, (2) challenging assumptions, (3) suspending judgment, (4) fractionation, (5) thought reversal, (6) brainstorming, (7) using analogies, and (8) random stimulation. He also describes three other characteristics of information processing in problem solving: (9) sequence of arrival of information, (10) choice of entry point, and (11) attention area. Let us now turn to briefly exploring the nature of these separate items.

While you may be familiar with aspects of vertical thinking (deductive syllogisms, conditional syllogisms, etc.) from logic or debate courses in high school and undergraduate or graduate school experiences, you may not know the meaning of the expression, "techniques of lateral thinking." Here are explanations of some of the techniques.

- **Generation of alternatives.** The most fundamental principle of lateral thinking is that any particular way of looking at things is *only one* from among many other possible ways. Using the generation of alternatives technique, you do not search for the best approach, but rather look for as many different approaches as possible. In the lateral search the alternatives generated do not have to be reasonable in themselves. Even if they are not reasonable, they may spark or precipitate reasonable solutions.

- **Challenging assumptions.** When using this technique, you challenge (1) the necessity of boundaries and limits in problem solving, and (2) the validity of concepts. Ask why. Once when someone asked the great mathematician Bertrand Russell how he accounted for his many new discoveries in what seemed to be a fully explored, fixed science, he answered simply, "I challenge the axioms."[15]

- **Suspending judgment.** You suspend judgment during the generative stage of thinking and apply it during the selective stage.

- **Fractionation.** Using this technique, you break down a situation into fractions and then restructure the situation by putting the fractions together in a new way. Ask, what if?

- **Thought reversal.** In the reversal technique, you take things as they are and then turn them around, inside out, upside down, back to front, and see what happens—what provocative

---

14. de Bono, supra at 44–45.

15. Anecdote adapted from Jacob M. Braude, *Speaker's Desk Book of Quips, Quotes and Anecdotes* (Prentice-Hall, Inc., 1963), 106.

rearrangement of information results. Ask, what's opposite? Thought reversal is also a technique of joke telling. Henry Ward Beecher, a famous New England clergyman, once applied this technique to delivering one of his famous sermons. It so happened that when he was opening his mail one morning, he pulled from an envelope a single sheet of paper on which was written one word: Fool. The next Sunday, in the course of his sermon, he referred to it in these words: "I have known many an instance of a man writing letters and forgetting to sign his name. But this is the only instance I've ever known of a man signing his name and forgetting to write his letter."[16]

- **Brainstorming.** This is more of a setting than a special lateral thinking technique. It encourages the application of lateral thinking techniques while providing an escape from the rigidity of vertical thinking. Brainstorming has three main features: a formal (or special) setting, suspended judgment, and cross-stimulation.

- **Using analogies.** You can use analogies to provide movement. The problem under consideration is related to the analogy, and then the analogy is developed along its own lines. At each stage the developed analogy is transferred back to the original problem to see if any aspects are useful to a solution. Ask, what's similar?

- **Random stimulation.** In the random stimulation technique, you use any information whatsoever, no matter how unrelated it may seem. No information is rejected as useless. The more irrelevant the information, the more useful it may be. Random stimulation occurs through: exposure and formal generation.

Dr. de Bono also describes three characteristics of information processing that affect the applications of lateral thinking techniques to problem solving:

- **Sequence of arrival of information.** The mind always arranges available information in the most stable or logical way. As more information comes in, the mind adds it to the existing arrangement. But there comes a time in problem solving that the problem solver cannot proceed further without restructuring the pattern. The deadlock can be averted only by breaking up the old pattern that has been so useful and arranging the old information in a new way. Thus the best possible arrangement of information in problem solving is quite independent of the sequence of arrival of the pieces of information.

---

16. Anecdote adapted from Jacob M. Braude, *Speaker's and Toastmaster's Handbook of Anecdotes By and About Famous Personalities* (Prentice-Hall, Inc., 1971), 280.

- **Choice of entry point.** In solving a problem where the desired alternative goals (solutions) after restructuring are prescribed but information concerning the current informational structure is missing, entering the information at the solution end and working backwards often facilitates resolution.
- **Attention area.** Very often in a problem-solving situation success is not just a matter of the order in which the information is attended to but the choice of the information parts that are going to be attended to at all. To restructure the problem, you may need no more than a slight shift in attention. On the other hand, if there is no shift in attention, it may be difficult to look at the situation in a different way.

You should use these techniques in your preparation for mediation and at the mediation conference itself. In that way you can enhance the climate for creativity and increase the opportunities for win-win, optimum, and superoptimum solutions.

3.14 DETERMINING YOUR NEGOTIATION STRATEGY AND RELATED TACTICS

If you have determined the goal, plan, and theme of your mediation presentation as described in section 3.5, then for all practical purposes you have also determined your negotiation strategy—the overall negotiation approach you will be taking during the mediation. Your chosen strategy may or may not coincide with your personal negotiating style—the default mindset or predominant approach you naturally take in negotiations if you do not consciously choose to alter it in a particular setting. The chart that follows shows characteristics of the two principal negotiating styles—competitive and cooperative.[17]

---

17. See Paul Michael Lisnek, supra at chap. 4.

COMPETITIVE AND COOPERATIVE STYLES

COMPETITIVE STYLE	COOPERATIVE STYLE
Views every opponent as an adversary	Does not view process as a game
	Desires an open exchange of information
Has high aspiration level	Views negotiation as a search for a mutually beneficial solution
Makes high initial demands	Avoids maneuvering against the opponent's emotions
Avoids making concessions	Avoids inappropriate manipulation
Believes concession means weakness	Will move off a position to consider other realistic options
Uses tactics and strategies directed *against* the other person in word and action	Is sensitive to the needs of the client
	Feels a high commitment to a reasonable and fair result

In your premediation planning, in addition to reflecting on your own negotiating style and that of your opponents and choosing the overall negotiation strategy you wish to take, you must review and consider tactics related to your strategy—those particular actions you may use in implementing your strategy. A premediation review of negotiation tactics will also prepare you to be able to identify specific tactics used by opposing counsel at the mediation session and to employ other tactics to neutralize them.

Negotiation tactics may be divided into three broad categories: competitive, cooperative, and avoidance. If you have decided on a competitive strategy, you will probably use related competitive tactics; conversely, if you have chosen to use a cooperative strategy, you will probably employ cooperative tactics. In mediation, avoidance tactics may be used with respect to certain issues or groups of issues. If you are using a combination of strategies—for example, beginning with a competitive strategy and then at an appropriate point in the mediation changing to a more cooperative strategy—then you may consider employing the corresponding tactics from each category.

3.14.1 Competitive tactics

Competitive tactics that you can use in mediation include the following:[18]

- **Alternative opportunities:** suggesting that there are opportunities for your client to cut deals or reach settlements with persons or companies not parties to the present dispute.

- **Belly up:** pretending to be less competent than the opposing advocate, thereby eliciting a first offer or first concession from the opposing advocate.

- **Bluffing:** stating an intention to do or not do something, seemingly without compromise, but which in fact may later be modified.

- **Brer Rabbit:** responding to an opponent's suggestion with "anything but that," when in fact it is exactly what you want. You later accept the concession in return for much greater concessions on the part of the opponent. In this way you get much more out of the bargain than the opponent.

- **Creating deadlock:** intentionally causing a mediation deadlock or impasse to force concessions or obtain delay.

- **Fait accompli:** taking action without consulting the other side to get the opponent to concede to something "already accomplished."

- **Feigning:** appearing to shift a position in a direction, the purpose being to divert attention away from the real goal or object for a time.

- **Good cop/bad cop:** giving the impression that one member of an advocate team is willing to compromise, while the other team member is stubborn and intransigent. The seemingly compromising team member eventually elicits major concessions from the opponent through charm and good nature.

- **Limited authority:** claiming a real or feigned limitation on your authority to settle beyond a certain value, to force an opponent's concession.

- **Media pressure:** suggesting that the media may be contacted is useful where your opponent fears adverse community reaction from publicity about the dispute.

- **Preconditions:** asserting demands to which all participants must agree before a mediation may proceed.

---

18. See generally, Schoenfield and Schoenfield, supra at 112–95; Lisnek, supra at 87–101; Donner and Crowe, supra at chaps. 11 and 12.

- **Reversal:** taking the offensive on a particular issue after being defensive on other ones, which allows you to gain at least temporary leverage in the mediation through a surprise move.
- **Threat or show of power:** stating an intention to take some action that will be harmful to other participants unless they comply with a condition or request.
- **Time Pressure:** relying on real or fabricated time constraints to obtain last concessions from the opponent.

3.14.2 Cooperative tactics

Cooperative tactics that you can use in mediation include the following:[19]

- **Association:** associating your negotiating position with the objectives, ideals, needs, or interests of the opponent.
- **Conditional proposals:** seeking closure by making offers that depend on the resolution of some or all of the remaining issues in the mediation.
- **Creating movement:** assuming the responsibility for pushing a deadlocked mediation forward without regard to which participant caused the impasse.
- **Cutting the salami:** obtaining what you want, slice by slice, rather than all at once.
- **Face-saving:** allowing your opponent to back away from a position or to make additional consessions without being embarrassed.
- **Focusing on process:** recognizing when a change of procedure might facilitate problem solving on the substantive issues.
- **Flexibility:** showing willingness "to look again" at a particular issue, without necessarily making a concession.
- **Logrolling:** subordinating or sacrificing lesser concerns to higher ones with a goal of higher mutual gain.
- **Participation:** demonstrating what other similarly situated people have received and arguing "me too."
- **Psychological commitment:** being enthusiastic about the benefits of a solution for both parties.
- **Reasonable deadlines:** suggesting reasonable time limits for opponents to respond to settlement proposals.
- **Reciprocity:** requesting a concession in return for a concession.

---

19. Id.

- **Romancing:** arguing that the solution in the present case should be better than those in past cases.
- **Splitting the difference:** suggesting, near the end of a mediation, to divide equally any remaining monetary difference.

Applications of these tactics are discussed in section 5.3.

3.14.3 Avoidance tactics

Avoidance tactics that you can use in mediation include the following:

- **Demanding to negotiate monetary issues first:** if money is a priority interest, insisting that monetary issues be negotiated first and that the nonmonetary issues be resolved through nonmonetary trade-offs.
- **Demanding to negotiate nonmonetary issues first:** if avoiding payment of a monetary settlement is a priority interest, insisting that the nonmonetary issues be resolved first so that their monetary worth can be valued before considering the monetary issues.
- **Declining to negotiate a related matter:** if your position is much weaker in a related dispute, refusing to combine that dispute with the principal dispute to avoid diminishing settlement possibilities for the principal dispute.
- **Withdrawing an Issue from Consideration:** refusing to discuss an issue because it is too emotionally painful for one party or the other.
- **Walking out:** expressing dissatisfaction with the other side's proposals or lack of them by leaving the negotiation or mediation session.

Applications of these tactics are discussed in section 5.3.

3.15 DECIDING WHO SHOULD ATTEND THE MEDIATION SESSION

Most mediators would agree that mediation is most effective when the clients themselves participate in the mediation session together with their lawyers. This is because reality testing and creative problem solving work best when the persons who ultimately have to "live with the solution" take an active, self-interested role in forging it. However, in those mediation situations where your client's presence is encouraged but not mandated, you must make a preliminary decision on whether to bring your client, and if you decide that your client should be present, then you must prepare your client so as to gain the optimum benefit from the mediation process.[20]

When there is a choice as to whether a *plaintiff* client should be brought to a mediation session, it is rare indeed that a decision is made not to bring the client. If you are representing a plaintiff in a personal injury case, for example, there are normally considerable advantages in having the plaintiff client present. The mediation session may offer the first opportunity for the insurance company representative to actually meet with the plaintiff client and hear the injured party's side of the case firsthand. The plaintiff's presence will humanize the "paper chase" and reveal, to the plaintiff's advantage, the emotional aspects and credibility of the case. Only in rare situations, such as where the client has severe incapacitating physical or mental disabilities or where a client might present himself as "too slick," "too senile," or "too naive," should you seriously consider attending the mediation session without the plaintiff client.

Similar considerations are involved in deciding whether to bring a *defendant* client to a mediation session. In many situations involving corporate defendants, you may choose to bring to the mediation session a company official with full settlement authority, even though that company official was not directly involved in the events giving rise to the dispute. In a personal injury case, for example, it is a routine practice for a claims adjuster to accompany the defense counsel to a mediation session instead of the actual defendant alleged to have caused an accident. Because the claims adjuster has a large role in deciding how much the insurance company will pay on a personal injury claim, she is the "real client" of the defense counsel. The claims adjuster assists the defense counsel in evaluating the claim and works with the defense counsel to present the mediator and the plaintiff's counsel with the best arguments supporting a settlement favorable to the insurance company's interests.

As a defense counsel in a personal injury case, you should always consider whether it would be beneficial to have the actual defendant present at a mediation session, in addition to the claims adjuster. Below are considerations that you may take into account in deciding whether to bring the actual defendant or not:[21]

- Liability is in issue, and the defendant is a credible, effective witness.

---

20. See generally Donner and Crowe, supra at, sec. 22:15.
21. These considerations are adapted from Haldeman, supra at sec. 5.3.

- The defendant is an especially likable and impressive witness who can testify to a simple and forgivable lapse in judgment that an average juror could easily see herself having.
- The defendant can testify to plaintiff's admissions against interest at the accident scene.
- The plaintiff is making an exaggerated or fraudulent claim that can be substantially contradicted by the defendant's statements.

A medical malpractice case against a physician poses special problems for a defense counsel, who must decide whether to ask the physician to attend the mediation or not. If the doctor desires to attend and is personable and professional in demeanor, you will most likely permit him to be present. If, however, the doctor is indignant, arrogant, and angry about being sued, you will probably be better off letting him tend to his patients on the day of the mediation, assuming of course that the doctor has given his consent to the insurance company and the defense counsel to settle the case. Thin-skinned doctors can be very dangerous to an insurance company's case. In a story about a medical malpractice case, a lawyer was questioning the defendant doctor. A bit maliciously, the lawyer quizzed, "Doctor, I hear that a man you treated for a liver ailment died of a heart attack." Outraged at this slur against his professional skill, the doctor shot back, "See here, my good man, when I treat someone for liver trouble, he dies of liver trouble!"[22] Needless to say, the plaintiff's lawyer had fun with this statement at the subsequent trial.

When you prepare for mediation, you should also be alert for situations where it might be helpful for persons in addition to your client to be present at the mediation session. For example, witnesses to critical events related to the dispute may be helpful.

More commonly, the presence of experts can help the mediator advance progress toward a settlement. Depending on the dispute, an expert—independent or corporate in-house—might come from one of any number of professions: medical, computer, accountancy, chemical, construction, economics, psychology, psychotherapy, etc. It is becoming more common for insurance defendants to have structured settlement experts either present at or on call for mediation conferences. If you decide that you need to have an expert present at the mediation, it is important that you advise the mediator and your opposing counsel of this decision in case they may have some objection that you have not anticipated. If one side is going to have an expert present, a mediator normally prefers that the other side has an expert available also—or at least be extended the opportunity to have one available. If the expense

---

22. Anecdote adapted from Edmund Fuller, ed. *Thesarus of Anecdotes* (Crown Publishers, 1942), 298.

of having an expert present is burdensome to one side, the mediator may suggest that no experts attend. If the schedule of the other side's expert precludes her attendance, the mediator may suggest rescheduling the mediation.

Chapter Four

PREPARING THE CLIENT FOR MEDIATION

"Advice is like snow; the softer it falls the longer it dwells upon, and the deeper it sinks into, the mind."

— *Samuel Coleridge*

Once, when President Ulysses S. Grant was visiting Scotland, his host gave him a demonstration of a game, new to Grant, called golf. Carefully, the host placed the ball on the tee and took a mighty swing, sending chunks of turf flying but not touching the ball. Grant quietly watched the exhibition with interest, but after the sixth unsuccessful attempt to hit the ball, he turned to his perspiring, embarrassed host and commented: "There seems to be a fair amount of exercise in the game, but I fail to see the purpose of the ball."[1] Like President Grant, a client who is inadequately prepared for what to expect at the mediation conference, in terms of the process, the players, the ground rules, and the potential results, may fail to fully comprehend its purpose and consequently may be unable to participate in it actively, meaningfully, and profitably. In this chapter we will explore several topics that you should cover when preparing your client for mediation: the nature of the mediation process; the roles of the mediator, the advocate, and the client; and miscellaneous logistical items. These topics should be covered in addition to those discussed in chapter 3, namely, the strengths and weaknesses of the case, your client's settlement goals, and your client's needs and interests.

4.1 ADVISING THE CLIENT ABOUT THE NATURE OF THE MEDIATION PROCESS

When preparing your client for mediation, you should describe the mediation process and the roles of the various participants in detail and encourage your client to ask questions if he does not understand something. This statement and other guidance provided in this chapter also apply of course to anyone who accompanies your client to the mediation, including corporate officials, experts, and interested nonparties. In

---

1. Anecdote adapted from Braude, *supra* at 143.

particular, you should advise your client whether the mediation is voluntary or court-mandated, and you should also describe the purpose and stages of the mediation process as outlined in section 2.1, with a special emphasis on the nature, purpose, and benefits of caucusing and the importance of confidentiality. Your client should know that mediation is not a trial and that any party has a right to request that the mediation be discontinued at any time. You should also explain who is going to be present at the mediation and that the objective of the mediation is for the parties to arrive at a voluntary agreement—a joint decision—on how the dispute should be resolved fairly. Also point out that the mediation process may not accomplish that objective, but that other, secondary objectives may be accomplished by experiencing the process, including acquiring a more accurate sense of the merit of the claims or defenses.

Further, be sure to advise your client of the differences between facilitative and evaluative mediation and specify the particular type of mediation that the mediator will be conducting. Inform your client that he will be asked to sign a mediation agreement at the beginning of the session that will cover such matters as confidentiality, immunity of the mediator from a lawsuit or subpoena to testify, and the manner and timing of the payment for the mediation services.

In addition, do not forget to explain the informal atmosphere of the mediation, the casual give-and-take discussions, and the lawyers' banter that may occur during the sessions. Emphasize that at some point during the mediation it may be appropriate and beneficial for the parties and their counsel to negotiate directly, without the presence of the mediator; for the mediator to meet with opposing counsel without the parties being present; and with the agreement of counsel, for the mediator to meet privately with the parties.

4.2 ADVISING THE CLIENT ABOUT THE ROLE OF THE MEDIATOR

In premediation discussions with your client, describe the mediator personally by explaining the mediator's general qualifications, background, practice experience, and style. Explain further that the mediator has an ethical duty to be impartial and neutral in the proceeding with respect to the parties and the subject matter of the dispute. If the mediator is a lawyer, you should emphasize to your client that, when serving as a mediator, the mediator is not practicing law. She will give no legal advice, and in fact, the mediator's ethical code prohibits it. Stress that the mediator's role is not to decide which party is right or wrong. Rather, the mediator is a facilitator of the parties' joint decision making. The mediator will assist the parties in identifying their issues, needs, and interests; exploring alternative solutions; focusing the discussion; and controlling any emotional outbursts.

The mediator will also lend structure to the parties' negotiations by chairing the discussion, clarifying communications, educating the parties, translating proposals into nonpolarizing terms, expanding the resources available for settlement, testing the reality of proposed solutions, insuring that the parties can comply with the proposed terms, serving as a scapegoat for the parties' vehemence and/or frustration, and protecting the integrity of the mediation process.[2] Moreover, the mediator is ethically bound not to disclose information given to her in confidence, either to any other party to the mediation or anyone outside the mediation proceeding.

In the appropriate case, also advise your client that the mediator is most effective when the *parties* can share with her suggestions for creative settlement solutions that neither the mediator nor the respective counsel may be able to perceive as the process unfolds. Tell your client that from time to time the mediator may play devil's advocate in caucuses, which should not be taken as indicative of the mediator's bias but rather as the application of a useful technique in aid of settlement. Also, inform the client that he may wait as much as an hour or more between caucuses, but that does not indicate that the mediator favors the opposing side. Sometimes one side possesses more information than the other that will be helpful to the mediator in reaching a settlement; in other instances, it takes longer for the mediator to help a party reframe her perceptions so as to accept a settlement proposal or to respond with a refinement of a proposal. In any event, it is a good idea for you to suggest that your client consider bringing some reading material along with him to the mediation conference to occupy the time during the waiting periods between caucuses.

Share with your client that the mediator, in performing her function, will spend a great deal of time listening to the parties but periodically will be apt to ask all sorts of questions—probing, clarifying, hypothetical, and open-ended. It may even seem at times that the mediator is cross-examining, ever so gently and deliberately—using a so-called velvet hammer approach. This aids the parties in reality testing—finding out what the real strengths and weaknesses of their cases are, eventually causing them to arrive at a consensus on fair settlement value.

---

2. See Joseph B. Stulberg, "Tactics of the Mediator," in *Donovan Leisure Newton & Irvine ADR Practice Book* (Wiley Law Publications, 1990), 138–39.

4.3   ADVISING THE CLIENT ABOUT THE ROLE OF THE ADVOCATE

If the mediation is to be facilitative, you should advise your client that your role will be different than it would be at trial or in an arbitration. Your goal in mediation will be the same as it is at trial or in arbitration—to obtain the best possible resolution for your client. Your method and manner of obtaining it, however, will be quite different.

If the mediation is to be a facilitative one, you should explain that the mediation will consist of a respectful conversation in an atmosphere of joint problem solving in which you will be expected to disclose, in caucus, the weaknesses of your case as well as its strengths. You will be doing a lot of listening as well as speaking. You may even express empathy toward opposing counsel in joint session, all this with the purpose of encouraging a mutually acceptable resolution. The law pertinent to the case will usually not be discussed at length. Creative solutions, having nonmonetary—yet valuable—elements may also be explored.

If the mediation is to be evaluative, stress that your goal will still be to obtain the best possible resolution on behalf of your client, but the relative strengths of the parties' legal positions will be emphasized, and the lawyers may even discuss the appropriate case law. You will be playing the more traditional advocate role in that you will be approaching the problem more legalistically and with the goal of persuading the mediator that her evaluation should favor your client's interests. You may be playing a role similar to an advocate in a mediation conference conducted in a case on appeal.

At times during the mediation, whether facilitative or evaluative, you will be speaking privately with your client to determine what move to make next. You will be seeking your client's impressions, feelings, and input as you proceed through the process. Together you may decide to use a strategy or tactic, to explore a settlement avenue, or to consider and even accept a settlement proposal that you had not previously considered. You should advise your client that flexibility is key to securing the best solution.

You should further advise your client that the ultimate decision on whether to accept a settlement offer or the mediator's evaluation will rest with your client, after taking your legal advice into account of course. If the case settles, you will work with opposing counsel in drafting a settlement agreement incorporating the joint decision of the parties.

4.4 ADVISING THE CLIENT ABOUT THE ROLE OF THE CLIENT

It is very important that your client know and be comfortable with his role at the mediation conference. Depending on the particular client, the nature of the case, and the personalities and style of the opposing parties or counsel, you may decide that your client will have an active verbal role, a limited verbal role, or no verbal role whatsoever. If your client is to have some verbal role, then you should advise him regarding the basic ground rules for a client's verbal participation.

4.4.1 Delineating the extent of the client's verbal participation

If your client is credible, likable, and persuasive, you may decide to employ his full and active verbal participation during the opening statement in the initial joint session and in the caucuses with the mediator. On the other hand, you may give an easily confused, unsure, and less-than-credible client, a very small role or perhaps no role in the factual presentation during the mediation session. If the case is complex technically or legally and your client is not intellectually sophisticated enough to understand it thoroughly and/or to discuss it meaningfully, then your client should have little or no verbal role. If allowed to speak in such a situation, your client may, at best, give the impression of being incompetent or unreliable, or at worst, do himself serious harm by unknowingly making an admission against his interest. Similarly, if the case involves emotional or sentimental matters that are difficult for your client to verbalize, then you should do most, if not all, of the talking. If the opposing party and/or counsel have aggressive personalities or are bullies and your client is either meek or withdrawn or has a penchant to meet force with force, you should probably do all the talking to keep the conversation on an even keel. Other considerations, of which you may be intuitively aware, may affect your decision on the extent of your client's verbal participation at the mediation.

If you decide that your client should stay silent during the mediation and that you should do all the talking, realize that keeping quiet may be very difficult for the client. You should discuss this potential difficulty with the client during the premediation preparation, giving him some inoffensive, reasoned basis for your decision to do all the talking. You should also counsel the client on the possible negative impact of nonverbal communication during the mediation. Your client's frowns, grimaces, sneers, scowls, mocking laughter, and the like during the presentations of either side do not advance the cause of a speedy favorable settlement. If your client is to remain silent, he should be counseled to appear interested, objective, and reasonable. A silent face can speak a thousand words.

If you decide that your client is to participate verbally at the mediation, discuss the nature and extent of the participation in detail prior to the session. For example, you may wish to discuss and coordinate with a client in a typical personal injury case the following areas of verbal presentation:[3] the facts of the accident; conversations with the opposing party at the accident scene or thereafter; initial injuries and treatment; doctor visits and treatment; the effect of injuries on employment; the effect of injuries on family life; residual and long-term pain and health problems, future treatment, future surgery, etc.; preexisting medical conditions; depression, fear, anxiety, embarrassment over injuries; and financial concerns caused by the accident. Clearly delineate for your client which of these topics you will discuss solely, which of them your client should be prepared to discuss, which ones documentary evidence should address, and which should be covered by a combination of your presentation, your client's presentation, and the documentary evidence.

4.4.2 Advising the client on participation ground rules—general

Meticulously rehearse your client on potential routine questions that either the mediator or counsel for the opposing party might ask. At least three reasons make it worthwhile to take the time to do this. First, it will put your client at ease knowing that he already has had a kind of "spring training" and has had an opportunity to field many of the factual or self-analytical questions that he might be expected to answer in the mediation. Second, it will put you more at ease knowing what answers he will be giving to those anticipated questions. And third, he will be prepared to make a good impression on opposing counsel, the opposing party, and the mediator. Regrettably, many advocates do not seriously undertake this kind of detailed preparation. Advocates who take their *art* seriously, however, are concerned about these kinds of details. They know that detailed planning and preparation defines the essence of their skill and competence and eventually pays dividends in terms of their enhanced professional reputation. When the acclaimed Athenian sculptor Phidias was carving the statue of Athena to be placed in the Acropolis and was working on the back of the head, he was careful to bring out with his chisel every strand of hair possible. An observer remarked, "That figure is to stand a hundred feet high, with its back to the marble wall. Who will ever know what details you are putting behind there?" Phidias turned to the observer, looked squarely into his eyes, and said pointedly, "I will know." He then turned back toward the

---

3.   See Haldeman, supra at sec. 5:3.

sculpture and continued with his detailed chiseling.[4]

Also be sure to impress on your client that the mediation session is not a trial and that the ordinary courtroom prohibitions against leading questions, narrative answers, and information irrelevant to claims or defenses do not apply. Furthermore, you need to counsel your client on the following eight specific ground rules that clients should observe during the course of the mediation session.

4.4.3 The client should face the mediator when speaking

It is important for you to advise your client to face the mediator when speaking. If your client talks across the table to the opposing party and opposing counsel, it is quite possible that either or both of them will interpret what your client is saying as accusatory or demeaning. This may arouse anger in one of them and perhaps cause an outburst and an interruption of your client's story. The opponent's outburst, in turn, may cause your client to react emotionally and perhaps say something in front of the mediator that is embarrassing or even harmful to your case.

Apart from avoiding these unpleasant happenings, having your client face the mediator when speaking has other benefits. Your client's eye contact with the mediator will help to make his message more persuasive to the mediator. Persuading the mediator is important because, even though mediators are duty-bound to remain neutral and impartial regarding the parties and the subject matter of the dispute, they are human beings whose perceptions and actions can have a great impact on the quality of the ultimate settlement. They are constantly vigilant for clues to finding the true heart of the conflict, the relative credibility and/or memory acuity of the parties, and their essential needs and interests. By maintaining eye contact with the mediator, your client can begin to build trust and rapport with the mediator and convey forthrightness of purpose, desire, and motivation to achieve a joint goal. This kind of bonding with the mediator has the effect of building a type of teamwork atmosphere that can spill over into caucuses and, through the mediator's shuttle pollination, positively reinforce the problem-solving efforts of both sides. Making sure your client faces the mediator also carries with it the added benefit of having the opposing party and counsel actually listen to what your client is saying without feeling threatened. Equally as important, it gives *you* the opportunity to observe the body language of the opposing party and counsel while your client is speaking. An opponent's frown or a smirk made while your

---

4. Anecdote adapted from James C. Humes, *Speaker's Treasury of Anecdotes about the Famous* (Harper & Row, Publishers, 1978), 69.

client is giving a factual presentation may communicate the opponent's denial or assent to your client's version of the events giving rise to the dispute.

There are exceptions to the "facing-the-mediator" ground rule. If a party wishes to make an apology to an opposing party across the table, it would be appropriate for the apologizing party to face the opposing party when speaking. Also, if a party wishes to express empathy to an opposing party, direct eye contact with that party would be appropriate. Finally, if a party wishes to express hope that the mediation will be successful, direct eye contact with the opposing party will enhance the credibility of that communication.

4.4.4   The client should speak to be understood

When preparing a client for mediation, allow him to rehearse the factual presentation in your presence. Listen very carefully while your client gives this practice presentation. Is it organized? Does it begin at the beginning and touch on all necessary points? Is it a fair, honest statement of what occurred? Does the client use terminology that can be understood by both the mediator and the opponents? This last question is a very important one. Clients with industrial, medical, or technical expertise may use words or expressions that are common to their everyday experience, but that are like a foreign language to others present at the mediation session. In the rehearsal session with your client, listen for such words, and when you hear one, stop your client and have him define it in simple terms. Impress on your client the importance of using words that everyone understands at the mediation conference. Point out to him that big words not only can communicate arrogance and insensitivity, but also can be boring, distracting, and misleading and in the worst case scenario, can precipitate very unpleasant results. When Benjamin Franklin was quite young, he once said to his mother, "I have ingested an acephalous molluscous." Fearful that the young Benjamin had swallowed something poisonous, his mother forced him to take a large dose of castor oil. The next day, the effects of the medicine having subsided, Ben confided to his mother that he "had eaten nothing but an oyster." While recuperating from the resultant vigorous spanking, young Ben vowed never again to use big words when little words would do.[5]

4.4.5   The client should state only facts

In the presentation rehearsal and at the mediation conference itself, your client should state only facts. He should be careful not to confuse facts with exaggeration and hyperbole. If your client finds it necessary to offer speculation or hearsay regarding a part of his story,

---

5. Anecdote adapted from Jacob M. Braude, *New Treasury of Stories for Every Speaking and Writing Occasion* (Prentice-Hall, Inc., 1959), 317–18.

he should label it as such when speaking to ensure that no one will be misled. Making these distinctions between fact and conjecture can have a very positive influence on listeners. It communicates that the speaker is making a determined effort to be fair and objective in his recollection of events. It also conveys an openness to have his recollection refreshed by the opponent, thereby imparting to the listeners an attitude of flexibility and an inclination to cooperativeness.

Conversely, a speaker's overstatement, embellishment, or stretching of the truth usually inspires listeners to be apprehensive and cautious about accepting all of the speaker's message. If the speaker misrepresents an important fact—even innocently—a listener may lose complete confidence in the speaker's ability to be truthful, may refuse to communicate with the speaker, or may become vindictive.

4.4.6 The client should never argue

Refraining from arguing is a cardinal rule everyone should observe at the mediation. "Arguing" carries at least two connotations. The first type of "arguing" makes a point persuasively with the purpose of convincing a listener to the speaker's point of view. That type of arguing is certainly well within the scope of permissible mediation behavior. What is taboo is "arguing" of the second type—making an argument, often anger-based, that is combative and offensive and does nothing but distract listeners from the task at hand. Most such arguments consist of isolated or periodic episodes of seemingly endless blustering and pointless discourse, resulting in a total waste of everyone's time. Admittedly, arguments of the first type and arguments of the second sometimes produce very similar effects. Consider the story of a young lawyer who had been talking for about four hours in court to twelve jurors who, when he had finished, felt like lynching him. After the young lawyer took his seat at counsel table, his opponent, a crusty old professional, rose slowly to his feet. After glancing quickly toward the jury, then down at his watch, he looked pleasantly at the judge and said, "Your Honor, I will follow the example of my friend who has just finished and submit the case without argument."[6]

4.4.7 The client should display no reaction to settlement offers

Because no one really knows what the true settlement value of a case is before the settlement agreement is actually reached, you should counsel your client not to display any reaction to any settlement offer—either verbally or nonverbally. If your client is the plaintiff, and the defendant's offer is much higher than anticipated, your client's

---

6. Anecdote adapted from Jacob M. Braude, *Braude's Second Encyclopedia of Stories, Quotations, and Anecdotes* (Prentice-Hall, Inc., 1957), 202.

reaction of shock and elation or statements of "sounds great!" or "hot dog!" may preclude you from later convincing your opponent that your client wants (or needs) more to settle the case. If your opponent makes what she thinks is a reasonable offer to settle and your client scoffs at it and verbally berates the opposing party, your client's reaction might anger the other side sufficiently to cause them to withdraw from the mediation. If your client is a defendant, impulsive reactions could do similar damage to the potential for successful negotiations. It should be emphasized that verbal reactions are not the only type of prohibited reactions to settlement offers. As pointed out in subsection 4.4.1, facial expressions can communicate what people are thinking. In the proper context, they can be a strong asset. In the wrong context, they can be a devastating liability. Counsel your client to display no body reactions—even facial reactions—to settlement offers.

4.4.8 The client should behave as if before a jury

Advise your client that, although he will not be under oath during a mediation session, he should speak narratively and answer questions as if under oath. Your client should make every effort to give the appearance to the mediator and opposing party and counsel alike that he is trustworthy and honest. The best advice to your client is "be yourself—don't try to be the person you think the mediator, or anyone else, wants or expects you to be." Tell your client to tell his story to the mediator "straightforwardly and sincerely," and if appropriate, "empathically." If your client tries to pretend to be someone he is not, the masquerade will undoubtedly fail, and it will probably adversely affect the success of the negotiations. No one easily tolerates a phony. That statement is as true with respect to mediations as it is with trials, and its truth was aptly demonstrated in an incident that occurred in a Kansas court some years back. A tall, awkward, somewhat timid fellow was called to testify as a witness for the defendant in a civil case. Defense counsel said to him, "Now sir, take the stand and tell your story like a preacher." "No sir!" roared the judge. "I want him to tell the truth!"[7]

4.4.9 The client should neither answer nor ask difficult questions

At times during the course of the mediation, the opposing counsel or the mediator may direct difficult questions to your client. Difficult questions might be defined as those that require some knowledge of the law to answer, seek information beyond the specific expertise of a client, or require a client to make or imply an admission against interest without having available the necessary information to give a full explanation.

---

7. Anecdote adapted from Edmund Fuller, ed., *2500 Anecdotes for All Occasions* (Avenel Books, 1978), 448.

During the premediation preparation, advise your client that when such questions are posed during the mediation session, your client should defer to you for an answer. You should also have an understanding with your client before you go to the mediation session that when someone asks your client a question during the course of the mediation, your client will pause slightly before answering to permit you to interject, if you think it necessary, to answer the question or to provide a reason why it cannot be answered at that particular time.

By the same token, you should caution your client not to ask the other side or the mediator difficult questions during the course of the mediation. Actually, better advice would be for your client not to ask the mediator or the other side any questions without first clearing the questions with you privately. After you screen the question, you may decide that it is appropriate to ask, and you may determine that your client is the appropriate one to ask it. Or, you may conclude that it would be better if you asked the question. Inappropriate questions posed by a client can sometimes have the effect of undermining a negotiating strategy, exposing a negotiation tactic, revealing the client's gullibility, threatening the other side, disclosing clues to your bottom line, or demonstrating the client's lack of knowledge, skill, ability, or competence. As to the last effect, consider this historical example. Mozart was once asked by a lad how to write a symphony. "You're a very young man," Mozart replied and then asked, "Why not begin with ballads?" "But you composed symphonies when you were ten years old," the youth urged. "Yes," said Mozart, "but I didn't ask 'how'."[8]

4.4.10 The client should listen carefully to the statements of the opposing party and should not interrupt

It has been said that when you talk you only say something that you already know; when you listen you learn what someone else knows.[9] Perhaps there should be a corollary to that saying as follows: when you intentionally interrupt another who is speaking, you do violence to everyone's learning. Most mediators, early in the mediation, will announce a ground rule requiring all participants to refrain from interrupting each other. They will normally accompany that ground rule with the suggestion that each participant take notes while another participant is speaking for use later in responding to that participant. Before the mediation, you should advise your client of this rule and urge his strict compliance with it during the mediation.

---

8. Anecdote adapted from Braude, *Speaker's and Toastmaster's Handbook of Anecdotes*, 277.

9. Adapted from Braude, *Braude's Second Encyclopedia of Stories, Quotations and Anecdotes*, 81.

Also, it is very important for you to advise your client to listen carefully to the statements of the opposing party and opposing counsel during the mediation session. Your client, having lived through the events giving rise to the dispute, normally knows much more about the subject matter of the dispute than you do. He may have told you much about the dispute during the course of several interviews but, for a variety of reasons, it is likely that he may not have told you everything. Most commonly clients do not tell their lawyers everything because they simply forget some of the details, or they do not realize certain details are important, or they do not want to share details that may detract from their litigating or negotiating position. By listening carefully to the statements of the other side during the mediation session, your client will be able to refresh his memory about certain details and will be able to alert you to statements of the other party that are inaccurate or perhaps intentionally false. With this new information, your client might be able to remember previously forgotten relevant events or point you to documents or other evidence that will verify and bolster your client's version of the story. By paying very close attention to the details of what the other party is saying, you and your client may discover that what you previously perceived her account of the facts to be might, in actuality, be something very different indeed. Consider, for example, the story about an old farmer who met with the railroad's young lawyer to file a claim against the railroad. The farmer told the lawyer that he "had noticed that his prize cow was missing from the field through which the railroad passed," and he wanted the railroad to pay the value of the cow. Without making any further inquiry of the farmer, the railroad's lawyer immediately began talking settlement, seemingly to take advantage of the farmer, who was unrepresented at the meeting. The young lawyer talked and talked and did a little arm-twisting, and finally the farmer agreed, reluctantly, to accept half of the value of the claim. After the farmer had signed the release and taken the check, the young lawyer just could not resist gloating over the old farmer a bit, saying, "You know, I hate to tell you this, but actually I put one over on you. The engineer was asleep and the fireman was in the caboose when that train went through your farm that morning. I didn't have a case." The old farmer smiled a bit and went on chewing his tobacco. Directly, he drawled, "Well, I'll tell you, young feller, I was a little worried about winning that case myself. You know, that durned cow came home this morning."[10]

---

10. Anecdote adapted from James C. Humes, *Podium Humor: A Raconteur's Treasury of Witty and Humorous Stories* (Harper & Row, Publishers, 1975), 169.

4.5   REVIEW OF THE CASE, SETTLEMENT GOALS, STRATEGIES, AND TACTICS

Before meeting with your client, you customarily will have considered privately most, if not all, of the topics covered in chapter 3. During that private preparation, you undoubtedly will have reached tentative conclusions in your own mind about the goal, plan, and theme of the mediation presentation; the documents you plan to show the mediator; the format of the presentation; a fair settlement value and reasonable settlement range of the case; and the negotiation strategies and tactics you will employ. It is important that you treat these initial decisions as tentative and retain the flexibility to change them after you have had the opportunity to have a premediation meeting with your client.

Lillian Hellman, the famous American playwright, once said, "People change and forget to tell each other."[11] This saying has direct relevance to preparing your client for mediation. When meeting with your client just prior to the mediation, you may discover that your client has redefined her needs and interests, has found some new evidence that is either favorable or unfavorable to your stance in the negotiations, has thought of some creative solution that will eliminate or minimize the need for a monetary solution, or has realized that other persons have information relevant to the conflict and should be brought into the mediation process. These changed circumstances may cause you to reconsider your whole approach to your case, including your previously contemplated settlement goals, strategies, and tactics. They may also cause you to reconsider whether premediation meetings with the opponents or premediation caucusing with the mediator would be helpful and/or whether the mediation should be rescheduled, for example, to allow you time to interview other persons whom your client believes should be brought into the mediation process. Other changed circumstances may cause you to consider speeding up the mediation process, as in the situation where your client, a plaintiff in a personal injury case, has fallen on bad financial times and needs proceeds from the personal injury settlement to cover basic living expenses.

Regardless of any changed circumstances, however, and the need for you to adjust your negotiation strategies and tactics to them, the premediation meeting with your client will help you both familiarize yourselves with the facts of the dispute and to reconsider the advantages and disadvantages of proceeding to mediation rather than initiating or continuing with litigation. You will also be able to review with your client the probability of succeeding in litigation and the remedies

---

11. As quoted in Carolyn Warner, *The Last Word: A Treasury of Women's Quotes* (Prentice-Hall Professional Publishing, 1992), 43.

available there in comparison with the potential solutions available in mediation.

This review process will give your client confidence in proceeding forward with the mediation and in the prospect of obtaining a just and fair result, or it will make her reconsider whether litigation may be the best negotiating tactic for the time being. Either way, your client, with your help, will be making fully informed decisions about her desires for the future. Knowledge of one's desires is the first step toward satisfying them. A former prime minister of Britain, the late Ramsay MacDonald, once was discussing the possibility of lasting peace with another government official. The official was unimpressed with the prime minister's viewpoint. "The desire for peace," the official said cynically, "does not necessarily insure peace." "Quite true," admitted MacDonald. "Neither does the desire for food satisfy hunger. But at least it gets you started toward a restaurant."[12]

4.6 ADVISING THE CLIENT ON MISCELLANEOUS MATTERS

When preparing your client for mediation, you need to cover several topics of a very practical, logistical nature. The most obvious one is the date, time, and place of the mediation. If the mediation is going to take place out of state or out of the country, make sure you check the time zone and have your client schedule his travel accordingly. Changes from regular to daylight savings time can also cause scheduling confusion. Considerations of jet lag also should be taken into account when scheduling air travel if the mediation is to be held out of the country.

If the place of the mediation is difficult to find or the lack of or similarities in street names is confusing, it is a good idea to provide your client with a map, and/or detailed directions on how to get there. Sometimes it is necessary to explain peculiarities of the building where the mediation is to be held. Large law firms often occupy several floors in a building and can have several reception areas on different floors. You should be very careful to advise your client about the specific floor and reception area to go to. In some buildings, certain banks of elevators service only certain floors; some elevators go to only a certain portion of a floor, and other elevators go to other portions of the same floor; and escalators sometimes provide the fastest route of all. Make sure to advise your client to take into account the effect of rush-hour traffic and/or weather conditions when planning the most direct route to the location of the mediation. Give your client a telephone number to call in case he gets lost.

---

12. Anecdote adapted from Humes, supra at 65.

This all seems like common sense, but as we have more life experiences, we soon discover that common sense is not so common after all. Taking a few minutes to remind your client about these matters may avoid delaying the beginning of a mediation, inconveniencing the mediator, angering the opposing parties, and contending with a flustered, embarrassed client who already seems to be off on the wrong foot in the mediation. Perhaps one way around all this is to meet your client at a known place and then proceed from there to the mediation location together. If you decide to do this, make sure *you* know how to get to the mediation. Detailed instructions, as just described, are important for any client, but they are imperative for the client who is disabled in some way. If your client is disabled, you will want to find out in advance of the premediation meeting the location of accessible entrances to the building and elevators inside the building so that you can advise her of these things and answer any questions.

Aside from these matters, you should also discuss with your client the appropriate dress for the mediation conference. What your client wears to a mediation session will vary from client to client and from situation to situation, and in some cases, it may even constitute an important aspect of your overall negotiating strategy. For example, if your client is wealthy and is a defendant in a securities case, you might want him to "dress down" to give the impression that he is an ordinary man of ordinary means. If your client is a person who believes that her employer has discriminated against her, you may suggest that she dress in her best business suit to convey a professional appearance that complements her claims of unusual leadership ability, high self-esteem, and quality job performance. These of course will be judgment calls on your part, but the judgments need to be made. There is practically nothing worse than having your client show up in a mediator's reception room in a T-shirt when you were expecting to see him in a three-piece suit. It is too late then to tell him what to wear.

You should also give your client an estimate of how long the mediation conference will last. Clients who take time off from work to come to a mediation need this information to advise their supervisors of how long they will need to be excused from their jobs. Supervisors need to know this so they can designate a substitute worker for your client. Also, if the mediation conference is going to last beyond the normal workday, your client needs to know this information in advance so that she can make appropriate adjustments in her personal schedule.

In premediation discussions, ask your client to identify any person or persons he might wish to contact before the parties reach a final settlement agreement, such as a spouse, partner, parent, relative, doctor, or banker. Arrangements should be made, if appropriate, to have the person available by telephone during the time the mediation is being held. You should also ascertain who, if anyone, will be accompanying your client to the mediation conference. If your client is not going to accompany you to the mediation, you should ensure that you obtain his written statement specifying the limits of your settlement authority. It is probably a better practice to obtain written settlement authority in advance of the mediation in all circumstances, to cover the eventuality that your client is unable to attend at the last minute but wants you to proceed alone.

4.7 BARRIERS TO EFFECTIVE ADVOCACY IN MEDIATION

There is a story told of a mediation attended by Farmer Tom and his lawyer and by an insurance adjuster and her lawyer, a senior partner in a silk-stocking insurance defense firm. After the opening statements of each side, the mediator, a former judge, permitted the attorneys to engage in cross-talk—a brief period in which each attorney had an opportunity to ask questions across the table. The insurance defense lawyer began and directed his question to Farmer Tom. "Didn't you say, at the scene of the accident, 'I'm fine'?" he asked. Farmer Tom responded, "Well, I'll tell you what happened. I had just loaded my favorite mule Bessie into the. . . ." "I didn't ask for details," the lawyer interrupted, "just answer the question. Did you not say at the scene of the accident, 'I'm fine'?" Farmer Tom said, "Well, I had just got Bessie into the trailer and I was driving down the road. . . ." The insurance lawyer interrupted once again and said to the mediator, "Judge, is it too much to ask that this plaintiff be required to simply answer the question of whether he admitted at the scene that he was 'fine'?" The mediator, now himself curious about what Farmer Tom had to say, said to the insurance lawyer, "I'd like to hear what he has to say." Farmer Tom thanked the mediator and proceeded, "Well as I was saying, I had just loaded Bessie into the trailer and was driving down the highway when this huge semi-truck and trailer ran the stop sign an smacked my truck right in the side. I was thrown into one ditch and Bessie was thrown into the other. However, I could hear ol' Bessie moaning and groaning. I knew she was in terrible shape just by her groans. Shortly after the accident a Highway Patrolman came on the scene. He could hear Bessie moaning an groaning so he went over to her. After he looked at her, he took out his gun and shot her between the eyes. Then the Patrolman came across the road with his gun still in his hand, and with barrel smoking, he looked at me and said, 'Your mule was in such pain and bad shape, I had to shoot her. How are you feeling'?"

As a lawyer representing a client in the mediation process you need to become familiar with the barriers that interfere with effective communication—impediments to your communicating effectively with clients and with opposing counsel in dispute and transaction settings. In the above example, Farmer Tom did not provide truthful or accurate information to the Highway Patrolman because of his fear of harm or retaliation. This communication barrier and others are discussed in this section 4.7 and sections 4.8 and 4.9, and the techniques you can use to neutralize the mediation advocacy barriers are discussed in section 4.10.[13]

Behavioral research has identified several reasons why people do not provide clear, accurate, and coherent information. These communication inhibitors include:

Fear of harm or retaliation. Some people fail to provide complete or accurate information because they fear, sometimes not realistically, that the information they provide will result in harm or some kind of retaliation against them.

Ego threat. People often avoid providing information that they feel will produce a negative image of themselves. For example, a client who has had a series of financial setbacks may be embarrassed to provide accurate information for fear of appearing incompetent or foolish.

Result threat. People often hold back information because they feel the information may adversely affect the outcome of the mediation. They fear that their opponents will selfishly use the information to enhance the results significantly in their favor.

Role expectation. Some people believe that their role in mediation is to be competitive at all times. They rarely provide information freely. Also, some people are intimidated by persons of perceived higher status, and therefore may be naturally impeded from sharing information easily.

Disclosure etiquette. A client may decline to disclose information because of a sense of etiquette—a feeling that a certain type of information is "taboo" or is inappropriate for disclosure to persons outside that party's age, family, or social groups. For example, a female employee who is alleging sexual harassment against a supervisor may not feel comfortable revealing the details of the supervisors alleged sexual advances.

---

13. The material in these four sections is adapted from Guernsey, supra at 77–79; Robert Bolton, *People Skills,* (Simon & Schuster, Inc., 1986) 15–26; Binder and Price, *Legal Interviewing and Counseling: A Client-Centered Approach,* (West Publishing Co., 1997) 8–19; *see also* Jean R. Sternlight, "Lawyers' Representation of Clients in Mediation: Using Economics and Psychology to Structure Advocacy in a Nonadversarial Setting," 14 *Ohio State Journal on Dispute Resolution* 269, 297–349 (1999).

Trauma. In personal injury, medical malpractice cases, and other disputes involving mental or emotional trauma, clients are often inhibited from discussing the details of the pertinent events and the consequences. Recall of such details evokes unpleasant or negative feelings such as anger, fear, guilt, or sadness.

Perceived irrelevancy. Often, people do not provide information because they do not consciously consider it relevant to the problem or to the solution.

Greater need. Sometimes, people decline to supply information about a particular topic because they perceive a greater need on their part to have some other need or interest satisfied. A plaintiff in a mediation session, for example, may first need to hear an apology from the other party before discussing the monetary aspects of a settlement.

Forgetting. It is not uncommon for mediating parties to be confused or forgetful about certain facts. Original perception can be modified over time by a variety of factors, including discussion with attorneys and other witnesses. Thus, a mediating party's recollection of actual events may be blocked and therefore not communicated.

Time and money. Some mediating parties will keep disclosure of information to a minimum in the mistaken belief that this behavior will hasten the mediation session to a successful conclusion in their favor. This tack actually inhibits communication and progress toward settlement.

Judging. Winston Churchill once remarked that "what most people call bad judgment is judgment which is different from theirs at a particular moment."[14] This human condition naturally evokes disagreement. Research bears out that people's judgment, bad or good, can impose a substantial barrier to communication. Psychologist Carl Rogers, for example, taught that a major barrier to interpersonal communication lay in the natural tendency of people to judge—to approve or disapprove of the statements or conduct of another person. Symptoms of judging surface as criticism, labeling, diagnosing, and manipulative praising. Criticism is a communication inhibitor when it amounts to persistent fault-finding. Labeling, negative or positive, is a mindset that focuses on "type" and it precludes a successful mediation result when it prevents a party from objectively evaluating the conduct or positions of himself or of others. Diagnosis, a form of labeling, inhibits effective communication when the diagnoser persists in playing emotional detective and probes, as an armchair psychologist, for hidden motives and psychological complexes of the other party.

---

14. Anecdote adapted from Bill Adler, *The Churchill Wit* (Coward-McCann, Inc. 1965), 50.

Unwarranted confidence. Advocates in mediation often place unwarranted confidence in their own predictions about future events, for example, often overestimating their own chances of winning at trial. Many reasons have been suggested as the causes of judgmental overconfidence. One of the principal reasons is that advocates normally have access to only some relevant information, and they may underestimate the importance of what they do not know.

Praise. Praise can be a facilitator or inhibitor of communication. If used honestly, praise can encourage communication; if it is used manipulatively, it can destroy effective communication. You should realize that sometimes a party may praise an opposing party in a mediation session in a manipulative way to obtain a favorable settlement result. If the party receiving the praise interprets the praise as manipulation (whether or not it is in fact manipulation), the praise-receiving party may become angry, less communicative, and less cooperative in subsequent caucuses.

Sending solutions. In mediation sessions, advocates sometimes make statements that can undermine subsequent effective communication. These statements may be categorized under the heading, "sending solutions" which consist of: ordering; threatening; moralizing; excessive or inappropriate questioning; and advising. An order is a demanded solution stated coercively and backed by an ultimatum. Orders make opposing parties resistant and resentful. An order implies that the other party's judgment is unsound and its purpose is to injure or destroy the other party's self-esteem. A threat is a solution communicated along with a high risk of punishment if the solution is not accepted. A party moralizes by backing his or her settlement proposals with the force of social, moral, or theological authority. Moralizing often fosters anxiety in the receiving party and, in addition, it arouses resentment, tends to thwart honest self-expression, and invites pretense. Sometimes an advocate will engage in excessive or inappropriate questioning of another advocate or party in a negotiation session. This tends to occur in mediations where a defendant feels that he has been falsely accused of illegal conduct. You should be careful to curtail such questioning immediately. Finally, a party (or counsel) "advising" the other side in a mediation session as to an appropriate solution often interferes with effective communication. Such advice frequently insults the intelligence of the other party. It implies stupidity on the part of the other party. Advising is destructive to the communication process because the advisor rarely understands the full implications of the problem—the complexities, feelings, and other factors that may lie hidden beneath the surface of the situation.

Avoiding the other party's concerns. Another type of barrier to communication is where one party, consciously or unconsciously, avoids the other party's concerns. Symptoms of avoidance are: diverting, logical argument, and reassurance. Diverting is characterized by a party's shifting a conversation from the other party's concerns to another topic of the speaking party's choice. Ironically, the phrase "speaking of ..." gives the impression of complementary conversation, but in fact often signals the beginning of a diversion. Logical argument made to an emotion-laden party carries with it a high risk of alienating that party. Logic tends to focus on facts and it communicates an avoidance of the other party's feelings. Where the problem is in the relationship between two parties, a logical argument constitutes a withdrawal from attending to the root of the problem—the parties' emotions. Such argument can have adverse effects on subsequent meaningful communication. Finally, reassurance may be used in a joint session by a party to seemingly comfort another person when, in fact, the intent of the speaker is to avoid emotional issues completely. Reassurance can easily be perceived as hollow by the receiving party, and can actually be a form of emotional withdrawal by the speaker. Such would be the situation where a defendant employer in an age discrimination case says to the plaintiff employee, "we at no time thought you were too old to be promoted—you're *definitely* not too old." The implication is that the employee was simply ineffective. This statement, even though well intended, could anger the employee and polarize the settlement situation.

Loss aversion. In general, behavioral research has shown that people are loss-averse—that is, they dislike losing money and therefore are willing to take an "irrational risk" in order to avoid a definite loss. Thus, loss-averse defendants may choose unwisely to litigate rather than settle out of court because they choose to risk a large loss rather than accept a smaller but certain one. Also, loss-averse plaintiffs may be more willing to accept a modest but certain settlement rather than gamble on the prospect of a potentially larger gain through continued litigation.

Risk aversion. Also, behavioral research has shown that people will give up a higher-value but riskier option to ensure they at least get something. Thus, in mediation, an advocate may be able to circumvent risk aversion/loss aversion barriers in the way that he or she frames a settlement proposal with respect to a "gain" or "loss" interpretation.

Endowment effect. Closely related to "loss aversion" is the concept of "endowment effect." If a person feels that he or she owns something, it may seem to that person to have a greater-than-market value. To that person, that "something"—if surrendered—may represent a special kind of loss—the loss of an endowment, for which the person may expect extra monetary compensation.

Reactive devaluation. The theory of reactive devaluation is that a party or an advocate may automatically devalue a settlement proposal made by an adversary, whereas he or she might accept they very same proposal if offered by an ally or neutral.

Zero-sum mindset. Advocates often assume that mediation is purely a distributive process—that is, if one side wins, the other side must lose. This zero-sum mindset often precludes the possibility of integrative bargaining or of value creation through consideration of non-monetary, but value-laden, possibilities.

4.8 THE PERCEPTION BARRIER

What we see depends on how we perceive the world—how our past perceptions have influenced our positive and negative mental sets, a topic discussed more fully in section 4.9. In both deal-making and dispute resolution, lawyers may easily see the other side's biased perceptions, but they are slow to recognize their own. Effective advocates make an effort to perceive and understand the true perspectives, interests, arguments, and concerns of the other side, as well as their own.

Human perception plays a vital role in: (1) creating informational illusions which spawn conflict; and (2) recognizing the reality that can lead to conflict's resolution. In this segment, we shall examine three types of perceptual illusions that routinely occur in conflict settings. Knowing what the illusions are is the first step in diluting their conflict-producing influence.[15]

It is relatively common knowledge that two people rarely perceive the same visual scenes or the same written words identically. Evidence of this, for example, is that eyewitness accounts of an automobile accident vary dramatically. One eyewitness may see something that another did not; another may see something that did not in fact exist or occur because the eyewitness was "programmed," mentally, to see it. Similarly, two people entering into a contract will think they are perceiving its terms identically, and even smile confidently as they sign the document binding themselves to its terms. Later, when events cause the parties to refer to the contract's terms for guidance, it is likely that the parties will perceive the pertinent contract provisions in somewhat different lights, interpreting the provisions, inclusively or exclusively, as best suits their separate needs. Thus, perception has at least two

---

15. For dialogue examples of conflict illusions, see John W. Cooley, *The Mediator's Handbook* (National Institute for Trial Advocacy, 2000), 189–99..

aspects: (1) an aspect that is totally visual; and (2) another, which involves beliefs or mental sets. Sometimes, these aspects combine to impair significantly the design of effective solutions to conflict.

As to the visual aspect of perception, we know that sometimes the eye plays tricks on the brain, or vice versa. In childhood, we knew these "tricks" to be optical illusions and we normally dismissed them as being fun, or perhaps curious, but as having no substantive effect on our lives. As adults, however, we should not be so quick to dismiss them, because they can, in part, contribute to design impairment and, at the very least, provide a useful analogy as to how beliefs and sets can interfere with design effectiveness and efficiency.

Information provided by the eye is not always precise or uncomplicated. Nearly every cue to spatial vision and distance—and thus nearly every visual situation—contains potential for ambiguity. Where ambiguity arises, it is called an illusion. Visual illusions are complicated and baffling. Most geometric or spatial illusions involve one or more of several basic phenomena, and they can be classified into three broad categories: (1) those which "fool" all observers identically; (2) those which are perceived differently by different observers (but eventually most observers can see both shapes); and (3) those which represent impossible objects which cannot be built in three dimensional space.

Illusions of the first type. Examples of the first category of visual illusions are shown here—those which fool all observers identically. Your brain is "programmed" by experience to think that two parallel lines converge in the distance and that if two or more objects of the same size are placed at varying distances from you, the closer one will appear larger. Thus, your brain does not accept the fact that in figure 1, the distant rectangle does not look smaller, so it compensates by making it look larger. Likewise, your brain functions similarly with respect to the human forms in figure 2. The human forms are all the same size and so are the rectangles in figure 1. This gives us some idea as to how the brain perceives in terms of background and relationships. It demonstrates how the brain does not always perceive things correctly, in situational contexts, such as here, where the rectangles and the human forms refuse to get smaller when they should.

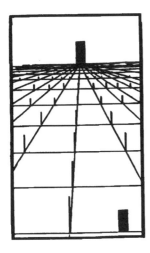

Figure 1   Figure 2

Similarly, the brain tends to underestimate the size of circles and overestimate lengths of straight lines. This is exemplified by figures 3 and 4.

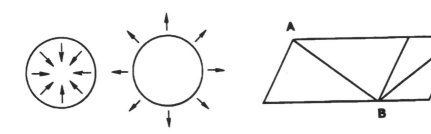

Figure 3   Figure 4

In figure 3, the circles are identical in size, though the left one looks smaller than the right one. In figure 4, the horizontal line AB is exactly equal to line BC in length. In figure 5 the horizontal lines are straight and parallel to each other, but in this depiction, the lines appear to be bent. In figure 6, the lines appear to form a spiral, but the apparent spiral is, in fact, a series of concentric circles. These effects are due to the fact that the brain perceives parallel lines and circles in terms of the relationship of the lines appearing behind them.

Figure 5   Figure 6

Another category of illusions that fools all persons identically are those which, though static, appear to be in motion.

For example, in figure 7, if you focus on the concentric circles in the middle of the other circles, the outer circles will appear to be moving back and forth on their centers. If you gaze at figure 8 for a few seconds, several parts of the figure will imply movement from side to side, when no movement is occurring.

Figure 7   Figure 8

By analogy, in any interpersonal situation each party perceives events and circumstances in terms of background, relationships, and interrelationships of people and events. Sometimes the perceptions of both (or, as the case may be, all) parties to the situation are incorrect. That is, they are viewing the situation (dispute or transaction) identically, but mistakenly. This problem of perception may interfere with effective design. For example, the parties may design a problem and solution differently if they know that the rectangles, as in figure 1, are the same size, instead of thinking that one rectangle is much larger than the other two. Recognition later that the rectangles, which in a real life negotiations may be buildings or floorspace, are identical in size may precipitate a dispute. Sometimes, negotiating or mediating parties will assume movement by another party when, in actuality, there is none. Sometimes opposing parties and their lawyers in a dispute situation will all be relying on a statutory provision or a particular contract clause when, in fact, another statutory provision or contract clause actually governs the situation in question. Usually the parties and their counsel, with appropriate investigation and inquiry, can discover their joint misperception, but sometimes the situation might require the assistance of a disinterested neutral party (and in the case of a dispute, a mediator) to detect the joint misperception.

Illusions of the second type: The second type of visual illusions are those figures or shapes which are perceived differently yet "correctly" by each of the observers. With additional study, however, each observer can eventually see the figure or shape which is perceived by the other observer. Consider the examples shown as follows.

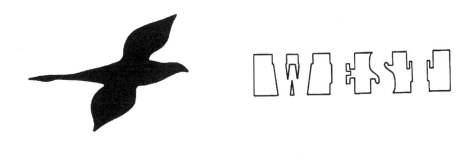

Figure 9   Figure 10

In figure 9, what do you see? You might say a goose. Another person shown the drawing might say a hawk, and another might say a dove. Other people might see something entirely different from a type of bird. Upon discussion, each person would be able to see and understand the other's perception of the drawing. Similarly, if asked what you see in figure 10, you might say "a series of puzzle or machine parts." If told that this configuration of lines and spaces spelled a word, could you perceive the word? If another person perceived the word and told you to focus on the spaces instead of the lines, could you see it? This is a word that often has "Wild" in front of it. Does that help? Do you see the word "WEST"? If not, show Figure 10 to a friend and see if he or she can help you perceive the word "WEST" from the information presented. This second type of illusion is quite prevalent in problem and solution design situations. Oftentimes, parties enter into interpersonal situations with "correct" perceptions about events or circumstances, but, at the same time, they are unable to "see" or appreciate the "correct" perceptions of their opponents. This often leads to a standoff or stalemate when, in fact, if each side could see the problem or transaction from the other's perspective, effective (unbiased) problem and solution design could commence. Again, this process of seeing the problem or transaction as perceived by the opponent often requires the assistance of a disinterested neutral party. Occasionally, even when there is a complete understanding of the perception of all parties, joint resolution is not possible. For example, if all parties see the possible forms in Figure 9 as either as goose, a hawk, or a dove, they may not be able to agree on which type of bird should be the agreed choice of all of them, but at least all parties will have had the opportunity to consider the possibility of selecting one or the other. Whereas, if one party thinks he or she is settling for a dove when in fact she's getting a hawk, there's bound to be trouble down the road. As a mediation advocate, you should endeavor to perceive as many depictions of the available information as possible.

Illusions of the third type: The third type of visual illusion is impossible objects. Visual impossibilities, unknown in direct vision or reality, can be depicted on paper in such a way that at first glance they appear to be logical. As they are examined more carefully, the visual cues create confusion. The triangular object shown below in figure 11 initially appears realistic and logical and is consistent over certain regions, but is nonsensical overall. Figure 12 has a middle element that initially appears to be an integral part of the fabricated object, but on closer examination it becomes clear that this is an impossible object, not able to be replicated in three-dimensional space.

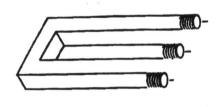

Figure 11   Figure 12

The brain struggles to make sense of these kinds of objects, but eventually accepts them for the illusions that they are. Similarly, in some interpersonal situations, the perceptions of one or more of the parties might be consistent in some respects, but design efforts may be doomed because of an unperceived impossible objective, due to personality conflicts, uncompromising philosophies, exaggerated expectations, and ineffective or nonexistent means to attain certain goals. The earlier the "impossible objective" can be discovered in such situations, the better for all parties concerned. A disinterested neutral party can often be of assistance in discovering the existence of an "impossible objective," but as a mediation advocate, you should be constantly alert to detect them when concluding a settlement and finalizing an agreement.

4.9 THE MENTAL SET BARRIER

Mental set is a person's readiness to respond to a situation in a set manner.[16] A negative set causes one to miss that which is not expected. For example, you may readily recognize the security guard who, in uniform, greets you as you enter your office building each morning. However, you may not recognize him when you see him out of uniform standing in the checkout line in the supermarket. The reason for this is that you do not expect to see him in the checkout line. Also, for example, if you are expecting someone to call you on the telephone, you will immediately recognize her voice. This is the effect of positive set. Mental set can be deceiving, and our belief systems, as discussed more fully below, can make us even more vulnerable to deception. Magicians and creators of special effects in motion pictures rely heavily on the mental set of their audiences. They raise expectations that they are doing or will do one thing, when in fact they are really doing something different. As observers, we tend to miss the "tricks." Consider the figure 1, below.

Figure 1

---

16. See John W. Cooley, "Mediation Magic: Its Use and Abuse," 29 *Loyola U. of Chicago L.J.* 1, 17–22 (1997).

Figure 1 is a visual example of negative set. Many people will not read the words as "I Love Paris in the the Springtime." They are familiar with the phrase "Paris in the Springtime" and they expect and are "set" to see that phrase in the triangle. But sometimes there are no externally created tricks—such as "the the"—in the above example, and our mental set still deceives us. Consider figure 2, below. Read the sentence inside the box and count the number of "F" letters present in the sentence. Do that before you read on.

FINISHED FILES ARE THE RE-SULT OF YEARS OF SCIENTIFIC STUDY COMBINED WITH THE EXPERIENCE OF MANY YEARS.

Figure 2

Most people are surprised to learn that there are six "F" letters in the sentence. Most people count three "F" letters and they miss the three "F" letters at the end of the three "OF" words. Again, our expectations—our mental sets—deprive us of seeing the facts as they are. Maybe we expect to see the letter "F" only at the beginning of words in the sentence, or maybe we have grown accustomed to skipping over small words like "OF" when we read, or perhaps because the word "OF" has a "V" sound at the end, our mind is not registering the "F" in "OF" as an F, but rather as a "V." Whatever the case, it is negative mental set that deceives us. Thus, negative set—our inclination not to see something that does exist—can be a formidable barrier to effective communication and problem solving.

Positive mental set, on the other hand, predisposes people to perceive something that actually does not exist. Consider the two figures below.

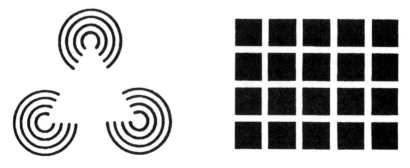

Figure 3   Figure 4

If asked whether there is a triangle in figure 3, most everyone would answer "yes" even though no lines of a triangle exist—only the *implication* of lines of a triangle. Most people who gaze at figure 4 will insist that there are dots at the intersections of the white lines, when in fact no such dots exist. Thus, positive set—our inclination to see something that does not exist—can be a formidable barrier to effective communication and problem solving.

Similar to the effect of mental set demonstrated by the visual illustrations presented above, people's belief systems cause them to notice events and facts that support their beliefs and ignore those that do not. This explains why two people can hold completely opposite views about religion, politics, education, state of the economy, and the "correct" interpretation of a contract. They unconsciously select supporting evidence that allows them to see the world in the way they believe it to be, and they *assume* that their view is the *only* correct view. Of importance to mediation advocates is the fact that mental set can significantly affect the way people see themselves, other people, and the world around them.

In general, the beliefs people have about themselves are usually self-serving or self-enhancing. People's need to enhance themselves stems from a need to maintain and develop positive self-regard. This can present problems for effective mediation because inflated perceptions about the reasonableness of one's negotiation position can lead perfectly normal people to expect that a completely neutral third party will favor their view. Inflated perceptions of one's own judgment can escalate destructive conflict behavior. And while people generally attribute their successes to themselves, they habitually are quick to blame others for their failures. The problem of this self-serving behavior is that it hinders people's ability to learn from experience and to adapt their behavior to what they learn.

Another ingrained trait of human behavior is to assume more responsibility for joint projects than is warranted. Thus, in a partnership, each partner will assume that he or she is more responsible than the other. Thus if each partner believes that he is working more than another partner, this can serve to escalate conflict.

People's belief systems also affect how they generally size up other people. Mediation advocates have to be on the lookout for what is called "halo and forked-tail effects." In general, people believe that if a person has one socially desirable characteristic—that is intelligence, sincerity, or the like—they also have other attractive traits. The converse of this is the forked-tail effect. If we learn something negative about a person, we tend to label that person with a number of undesirable characteristics. These generalizations are often wrong and can affect the quality and durability of settlements. There is a proven tendency of people to be influenced by their first impressions of other people. Research studies have shown that negative information about a person has more lasting effects on people that does positive information.

Another belief of people which directly affects their behavior in a conflict situation is the "fixed-pie" perception. That is the belief that the other party's interests are directly opposed to your own. In many situations, just the opposite is true. Still another type of pervasive false belief is people's thinking that other people—the majority—are similar to themselves. This belief inhibits a person in conflict to step in her opponent's shoes and view the problem from the opponent's perspective.

Finally, belief systems significantly affect how people generally view the world, and their beliefs about how the world works greatly affect what they do. In general, people tend to have a hindsight or "I told you so" bias. Once people know the outcome, they perceive it to be the inevitable consequence of factors leading up to the outcome. When a mediator achieves a novel solution, the parties, in hindsight, believe it to be "obvious"—when in fact they could not perceive the intervening steps. This type of hindsight bias often inhibits forward thinking, integrative solutions.

Another common belief of people that interferes with settlement of disputes is their tendency to infer an unwarranted causal connection between two events. This tendency toward simple solutions causes people to become entrenched in their positions and uncooperative in their conflict behavior. And it is strange, but true, that people often tend to persevere in a belief even though they are confronted with evidence conclusively proving that their belief has no valid basis. In a mediation, sometimes a mediator has to work hard with one or more parties until they "let go" of these erroneous beliefs that block settlement.

Finally, there's the "serves 'em right" belief. Many people believe that the world is a fair place: people get out of life what they deserve and they deserve what happens to them. Actually, the opposite is frequently true. Life is hardly predictable; and it is rarely completely fair.

4.10 TECHNIQUES FOR NEUTRALIZING THE BARRIERS TO EFFECTIVE MEDIATION ADVOCACY

Among techniques available for neutralizing communication barriers are: (1) education and discussion; (2) cost-benefit analysis; (3) empathic understanding; (4) honest praise and recognition; (5) altruistic appeals; (6) curtailment; (7) active listening; and (8) effective questioning.

Education and discussion. If you sense that ego threat, result threat, role expectation, or disclosure etiquette is inhibiting a client's effective communication with you, you should, in most instances, share your observations in a caucus with the client and discuss the validity of your perceptions. If your impressions are deemed to be valid, you can then discuss how he or she may overcome these barriers. To overcome a client's inhibitions caused by embarrassing details, adverse outcomes, or low self-esteem, it is often helpful for the lawyer to emphasize that he or she is ethically obliged to keep confidential any information designated as such by the client. It is also helpful for the lawyer to emphasize that a client's disclosure to the lawyer can assist the lawyer in generating possible solutions to the problem. Making a client consciously aware of the communication barriers and discussing ways to deal with them frequently are the first steps in dissolving the barriers and engendering open communication flow between a client and the lawyer.

Cost-benefit analysis. If you sense that greater need, time, and money are factors inhibiting effective communication between a client and yourself, you might consider discussing the matter with the client from a cost-benefit viewpoint. In this discussion, you can point out that you cannot help the client solve the problem unless all pertinent information is disclosed. You can also emphasize that by disclosing the information to you, the client may acquire extrinsic rewards in the form of an accelerated, satisfactory settlement and the avoidance of continued litigation and a costly trial.

Empathic understanding. Researchers contend that there are three key qualities that foster improved communication: genuineness, nonpossessive appreciation (or love), and empathy. Genuineness means being honest and open about one's feelings, needs, and ideas. Non-possessive appreciation involves accepting, respecting, and supporting another person in a nonpaternalistic and freeing way. Empathy refers to the ability to see and hear another person and understand him or her from his or her perspective. To be completely understood, empathy must be contrasted with apathy and sympathy. Apathy is a lack of feeling or a lack of interest or concern. Sympathy is a "feeling for" another person, as opposed to empathy which is a "feeling with" the other. The continuum described in the table below assists in distinguishing the three concepts.

The Apathy-Empathy-Sympathy Continuum

APATHY	EMPATHY	SYMPATHY
"I don't care."	"Looks like you're really feeling down today."	"You poor thing . . ."
"That's your problem."	"Sounds as if you were really hurt by that."	"I feel just dreadful for you!"

Empathy is comprised of three components. The empathic person: (1) has a sensitive and accurate understanding of the other person's feelings while maintaining a separateness from the person; (2) understands the situation that contributed to or triggered those feelings; and (3) communicates with the other person in such a way that the other person feels accepted and understood. This last component—communicating one's empathic understanding—is crucial to removal of communication barriers and to the fostering of effective communication. Effective advocates practice and model genuineness, nonpossessive appreciation, and empathy in their mediation communications and encourage the development and display of these communication-enhancing qualities by parties and counsel in mediation. Empathic understanding may be used to neutralize any of the communication barriers, but it is especially effective when disclosure etiquette and client trauma are the operative communication inhibitors.

Honest praise and recognition. In general, the performance of human beings improves when they are praised or recognized for their action. Sometimes, you may be able to break through a communication barrier and elicit substantial, helpful information by praising a client's disclosure of a few factual details. As the client discloses additional information, you can encourage further disclosure by additional praise and recognition, such as, "Those facts are very helpful," or "You're really doing a good job of providing the information needed to settle this case."

Altruistic appeals. Many people need to identify with some high value or cause that is beyond immediate self-interest. The high value or cause may be as abstract as "truth" or a "sense of justice" or as concrete as the "stated goals" of an organization or company. In the appropriate situation, you can make such altruistic appeals if it seems probable that they will facilitate a client's or an opposing counsel's disclosure of significant information.

Curtailment. It may be necessary for you in a mediation session to curtail communication that will have injurious, inhibiting, or destructive effects on subsequent communication in the mediation process. Most often curtailment is used when an advocate senses comments or behavior of another advocate indicating judging, sending solutions, or avoiding the concerns of the other party or parties.

Active listening. You can employ techniques of active listening to identify and categorize all of the communication barriers discussed in sections 4.7, 4.8, and 4.9 above. First, as described in subsection 5.5.2 below, you should be familiar with the six styles of listening and you should know what your dominant listening style is. Second, as explained more thoroughly in subsection 5.5.4 below, you should understand that hearing and listening are two different processes. The former is the ability to record transmitted sound vibrations. The latter involves making sense of what you hear. In the mediation environment, you will normally engage in two types of listening: critical and active. Critical listening occurs when you are listening to evaluate, not for pleasure. This type of listening takes effort, time, and planning. It is necessary to recognize and weigh the facts as presented by the speakers and to determine the validity of the conclusions which the speakers are presenting.

As explained in subsection 5.5.4 below, there are several ways to improve your ability to listen critically. To engage in active listening, however, you must continuously try to determine the true meaning of the speaker's message. It involves an effort to understand and attribute meaning to the content of both the speaker's substantive concern and emotional state. Active listening requires two steps: (1) hearing and giving meaning to the content of the speaker's statements; (2) communicating the interpreted meaning back to the speaker.

Effective questioning. You can assist a client or an opposing counsel to overcome communication barriers by applying effective questioning techniques. Abe Lincoln used such questioning techniques frequently. On one occasion, having failed to make a stubborn opposing counsel see the error of his own reasoning, Lincoln said, "Well, let's see. How many legs has a cow?" "Four, of course," replied the opponent. "That's right," said Lincoln. "Now suppose we call the cow's tail a leg, how many legs would the cow have?" "Why, five, of course," was the ready response. "That's where you make an error," said Lincoln. "Simply calling a cow's tail a leg doesn't make it a leg."[17]

Questions provide you with tools to accomplish five tasks in your efforts to negotiate a settlement of a dispute: (1) gain a party's attention;

---

17. Anecdote adapted from Bill Adler, *Presidential Wit from Washington to Johnson* (Trident Press, 1966), 64.

(2) get information; (3) give information; (4) stimulate thinking; and (5) bring discussion to a conclusion. Attention questions set the mood of the conversation and put people at ease. They are ritual questions like, "did you have any trouble finding the conference room?" "hasn't the weather been wonderful the last few days?" "have you been to Chicago before?" The second type of question is designed to acquire information. Words that begin this type of question include: who, what, when, where, should, shall, is, and do. Questions of the third type supply information to the listener. They communicate where the questioner is headed with a succession or line of questions. For example, questions communicating a questioner's focus on the answerer's ability to have avoided an automobile accident would be: "on the morning of the accident, were you wearing your glasses?" "was your car stereo playing at the time?" "were you driving into the sun?" "were you using your cellular telephone at the time?" Questions of the fourth type stimulate a client or an opposing counsel, or another party to start thinking about a topic. Such questions are intended to be nonthreatening and are normally used to open up a new topic area in the discussion. Examples are: "can you describe the first time you met with Mr. Thompson?" "would you explain what happened in the emergency room?" "prior to the first shipment of semiconductors, what kind of interactions did you have with Ms. Waldorf?" Questions of the fifth type are designed to lead an answerer to a conclusion. These questions fall into the category of gentle cross-examination. Advocates must carefully frame such questions so as to avoid creating excessive anxiety or anger in the answerer. It is through this type of questions that the advocate helps a client or a party to reality test and to reframe their perceptions.

Apart from these five functional descriptions, questions can also be categorized by their structures. Questions are open, closed, and reflective by virtue of their structure. Open questions prompt answerers to relax and open up in the discussion. Most commonly they are used by advocates to seek clarification, to gain more information, and to foster a detailed response. Open questions usually begin with *how, what, when, where, who,* and *why.* Examples are: "how do you feel about the defendant's proposal?" "what are your ideas for dealing with plaintiff's financial concerns?" "who else in your department might be able to work with Nancy to finish the project before December?"

Closed questions usually yield an unqualified yes or no answer. Effective advocates use closed questions to get a quick response and to check details. They are predominantly data-oriented, not feelings-oriented. Examples are: "did you call the police?" "did you call Acme to repair your roof?" "have your read the defendant's settlement proposal?" When effective advocates employ the third type of question structure—the reflective questions—they incorporate an answerer's response to a prior question both to confirm their understanding of that response and to allow the answerer to think about and perhaps modify the response. For example, suppose a defense advocate asks her plaintiff counterpart, "Would you accept $22,000 to settle both matters in dispute?" The counterpart responds, "That offer is too low." The defense advocate then asks a reflective question: "You feel that the offer is too low?" This question allows the counterpart to rethink the former response and provide reasoning as to why the defense advocate's offer is too low or what the plaintiff needs in addition to that amount to settle. By using this reflective question, the defense advocate does not indicate that she has made a judgment either about her own settlement offer or the counterpart's response.

Chapter Five

EFFECTIVE ADVOCACY IN THE MEDIATION SESSION

*"Every now and then, when you're on the stage,
you hear the best sound a player can hear. . . . It is
the sound of a wonderful, deep silence that means
you've hit them where they live."*
— *Shelley Winters*

Lawyers who participate in a mediation for the first time are quite often unsure about their specific role at the mediation session. Even experienced trial lawyers are initially daunted by the lack of rules and the flexibility of the process. As a result, many of them assume a passive role on their first foray into the world of mediation, content with merely observing the mediator, studying the mediator's techniques, and attempting to glean from the mediator's conduct a sense of the proper protocol for counsel in this foreign setting. In a way they are much like the Italian ambassador who was having breakfast one day with President Calvin Coolidge. The ambassador was somewhat puzzled when the president carefully poured his cup of milk into his saucer, but being the diplomat that he was, he did precisely the same thing with his milk. The president smiled slightly but said nothing as he stooped down to give his saucer to a gray cat waiting patiently at his feet.[1] The point of this chapter is that in mediation the advocates need not follow, they should *lead*! And they should also do what they do best and most often—*negotiate*! If you bring only that much away from this chapter, you will have an edge in every mediation in which you participate.

5.1 PREPARING THE PREMEDIATION SUBMISSION

Your effectiveness in the mediation session may depend a great deal on the care you take and the time you devote to the preparation of the written materials you submit to the mediator in advance of the mediation session. Drafting this submission and collecting documents pertinent to it will require you to think through many of the topics covered in

---

1. Anecdote adapted from Humes, *Speaker's Treasury*, supra at 167.

chapter 3 and to organize your presentation both mentally and on paper.

You may not need to prepare a premediation submission in every mediation situation. Different mediators and dispute resolution organizations have differing requirements. Some mediators like detailed submissions, including relevant documents, others prefer short position statements, and still others do not want any premediation submissions, believing that such submissions may have a tendency to bias them one way or the other before the mediation begins. To avoid unnecessary work for yourself and expense to your client, you would be well advised to contact the mediator or the appropriate dispute resolution organization long before the scheduled mediation date to determine if they desire a premediation submission, and if so, what format, content, and length they prefer. The remainder of this section will describe the suggested content of a typical premediation submission in a case of average size and complexity. Whether you can put together a submission of the type described below will of course depend on the amount of time you have available and what your client can afford to spend to allow you to produce it.

In the average case, the nature and the content of a premediation submission will vary depending on its specific purpose and on the stage of litigation, if any. If the purpose of the submission is to give the mediator an overview of the facts and law of the case and if the parties are to serve these documents on each other, then the submission will resemble a position statement or a condensed brief with perhaps an appendix of relevant documents and copies of any critical appellate court opinions. If, however, by agreement of the parties or by direction of the mediator, the parties are to make confidential, ex parte submissions to the mediator, then those submissions will likely contain more personal analyses of the parties, of their relationship if appropriate, and of the nature of the dispute, in addition to the parties' condensed briefs and appendices. For example, an ex parte premediation submission in a partnership dissolution situation may, in addition to other documents, consist of the following: a history of prior negotiations; an objective assessment of the parties' strengths and weaknesses; a list of highly sensitive issues; a description of any communication problems existing between counsel; the root causes of the conflict; the nature and extent of the prior good relationship enjoyed by the parties; the negotiating styles of the parties and counsel; suggested approaches for the mediator to take in attempting to resolve the dispute; and suggestions for creative solutions.

Apart from the purpose of the submission, the timing of the mediation in relation to any proposed or ongoing litigation may also dictate the submission's content. If the mediation occurs before any lawsuit is filed and therefore before any discovery has taken place, the plaintiff's premediation submission in the above-described partnership dispute might reasonably consist of (1) a summary of the events precipitating the dispute, (2) the plaintiff's contemplated legal claims and the relief to be requested if a lawsuit is filed, (3) the partnership agreement and the accounting records that define the heart of the conflict between the partners, and (4) a short legal memorandum and copies of any critical appellate court opinions. If the mediation occurs during ongoing litigation, a defendant's premediation submission in the same partnership dispute might, in addition to specific documentary evidence and critical appellate court opinions, include some or all of the following: (1) an overview of the history of the dispute and the litigation, together with a description of the status of the litigation; (2) pertinent court pleadings (e.g., Complaint, Answer, and Counterclaim); (3) any motion for summary judgment and responsive memorandum, together with pertinent court rulings; (4) court-filed legal briefs or excerpts of them on aspects of law important to discussions during the mediation; and (5) a legal memorandum regarding the lack of the plaintiff's entitlement to damages. If a mediation occurs in the same case after judgment and while the case is pending on appeal, the parties' premediation submission may include any or all of the following: (1) judgment being appealed (with any Memorandum Opinion); (2) jury instructions; (3) general and special verdicts; (4) motion for new trial, response, and ruling; and (5) appellate briefs.

Of course, any of the just-described premediation submissions may also contain a more personal analysis of the parties and the dispute if the submissions are to be ex parte.

5.2 THE OPENING STATEMENT IN MEDIATION

There are two types of opening statements that are made in the beginning of the mediation session. One type is given by the mediator; the other is given by the advocates alone, by the advocates together with their clients, or by the clients alone (referred to collectively as the parties' opening statements). The mediator's opening statement usually takes about ten minutes and has several purposes: educating the parties on the mediation process, the mediator's role, and what to expect during the course of the mediation; setting the tone for the mediation session; establishing rapport and credibility with the parties; obtaining a commitment from the parties to negotiate in good faith; establishing an initial pattern of agreement; outlining procedural considerations, including those related to caucusing and confidentiality; and suggesting an agenda for the mediation session. Although opening statements vary from mediator to mediator, the content of the statement routinely includes the following: introductions of the mediator and the other persons present; a description of the mediator's background and experience; a disclaimer of any bias, prejudice, or conflict of interest on the mediator's part or a disclosure of possible conflicts of interest that the parties may consider in deciding whether to proceed with the mediation or not; an estimate of the length of the mediation session; and certain "housekeeping" matters such as rules about smoking, interruptions, the presence of outside observers or witnesses, understandings regarding talking to the media, and when breaks will be taken for meals. During the opening statement the mediator may also ask the parties and their counsel to sign a premediation agreement if they have not previously done so. As explained in a prior chapter, the premediation agreement covers such matters as the parties' consent to participate in the mediation with a particular mediator, to keep the information generated in the mediation confidential, to refrain from suing or subpoenaing the mediator, and to share the cost of the mediation.

The parties' opening statements provide an opportunity for the advocates (or the parties themselves) to educate the mediator and the opposing parties and their counsel on the factual background of the dispute and on their respective thoughts about how the dispute should be resolved. Typically, a party's opening statement in a case of average size and complexity may take between fifteen and thirty minutes. In a complex, high-stakes case, the opening statement of each side may take an hour or more. In some ways, a party's opening statement is similar to an opening statement at trial. The advocate identifies herself and the client(s), discusses the facts of the case, identifies disputed and undisputed facts, outlines the claims or defenses, and states the nature of the relief sought. But that is where the similarity ends. From that point on, a party's opening statement in a mediation is markedly different from the type of opening statement given by counsel at trial. Unlike a trial opening statement, in a party's opening statement in mediation, the advocate may have her client speak, may present documentary evidence, including affidavits and deposition transcripts, and may use audio or visual aids. Further, the advocate may discuss the applicable law and, if representing a plaintiff, may discuss in detail how the amount of damages was computed. If representing a defendant, an advocate in a party's opening statement may present evidence to show that plaintiff's claims are without merit, may discuss applicable law supporting defendant's position, and may make legal arguments as to why plaintiff is entitled to no recovery or a lower recovery, as appropriate. Moreover, unlike a trial opening statement, advocates representing both sides will be expected to discuss the prior negotiation history in the case, including current demands and offers and reasons why prior settlement overtures have failed to achieve settlement.

It is very important for you to realize that *the party's opening state-ment in mediation is like a trial opening statement and a trial closing argument wrapped into one.* Unlike the trial setting, rarely if ever do you have the opportunity in mediation to make a trial-like "closing argu-ment" at the end of the mediation session. Many times a case will settle during the course of caucusing, and if it does not settle midmediation, normally the final joint session with the mediator is taken up with the mediator giving his evaluation of the case and with discussion of further necessary discovery, of the future course of negotiations, and the like. Thus the party's opening statement is a one-of-a-kind opportunity in mediation to make your most complete, persuasive settlement pitch to the mediator and to the opponents on behalf of your client. It should be well planned and well executed. Review all the communication and per-suasion advice provided in section 5.5 prior to the mediation session and apply it during the course of your opening statement.

5.2.1 Using the client to tell the story

If you decide to have your client tell her own story, you may want to introduce yourself and your client and make some brief introductory remarks to assure the mediator and the other side that you and your cli-ent are at the mediation with the good-faith purpose of coming to an agreed solution to the dispute (or part of it, as appropriate). In this in-troduction, you may also want to give the mediator any pertinent back-ground information that you think is necessary to put your client's story in context.

Allow your client to tell her story in a narrative style. A question-and-answer format is not recommended because it is unnecessarily time consuming and does not ordinarily allow the client to use her persua-sive speaking abilities. While the client is telling the story, you should listen carefully and take notes of any important facts that the client has inadvertently omitted. When the client is finished telling the story, then you can ask follow-up questions from your notes. After that occurs, you may want to add any concluding remarks, including information about the status of the litigation and about the status of any settlement nego-tiations. Finally, you should ask the mediator if he has any questions. You should be aware that the mediator may ask several questions, and then the mediator may ask if anyone on the other side has any questions for you or your client. Do not assume that what you planned to give them by way of the opening statement is all that the mediator and the others will want or need. You may have overlooked something very basic—like the doctor who was busy in his study when his small son came in and stood silently by. The doctor, preoccupied with his work, put his hand into his pocket, took out a coin, and offered it to the boy. "I don't want any money, Daddy," the boy said. After a few moments the doctor opened a desk drawer, took out a candy bar, and offered it to his son. Again the boy refused. A little impatient, the busy doctor asked, "Well, what *do* you want, my son?" "I don't want anything," replied the boy. "I only wanted to be with you."[2]

5.2.2 Using documents

If your client is comfortable referring to documentary evidence or demonstrative exhibits while telling the story and the documentary evidence will significantly aid the mediator in understanding the story, then you should allow your client to do it. If you take that tack, you and your client should preorganize the documents to match the logical flow of your client's story. Of course, it is important that the mediator and opposing counsel also be provided with a set of the documents to which your client will be referring. Another way to deal with the documents is for you to "feed" the documents to your client at appropriate points in her story and then have her discuss the relevance of the document at that time. If you have multiple documents and you appropriately space and time the "feeding," then you effectively guarantee that your client follows the preagreed organization of her opening statement. The simplest way to do this is to provide your client with a tabbed binder of documents. Still another way to use documents is for your client to tell the story and for you to discuss pertinent exhibits following your client's presentation. How you work documents into the party's opening statement depends to a large degree on your client's communication ability, the nature of the documents, and the need for the documents in actually telling the story.

5.2.3 Using audiovisual aids

Occasionally the party's opening statement would benefit from the use of audio or visual aids. If you decide to employ such aids, you should carefully coordinate their use with your client. Large charts, models, blowups of documents, video playback equipment, and the like should be situated in the room so that all participants have an unobstructed view of them during the course of the storytelling. If an overhead projector, a slide projector, or a computer projection device is going to be used, you need to decide whether you or the client will activate screen changes during the course of the presentation. You should also arrange for such equipment in advance and arrive early enough at the mediation session to test the equipment and meet briefly with your client to make sure that he understands how the equipment is to be used during the storytelling.

---

2.   Anecdote adapted from Braude, *Speaker's Desk Book*, supra at126.

5.3 APPLIED NEGOTIATION TACTICS—KNOWING WHAT TO DO AND WHEN TO DO IT

In section 3.14 we reviewed some of the common competitive and cooperative negotiation tactics. In this section we will consider the specific circumstances and the timing of the use of such tactics during the course of the mediation. We will also consider how to respond to certain negotiation tactics of the opponents in mediation.

As pointed out in section 3.14, the three principal types of negotiation tactics are competitive, cooperative, and avoidance. They correspond to three broad types of conflict behaviors: competing, cooperating, and avoiding. Cooperating conflict behavior consists of three subtypes: accommodating, compromising, and collaborating. Thus the five principal conflict behaviors potentially operating in any mediation are:[3]

- Competing.
- Accommodating.
- Compromising.
- Collaborating.
- Avoiding.

To determine when to use a particular negotiation tactic identified in section 3.14 and in this section, you need to know and understand the five basic conflict behaviors and the criteria for choosing the most effective behavior for a particular situation.

---

3. The discussion regarding conflict behaviors here is in part adapted from Ralph H. Kilmann and Kenneth W. Thomas, "Interpersonal Conflict-Handling Behavior as Reflection of Jungian Personality Dimensions," *Psychological Reports* 37 (1975): 971–80. See also Thomas-Kilmann Conflict Mode Instrument (Tuxedo, N.Y.: XICOM, Inc., 1974), a self-discovery device for conflict behaviors, used widely to train negotiators and mediators; and John W. Cooley, "Geometries of Situation and Emotions and the Calculus of Change in Negotiation and Mediation," *Valparaiso University Law Review* 29 (1994): 32–39.

5.3.1   The five principal conflict behaviors

The chart below summarizes the five principal conflict behaviors in terms of their qualities of assertiveness (attempting to satisfy one's own concerns) and cooperativeness (attempting to satisfy the other person's concerns).

ASSERTIVENESS AND COOPERATIVENESS OF THE FIVE PRINCIPAL CONFLICT BEHAVIORS

BEHAVIOR	ASSERTIVENESS	COOPERATIVENESS
Competing	High	Low
Accommodating	Low	High
Compromising	Medium	Medium
Collaborating	High	High
Avoiding	Low	Low

Note that both competing and collaborating are high in assertiveness, whereas both competing and avoiding are low in cooperativeness. Accommodating and avoiding are low in assertiveness. Collaborating is high in both assertiveness and cooperativeness. Knowing these relative qualities should aid your understanding of the Behavior Analysis Chart later in this section. The following chart shows the specific characteristics of the five behaviors.

CHARACTERISTICS OF THE FIVE
PRINCIPAL CONFLICT BEHAVIORS

BEHAVIOR	CHARACTERISTICS
Competing	Power-oriented Pursuing own goals at another's expense
Accommodating	Neglecting own concerns to satisfy other's concerns Self-sacrifice; selfless generosity; charity Obeying orders against one's will Yielding to another's point of view
Compromising	Seeking some expedient, *partially satisfactory* solution Splitting the difference Exchanging concessions Seeking a quick middle-ground position
Collaborating	Attempting to find a *fully satisfactory* solution Identifying underlying concerns to find mutual satisfaction Seeking creative solutions
Avoiding	Not immediately pursuing own concerns or others' concerns Not addressing the conflict Sidestepping an issue Postponing an issue Withdrawing from a threatening situation

5.3.2 Criteria for choosing a specific behavior in mediation

Determining the appropriate conflict behavior and associated tactic to use at any particular point in the mediation session involves two considerations: (1) your goal at that time on a particular issue or issues and

(2) the conflict behavior and associated tactic your opponent is using at that time.

The following series of charts shows the circumstances prompting the use of a specific behavior to satisfy your immediate mediation goals.

COMPETING

CIRCUMSTANCES PROMPTING USE OF BEHAVIOR			
You need a quick solution	You have power in a situation and wish to use it	You need a favorable resolution on an issue vital to client	You need to protect your client

COOPERATING

SPECIFIC COOPERATIVE BEHAVIOR	CIRCUMSTANCES PROMPTING USE OF BEHAVIOR			
Accommodating	You are wrong or you want to avoid disruptions	Issue is more important to other side	Build credits for later	Competition would damage cause
Compromising	Goals are moderately important	Temporary settlement	Time pressures	Back-up mode
Collaborating	Find integrative solution	Merge insights	Gain commitment	Work through hard feelings

AVOIDING

CIRCUMSTANCES PROMPTING USE OF BEHAVIOR			
Trivial issue or low power	Possible damage outweighs negotiated result	Gain time to cool down	Gain time to gather information

You must check your choice of a behavior in relation to your goals against your perception of the behavior or tactic your opponent is employing at the time. For example, if at some time during a mediation you determine to use accommodating behaviors and/or tactics to avoid disruptions or to speed up the mediation and your opponent is consistently using highly competitive behaviors and/or tactics, you may find that as the process gains momentum toward resolution, you have given up too much without the possibility of recoupment or reciprocity.

The Behavior Analysis Chart that follows depicts the chances of achieving a minimally acceptable result when you are using a particular behavior vis-à-vis a particular behavior your opponent is using. The chart has been designed—and this is important—from *your* perspective, giving you the appropriate advantage that accompanies conscious choice of a particular behavior. To use the chart, enter it from the top (the "You" side) with the particular behavior you intend to use. The five behaviors are abbreviated as follows:

> Av = Avoiding
>
> Ac = Accommodating
>
> Cr = Compromising
>
> Cl = Collaborating
>
> Cp = Competing

After entering the chart at the point corresponding to your behavior, proceed vertically to the cell corresponding to the behavior you perceive your opponent is using. The letter inside the cell represents the chance you will achieve a minimally acceptable result if the respective behaviors do not change:

> L = Low chance (0% to 25%)
>
> M = Medium chance (26% to 75%)
>
> H = High chance (76% to 100%)

Note that the highest chance of achieving a minimally acceptable result occurs in the cells relating to your use of collaborating and competing behaviors, both having high assertiveness qualities. Note also that whenever you or your opponent uses avoiding behavior (low assertiveness, low cooperativeness), the chance of a minimally acceptable result is low—usually zero. Equally low chances of a minimally acceptable result occur when you and your opponent are both competing (high assertiveness, low cooperation). Cells reflecting the remaining combinations normally have medium chances of minimally acceptable results.

137

BEHAVIOR ANALYSIS CHART

YOUR OPPONENT	YOU				
	Av	Ac	Cr	Cl	Cp
Av	Low	Low	Low	Low	Low
Ac	Low	Medium	Medium	Medium	Medium
Cr	Low	Medium	Medium	Medium	Medium
Cl	Low	High	High	High	Medium
Cp	Low	High	High	High	Low

After choosing an appropriate negotiating behavior, then all that remains is determining which specific tactic—corresponding to the chosen behavior—may be appropriate in the specific situation. The chart on the following page presents the five principal conflict behaviors in relation to their associated negotiation tactics.

TACTIC SELECTION CHART

FIVE PRINCIPAL CONFLICT BEHAVIORS	RELATED NEGOTIATION TACTICS
Competing	Alternative Opportunities Belly-up Bluffing Brer Rabbit Creating Deadlock Fait Accompli Feigning Good Cop/Bad Cop Limited Authority Media Pressure Preconditions Reversal Threat or Show of Power Time Pressure
Accommodating	Association Creating Movement Face-Saving Reasonable Deadlines
Compromising	Conditional Proposals Log-Rolling Reciprocity Cutting the Salami Splitting the Difference
Collaborating	Focusing on Process Flexibility Participation Psychological Commitment Romancing
Avoiding	Declining to Negotiate Monetary Issues Declining to Negotiate Nonmonetary Issues Withdrawing an Issue Walking Out

You will not, of course, review these charts during the active negotiating portions of mediation sessions. However, you may find them very helpful in generating ideas for strategies and tactics during premediation preparation and during waiting periods that routinely occur in the course of a mediation session when the mediator is caucusing with the other side.

5.4 DERIVING THE MOST TACTICAL ADVANTAGE FROM CAUCUSES

Your chances of obtaining a good result for your client will be increased significantly if during the course of the mediation session you keep firmly in mind that you—not the mediator—own the process. You must take and keep control of it. You must be proactive, rather than merely reactive, particularly during the caucuses. You must remember that you are *negotiating* at all times on behalf of your client—in part, with the mediator, through the mediator, and with the other side. In negotiating *with* the mediator, you should be collaborative at all times—both cooperative and assertive. In negotiating *through* the mediator and *with* the other side, you may use the whole range of tactics discussed in sections 5.3 and 3.14. Realize that the mediator also will be using strategies and tactics with the goal of achieving settlement.[4] You need to know (1) how to identify and deal with the mediator's caucus strategies and tactics and (2) how to use the mediator as a vehicle for deriving the best settlement possible for your client.

5.4.1 Identifying and dealing with the mediator's strategies and tactics

Stated simply, the mediator has three basic strategies that operate in a continuing iterative cycle during the course of a mediation: gathering information, interpretation and diagnosis, and encouraging movement. In carrying out the first two strategies the mediator uses active listening and intuitive and rational thinking skills. For those two strategies to be effective, the parties must share with the mediator as much relevant information as possible regarding the source and status of the dispute and suggested proposals for resolution. In carrying out the third strategy—the movement strategy—the mediator typically uses a variety of tactics that may be categorized under three headings: communication, substantive, and procedural.

Typical communication tactics include (1) the conduit tactic, in which the mediator merely reports the settlement proposals from each side to the other; (2) the surrogate tactic, in which the mediator additionally provides justification for the proposals; (3) the reshaping tactic, a more extreme tactic in which the mediator alters or embellishes the

---

4. See generally Deborah M. Kolb, *The Mediators* (MIT Press, 1983) 72–74, 96–100. See also John W. Cooley, "A Classical Approach to Mediation—Part II: The Socratic Method and Conflict Reframing in Mediation," *University of Dayton Law Review* 19 (1994): 589.

proposals with his own ideas about how the dispute may be resolved; and (4) the clarification tactic, in which the mediator obtains responses to specific questions or reiterates or highlights something that has already been said.

For the most part, mediators do not employ these tactics abusively. However, in order to avoid any possibility that the mediator will communicate something to the other side that is not in keeping with your overall strategy or tactics, you must be very explicit regarding your desires. At the end of each caucus with the mediator remind the mediator, in a respectful way, how important it is to use specific wording when relaying a proposal. If the proposal is long or complex, write it for the mediator. Also, listen carefully to how the mediator communicates proposals from the other side to you. You may obtain some insight into whether the mediator tends to exaggerate or overembellish the other side's proposals. Ask for a joint session to clarify proposals directly with the other side if you think it is necessary.

Substantive tactics are usually mediator-initiated and consist of commentary about some facet of the issues in dispute. These tactics include (1) the translation tactic, in which the mediator redefines seemingly noncomparable issues in order to effect trade-offs; (2) the norm-deviating tactic, in which the mediator points out that a party's demands are unrealistic in that they deviate substantially from the norm in other similar situations or settlements; (3) the opinion tactic, in which the mediator offers an independent opinion about the merit or lack of merit of a proposal; and (4) the recommendation tactic, in which the mediator strongly suggests that a party make or accept a settlement proposal.

A mediator who offers an unwanted opinion in a mediation can greatly disadvantage one side and sometimes erect a formidable barrier to settlement. For example, if the parties have opted for a facilitative mediation and the mediator offers her unsolicited opinion on a fair settlement value that is much more than the defendant wishes to pay, the plaintiff may take that value as "gospel," and the defendant may have no choice but to defend the case in a trial. In the initial joint session with the mediator, it is a good practice to advise the mediator of the type of mediation—facilitative or evaluative—the parties have chosen. A busy mediator may not remember which type of mediation was requested, and she will welcome your reminder. At the same time, make sure your opposing counsel acknowledges the type of mediation agreed to so that he does not dispute it later in the mediation.

Finally, procedural tactics are those actions that the mediator takes to control and to facilitate the process. Tactics in this category include setting the time and location of the mediation, proposing extramediation activities, such as separate meetings of aligned parties or site visits, and threatening to withdraw. If you believe that the mediator is using procedural tactics unfairly to encourage a speedier settlement, you should request a caucus with the mediator so that you can discuss the matter directly. In a respectful way, you can share your concerns with the mediator and request that she be more flexible regarding the procedural matters. If the mediator is threatening to withdraw because of the conduct of the other side, you may be unable to prevent the withdrawal. However, if the threatened withdrawal is premised on your client's statements or stance, you should caucus with your client first, and then as appropriate, request a caucus with your client and the mediator.

5.4.2 How to use the mediator and the caucusing process for the best results

The caucus is an important instrument that the mediator uses to achieve settlements. The main virtue of the caucus is that it eliminates one of the principal barriers to dispute settlement—direct confrontation between the parties. By following the guidelines suggested below, you can, from behind the scenes, use the mediator's negotiating prowess and the nonconfrontational benefits of the caucusing process to orchestrate optimal settlement results for your client. But make sure that you alert your client to what you are doing so that he does not inadvertently spoil the symphony. Once when Leopold Stokowski was conducting the Philadelphia Orchestra in the Leonore Overture no. 3, a famous off-stage trumpet call twice failed to sound on cue. When the performance concluded, Stokowski rushed into the wings, ready to give the delinquent trumpet player a tongue-lashing. To his surprise, he found the tuxedoed musician struggling in the arms of a burly security officer. "I tell you, you can't blow that darn thing in here," the officer was saying, "there's a concert going on!"[5] The moral of this story is, first and foremost, let your client know what is going on at all times during the course of the mediation.

- **Take charge of the initial caucus.**

From the beginning of the very first caucus, let the mediator know that the mediator and you are on the same team. You both have the goal of settling the case. Be collaborative. The mediator is your teammate and messenger. Whether representing a plaintiff or defendant, you should begin by giving an honest summary of the strong points of your case and its weak points together with the strong and weak points of the other side's case. If you do this, the mediator will be impressed with your preparedness and reasonableness. If you do not do this, the mediator will ask questions that will elicit precisely the same information but over a longer period of time. By acknowledging your weaknesses and

5. Anecdote adapted from Humes, *Speaker's Treasury of Anecdotes about the Famous, supra at* 139.

the other side's strengths you deprive the mediator of an opportunity to use them to adjust your first offer or demand. Also, immediately after you give your summary of strengths and weaknesses, go right into making your first proposal for settling the case. You need not hem and haw about it. You have given the matter a lot of thought in your preparation.

- **Make a reasonable first offer or demand through the mediator.**

If the first settlement offer or demand is a dollar figure, explain to the mediator in detail how you arrived at the figure. The first offer or demand should be highly favorable to your client and reasonable in the sense that it should not offend or insult the other side. A $500 response to a $50,000 demand would most likely insult the ordinary plaintiff. It may even cause the mediation to terminate. If the mediator has any questions, answer them directly and succinctly.

- **Do not disclose your bottom line to the mediator up front.**

If you are an advocate for the plaintiff, do not tell the mediator in the initial caucuses the minimum amount you would accept to settle the case. First of all, the defendant, despite his prior statements to the contrary, may be willing to pay much more than you think to resolve the matter. If, as plaintiff's advocate, you tell the mediator up front your minimum acceptable figure, the mediator will not feel compelled to settle the case at a figure much more than that and will feel satisfied if the case settles at or near your figure. Second, you should not reveal your minimum acceptable figure up front because it may change during the mediation session. The defendant may reveal information that greatly increases the value of your case or that significantly undermines his position. Or, you may discover information which causes you to value your case at a lower level. If you committed to a minimum acceptable figure at the beginning of the mediation, you may feel psychologically inhibited from moving off it, thus sacrificing an opportunity to settle at a slightly lower amount. If you are an advocate for the defendant, do not disclose to the mediator the maximum amount you are willing to spend on the case and then expect the mediator to "play" within that constraint during a series of caucuses. First of all, by doing that you surrender to the mediator most, if not all, of your control over the ongoing negotiation and mediation processes. Second, it places the mediator in an awkward ethical position vis-à-vis the opposing side. As the process progresses, the mediator cannot be totally honest with the opposing side if asked by that side whether there is any flexibility in the offers. In effect, the opposing side will be negotiating directly with the mediator without even knowing it. A mediator in that position will have a great deal of difficulty remaining neutral. If the opposing side will accept in full settlement half of the maximum amount the mediator knows is available for settlement, does the mediator have a duty to disclose that more money is available? If asked? If not asked? Does the mediator in such a situation have a duty to withdraw? These are difficult ethical dilemmas. The better practice is not to put mediators in these ethical predicaments.

- **Listen carefully to the mediator and watch for clues about the other side's strategy or bottom line.**

When the mediator reports back with the other side's response to your proposal, the mediator will have gained much information about the other side's strategy, tactics, and maybe even its bottom line. The mediator will be primarily engaged in communicating the substance of the other side's response to you. However, the mediator's tone of voice, word selection, or body language may provide useful clues about what the other side is really thinking. As to word selection, the mediator may use the following phrases, which may in fact have the meanings shown:

Mediator Statement	Possible Meaning
"...*finally* they've made some movement."	"They should and could have made more movement."
"The defendant says he *personally* cannot pay a penny more."	"Defendant may get someone else to contribute to the settlement."
"The defendant says there's no way plaintiff can be reinstated to his job *at this time.*"	"Reinstatement may be possible later when the company reorganizes."
"Plaintiff wants as much as he can get, *no matter how long it takes.*"	"Plaintiff would accept payment of the settlement in installments."
"The plaintiff *cannot forgive* the defendant for humiliating her by those sexual remarks."	"Plaintiff needs an apology before she can settle the case."

Through body language the mediator might unconsciously provide clues to the other side's true interests or concerns. (See section 5.5.5.) Also, if you simply ask them, some mediators will freely share their perceptions of the emotional state of participants on the opposing side during caucuses.

- **Orchestrate your mediator-carried messages to effectuate your changing strategy and tactics.**

Before going into the caucusing phase of a mediation session, you should consider in advance and discuss with your client the possible caucusing scenarios and what your caucusing tactics might be for various scenarios. Assume that you represent a plaintiff in a personal injury case and that you have decided to adopt a competitive strategy in the mediation. Assume further that your premediation demand was $50,000 and the insurance company's offer was $5,000. In keeping with your competitive strategy, you have determined that you will make very minor monetary concessions in the first three caucuses. You have determined the reasonable settlement range to be somewhere between $20,000 and $25,000.

During the mediation, after the first caucus, assume that you authorize the mediator to communicate a reduction of your premediation demand by only $2,500 to $47,500 "because of the strength of your case on the liability issue." The insurance company, acknowlodging to tho modi ator in caucus that the plaintiff will probably be able to establish liability and that the insurance company's first offer was intentionally nominal, responds by doubling its first offer and authorizing the mediator to communicate a $10,000 offer.

Maintaining your competitive strategy, you move to $45,000 after the second caucus, and the insurance company responds competitively by increasing its offer only to $12,000. In the third caucus, you remain competitive, reducing your demand only to $40,000 and using the competitive tactic of threatening a walkout by having the mediator communicate to the insurance company counsel, "If the insurance company does not get more realistic in its offer, the plaintiff is going to walk out of the mediation."

The insurance company counsel responds by moving to $17,000 but tells the mediator to communicate to you, "She's nearing the limit of her authority." Hearing that, you interpret it to mean that the insurance company is approaching the lower end of the settlement range estimated by the insurance company. It appears that your estimated settlement range and the estimated settlement range of the insurance company overlap. You have two choices now: (1) continue your competitive strategy and reduce your demand by a small increment, or (2) become more cooperative by reducing your demand by a significant increment (using the accommodating tactic of creating movement), but still not within your estimated settlement range. If you follow strategy 1, the insurance company may terminate the mediation. If you follow strategy 2, you may get the insurance company to make an offer within your estimated reasonable settlement range.

You decide to go with the more cooperative strategy 2 and reduce your demand from $40,000 to $30,000 with instructions to the mediator to convey to the insurance company, "The plaintiff is approaching its movement limit." You also use the compromising tactic of reciprocity by asking the mediator to communicate, "The $10,000 reduction represents plaintiff's good-faith interest in settling the case, and plaintiff expects a reciprocal expression of good faith by the defendant." The insurance company counsel moves to $22,000 and conveys to the plaintiff through the mediator that counsel has reached the limit of its authority.

At this point, you decide to use the compromising tactic of splitting the difference and instruct the mediator to suggest that solution—$26,000—to the other side. The insurance company counsel asks for a recess, calls the supervising adjuster on the case, and tells the mediator to convey to the plaintiff its final offer—$23,500. After discussing the pros and cons with your client, you accept the insurance company's offer, which in fact falls within your estimated reasonable settlement range.

The important point to remember is that the mediator is your negotiation conduit. Convey through the mediator to the other side those statements that effectuate your chosen tactics and that you would ordinarily say to opposing counsel personally if negotiating face to face.

- **Refrain from using the mediator to communicate extramediation threats.**

Do not expect the mediator to be willing to communicate extramediation threats to the other side. Extramediation threats are those that relate to topics or people not directly related to the dispute or to the commonly understood consequences flowing from the nature of the dispute, its processing, and its resolution. Parties make such extramediation, irrelevant threats for the specific purpose of gaining an unfair advantage in the mediation. For example, to encourage a defendant to accept the plaintiff's settlement proposal, a mediator could not ethically communicate a threat by the plaintiff to expose defendant's alleged illicit conduct (marital cheating, alcoholism, tax evasion) to his wife, his employer, or the government, respectively. Communicating these types of threats would place the mediator squarely in the role of a blackmailer or an accessory to blackmail.

Mediators, of course, routinely communicate to one side or the other threats directly related to the dispute or the process. These types of threats merely reflect the existing power, authority, or opportunities available to one party vis-à-vis the other in the particular dispute and would ordinarily be legitimate tactics in conventional dispute negotiation. Sometimes the threats are present in the minds of the mediation participants but are not verbalized. Threats that are related to the dispute include the following: to contract with alternate suppliers (in a business dispute mediation); to strike (in a labor mediation); and to withdraw financing (in a construction case). Threats related to the process might include threats to conclude the session, to walk out of the mediation, and to proceed to trial.

- **Hold back some information favorable to you or unfavorable to the opposing side until the final caucuses.**

The timing of the release of information can be a very powerful settlement tool for you in mediation, just as one move in chess or the calculated playing of one bridge hand can change the whole complexion of victory and loss. It is not necessary to show the mediator every relevant document in the initial joint session. In many situations it is most effective to show some documents in the initial joint session and mention others. Then in the sequential caucuses have the mediator read the critical documents with you, answer the mediator's questions, and suggest that the mediator have the other side respond to or explain passages in the documents in a subsequent caucus. These critical documents contain either information favorable to you or unfavorable to your opponents. The other side, after being presented with the documents you have supplied to the mediator, may indeed respond with other documents that the mediator will bring back to you for explanation. Be prepared for that, and either show the mediator those documents up front or know in advance precisely what you are going to say in response to them. If the other side has no adequate response to your documents, you may have provided the mediator with exactly what he needs to elicit a major concession from the other side regarding settlement.

- **Take the time necessary to caucus with your client privately.**

In caucus when the mediator brings you the other side's response to your settlement proposal, and after you have assured yourself that you fully understand it, consider telling the mediator that you need a few minutes to caucus with your client. Caucusing with your client not only will assist you in determining your client's needs and interests *at that particular time* in the mediation, but also may assist you in better evaluating the proposal and in formulating a reasoned response to it.

- **When you state a proposal or make a movement off a demand or offer, provide the mediator with several supporting reasons why you did it and why the new proposal should be acceptable to the other side.**

When you provide the mediator with a settlement proposal in response to one from the other side, it is very important to state several supporting reasons why you are modifying your former proposal and why the newly formulated proposal should be satisfactory to the other side. This will assist the mediator in explaining to the other side that your new proposal is principled—that is, that your movement is rationally based and that you are not simply "caving in" to the other side's more meritorious demands.

- **Know what aspects of your case are confidential and advise the mediator at the end of each caucus concerning what information should not be disclosed to the other side.**

Normally, at the end of each caucus the mediator will ask you if any of the information discussed in the caucus is confidential. The mediator does this so that she knows what information you do not want communicated to the other side with your counterproposal for settlement. If the mediator fails to ask about confidential information, make sure that you remember to tell her the specific information you want to keep confidential. If, as the mediation proceeds, you believe that certain confidential information may give you increased leverage at a particular stage, you can authorize the mediator to disclose it to the other side at that time.

- **Do not tell the mediator that you want to make or accept a settlement proposal that you have no authority to make or accept.**

When you communicate a firm settlement proposal to the mediator with instructions to convey it to the other side, make sure that you have authority from the client to make the proposal. If the proposal is unauthorized, you may destroy the chance to settle the case, cause the other side to become antagonistic and adversarial, or worse yet, cause the other side to hold your client to the agreement or suffer adverse consequences. This situation sometimes arises when the advocate is present at the mediation with a corporate representative who believes that a proposal will be authorized by the company but later finds out that the company will not back it up. Likewise, when you agree to accept a proposal conveyed by the mediator to you from the other side, make sure that you have the authority to accept it. If you are not sure that you have the authority to make or accept a settlement proposal, simply tell the mediator to relate to the other side that your offer or acceptance of the proposal is contingent on your client's approval.

- **Refrain from talking about your fees or the mediator's fees as elements of the settlement.**

In the caucuses do not include the mediator in your discussions about how your fees and the mediation expenses need to be factored into the settlement equation. These may be appropriate topics for discussion between you and your client, but they are irrelevant to the mediator. Discussing the mediator's fees in his presence is embarrassing to the mediator and actually puts the mediator in the position of possibly having or appearing to have a monetary stake in the continuing caucusing with the other side. This may impact, either actually or impliedly, on the mediator's duties of neutrality and impartiality to the parties.

5.5 PERSUASION THROUGH EFFECTIVE COMMUNICATION

As an advocate in mediation, you will be more successful on behalf of your client if you can persuade your multiple audiences through effective communication techniques. In this section we will explore the four elements of effective communication and gain an understanding of how you and your client can combine these elements in mediation to persuasively communicate your own settlement proposals or to persuasively and constructively critique your opponent's settlement proposals.

In its most basic sense, communication consists of four component elements:

- Transmitting information verbally (speaking).
- Transmitting information nonverbally (use of body language).
- Receiving and interpreting verbal information (listening).
- Receiving and interpreting nonverbal information (processing sensed body language).

You (and your client) perform the first two tasks above as speaker; the second two tasks, as audience. During a mediation, if you consciously expend effort to accomplish each of these four tasks effectively, your chances of persuading your audiences (opposing counsel, opposing parties, and the mediator) to your point of view will be greatly enhanced. Thus to be a persuasive mediation advocate, you must concentrate on (1) speaking effectively, (2) using body language effectively, (3) listening effectively, and (4) processing sensed body language effectively. Each of these topics are discussed separately. But first it might be helpful to review a few of the classical principles of persuasion.

5.5.1   Persuasion in general

- **The five objectives of persuasive messages.**

Persuasion in its broadest sense may be described as the art of moving human beings to action.[6] Persuasion starts by creating a relationship between yourself and others. The primary purpose of creating such a relationship is not merely to connect people who were previously unconnected; rather, its primary purpose is to make them aware of the connections that they already have. An artful advocate accomplishes this task by mastering the five objectives of persuasive messages: (1) to command the attention of the receiver, (2) to be understood by the receiver as intended by the sender, (3) to warrant the receiver's belief that the information presented is credible or accurate, (4) to present information that conforms to the receiver's values of what is right and wrong, and (5) to motivate the receiver to act. Persuasive messages influence how receivers choose or decide which information to process. This implies the utility of strategy and theory and the importance of audience analysis. Thus, as an advocate in mediation you must analyze your audiences and apply those analyses when determining how best to achieve the five objectives of the persuasive message.

- **The three artistic means of persuasion.**

Aristotle's teachings about persuasion are as relevant today as they were when he first conceived them. As early as the fourth century B.C., Aristotle identified and labeled three "artistic means of persuasion": *ethos* (character of speaker), *pathos* (emotions aroused in audience), and *logos* (logic—true or probable argument). These three means of persuasion bear a striking resemblance to the three dimensions of attitude in modern-day psychology: behavioral (*ethos*), affective (*pathos*), and cognitive (*logos*).

Of major importance to you as a mediation advocate is the behavioral component of persuasion, *ethos*, which concerns the analysis of a speaker's character and credibility. *Ethos* encompasses the personal characteristics of the speaker and how perceptions of wisdom, decency, and personal goodness influence a listener's motivation to act or think in consonance with the speaker's urgings. According to Aristotle, the speaker's trustworthy character was the test of the *truth* of what was being said. *Ethos* was the "controlling factor" in persuasion. He identified two aspects of *ethos*: (1) personal qualities of the speaker by which the audience can judge the character of the speaker, and (2) the stereotypes by which the audience may judge the character of the speaker. Thus in a mediation you must be continually conscious of your own

---

6.   For a more complete explanation of persuasion in mediation, see John W. Cooley, "A Classical Approach to Mediation—Part I: Classical Rhetoric and the Art of Persuasion in Mediation," 19 *U. of Dayton L.Rev.* 83 (1993).

personal qualities that project trustworthiness and those qualities of stereotypes that detract from your trustworthiness, which you should therefore avoid, and those that enhance your trustworthiness, which you should therefore exhibit.

As a mediation advocate you also need to have an intimate understanding of the affective component of persuasion, *pathos*. Simply defined, pathos is the art of putting the audience in a desired frame of mind by appealing to their emotions, personal involvement, or needs reduction or satisfaction. At its foundation, *pathos* is an appeal to how the audience feels about concepts, values, conduct, and situations generally.

Finally, you need to know, understand, and apply *logos* in the mediation setting. *Logos*, the cognitive component of persuasion, refers to how the listener thinks, and is probably best described as an appeal to an audience's sense of reason through structured argument and evidentiary proof, which favors logical consistency. The interrelationship between Aristotle's three means of persuasion and the three psychological components of persuasion is demonstrated in the diagram appearing below.[7]

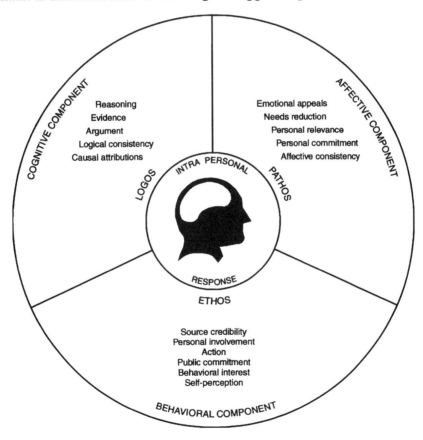

7.   This chart is from Raymond S. Ross, *Understanding Persuasion*, 3d ed. © 1990 by Allyn and Bacon. Reprinted by permission.

By knowing your audiences in mediation, you will be able to adjust the amount of each ingredient—*ethos, pathos, and logos*—in conveying a persuasive message to accomplish your goal in a particular interchange. If there is no opportunity to analyze your audience, or if you are unable to accurately classify it, you will probably want to use a balanced approach and incorporate all three means, realizing at all times that *ethos* will be the controlling factor in the persuasiveness of your message.

   • **Aristotle's Twenty-eight Strategies of Argument.**

   Aristotle described twenty-eight strategies of argument as presented in the chart immediately below:[8] The examples in this chart will help you understand the types of arguments that you can make in the opening joint session and in caucuses with the mediator.

STRATEGIES	DESCRIPTION AND EXAMPLES
1. ARGUING: From opposites;	1. Seeing whether the opposite predicate is true of the opposite subject; thus refuting the argument if it is not, confirming it if it is; Example: To be temperate is a good thing; for to lack self control is harmful. Argument confirmed.
2. From different grammatical forms of the same word;	2. The same predicate should be true or not true; Example: My friend argues that what is done justly would be a good; but to be put to death justly is not desirable (at least to the one executed); therefore, the just is not entirely good.
3. From correlatives;	3. If the person harmed deserved to suffer, then the agent of the suffering acted honorably and justly (so long as he/she was the appropriate person to have acted); Example: It was not unjust to kill someone who justly deserved to die (i.e., execution by state after a trial).

---

8.   This chart is developed from information contained in George A. Kennedy, *Aristotle on Rhetoric: A Theory of Civic Discourse* 190–203 (1991); see also John W. Cooley, "A Classical Approach to Mediation—Part I: Classical Rhetoric and the Art of Persuasion in Mediation," 19 *U. of Dayton L.Rev.* 83 (1993).

4. From more or less;	4. If the greater thing is true, the lesser is also true (and vice versa); or if something is not the fact in the case where it would be more expected, it clearly is not the case where it would be less expected; Example: If not even the judges know everything, attorneys can hardly do so.
5. From a view of time;	5. Arguing from what was true in the past to what is more true in the present; (a fortiori—from the stronger); Example: Yesterday, you agreed to consent to the entry of an injunction because, as you admitted, "my client's conduct is predatory"; today you refuse to consent to the injunction, even though your client, in the meantime, has expanded his unlawful conduct into other sales territories?
6. From turning what has been said against oneself upon the one who said it;	6. Discrediting the accuser; Example: Even the prosecutor has had speeding tickets.
7. From definition;	7. Making arguments from the essence of meanings of words; Example: What is divine? Is it not either a god or the work of a god? If it is the work of a god, does not a god exist?
8. From varied meanings of a word;	8. Example: The word "sharp" has several meanings: capable of cutting, intelligent, and a notation in music.
9. From division;	9. Limiting the available alternatives, and excluding most, if not all, of them; Example: All people do wrong for one of three reasons: either this, or this, or this; now two of these are impossible in this case, but even the plaintiff's counsel herself does not assert the third.

10. From induction;	10. To prove on the basis of many similar instances; Example: Three times in the past the respondent has been found guilty of sabotaging parts shipments delivered by strike-breakers, yet he asks management to believe that he was home watching television by himself when the latest sabotage occurred.
11. From a previous judgment about the same or a similar or opposite matter;	11. Argument based on precedent; Example: The agreement we reached previously in *Jones v. Acme* is ideally suitable to resolve the issues now before the mediator.
12. From the parts;	12. Arguing by shifting focus to a species within a defined genus; Example. Defense counsel has argued that plaintiff could not prove his case if this dispute went to trial, but which element of the plaintiff's prima facie case could not be proved?
13. On the basis of the consequences;	13. Exhorting or dissuading, accusing or defending, praising or blaming on the basis of the good or bad which will result from some conduct; Example: Ms. Mediator, if the employee is not suspended for a substantial period of time, other employees will be tempted to engage in the same kind of misconduct.
14. From equally undesirable alternatives; ·	14. Argument by posing a dilemma in which the same or opposite act performed in each of two (or more) situations presented yields an undesirable consequence; arguing a "Catch-22 situation"; Example: Since my client did not report the alleged child abuse to the authorities as required by law, she is subject to a fine and incarceration; but if she had reported the child abuse she would have suffered physical abuse personally from her spouse, and possibly death.

15. From exposition of opponent's true position or motivation;	15. <u>Example</u>: Plaintiff does not want her deposition postponed because of a previously scheduled appointment here at Bel-Nor Hospital for minor surgery. I have evidence that she made preparations to go on a 10 day trip to the Bahamas after she received the notice of deposition.
16. From consequences by analogy;	16. Argument by showing the irrationality of the reverse proposition; <u>Example</u>: If underage boys can be drafted into military service because they are tall, tall boys must be men; if so, short men must be boys.
17. From same results to same causes;	17. Arguing that "you can't have it both ways" or "either way"; <u>Example</u>: Mr. Mediator, the government contends that even though there was a technical defect in the way this law was enacted, it became effective before my client allegedly violated it. I respectfully suggest that this law could not have been defective and effective at the same time.
18. From contraries;	18. Arguing that it is not always appropriate to choose the same thing before and after an event, but rather the reverse; <u>Example</u>: Was it not shameful that this young mother, while staying with her parents, fought to come home to see her children, and having come home, was forced by her husband to go back to her parents in order not to fight?
19. From purpose to cause;	19. Arguing that the purpose for which something might exist or might happen is the cause for which it does exist or has happened; <u>Example</u>: Is it not possible that Mr. Ford promised his estranged grandson the property in Acapulco in life so that his will, which mentioned nothing of it, would communicate his real intentions in death?

20. From reasons why people act and why they avoid action;	20. Arguing as to what turns the mind in favor or against something; Example: Would not a man such as Mr. Smith, who had a serious gambling habit and who was about to experience a foreclosure of his home mortgage, be tempted, if not inclined to "borrow" money from his employer without his employer knowing it?
21. From things which have happened previously, though implausible;	21. Arguing that truth is often stranger than fiction; Example: Who, in 1985, would have predicted that the Berlin Wall would be rubble by 1992? Why then is it not possible for Ms. Murphy, against all odds, to have made $3,000,000 investing in the stock market on one day without access to any inside information?
22. From the refutative;	22. Argument by looking at contradictions in three separate ways: (1) as applying to the opponent; (2) as applying to the speaker; and (3) as applying to the speaker and the opponent; Example 1: He says he loves his company; yet he gives his company's secrets to his company's enemies. Example 2: She says that I am litigious, yet she cannot state the name of a single case which I allegedly have filed. Example 3: Her employer has never lent her any money, but I have rescued her from foreclosure.
23. From the possibility of false impression;	23. Arguing by analogy from the possibility of false impression; Example: For centuries, many people believed the world to be flat. When the facts became known, the people discovered that they were initially wrong. So, too, of my Mr. Walton's alleged misconduct.

24. From cause and effect;	24. Arguing that if the cause exists, the effect does; if it does not, there is no effect; Example: It is clear that the Ms. Carlton's preoccupation with tuning her car radio resulted in her driving through the red light and crashing into Mr. Fenster's car, broadside.
25. From the possibility of an untried, better plan;	25. Arguing that there is possibly a better way of doing something than the present way; Example: Perhaps this case is more suitable for mediation than for court litigation.
26. From a comparison to things done in the past;	26. Argument by focusing on the comparison between what is being proposed to be done, and what has been done in the past; Example: You have given us 10 days in the past to submit a settlement proposal, rather than the 5 days which you have just proposed.
27. On the basis of mistake;	27. Accusing or defending on the basis that mistakes have been made; Example: Because all the other identically phrased clauses in the contract were scratched through with initials of the contracting parties, it must have been a mistake that this single identical clause remained.
28. From the meaning of a proper name;	28. Argument by association with a proper name of a person, place, or thing, known generally to the audience; Example: Management's decision on this matter has created a Loch Ness in the workplace.

- **Aristotle's Nine Fallacious Arguments.**

Aristotle identified nine fallacious arguments. As an advocate in mediation, you should be aware of them in order to avoid using them and to be able to detect when a speaker is employing them. Some of the examples appearing in the chart below are those of Aristotle, some are those of this author, and some are combinations of both.[9]

FALLACIES	DESCRIPTIONS AND EXAMPLES
1. FALLACY RESULTING: From the shape of the expression;	1. Using words that sound the same but have different meanings; Example: Plaintiff's counsel: "After the injury to my client, the barber admitted his 'sheer' misfunction." Opposing counsel: "That's not true. What my client said was 'my shears malfunctioned.'"
2. From combining what is divided and dividing what is combined;	2. Connecting facts or arguments, and then drawing an inference without basis in fact; dividing facts or arguments to make things seem what they are not; Example: Defendant was not at work and not at home, so he must have sabotaged his employer's power station.
3. From exaggeration;	3. The absence of argument or enthymeme; opponent attempts to persuade by bombast; amplification of alleged action without proof; Example: What defendant did here has sent a clear signal to every last teenager in the country that they can engage in computer piracy and become rich doing it.
4. From an unnecessary sign;	4. A nonsyllogistic statement; Example: Every wicked man is a thief.

---

9.   This chart is developed from information contained in Kennedy, id. at 204–210; see also Cooley, id at 19 *U. of Dayton L.Rev.* 83, 115–16 (1993).

5. From an accidental result;	5. Drawing a conclusion based on seeming circumstances and not on the facts or reason; Example: The Chief Executive Officer was angry because he felt the Union leaders intentionally dishonored him by not inviting him to the retirement luncheon, when, in fact, his name was overlooked completely by mistake.
6. From a fallacious assumption;	6. Example: Because the beggars sing and dance in the subway station, they are happy.
7. From treating a non-cause as a cause;	7. Treating what happens later as though it happened because of what preceded; Example: Three hours after the train blew its whistle, the shop owner found his front window cracked from top to bottom. There is no question that the railroad is responsible for the damage.
8. By omission of consideration of when and how;	8. Example: A person may always kill another in self-defense. [In the pertinent jurisdiction, the proposition is valid only if the person does not use excessive force and does not initially provoke hostility].
9. By confusing what is general and what is not general with the particular;	9. Arguing that the improbable will be probable because some things happen contrary to probability; arguing a qualified (rather than a general) probability without clearly saying so; Example: If a strong man is charged with assault, he should be acquitted because it is not likely that he would start the fight for the very reason that it would seem probable that he would be accused of starting it.

5.5.2 Persuasion through effective speaking

When speaking in the mediation session you and your client should keep in mind some practical delivery or "packaging" techniques to enhance the persuasiveness of your message.

- **Voice.** Vocal tone, pitch, volume, and speed help create an environment in which your opponent may feel more comfortable and thus may be more open to your message. The potential for miscommunication increases when, for instance, a person who speaks loudly attempts to communicate a certain idea to a recipient who prefers a more subtle approach. Your desire to create an atmosphere in which your opponent feels more comfortable will naturally enhance your credibility and effectiveness.

• **Concrete language.** State your message in simple, concrete language to which the recipient can easily and comfortably relate. If you use abstract language, you will force the mediator or your opponent to translate that abstraction into her own vision of concreteness, which may vary from your intended meaning. Avoid legalese at all costs.

• **Knowledge.** To be persuasive, your message must demonstrate your accurate knowledge of the subject matter. Furthermore, your message must reflect common sense and diplomacy. In the mediation setting, you must particularly gauge your speech to reflect your knowledge of your opponent's needs and interests and his priorities among them. Not knowing your opponent's priorities can impact negatively on your effectiveness in communicating unpleasantness or "bad news" to your opponent—for example, that your client will not meet your opponent's settlement demand. The importance of knowing the recipient's priorities when you are delivering bad news is probably no better illustrated than by the story of the tourist who was driving through eastern Kentucky. The tourist, passing the cabin of a mountaineer, had the misfortune of running over and killing a hound that happened to be the mountaineer's favorite hunting dog. The tourist went into the cabin and told the mountaineer's wife what had happened and how sorry he was. The mountaineer was out in the fields, and the tourist decided he had better go tell him of the accident, too. "Better break it to him easy like," advised the wife. "First tell him it was one of the kids."[10]

• **Enthusiasm.** If you are reasonably enthusiastic about your perception of the problem and your proposals for settlement, you will convey your self-confidence and inspire the other side to become engaged in the problem-solving process. But be aware that excessive enthusiasm and exuberance can draw hecklers and naysayers. You have to be prepared to deal with these types. Here are a couple examples of how noted historical figures dealt with them. Once when the famous American clergyman, Henry Ward Beecher, was enthusiastically delivering a Sunday sermon, a drunken spectator interrupted him by crowing like a rooster. Beecher was imperturbable. Looking at his watch and without skipping a beat in his delivery, he said, "What! Morning already? I would never have believed it, but the instincts of the lower

---

10. Anecdote adapted from Humes, supra at 171.

animals are infallible."[11] The second example involves Senator McGovern, who was reprimanded by his wife for using bad language to a young heckler during a fiery and enthusiastic speech in the 1972 political campaign. In defending against his wife's criticism he explained that "it was only an eloquent admonition delivered in great passion to the young man, who was invited to approach a strategic part of my anatomy with some tenderness."[12] Perhaps Senator McGovern's revisionist description would have been a better response to the heckler. In any event, you should realize that over-enthusiasm can trigger resentment in others, and you should be prepared to respond to negative feedback.

- **Emphasis.** Although you hope that your opponent will be intensely listening to your entire message, it is more realistic to realize that he will remember the beginning and end of your argument better than the middle. Thus it may be useful to begin and end with the most strength. But be mindful that emphasis through repetition can be self-defeating. In his early years in politics, President Coolidge had been a Massachusetts legislator. In one legislative session, a legislator noted for his long-winded speeches gave a lengthy and tiresome address in emphatic support of some measure. The speech included a long series of repetitive affirmations, all beginning with the words "Mr. Speaker, it is. . . . " When the legislator eventually concluded, Coolidge rose and simply said, "Mr. Speaker, it is not!" and sat down. Everyone laughed, and the measure was defeated.[13] Coolidge won because he used the persuasion technique of emphasis incisively and brilliantly, while his competitor did not.

- **Alignment.** Researchers have found that (1) a person is more apt to accept a message from an unknown source if the message begins with a position that is similar to her own, (2) a communicator's effectiveness will increase if he initially expresses some views that are also held by his audience, and (3) people are more persuaded by a communicator they perceive to be similar to themselves.[14] Thus it may be beneficial for you to begin your opening statement by agreeing with some aspect of your opponent's view or case. However, you must be careful how you do it. If you appear to be merely patronizing, you may only succeed in antagonizing your opponent.

---

11. Anecdote adapted from Fuller, supra at 135.
12. Anecdote adapted from Humes, supra at 97.
13. Anecdote adapted from Paul F. Boller, Jr., *Presidential Anecdotes* (Oxford University Press, 1981), 238.
14. See generally Marvin Karlins and Herbert I. Abelson, *Persuasion: How Opinions and Attitudes Are Changed*, 2d ed. (Springer Publishing Co., Inc., 1970), 120, 128.

- **Optimism.** If you speak with optimism, your message will be naturally appealing to your listener. Mediators use this technique when advising the parties of revised settlement proposals in sequential caucusing. You can also use this technique in your joint session discussions. Optimism has the tendency to move parties toward a mutually acceptable solution, or if they cannot find a totally acceptable solution, to see the good aspects of a lesser solution and find satisfaction in that. A good example of the power of optimism occurred some years ago when an American engineering company and a Chinese engineering company were working toward each other in a tunnel-making project in China. When the headings were finally broken through, a slight error in the alignment was apparent. On being advised of this, the American chief engineer and the Chinese chief engineer met to determine how the problem could be solved. The American chief engineer remarked that in America such an error would have caused a congressional inquiry. The Chinese engineer replied that in China there would be nothing but pleasure at the tunnels meeting at all. Startled by his remark, the American engineer asked incredulously, "Did the Chinese, when working toward each other, ever bypass each other?" "Oh, sure—but when that happens it's even better. When the project is completed we have *two* tunnels!"[15] The following page contains suggested "can do" responses to "can't do" statements typically made by opposing parties, their counsel, or even your client prior to, during, or after a mediation session.

---

15. Anecdote adapted from Braude, *Lifetime Speaker's Encyclopedia*, supra at 218–19.

Can't do.	Can do!
We've never done it before	We have the opportunity to be first.
It's too complicated.	Let's look at it from another angle.
It will never work.	Let's give it a try.
There's not enough time.	We'll reevaluate some priorities.
We already tried it.	We learned from the experience.
It's a waste of time.	Think of the possibilities.
We don't have the expertise.	Let's network with those who do.
We can't compete.	We'll get the jump on the competition.
The old way is good enough.	There is always room for improvement.
We're understaffed.	We're a lean, mean machine!
We don't have enough room.	Temporary space may be an option.
We don't have the equipment.	Maybe we can sub it out.
No one communicates.	Let's open the channels.
I don't have any ideas.	I'll come up with some alternatives.
Let somebody else deal with it.	I'm ready to learn something new.
It's too radical a change.	We'll never know until we try.
It takes too long for approval.	We'll walk it through the system.
It doesn't fit us.	We should look at it.
It's not my job.	I'll be glad to take the responsibility
No can do.	Can do!

• **Speak to engage the recipient's listening style.** Research has identified at least six different styles of listening:[16] leisure, inclusive, stylistic, technical, empathetic, and nonconforming. One or more of these styles may predominate in a person's listening behavior. If you can identify a person's listening style and construct your verbal message so that it is compatible with that style, you will heighten the probability that your listener will completely understand both the thrust and the subtleties of what you are attempting to convey. Below are abbreviated descriptions of each listening style.

Leisure listener:	Attends to pleasant stimuli and tunes out spoken communication that demands intensity of effort or undue discomfort.
Inclusive listener:	Has a wide "listening band" and listens most intensely at the beginning of an interaction, searching for a key idea, after which she can relax.
Stylistic listener:	Is interested in the speaker's background or credentials as a basis for evaluating the worth of what the speaker says, and lacks confidence in or rejects the message of a speaker who does not conform to the listener's preferred speaker style.
Technical listener:	Listens more frequently in fields that draw from the physical sciences, where specialized knowledge has been systematized, researched, and expanded into processes and procedures.
Empathetic listener:	Has an acute ear for the emotional states of others and is so busy processing the multitude of nonverbal messages that the actual meaning of the spoken words may become garbled or lost.
Nonconforming listener:	Evaluates whether the speaker's facts justify the speaker's position and how strong that position is compared to his own.

---

16. See generally Cooley, *Appellate Advocacy Manual*, supra, chap. 11, pp. 33–37 and sources cited there.

- **Power of example.** One of the most powerful persuasion techniques is for the speaker to present examples from the past to show how injustices of the past are the same as current ones or how the remedies in those situations could be applied to rectify the current situation. The persuasive power of example is greatly magnified when the speaker is able to have the listener mentally and physically experience the former injustice or the former remedy through a simple exercise. In the early nineteenth century, when General Benjamin Lincoln went to make peace with the Creek Indians, one of the chiefs asked him to sit down on a log. He was then asked to move and in a few minutes to move still farther. The request was repeated until the general got to the end of the log. The Indian said, "Move farther," to which the general replied, "I can move no farther." "Just so it is with us," said the chief. "You moved us back to the waters, and then ask us to move farther."[17]

- **Power of apology.** Do not underestimate the power of an apology, made either in the beginning of the mediation session, or at some other point in the process, as appropriate. A story from the life of George Washington best makes the point. In 1754, when Washington was a colonel stationed with his men in Alexandria, there was an election held for the Virginia Assembly. A man named William Payne opposed the candidate supported by Washington. Washington got into a heated argument with Payne about the election and said something extremely offensive to him. In a fury, Payne knocked Washington to the ground. But when Washington's men came running to avenge their commander, Washington intervened and persuaded them to return peacefully to the barracks. Early the next morning, Washington sent Payne a note requesting his presence at a local tavern. Payne went to the tavern expecting a duel. To his surprise, he saw wine and glasses instead of pistols. When Payne arrived, Washington rose to greet him and, smiling, he offered Payne his hand. "Mr. Payne," he said, "to err is nature; to rectify error is glory. I believe I was wrong yesterday; you have already had some satisfaction, and if you deem that sufficient, here is my hand—let us be friends." From then on, Payne was an enthusiastic admirer of Washington.[18]

    In a mediation, an apology need not include an admission of responsibility for injuries suffered. A defendant, for example, can acknowledge that the plaintiff suffered injuries, can sympathize with the loss or injuries suffered, and can acknowledge the basis for the plaintiff's negative feelings toward the plaintiff. In many

---

17. Anecdote adapted from Humes, *Speaker's Treasury of Anecdotes about the Famous,* supra at, 63
18. Anecdote adapted from Boller, supra at 8.

cases, even complex commercial disputes, a verbal and/or a written apology can carry great value in settlement if properly planned and effectuated by defense counsel.

- **Power of humor.** Advocates can employ humor to accomplish many objectives in mediation. Research has shown that the use of appropriate humor tends to increase the likability (ethos) of the communicator. It can be used prior to and at the mediation session to build rapport and more open and trusting relationships with the opposing counsel. Advocates can use humor to obtain concessions. Research has shown that persons who receive settlement offers accompanied by humor are more likely to acquiesce in those offers than persons who receive offers unaccompanied by humor. Humor can also be used by an advocate to soften the blow when rejecting an undesirable settlement offer made by opposing counsel. For example, when Abe Lincoln was President, friends were always offering him endless, and to him useless, suggestions on how to run the White House. To some of them, he would tell the story of a man trying to get on a horse. As the man climbed aboard, the animal picked up one of its rear feet friskily and got it caught in a stirrup. Said the man to the horse, "All right, if you want to get on, I'll get off!"[19] That usually worked. The suggestions stopped, and Lincoln still had a friend.

5.5.3   Persuasion through effective use of body language

Ben Franklin was a great believer in the utility of body language as a persuasive device. He once remarked:

> The way to convince another is to state your case moderately and accurately. Then scratch your head, or shake it a little and say that is the way it seems to you, but that of course you may be mistaken about it. This causes your listener to receive what you have to say, and as like[ly] as not turn about and try to convince you of it, since you are in doubt. But if you go at him in a tone of positiveness and arrogance, you only make an opponent of him.[20]

Modern behavioral research confirms Ben Franklin's intuition that nonverbal behavior is a major factor in effective communication and persuasion. Communication studies have revealed that humans take meaning from the messages they perceive in the following manner: 7

---

19. Anecdote adapted from Vic Fredericks, *The Wit and Wisdom of the Presidents* (Frederick Fell, Inc. 1966), 36.
20. Braude, *Braude's Second Encyclopedia of Stories, quotations, and Anecdotes*, supra at 35.

percent from the actual words, that is, the dictionary meaning of the vocabulary; 38 percent from the voice and vocal qualities, including rate, pitch, tone, volume, and intensity; and 55 percent from nonverbal cues, including posture, stride, gestures, eye contact, facial expressions, mannerisms, and movement.[21] Because more than half of the effectiveness of your message is likely to be dependent on nonverbal cues, you need to pay very close attention to them. They can either enhance, distort, or destroy the content of your intended message.

- **Dress and demeanor.** It is unfortunate but true that people's credibility is often judged solely on the basis of their dress and demeanor. For this reason it is important for both you and your client to dress in a manner compatible with the nature and location of the mediation. As to your demeanor, it is important to be controlled and professional at all times toward all involved in the mediation process. Although it may be true that in court an aggressive manner or demeanor may win points with some juries, in the mediation process such tactics will most likely be ineffectual.

- **Eye contact.** Eye contact is an essential aspect of nonverbal persuasion. Through eye contact you establish that your communication channel is open and that you want feedback from another person concerning her reaction. If you are looking at your opponent while she is speaking, your gaze will likely be interpreted as a sign of attention to what your opponent is saying. Furthermore, your opponent may form opinions, valid or not, regarding your personality as a result of the number of times you look at her or do not look at her.

- **Facial expressions.** Your face has the potential for communicating vast amounts of nonverbal information, and it is important for you to be mindful of this fact during mediations because it has been shown that when communicating verbally people tend to pay more attention to the face than any other communication channel.[22] Your face has the capability of displaying your emotional states, reflecting interpersonal attitudes, and providing nonverbal feedback to other people's comments.

- **Other body language to enhance the persuasiveness of your verbal message.** Following are examples of body language that are in harmony with the indicated verbal statements and the attitude of the speaker and therefore would positively reinforce the speaker's message.

---

21. Margaret McAuliffe Bedrosian, *Speak Like a Pro in Business and Public Speaking* (John Wiley & Sons, Inc., 1987), 52.
22. Mark L. Knapp and Judith A. Hall, *Nonverbal Communication in Human Interaction*, 3d ed. (Harcourt Brace Jovanovich College Publishers, 1992), 262. See also Guernsey, supra at chap. 6, sec. I.

Appropriate Body Language for a Speaker's Statement and Attitude

STATEMENT	ATTITUDE	BODY LANGUAGE
"I do not appreciate the unkind remarks you have made about my client, but we are committed to staying here today until this dispute is resolved."	Self-controlled	Hands on table, interlaced fingers
"We are offering $50,000; take it or leave it."	Confident	Steepling of hands
"Fifty thousand is close, but it will take fifty-six for us to sign on the dotted line."	Interested	Leaning forward
"Okay, we will pay you fifty-six if you will accept payment in four equal installments over a one-year period."	Open, Acceptant	Open arms and hands
"We'd have to think long and hard about a payment period of that duration."	Evaluating	Index finger to cheek; taking glasses off and cleaning them
"We don't have all day."	Ready	Sitting on edge of chair
"Well, maybe we should adjourn until tomorrow."	Defensive	Crossed arms on chest

5.5.4   Persuasion through effective listening

Albert Einstein knew well the importance of effective listening in communication. He once shared what he considered the best formula for success in life. If "a" is success in life, he posited, then the formula is $a = x + y + z$; "x" being work and "y" being play. When asked what "z" was, Einstein mischievously remarked, "That, my dear sir, is keeping your mouth shut."[23] In mediation it is important at times not only to keep your mouth shut, but also important to know what your mind should be doing when your mouth *is* shut.

Hearing and listening are two different processes. The former is the ability to record transmitted sound vibrations; the latter involves making sense of what you hear. Listening with your mind fully engaged and your complete attention directed to the speaker can be more powerful than the spoken word. By listening to the mediator or your opponent, several goals can be accomplished. First, listening makes the other person believe that his point of view has enough validity to be considered. Second, this respect for the opponent's disclosures helps create an atmosphere that is conducive to open and collaborative discussions. Third, patient listening often induces less skilled adversaries to disclose more information than intended because of a seemingly supportive environment.

As an advocate in mediation, you need to have some idea of your predominant style of listening as described in subsection 5.5.2, and you need to understand that you may have to modify that listening style to be effective in each separate mediation experience. In the mediation environment you will normally engage in two types of listening: critical and active. Critical listening occurs when you are listening to evaluate, not for pleasure. This type of listening takes effort, time, and planning. It is necessary to recognize and weigh the facts as presented by your opponent and to determine the validity of your opponent's conclusions.

You can improve your ability to listen critically in several ways. First, you must mentally and physically prepare yourself to listen. Physical preparation may include sitting upright and focusing your eyes on your opponent. This type of preparation, while helping your own listening ability, also presents the image to your opponent that you are really listening. It is also important for you to let go of the hundreds of other thoughts running through your mind and concentrate solely on what your opponent is saying. This type of preparation is difficult work and may take some practice. Therefore it may be beneficial to practice with your family or office colleagues. Second, it is important to refrain from making emotional responses to your opponent's behavior or words. These types of reactions detract from your attentiveness and may hurt your client and your case later.

To engage in active listening you must continuously try to determine the true meaning of the speaker's message. This involves an effort to understand and attribute meaning to the content of both the speaker's substantive concern and her emotional state. Active listening requires two steps: (1) hearing and giving meaning to the content of the

---

23. Anecdote adapted from Morris Mandel, *Story Anthology for Public Speakers* (Jonathan David, Publishers, 1966), 257.

speaker's statements, and (2) communicating the interpreted meaning back to the speaker. The reflection back is more a mirroring of what you heard rather than a parroting of what the speaker said.[24]

5.5.5 Persuasion through effective processing of sensed body language

As implausible as it may seem, your ability to be persuasive in a particular mediation setting may be significantly enhanced by your skill in accurately sensing your opponent's body language. The more you are able to correctly sense and interpret that body language, the better you will be able to understand what your opponent is really feeling or thinking and to respond appropriately.

INTERPRETING BODY LANGUAGE

ATTITUDE	BODY LANGUAGE
Suspicious	Not looking at you; sideways glance
Nonreassuring	Chewing on pen; rubbing thumb on thumb Biting fingernails
Bored	Doodling; drumming; blank stare
Expectant	Rubbing palms
Doubtful	Straight finger touching nose; hands over mouth
Deferent	Stepping aside; backing away
Nervous	Clearing throat; hands covering mouth while speaking; tugging at ear; wringing of hands
Frustrated	Tightly clenched hands; rubbing back of neck

---

24. See generally Paul Michael Lisnek, *Lawyer's Handbook for Interviewing and Counseling*, CLE ed. (West Publishing Company, 1991), 3–17.

5.5.6 Persuasion through application of social psychology—the power of social influence

The scientific study of the process of social influence has been underway by social scientists for well over half a century.[25] Numerous social psychologists, in particular, have investigated ways in which an individual can influence another person's attitudes and actions to accept the individual's proposals. This investigation has yielded six tendencies of human beings that cause them to respond positively to proposals made to them by other human beings. These six behavioral tendencies are reciprocation, commitment/consistency, social validation, liking, authority, and scarcity. Knowledge of these six sources of influence and persuasion can truly be thought of as empowerment in your representation of clients in negotiation and mediation. Knowledge of these six behavioral tendencies of people can affect the way we can persuasively present acceptable proposals in negotiation and mediation and can suggest pitfalls to be avoided when considering proposals advanced in these processes by other parties. These six behavioral tendencies are discussed separately below.

- **Reciprocation.** One essential rule of human conduct is the code of reciprocity. Under the norm of this code, individuals feel obligated to repay value for what they perceive as value received from another. The reach and power of the unsolicited gift should not be underestimated. Charitable organizations have found that contributions they receive double when they include a set of free personalized address labels in their mailings. Similarly, other industries profit from the unsolicited gift rule. Food and liquor stores offer free samples, exterminators offer free home inspections, health clubs offer free workouts. They profit when customers purchase their product or service for the first time or more of their products and services over time. The reciprocity rule applies to more than merely gifts or favors. It also applies to concessions people make to one another in their everyday interactions and in negotiations. Behavioral research has shown that if people are first confronted with an extremely distasteful proposal, they will reject it; but if immediately after rejection, they are confronted with a discernibly less distasteful proposal as concession by the offeror, they will normally accept the less distasteful proposal. One lesson we can gain from this explanation is that when representing clients in negotiation and mediation, we may be able to obtain the opposing party's acceptance of our reasonable proposal if we advance an unreasonable one first and, if rejected,

25. The information in this Subsection is adapted from Robert B. Cialdini, *Influence: The Psychology of Persuasion* (William Morrow, NY, 1993) and Robert B. Cialdini, "Persuasion," 284 *Scientific American* 76 (Feb. 2001).

immediately advance the more palatable, reasonable one—the one that will satisfy our client's interests. Another lesson to be learned here is to be wary of this technique when we see it being used by others in negotiation and mediation. It is important not to let yourself be lured into accepting a proposal on behalf of your client that less than satisfies his or her needs and interests.

- **Commitment/consistency.** Two more related potent human motivations are commitment and consistency. Because people believe that it is typically in their best interests to be consistent, they fall into the habit of being automatically consistent all of the time—even when it is unreasonable to be consistent. For example, in one psychological study, bettors in a racetrack experiment were much more confident about their choice of a horse in a race thirty seconds after they bet their money than they were thirty seconds before they placed their bet. Before they put down their money they were tentative and uncertain; afterwards they were significantly more optimistic and self-assured. The act of making a final decision—here choosing a horse and placing the bet—was a critical factor in their change in attitude. Once they took a stand, their need for consistency pressured them to bring what they felt and believed into line with what they had previously done. They simply convinced themselves to continue to believe that they had made the right choice because their continuing belief was consistent with their decision to act. Mechanical consistency functions as a shield against effective thinking and it can be exploited by those who would prefer that people not think too much in response to their requests for compliance. Social psychologists believe that it is a person's feeling of commitment that forces the person to be consistent. Also, research has shown that when people must display their initial decisions publicly (to others of a group), they are very reluctant to change those decisions later. This is especially so when their decisions were initially displayed in writing. Thus in one jury study, hung juries were significantly more frequent in close cases where jurors had to express their opinions with a visible show of hands rather than by secret ballots. Once they indicated their opinions to the other jurors publicly, they were committed to those opinions and not inclined to change them. In another study, persons engaged in door-to-door charitable fund raising reported that contributions nearly doubled when the charitable solicitors got residents to sign a petition generally supporting the handicapped two weeks before asking residents for contributions for the handicapped, thus making a public commitment to that same cause. A lesson to be taken from this explanation in relation to negotiation and mediation is not to show your bottom line to the mediator or the other parties too soon in the process. You will feel committed to it even though new evidence emerges in the process which should reasonably alter your thinking. Another lesson to be learned here is to avoid urging the opposing party to take a firm position on a particular settlement result too early in the process because it may be impossible to sway the opposing party's commitment to that amount, formula, or format later. That party may see a need to remain consistent with that position, as irrational and self-defeating as it may be for him or her to do so.

- **Social validation.** If many individuals have decided in favor of a particular idea, other individuals are more likely to follow because they perceive the idea to be more correct or more valid. An interesting behavioral study conducted in New York City showed that when one individual stopped on a busy sidewalk and looked skyward for sixty seconds, 4 percent of passersby joined him looking upward. When five individuals did likewise, 18 percent of passersby followed suit; and when 15 individuals looked at nothing in the sky, 40 percent of passersby joined them. Marketers rely on social validation when they emphasize, through televised throngs of purchasers at department stores, that their product is the largest-selling of its kind. Fund raisers often successfully rely on this human behavioral trait when they show potential contributors a list of their own neighbors who have donated to their cause. In general, the longer the list of neighbors, the greater the persuasive effect. This human tendency toward social validation— a type of peer pressure—can be a powerful tool to influence people's behavioral conduct. Peer pressure can lead to beneficial or harmful results, depending on the goals toward which the pressure is directed. Some peer pressure, for example, can influence people to achieve academically while other types of peer pressure can influence harmful results such as the use of alcohol or illegal drugs. But the important point for you to remember is that one way to get people to comply with your requests or to accept your proposals is to demonstrate or imply that a significant number of other people have complied with your similar requests or accepted your similar proposals in the past. The other lesson to be learned here is to be careful not to be overly influenced by a showing that other people have complied with or have accepted that which is being proposed by an opposing party.

- **Liking.** People prefer to say "yes" to those whom they like, for whom they have an affinity or affection, or with whom they have a rapport. A Tupperware party begins somewhere in the world in some person's home every 2.7 seconds. The reason for this is that

Tupperware has capitalized on the "liking" tendency of people. The Tupperware Company is living proof of the simple fact that people generally prefer to buy products from a liked friend—the host of a Tupperware party—rather than from some unknown salesperson. Studies have shown that physical attractiveness; similarity; personal, historical, or geographical connections; compliments; and cooperation can influence people to comply with a person's request or to accept a person's proposal. Even when cooperation is feigned, it can be a powerful component in closing a deal. Salespersons, for example, sometimes attempt to be perceived by their sales prospects as cooperating partners. Indeed, automobile salespersons are notorious for "doing battle" with their "villainous" sales manager on behalf of their prospective car buyers. The lessons to be drawn from this research for advocates in negotiation and mediation are (1) to use the "liking" principles (similarity, connections, compliments, cooperation, etc.) when appropriate in order to assist opposing parties to "get to yes"; and (2) to be vigilant to avoid "getting to yes" prematurely as a victim of the "liking" principles, without achieving sufficient benefit to your client in the process.

- **Authority.** Human beings are moved by the power of authority. "Four out of five doctors recommend" is a common advertisement that is used successfully by pharmaceutical companies and health product suppliers to persuade people to buy their products. Those touting their experience, expertise, or scientific credentials marshal substantial power in influencing other people to comply with their requests or to accept their proposals. People in uniform—such as security guards and mail carriers—serve as authority figures for some people, causing them to change their behavior. Remarkably, research has shown that what people wear can have a significant effect in controlling the behavior of other people. In one study, it was discovered that a man could increase by 350 percent the number of pedestrians who would follow him across the street against the light by changing one simple thing about himself. In the first part of the study he wore casual dress; in the second part, he donned indices of authority: a suit and tie. What can we learn from this behavioral research that is applicable to representing clients in negotiation and mediation? First, we should understand that our experience, expertise, and credentials can, if properly communicated during the course of settlement discussions, have an important influence on the other side. This communication must be subtle, however, and not done in a braggadocios way. Also, in a mediation, the mediator's experience and expertise can be used to authoritative advantage, particularly if your settlement proposal is communicated to the other side accompanied by the recommendation and good will of the mediator. Second, we should be alert to avoid being urged by a domineering lawyer, mediator, or judge into agreeing to a settlement proposal that is not in the best interest of our client, merely because we perceive that this person has more experience or expertise in the matter and therefore speaks with authority. Oftentimes, people who claim experience and expertise have no more understanding of or insight into a matter than we do.

- **Scarcity.** A great deal of research evidence shows that as items and opportunities become less available to us, they become more desirable. Advertisers rely on this principle when they engage in "one of a kind" or "limited time only" promotions. Scarcity affects the value of information as well as commodities. In one research study examining the effects of scarcity and exclusivity on behavioral compliance, an owner of a company that imports beef into the U.S. and sells it to supermarkets had his salespeople call different randomly selected groups of customers and gave them differing instructions as to what to say to the customers. As to the first random sample, the salespeople made a standard request of them to purchase imported beef. As to a second random sample, the salespeople added to the standard request that a shortage of Australian beef was anticipated. The added information of scarcity of the beef caused purchases by the supermarkets to more than double. As to a third random sample, the salespeople not only told the supermarkets about the impending shortage of Australian beef, but also that the information came from his company's *exclusive* sources in the Australian National Weather Service. These supermarkets increased their beef orders by 600 percent. They were influenced to comply with the importer's purchase request not only because they perceived the beef to be scarce—and therefore valuable—but also because they perceived the information that the beef was scarce was itself scarce and exclusive, and therefore more valuable and reliable. Advocates in negotiation and mediation are often confronted with situations of alleged scarcity, not only with respect to items or opportunities at issue in the dispute or transaction, but also with respect to information relating to those items and opportunities. Advocates who wish to increase value of an item, an opportunity, or content or source of information under discussion can successfully do so by emphasizing its scarcity or exclusive nature. Conversely, advocates who wish to devalue these things can emphasize the existence of identical, similar, equivalent, or fungible substitutes.

From an evolutionary point of view, each of these six behavioral tendencies described above would naturally be expected to be markers of conduct by human beings who must find the best ways to survive while living in social groups. In many situations, it is wise counsel for human beings to repay favors, behave consistently, follow the lead of others, favor the requests of those we like, heed legitimate authorities, and value scarce resources. The effective advocate in negotiation and mediation recognizes these facts, but at the same time maintains vigilance to avoid being manipulated unknowingly in any dispute or transaction by people who might unfairly capitalize on these behavior-influencing tendencies.

5.6 APPLYING CREATIVE PROBLEM-SOLVING TECHNIQUES

In section 3.13 we reviewed some principles of lateral thinking, the creative problem-solving techniques that you can use to achieve mutual gain solutions for your clients. In this section we will explore in greater depth how you, as an advocate in mediation, can successfully apply these techniques to actual dispute situations.

5.6.1 Designing the problem, the process, and the solution

A dispute is merely a problem, and it is susceptible to resolution through the application of well-known problem-solving techniques. It is important for you to understand that resolution of any dispute requires the solving of three separate design problems: (1) designing (or, if you prefer, defining) the problem itself, (2) designing the process for solving the defined problem, and (3) designing the solution to the defined problem by using the process you designed. Sometimes, depending on the particular situation, the mind solves these three design problems in sequence; at other times it resolves them simultaneously. The application of lateral thinking techniques enhances their resolution.[26]

• **Designing the problem.**

The concept of *designing* a problem may be difficult to grasp at first. Every time you attempt to solve a problem, you have already designed the problem in your mind. If the problem is a dispute, your perception of the disputants, their conduct, and related events has played a significant role in this design process, along with your assumptions, emotions, and in most cases, your cliché patterns of thinking. Your interpretive "design" of the dispute may occur instantaneously and may be only one

---

26. This section is adapted from Cooley, *Appellate Advocacy Manual,* supra at secs. 2:04, 2:16. See also Cooley, "Mediation and Joke Design," supra at 265–69.

of myriad designs available. What your instantaneous design powers produced as a problem may in fact, if viewed or perceived from a different angle, be an opportunity for change—a betterment of some kind. What you initially perceived as a problem may be no problem at all—and any time you spend in solving it will be wasted.

The idea of problem design may additionally seem foreign because our culture and educational system (particularly mathematics and science courses) traditionally present to us single-solution problems already designed. We are rarely given an opportunity in school to design problems. Yet this is a primary task in everyday life—particularly for the lawyer. Let's take a closer look at what "problem design" means.

At the root of all disputes are human needs or interests that appear to conflict or that are unsatisfied to some extent. For example, your client's neighbor, a self-styled mechanic, tinkers with his car late into the night and "revs up" the engine in the driveway under your client's bedroom window. Your client's problem is not her neighbor or his car; the problem is the conflict between your client's neighbor's need to repair his car at that particular time and your client's need for sleep. This simple example can be extrapolated to the problems precipitating the most complex of lawsuits filed in any of our courts today. At the core of these lawsuits is a simple conflict of the parties' needs. That is what makes the first aspect of problem solving (i.e., problem design) so important. Parties' needs or interests in any particular situation may be satisfied in a variety of ways, and sometimes a conflict spurs a solution that is better than the one that the parties would have reached had the conflict or encounter not occurred.

After full consideration of all facets of a particular dispute, you may conclude that satisfaction of your client's needs may be best achieved by allowing a third party to determine which disputant has a *right* to have his needs satisfied or a duty to satisfy the other disputant's needs. This will require resorting to "the law." Then the problem-design problem shifts from a "needs"/"resources" analysis to a "rights"/"duties" analysis. Many problem designs are possible under a "rights"/"duties" analysis, just as there were under the "needs"/"resources" analysis. All these possibilities are explored and evaluated in the problem-design mode.

- **Designing the process.**

After designing the problem—defining the parties' root needs and interests—the next step is to design the process for solving it. The number of approaches you can take to solve a problem is limited only by the extent of your insight and creativity. As lawyers, many of us are prone to see only one or two possible approaches to solve a problem, even though many more might exist. Normally, we try first to negotiate a solution to a problem, using methods and techniques that have succeeded for us in the past. However, depending on the parties, lawyers, and nature of the problem involved, a different negotiation approach or combination of approaches might be necessary to achieve success. We are often blind to these combined approaches because of our past negotiation ritual. In these situations, a mediator can be helpful in adjusting the process to meet the needs of the redefined problem and in facilitating the generation of creative solutions.

- **Designing the solution.**

After designing the problem and the process for solving it, the next step is to design the solution. Lawyers generally feel much more comfortable with this third design problem because they normally take a solution-oriented approach to a problem before they have designed the problem (given full consideration to defining the problem) and before they have designed the process for solving it (explored and evaluated alternative processes). Actually, properly solving the first two design problems (problem design and process design) makes designing a solution to the problem much easier.

Revisiting the simple example of the mechanic/insomniac dispute, assume that you represent the insomniac. After interviewing her, you conclude that an optimal solution to this dispute cannot be reached if you design the problem in terms of the insomniac's rights, select the traditional process (courts) for securing the rights, and solve the problem by securing an injunction. Although an ordinance in your client's community prohibits residents from engaging in loud activities after 11:00 P.M., you conclude that a court injunction, although obtainable, would probably not be an adequate solution. What if the insomniac wanted to go to bed at 10:00 P.M. on some nights? The court injunction would probably not cover that situation. Besides, the injunction solution would further alienate these neighbors and cause animosity and other interpersonal problems in their relationship. You decide to take the matter to mediation. You think the mediator will be able to convince your client's neighbor to stop repairing his car at night. At this time, you see this as being the only plausible solution to the problem.

5.6.2 Applying lateral thinking techniques to achieve optimal solutions in mediation

Now assume further that the mechanic and his lawyer agree to mediate the above-described dispute. The mediator, through challenging assumptions, thought reversal, and brainstorming separately with the parties and counsel in caucuses, has developed—much to your surprise—this additional information that you and opposing counsel now share:

- The mechanic has a teenage daughter who could walk the insomniac's six-year-old son to school each weekday morning.
- The insomniac attends bridge and chess club meetings two nights a week until 10:30 P.M.
- The insomniac has a "classic car" that needs engine work.
- The insomniac has an extra garage behind her house that is vacant and unused.
- The insomniac has a van that the mechanic borrows from time to time to haul materials, products, and furniture.
- The mechanic and his family go to their lake cottage on most weekends.
- The insomniac and her family never go away on trips.
- The insomniac's teenage son stays out late most nights and sleeps "like a rock."

The goal now is for you to use this information and other known information about the parties to develop a mutually acceptable, optimal solution. To accomplish this most effectively, you may want to apply fractionation, the lateral thinking technique commonly used in mediation to develop integrative (nonmonetary or combined nonmonetary and monetary) solutions.

Fractionation, as applied to mediation, is the process of disturbing perceptions, exploring options and possibilities, and then reframing and repatterning perceptions. It can be used here to disturb the perception (or assumption) of the parties' limited needs and resources, to explore the possibilities of matching resources to needs, and to repattern the needs-resources possibilities into realistic solution configurations. The discussion that follows explains how you might apply fractionation to develop an optimal solution on behalf of your client during the mediation of the mechanic/insomniac dispute.

In employing fractionation, your first step is to break down the problem into the component needs and resources of the parties. You do this by *listing the specific and general needs of the parties and the resources available to each to satisfy the party's own needs and the needs of the other party.* Using a matrix format, as shown on the next page, will facilitate this task. This is something you can sketch out during one of the caucus wait-periods.

Fortunately, the mechanic/insomniac conflict is relatively simple because each party has a single specific need. For the insomniac, it is to substantially reduce or eliminate noise to permit sleep; for the mechanic, it is to repair his car. In other situations, each party may have multiple specific needs with multiple corresponding resources to satisfy those needs. With respect to each single specific need of the parties, multiple resources are available to satisfy it, as shown below.

SPECIFIC NEEDS MATRIX
INSOMNIAC

Specific Need: Substantially Reduce or
Eliminate Noise to Permit Sleep

INSOMNIAC'S AVAILABLE RESOURCES TO SATISFY OWN NEEDS	MECHANIC'S AVAILABLE RESOURCES TO SATISFY INSOMNIAC'S NEEDS
Sleep in another part of the house	Get more effective muffler
Wear earplugs	Work on car in street
Take sleep-inducing medication	Work on car on weekends
Wear stereo headset	Use rubber hammer and other rubberized tools
Wear earmuffs	Work on car earlier in the evening
Go to bed later	
Sleep earlier in the evening	
Move to another house	

SPECIFIC NEEDS MATRIX
MECHANIC

Specific Need: Repair Car

INSOMNIAC'S AVAILABLE RESOURCES TO SATISFY OWN NEEDS	MECHANIC'S AVAILABLE RESOURCES TO SATISFY INSOMNIAC'S NEEDS
Continue current behavior	Allow mechanic to use garage in back of insomniac's house
See mechanic's available resources to modify behavior in insomniac's specific needs matrix	Be our of house until 10:30 P.M. two nights per week

GENERAL NEEDS MATRIX
INSOMNIAC

GENERAL NEED	OWN RESOURCES	MECHANIC'S RESOURCES
Person to take six-year-old son to school	None	Teenage daughter; Mechanic drives to work, past school
Person to repair classic car	None (except to pay for repairs)	Interest in classic car; Mechanical ability

GENERAL NEEDS MATRIX
MECHANIC

GENERAL NEED	OWN RESOURCES	INSOMNIAC'S RESOURCES
Van to transport materials	None (would have to rent)	Van
Someone to watch home and take in mail when out of town on weekends	None	Insomniac and husband never go out of town

The next step is to place all the matrices in front of you and scan them for a few minutes. Allow your mind to see relationships and inter-relationships between the various specific and general needs and available resources. Then, by using the tool "what if," begin to reframe the situation and restructure it into a new arrangement. You should attempt several "what if" repatternings until an arrangement emerges that tends to optimize satisfaction of the parties' needs and the use of available resources. No arrangement is sacred; any arrangement may at any time be repatterned in this reframing process. One possible "what if" repatterning that might emerge from your scanning of the matrices is as follows:

- The mechanic works on his car in the driveway until 10:30 and only on nights that the insomniac is participating in her club activities.
- The mechanic is allowed to use the insomniac's van on request in exchange for occasional repair service on the insomniac's classic car.

- The insomniac pays the mechanic's daughter a weekly stipend to walk the insomniac's son to school.

After another "what if" repatterning, another arrangement might be the following:

- The mechanic can use the insomniac's spare garage to work on his car at any time.
- The mechanic's daughter walks the insomniac's son to school; the mechanic gives his daughter a modest increase in her weekly allowance.
- The insomniac watches the mechanic's house and takes in the mail when the mechanic's family goes to the lake on weekends.

Another repatterning might yield this arrangement:

- The insomniac and her husband switch bedrooms with their teen-age son, who is out late most nights and sleeps "like a rock."

The matrices could of course yield many other arrangements through repatterning. The point of this section is to illustrate how lateral thinking—particularly fractionation—can assist you in developing many potential solutions to a dispute that initially appears to have but a single solution. If you apply these techniques, your only problem might be the difficulty of choosing from among several good solutions. But of course that is a problem you can easily tolerate.

5.7   STRUCTURED SETTLEMENTS AND DECISION TREE ANALYSIS

5.7.1   Structured settlements

To understand the concept of the time-value of money and the benefits of a structured settlement, perhaps it would be well to consider the story of husband and wife, Morris and Esther who operated a delicatessen in the city. Every year during their sixty years of marriage, Morris and Esther went to the State Fair, and every year Esther pleaded with Morris to let her "ride in that single-engine airplane" to observe the fairgrounds and the rural landscape. Every year Morris had the same response, "Esther, I know you want to ride in that airplane, but it costs 50 dollars, and 50 dollars is 50 dollars." Last year Morris and Esther went to the State Fair and Esther said, "Morris, I'm eighty-five years old. If I don't ride that airplane this year I may never get another chance." Morris replied, "Esther, that airplane ride costs 50 dollars, and 50 dollars is 50 dollars." Esther kept begging Morris to let her ride, and the airline pilot overheard their debate, and approaching them, said, "Folks, I'll make you a deal. I'll take you both up for a ride. If you can stay quiet for the entire ride and not say one word, I won't charge you; but if you say one word, it's 50 dollars." Morris and Esther agreed and up they went. The pilot did all kinds of twists and turns and rolls and dives with the airplane, but he heard not a word. He did all his acrobatic tricks over again, but still not a word. When he landed the plane, the pilot turned to Esther and said, "By golly, I did everything I could think of to get you to yell out, but you didn't." Esther replied, "Well I was gonna say something when Morris fell out, but 50 dollars is 50 dollars."

Well, in fact, Morris—and Esther—were unfortunately (dead) wrong. Fifty dollars is not merely 50 dollars; it has the potential of being much more. Had Morris invested the $50 at his first visit to the State Fair at 5 percent interest, in sixty years that 50 dollars, compounded annually, would have grown to nearly $1,000 (actually $933.96). They could have taken an airplane ride many times in the last couple of decades, and still had several hundred dollars left over. What Morris and Esther did not know about the time-value of money can be of help to you when you are advising your client on the appropriateness of designing a structured settlement in a particular mediated resolution.

Many personal injury and wrongful death cases are prime candidates for the use of structured settlements.[27] These are simply settlements in which all or some of the payments made to a plaintiff are deferred. They are particularly useful in mediated settlements involving minors, spendthrifts, or other persons incapable of prudently managing large cash settlements. For a plaintiff, the principal advantages of a structured settlement include periodic guaranteed payments and the avoidance of federal income tax liability. The principal advantage to a defendant is that the amount of cash needed to settle a case will be a small percentage of the actual dollar amount the plaintiff will be receiving over time. Thus the structured settlement is a true mutual gain solution—the plaintiff receives substantially more dollars over time than the defendant is willing to pay currently in a cash settlement, and the defendant benefits currently from a limited cash outlay requirement.

The design of a typical structured settlement has three aspects: (1) cash paid at the time of settlement, (2) future lump sums paid periodically, and (3) annuities (annual, monthly, weekly, or some other uniform method of future payment). Cash paid at the time of settlement includes money to cover legal fees and unpaid health care and related expenses that the plaintiff incurred between the time of the accident and the settlement. A plaintiff's individual circumstances govern the timing and amount of future lump sum and annuity payments, which

---

27. See generally James R. Eck and Jeffrey L. Ungerer, *Structuring Settlements* (Shepard's McGraw-Hill, Inc., 1987).

may vary dramatically from case to case. When designing the periodic lump sum structure as plaintiff's counsel, you need to think creatively to ensure that you have taken into account all the future needs of your client. If your client is a minor, those needs might include future medical, surgical, and rehabilitative expenses, private prep school expenses, college, postcollege European travel, postgraduate education, wedding expenses, the purchase of a first home, funds needed to start a new business, retirement, and so forth. If a married person or couple are to share in the proceeds of the settlement, you need to take special precautions to ensure that each spouse has the opportunity to protect his or her interest in the proceeds as they are being paid over time. It is very important for you to explore with your client, in detail, what his projected needs will be. You do not want your client to be caught in the lurch sometime in the future without sufficient funds to satisfy a need that could have been easily anticipated. As to the structuring of annuities, you may want to consider a built-in escalator to offset possible future increases in the cost of living.

Finally, as plaintiff's counsel, you need to know or be able to reasonably estimate what the structured settlement is costing the defendant. This information is necessary for at least two reasons: (1) so that you can determine whether the defendant's offer is an equitable settlement of the claim, and (2) assuming your fee is contingent so that you can calculate what that fee will be. Ordinarily, a liability insurance company purchases a structured settlement from a life insurance company. To determine the cost of the structured settlement to the liability insurance company, you need to understand how a life insurance company calculates annuity premiums. This calculation typically takes into account the following factors: the interest rate, mortality data, the value of uniform periodic payments, the value of future lump sum payments, the growth of future payments, and the present value of lost income. A discussion of the specific formulas for computing these values is beyond the scope of this work. However, you should be aware that various publications and computer programs are available to assist you in performing these calculations.[28]

5.7.2   Decision tree analysis

Decision tree analysis (also called "decision analysis") is a tool that you should consider using in your preparation for mediation and, in the appropriate situation, during the course of the mediation itself.[29] Decision tree analysis is not a new concept. It has been used in the corporate

---

28. See, e.g., chaps. 2, 3, 4, 10, and 13.
29. *See generally,* David P. Hoffer, "Decision Analysis as a Mediator's Tool," 1 *Harvard Negotiation Law Review* 113 (1996); Marjorie Corman Aaron, "The Value of Decision Analysis in Mediation Practice," 1995 *Negotiation Journal* 123.

world for decades to model complex decisions that involve multiple un-certainties. Increasingly, it has been used by litigators as a systematic method of determining whether a case should be settled or litigated. And in the latter part of the 1980s, mediators and advocates in media-tion have turned to this tool to aid in the settlement of cases. The key to success in using a decision tree analysis to help settle a case is persuad-ing the lawyers using it to be realistic in estimating the probabilities of events occurring as they move through the analysis. Also, if you intend to use decision tree analysis in a mediation, you should ensure that the mediator you select knows how to facilitate such an analysis and is will-ing to do so.

Overcoming obstacles to using decision analysis. You should be aware that parties or their lawyers may resist your suggestion of using decision trees in evaluating a case for several reasons. Some of these reasons and ways you can make parties and lawyers more com-fortable with this decision-aiding technique include:

- **Lawyers' and/or parties' discomfort with mathematics.** To overcome this obstacle, the mediator can begin by drawing a deci-sion tree on a flip chart and explaining how it works conceptually without using numbers.

- **Lawyers' and/or parties' discomfort with computers.** The mediator begins with flip chart as explained above. When the par-ticipants tire of computations by hand, the mediator then shows them how easy and fast the computer makes the tasks. The medi-ator can also emphasize that the computerized numerical analy-sis is only a preliminary attempt to find a fair settlement value and it represents only possible points in a range of reasonable fig-ures. The mediator can also explain sensitivity analysis early in the process, and that the participants should reserve judgment on the accuracy of the technique until after initial analyses have been performed.

- **Lawyers' dislike of "losing control" of the evaluation of his/her case.** Fear of a computer click destroying the lawyer's opinion of a case may be a formidable obstacle to the use of com-puterized decision analysis. To overcome this fear, you can sug-gest that the mediator conduct the evaluations separately in caucuses so that the lawyers can "experiment" with the outcomes before they are imposed on them by a "black box." By caucusing, they can also avoid the effect of an opponent anchoring his bar-gaining position to the computer-generated evaluation.

- **Lawyers' and parties' unwillingness to share realistic probability estimates with the mediator.** Again, use of the caucus procedure normally helps to make the participants be more realistic about the strengths and weaknesses of their respective cases, and thereby more realistic about probability estimates. Where participants are very unrealistic, the mediator can run the analysis with the party's probability estimates and the mediator's probability estimates, and then allow the participants to compare and discuss the estimates while the mediator is absent from the room.

- **Fundamentals of decision analysis.** The text that follows briefly explains the fundamentals of decision analysis:[30]

A decision tree is a graphical representation of a complex decision. Developed in the 1960s for use in business education, decision trees are flexible enough to be used for many types of decisions. Professionals in the fields of business, economics, medicine, public policy, engineering, and law all use decision trees when multiple uncertainties complicate the decision process.

A. *Structure*

Decision trees are organized chronologically, from left to right. They contain certain "nodes" of three different types: decision, chance, and terminal. A decision node (represented by a square) denotes a point at which the decision maker must choose between two or more options. A chance node (represented by a circle) denotes a point where the decision maker has no control over the outcome; each event following a chance node has a probability associated with it that reflects how likely it is to occur. Terminal nodes (represented by triangles) denote final outcomes, after which no events relevant to the decision are considered.

The following simple decision tree represents a situation in which a personal injury plaintiff must decide whether to proceed to trial with a chance of recovering $1,000 or settle for $500. (See Fig. A.) Assume that you represent the plaintiff in this lawsuit.

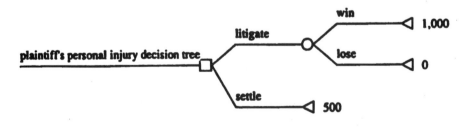

Figure A

---

30. The explanation of decision analysis is reprinted with permission of the *Harvard Negotiation Law Review.: Hoffer, Decision Analysis as a Mediator's Tool*, id. at 134–37 (1996).

The plaintiff faces two choices—litigate or settle—which are represented by branches emanating from the decision node at the left. If the plaintiff settles, the inquiry is complete: he gets $500 and the dispute ends. If he chooses to litigate, there are two possible outcomes: win (a terminal node with payoff of $1,000) or lose (a terminal node with a payoff of zero). For purposes of this example, all of the uncertainties associated with litigation (other than liability), as well as costs, are ignored.

To make this decision intelligently, the plaintiff must assess how likely he is to win if litigation is pursued. A $500 settlement offer may seem inadequate if the plaintiff has an excellent chance of winning $1,000; however, the offer may be very attractive if a successful outcome is less certain. In order to be more precise, we must assign probabilities to the uncertain events modeled by the tree. In this simple case, we must assess the likelihood that the plaintiff will win at trial.

Assume that, in your professional judgment, your client has a 40 percent (.4) chance of winning at trial. This probability would be displayed beneath the node labeled "win." Accordingly, a probability of 60 percent (.6) would be displayed beneath the node labeled "lose." (See figure B.)

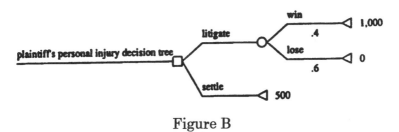

Figure B

B.   *Calculation*

Settlement is apparently preferable to litigation in this case because the probability of winning is not high enough to risk the gamble of trial. This evaluation is based on a concept called expected value or expected monetary value. The expected value of a node is defined as the sum of the products of the probabilities and payoffs of its branches. In other words, the expected value of a course of action is the average value of taking that course of action many times. If one were to try cases identical to this case one hundred times, about forty would result in a victory while sixty would result in a loss. The average recovery would be forty victories at $1,000 per victory, or $40,000, plus sixty losses at $0 per loss, divided by 100 cases tried, for an average recovery of $400.

Thus, the expected value associated with the "litigate" node is $400. (See figure C.)

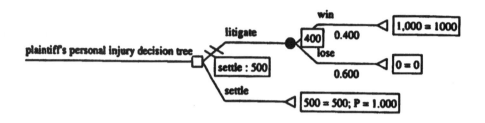

Figure C

C.   *Different Kinds of Trees*

A distinction must be drawn between decision trees and chance trees. A decision tree is a tree whose first node (the "root" node) is a decision node; thus, it models a situation in which the events being modeled are triggered by an initial decision to be made by the decision maker. A chance tree (or "event tree") is a tree whose root is a chance node; in other words, no decision is required. It is used to model events over which the decision maker has no control, and its value represents the value of being faced with the modeled set of uncertainties.

Chance trees are often embedded in decision trees. For example, one can examine the chance tree that represents the litigation alternative in the example above. Its expected value, $400, represents the expected value of litigation. (See figure D.)

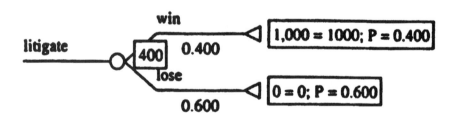

Figure D

D.   *More Complex Trees*

The concept of expected value is at the core of all decision analysis. In more complex trees, the expected value is calculated in stages. In the example below, a motion for summary judgment is interposed between the decision to litigate and the outcome of the trial. (See figure E.)

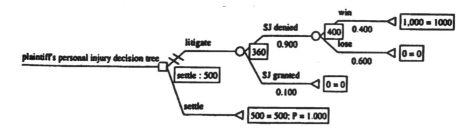

Figure E

If your client chooses to litigate, the defendant will move for summary judgment, with a 10 percent chance of winning. If summary judgment is denied, the same win/lose chance tree from figure D follows the denial of summary judgment.

To calculate the expected value of this tree, the decision analyst starts at the right side. As discussed above, by multiplying the probability of winning by the damage award, multiplying the probability of defeat at trial by the payoff, and adding the two figures together, an expected value of $400 is calculated and displayed next to the node "SJ denied." Thus, the expected value of the case upon denial of summary judgment is $400.

The plaintiff's expected value of litigation must also take into account the possibility of losing on summary judgment. Thus, the expected value of litigation is calculated by multiplying the expected value associated with the denial of summary judgment, $400, by the probability that summary judgment will be denied, 90 percent. This figure, $360, is added to the product of the zero value of losing on summary judgment and the 10 percent probability of losing on summary judgment. The expected value of litigation is thus $360. The $40 difference between this expected value and the expected value in the simpler example reflects the risk that the plaintiff will lose on summary judgment. Since a $500 settlement offer is preferable to a litigation alternative whose expected value is $360, your client would be well advised to settle the case.

5.8 ASSISTING THE MEDIATOR TO ACHIEVE CLOSURE

By and large, mediators are very creative and resourceful people, but they need the parties' and the advocates' help on many occasions to achieve closure in mediation. Often the parties have insights and perspectives on the conflict and on potential solutions that the mediators do not know or perceive. Mediators routinely use a number of tools to effect closure, some of which are discussed below. If you perceive that one or more of these tools might be applied in a particular case to achieve settlement, make sure that you bring it to the mediator's attention at an appropriate time during one of the final caucuses.

- **Suggest that the mediator present the proposal as if it were her own idea.**

It is not uncommon that conversations with the mediator during caucuses generate ideas for possible ways to settle the case. Some of these ideas might initially seem absurd or arrogant to the receiving side if presented as the idea of the proposing side. If the mediator presents the idea to the receiving side in such a way as to imply that she is making the suggestion, it is likely that the other side will give the idea serious consideration. For example, assume that a Fortune 500 manufacturer is in a mediation where the other side is a small electronics company that supplies critical parts for the manufacturer's products. The manufacturer has sued the small company for supplying defective parts. Assume further that during one of the mediator's caucuses with the small company, the CEO of the small company discloses that, because of bad economic times, he would consider a buyout of his company by the manufacturer. In a caucus with the other side, if the mediator presents the idea as that of the small company, the manufacturer may scoff at it and reject it out of hand. But if the mediator says to the manufacturer in a caucus, "Would you ever consider the possible cost-benefits of buying the electronics company outright?" The manufacturer will probably objectively evaluate the suggestion, if for no other reason than out of respect for the mediator's attempts to help the parties find a mutually agreeable solution.

- **Suggest that the mediator make the proposal conditional without communicating a commitment on your part.**

Mediators frequently use a tactic of saying to one side in caucus, "If I can get the other side to do X, will you do Y?" or "If I can get the other side to pay Z, will you accept it in full settlement?" Of course the mediator already knows when he asks those questions that the other side will do X or that the other side will pay Z. In this way, the mediator can make a proposal without having the proposing side actually make a concession that would alter its bargaining position. If the receiving side accepts, settlement results. If the receiving side says it cannot do Y or cannot accept Z, then the proposing side has lost nothing and can consider other possible proposals to have the mediator communicate to the other side. If the mediator does not offer to use this tactic, you may want to suggest it, if appropriate.

• **Suggest that the parties split the difference.**

As a final gesture to avert a failed settlement attempt, mediators often suggest, where the final bargaining bracket is relatively narrow, that the parties split the difference. If the mediator fails to make this suggestion, you should consider raising it yourself.

• **Suggest a structured settlement or payment in installments.**

In situations involving large money resolutions where the plaintiffs are young and healthy enough to have a long life expectancy, structured settlements can provide a mutual gain solution. As discussed in more detail in section 5.7, through a structured settlement the insurance company can deposit an agreed amount now, and a plaintiff can receive annuity payments over a period of time that total perhaps much more than the plaintiff could have received in a lump sum payment. Also, the settlement can be structured so that the payments are tailored to the foreseeable needs of the plaintiff at various points in the future—college, marriage, having children, and so forth. Aside from structured settlements, sometimes merely suggesting that an agreed settlement be paid in equal installments over a period of time or in a lump sum plus periodic installments can precipitate a resolution of a dispute.

• **Suggest a future business arrangement.**

In an intercompany dispute, opportunities for the disputants to resolve their differences through future business transactions often allow the aggrieved party to recoup any present losses over time. These types of solutions are particularly attractive where there is an advantage, because of the specific market or of the status of industry competition, in the companies' continuing to do business together.

• **Suggest a portion of the settlement be paid to a mutually acceptable charity**.

Occasionally there arises a situation where a defendant, such as a corporation, believes that it did nothing to injure the plaintiff and therefore rejects the idea of paying very much in settlement, but at the same time it desires very much to settle the dispute to avoid adverse publicity.

This situation tends to arise in civil rights or discrimination cases. Suggesting that a portion of the settlement be paid to a mutually acceptable charity or civil rights organization can sometimes satisfy both parties' interests to ensure that some future good can result from their joint solution.

- **Suggest payment in kind instead of in dollars.**

In many types of disputes, resolution can be achieved through settlements permitting a transfer of goods or property or a performance of services instead of a payment of money. You should always be on the alert for these closure-aiding opportunities.

- **Suggest substitution of goods.**

In any dispute involving a purchase or lease of goods or of property that later proves unsatisfactory to the purchaser or lessee, a solution can often flow from a suggestion that goods or property of higher quality be substituted for the alleged unsatisfactory goods or property. A guarantee or warranty might also accompany the substituted goods or property.

- **Suggest an apology.**

A simple apology may be of great value to a complaining party. Indeed, in a defamation case for instance, an apology might be worth millions if coupled with a public retraction. Even in a small personal or business dispute, a sincere apology, particularly in written form, can provide an important element of a settlement package. Be vigilant for situations appropriate for its use.

- **Suggest a change in title, label, or description.**

For many people, a title or label has intrinsic value for self-identity, self-esteem, or other reasons. Thus in an employment dispute, a change in an employee's title to reflect supervisory status may be as important to the employee as an increase in salary. Similarly, in a consumer class action against a manufacturer in a product liability case, an element of the settlement might reasonably be an agreed change in the label for the product, including a detailed description of the appropriate use of the product and a warning to the consumer of the consequences of inappropriate use. Other simple "label" changes might facilitate a settlement. For example, in a residential lease, changing the description of the living space to read "penthouse apartment" with a corresponding reference in the lobby directory, may, with other concessions, be a sufficient inducement for a celebrity tenant to drop a lawsuit for the landlord's failure to deliver timely possession of the premises.

- **Suggest extradispute resources for satisfying a party's extradispute interests.**

In certain situations, resources for satisfying all or a part of a dispute lie outside the resources or power available to the actual parties in conflict. For example, in a sexual harassment case brought by a female lawyer against a male partner and the law firm itself, part of a settlement could consist of satisfying the female partner's long-held desire to become a member of a highly exclusive country club or to be appointed as an adjunct professor of law at a local law school. Senior partners in the firm could, through their network of well-placed contacts, perhaps see to it that those extradispute interests of the female lawyer were quickly satisfied.

- **Suggest a confidentiality agreement.**

A defendant's fear that the settlement in the present case will cause many other individuals to file claims and seek similar settlements often constitutes a formidable barrier to a settlement. As part of the settlement, the parties may enter into a confidentiality agreement that imposes severe sanctions for violating confidentiality. This can sometimes overcome the fear of additional claims and allow the parties to reach settlement.

- **Suggest a change in language or in the interpretation of language.**

In some contract or lease disputes, resolution can be achieved through an agreed change in language or an agreed interpretation of language as part of a settlement package. Thus in a manufacturer-supplier contract where a supplier is sued for failure to expressly comply with a contract term requiring the supplier to "ship the goods within ten days of the date of the purchase order," a settlement might in part consist of changing the contract to read "ship the goods on the tenth day following the date of the purchase order unless that day is a nonbusiness day, in which case the goods will be shipped on the next business day." The new language could then be interpreted to permit the supplier to ship goods on the Tuesday following a three-day holiday weekend, whereas a strict reading of the old language would have required goods to be shipped on the Saturday of a three-day weekend, even though all three days were nonbusiness days.

5.9   ETHICAL CONSIDERATIONS

To represent your client effectively in mediation you need to be familiar with two types of ethical standards—those that guide mediators

in performing their function and those that govern the conduct of lawyers engaged in negotiation. You need to understand the ethics of the
mediator function so that you will know when a mediator is exceeding
his ethical bounds and thus when it may be appropriate to advise your
client of the necessity to conclude participation in a particular mediation. You need to understand the ethics of the lawyer's function in negotiation so that you will know the constraints on your own conduct as an
advocate and on the conduct of opposing counsel. This section discusses
these two types of ethical standards.

5.9.1   Standards of ethical conduct for mediators

Mediator ethical standards are defined in relation to the mediator's
duties to the parties, to the process, to nonparties, and to other professionals. Several professional dispute resolution organizations currently publish mediator standards. The American Arbitration
Association, the American Bar Association, and the Society of Professionals in Dispute Resolution have jointly published Model Standards
of Conduct for Mediators, a set of ethical standards for mediators. In the
discussion that follows, references to numbered standards reflect the
Model Standards. A complete set of these standards is reproduced in
appendix I.

- **Duties to the parties**

Mediators must recognize that the mediation process is based on the
principle of self-determination by the parties (Standard I). The purpose
of the process is to allow the parties to reach a voluntary, uncoerced
agreement. The role of the mediator is to facilitate a voluntary resolution of a dispute. A mediator can educate the parties about the mediation process and help them make informed decisions but may not advise
them on the law. And she must have the necessary qualifications to satisfy the reasonable expectations of the parties (Standard IV).

A mediator must conduct the mediation in an impartial manner
(Standard II). A mediator may mediate only those matters in which he
can remain impartial and evenhanded with respect to the subject matter of the dispute and the participants' personal characteristics, background, or performance at the mediation. A mediator is further
required to disclose all actual and potential conflicts of interest reasonably known to the mediator and afterwards decline to mediate unless
all parties choose to retain the mediator (Standard III). The need to protect against actual or apparent conflicts of interest also governs the conduct of mediators both during and after the mediation.

A mediator must maintain the reasonable expectations of the parties with regard to confidentiality and may not disclose any confidential
matter to the opposing party or to anyone outside the mediation unless

given permission by the pertinent party or parties or unless required by law or other public policy (Standard V). The mediator's duty of confidentiality arises from at least four types of laws: specific statutes or court rules related to mediator confidentiality or mediator privileges, rules related to evidentiary exclusion of settlement discussions, discovery limitations, and laws regarding the enforcement of agreements not to disclose.

A mediator must conduct the mediation fairly, diligently, and in a manner consistent with the principle of the parties' self-determination (Standard VI). A mediator must withdraw from a mediation when incapable of serving, when unable to remain impartial, when the mediation is being used to further illegal conduct, or when a party is unable to participate due to drug, alcohol, or other physical or mental incapacity.

A mediator must to be truthful in advertising and solicitations for mediation (Standard VII) and must fully disclose and explain the basis of compensation, fees, and charges to the parties (Standard VIII).

Included in the mediator's duties under Standards I and VI is the responsibility to see that checks are performed to guarantee that the settlement is fair and equitable within the perceptions of the parties. Under those standards, a mediator is also expected to deal appropriately with power imbalances causing advantages to one or more parties resulting from wealth, social position, access to legal expertise, access to facts, negotiating ability, physical intimidation, or an opponent's avoidance of conflict. Methods by which mediators deal with power imbalances include (1) enlisting the aid of the parties' counsel, (2) convincing parties to stop the intimidating tactics or other abusive behavior, (3) encouraging parties to obtain legal representation if they are unrepresented, (4) educating the parties in effective negotiation techniques, and (5) advising the parties of the mediator's obligation to withdraw if the adverse effects of the imbalance cannot be resolved.

- **Duties to the process**

Mediators have a duty to improve the practice of mediation (Standard IX). They also have the duty of nonownership of the problem, of the process for solving it, and of the solution. They have a duty to protect the integrity of the mediation process and the duty to withdraw when appropriate.

- **Duties to nonparties**

Mediators may, in some circumstances, owe duties to identifiable nonparties who do or may have an interest in, or who will or may be affected by the outcome. Before they commence mediations, mediators often ask whether there are other individuals or organizations that should be invited to participate. If all the necessary individuals or organizations do not participate, the mediated agreement may risk being challenged in court. Mediators may also in certain circumstances owe duties of protection or notice to the general public. This occurs in situations involving a risk to public safety, for example, where the mediation concerns the environmental risks associated with toxic waste storage or removal.

• **Duties to other professionals**

A mediator owes a duty not to interfere with professional relationships between the parties and other professionals—lawyers, physicians, psychotherapists, and the like—and also a duty to appointing judges and to the judicial process generally.

5.9.2   Standards of ethical conduct for lawyers in negotiation

Codes of professional conduct for lawyers vary from state to state, and although a few still follow variations of the American Bar Association's Model Code of Professional Responsibility, many have adopted the more recent ABA Model Rules of Professional Conduct (Model Rules). The discussion that follows addresses the lawyer's ethical duties in negotiation under the ABA Model Rules (MR) and includes references to the relevant rule numbers. The duties covered include advising the client, advocacy, truthfulness, confidentiality, and drafting agreements.[31]

• **Advising the client**

Under the Model Rules a lawyer must keep a client reasonably informed about the status of a matter and must promptly comply with reasonable requests for information from the client (MR 1.4(a)). Furthermore, a lawyer must explain a matter to the extent reasonably necessary to permit the client to make informed decisions regarding the representation (MR 1.4(b)). Initial discussions with the client should normally include (1) the extent to which the lawyer's professional background is either necessary or superfluous to the negotiation, (2) when and to what degree the client can expect to be consulted regarding how the negotiation is progressing, and (3) whether the subject matter of the negotiation is one in which the attorney is qualified to be involved. If a lawyer becomes aware that the client intends to engage in criminal or fraudulent conduct, many jurisdictions allow the lawyer to discuss the legal consequences of any proposed course of conduct with a client and

---

31. See generally Donner and Crowe, supra at chap. 14, pp. 1–15. Selected ABA Model Rules of Professional Conduct appear in appendix J.

to advise the client to make a good-faith effort to determine the validity, scope, meaning, or application of the law(MR1.2d). But of course the lawyer may not do anything that can be construed as aiding or abetting the client in committing a criminal or fraudulent act. If a lawyer asks a client to consent to a representation affected by a conflict of interest, the client must give informed consent.

- **Advocacy**

The lawyer is expected to exercise independent professional judgment on behalf of her client and to advocate the client's interests and positions, so long as the positions can be argued in good faith and are supported by existing law. The lawyer not only has an ethical duty of advocacy on behalf of the client, but she also is an officer of the legal system and a public citizen having special responsibility for the quality of justice (MR, preamble). Thus the lawyer's duty of advocacy for the client is defined, in part, by the expectations of the community and the court in which the lawyer practices.

Limitations on the extent to which a lawyer may vigorously advocate her client's interests or positions in negotiation include the following: (1) a lawyer may not contact the other side directly, or advise the client to do so, if that party is represented by a lawyer unless the lawyer has the consent of the other lawyer or is authorized to do so by law or a court order (MR 4.2); (2) a lawyer may not request that persons other than the client (or his relatives or agents) refrain from voluntarily giving relevant information to another party (MR 3.4(f)); and (3) a lawyer must make reasonable efforts to expedite litigation consistent with the interests of the client (MR 3.2).

- **Truthfulness**

In the course of representing a client, a lawyer may not knowingly make a false statement of material fact or law to a third person or fail to disclose a material fact to a third person when disclosure is necessary to avoid assisting a criminal or fraudulent act by a client (MR 4.1). Under generally accepted conventions in negotiation, certain types of statements normally are not taken as material facts. They include estimates of price or value, a party's intention regarding an acceptable settlement of a claim, and the existence of an undisclosed principal except where nondisclosure of the principal would constitute fraud. The Comments to the Model Rules suggest that puffing in negotiations is permissible. Nevertheless, the line between impermissible lying and permissible puffing is not bright. Regardless of the precise contours of the concept of puffing, there is wide agreement that the Model Rules prohibit a lawyer from knowingly falsifying facts, evidence, or legal precedent.

- **Confidentiality**

A lawyer may not reveal information relating to representation of a client unless the client consents after consultation, except for disclosures that are impliedly authorized in order to carry out the representation (MR 1.6). As to impliedly authorized disclosures, in litigation for example, a lawyer may disclose information by admitting a fact that cannot properly be disputed, or in negotiation a lawyer may make a disclosure that facilitates a satisfactory conclusion. The mediation process stretches the application of this rule. For example, lawyers routinely share confidences of clients with a mediator—with or without the client's explicit authorization. This convention is widely accepted because the mediator has an ethical duty to keep such information confidential if instructed to do so. Even though the mediator cannot disclose such information to the other side, the mediator can use confidential information to suggest solutions to the parties that the parties would not discover through direct communication. Of course a lawyer must honor his client's requests not to disclose particular information to a mediator.

- **Drafting agreements**

A lawyer may not prepare a settlement agreement giving the lawyer or a person related to the lawyer any substantial gift from a client, including a testamentary gift, except where the client is related to the donee (MR 1.8(c)). Furthermore, a lawyer may not make or negotiate an agreement giving the lawyer literary or media rights to a portrayal or account based in substantial part on information relating to the representation (MR 1.8(d)). Finally, a lawyer may not participate in the making of a partnership or employment agreement that restricts the rights of a lawyer to practice after termination of the relationship (except an agreement concerning benefits upon retirement) or in the making of an agreement in which a restriction on a lawyer's right to practice is part of the settlement of a controversy between private parties (MR 5.6).

5.9.3   Civility guidelines

Some of our presidents have provided us lawyers with fine examples of diplomacy and civility in action. Abraham Lincoln once described diplomacy as the "ability to describe others as they see themselves." He was a master at treating his fellow man, professionals and laypersons alike, with the utmost civility. On one occasion, Lincoln's law colleague was very angry with a lawyer whom he felt had mistreated and misled him in prosecuting a particular case. The colleague asked Lincoln for advice. Abe told his colleague to write a letter to the offender, explaining the matter and letting the offender know exactly how victimized the colleague felt. "Tell him everything that bothers you," Abe said, "and in no uncertain terms." The colleague asked, "Should I mail it or have it delivered by messenger?" "Neither," said Abe. "Rip it up when you finish. You'll feel much better."[32] Another President, Calvin Coolidge, liked to use humor to encourage civility among lawmakers. Once, when he was Governor of Massachusetts, Coolidge sat patiently while two state senators were arguing vociferously. It reached such a peak that one finally told the other to "go to hell." The insulted senator turned to Coolidge, who had been flipping rather idly through a legal-looking tome, and shouted, "Well, what are you going to do about it, Governor? He told me to go to hell." Coolidge, calm and collected, replied, "Don't worry, Senator. I've looked up the law. You don't have to go there."[33] As advocates in mediation, we can learn lessons in civility from these and other historical examples. We can also receive guidance on civility from our professional organizations.

In 1998, the American Bar Association's Litigation Section issued a set of Guidelines for Litigation Conduct to address what it viewed as a decline in professionalism and civility among lawyers. Modeled on the Standards of Professional Conduct adopted by the United States Court of Appeals for the Seventh Circuit, the ABA Section of Litigation's Guidelines are purely aspirational and are not used as a basis for liability or discipline. You should draw these guidelines to the attention of lawyers, as necessary when inappropriate or unprofessional behavior of lawyers tends to threaten the intended purpose, the integrity, or the character of the mediation process. Guidelines that appear to directly pertain to the negotiation and mediation processes include:

1. We will practice our profession with a continuing awareness that our role is to zealously advance the legitimate interests of our clients. In our dealings with others, we will not reflect the ill feelings of our clients. We will treat all other counsel, parties, and witnesses in a civil and courteous manner, not only in court, but also in all other written and oral communications. We will refrain from acting upon or manifesting bias or prejudice based upon race, sex, religion, national origin, disability, age, sexual orientation, or socioeconomic status toward any participant in the legal process.

2. We will not, even when called upon by a client to do so, abuse or indulge in offensive conduct directed to other counsel, parties, or witnesses. We will abstain from disparaging personal remarks or acrimony toward other counsel, parties, or witnesses. We will treat adverse witnesses and parties with fair consideration.

---

32. Anecdote adapted from Fredericks, supra at 48, 49.
33. Anecdote adapted from Fredericks, supra at 84.

* * *

6. We will in good faith adhere to all express promises and to agreements with other counsel, whether oral or in writing, and to all agreements implied by the circumstances or local customs.

7. When we reach an oral understanding on a proposed agreement or a stipulation and decide to commit it to writing, the drafter will endeavor in good faith to state the oral understanding accurately and completely. The drafter will provide other counsel the opportunity to review the writing.

    As drafts are exchanged between or among counsel, changes from prior drafts will be identified in the draft or otherwise explicitly brought to other counsel's attention. We will not include in a draft matters to which there has been no agreement without explicitly advising other counsel in writing of the addition.

8. We will endeavor to confer early with other counsel to assess settlement possibilities. We will not falsely hold out the possibility of settlement to obtain unfair advantage.

9. In civil actions, we will stipulate to relevant matters if they are undisputed and if no good faith advocacy basis exists for not stipulating.

* * *

16. We will promptly notify other counsel, and . . . other persons, when . . . meetings, or conferences are to be canceled or postponed.

* * *

29. We will not ascribe a position to another counsel that counsel has not taken.

Chapter Six

POSTMEDIATION ADVOCACY

"You cannot shake hands with a clenched fist."
— *Golda Meir*

Your use of negotiation skills does not terminate with the adjournment of the mediation. If the mediation is successful, a settlement agreement must be drafted. This often requires a great deal of negotiation. If the mediation is not successful, then discussions relating to the disputo may continue, the parties may reach a settlement, and they may reduce its terms to writing—all through negotiation. If for some reason the settlement agreement breaks down sometime later, then the parties will probably first use negotiations to mend the problems.

Negotiations after a successful mediation often take on a very positive aura. Advocates tend to collaborate more easily in trying to ensure that all parties' interests are satisfied. For this very reason, you need to be on your guard not to give up too much. Consider the famous negotiation involving Solon Spencer Beman and the Pullman Company. Beman, a New York architect, was the master builder of the model town built for the Pullman Company south of Chicago. When the town was nearing completion in 1884, Beman was so proud of his new self-contained town he went to Mr. Pullman one day and suggested that it would be quite appropriate to name the town "Beman" after its architect. Mr. Pullman readily admitted that Beman was a fine name but suggested a compromise. Beman, caught up in his own success, said that he would embrace any compromise. "Good," said Mr. Pullman, "We will use the first syllable of my name and the second syllable of your name. The city will be called 'Pullman'."[1]

6.1 CONTINUING THE NEGOTIATIONS

If mediation does not resolve a dispute, then you have several alternatives: proceeding to arbitration or some other third-party dispute resolution mechanism, preparing for and going to trial, or continuing to negotiate directly with the other side. If you decide to pursue

---

1. Anecdote adapted from Braude, *New Treasury*, supra at 76.

negotiations, then you probably should carefully consider (1) the dynamics of the prolonged deadlock and (2) techniques and tactics to counter those dynamics.

Research has revealed that the dynamics of prolonged deadlock have seven characteristics: feelings of anger, resentment, tension, hostility, mistrust, frustration, and/or futility; expressions of criticism and blame and attempts to block them; a blurring of the issues; personalization of the conflict; focusing on areas of wide disagreement instead of on areas of agreement; each side locking into its positions; and each side tending to unite as a team against the other side.[2] The essence of these dynamics is the playing out of the parties' logic-draining, perception-distorting emotions. To effectively counter these dynamics you must use techniques that deal directly with these emotions. Sometimes the tactic of changing the negotiator or negotiation team leader may substantially relieve the debilitatingly emotional component of a conflict. Other general techniques for dealing with the parties' emotions include the following:[3]

- Focus on the process to acknowledge the legitimacy of feelings, enhance understanding, and, if possible, depersonalize the situation.
- Use selective information disclosure and information bargaining, instead of making accusations.
- Create an environment for a "fresh start."
- Redefine the issues.
- Emphasize the problem-solving approach.
- Jointly develop win-win proposals.

Specific focusing tactics that may help distract the parties from their emotions and allow them to deal more directly and rationally with finding a solution include guiding discussions toward:[4]

- Modifying the payment terms.
- Altering the allocation of risk.
- Modifying the time of performance.
- Adding guarantees of satisfaction.
- Adding a grievance mechanism.
- Changing the specifications.
- Adjusting the terms.
- Recognizing inaccurate information.
- Obtaining correct information.

---

2.   Schoenfield and Schoenfield, supra at 180.
3.   Id. at 180–81.
4.   Id. at 164.

By using these and other techniques and tactics, you may be able to negotiate a favorable result. If resolution is not completely possible, you may be able to bring the parties closer together on some of the issues to generate interest in a follow-up mediation session.

6.2 DRAFTING THE SETTLEMENT AGREEMENT

Once you and your opposing counsel, in consultation with your respective clients, have reached agreement as to a settlement, the next task is to put it in writing. Producing a durable, enforceable settlement agreement involves several important considerations.[5]

The first question you will confront is: who is going to draft the agreement? Your first impulse may be to let the other attorney draft the agreement. This may be a good idea, for example, if your client cannot afford the expense of having you draft it. Besides, a few tricky provisions may need to be worked out, and it may be beneficial to have the other advocate think through all the alternatives and come up with proposals first, which you can refine later. Indeed, the other advocate, happy that the dispute is resolved, may propose language that you have not considered that is quite favorable to your client. Another advantage of having the other advocate draft the settlement agreement is that if there ever is an alleged breach, the judge or arbitrator will be inclined to interpret the agreement against the interests of the side who drafted it.

Getting beyond your first impulses, however, you may conclude that you have very good reasons to volunteer to draft the settlement agreement in the first instance. The circumstances may be such that the choice of terms to be used in the agreement is critical, and your client would benefit from your preparing the first draft. For example, if you represent a publisher in the settlement of a scope of rights dispute with an author, you would probably opt to prepare the first draft of the contract so that you could use standard publishing industry terms to better aid later interpretation of the agreement. Another advantage of preparing the first draft is that you have the opportunity to create provisions in the agreement addressing issues that were not specifically addressed in the mediation or settlement negotiations.

When drafting the agreement, use commonsense writing techniques, as follows:

- Organize the document logically.
- Use simple and direct language.
- Provide a definitions section.

---

5.   See generally Roger S. Haydock, *Negotiation Practice* (John Wiley & Sons, 1984), 181–92.

- Use the same word to describe the same idea or concept throughout.
- Use short paragraphs with boldface topic headings.
- Use the active voice.
- Say what you mean.
- Be careful of possible dual interpretations.

As to the last item on the list, you should definitely *not* follow the example of a church fund-raiser who once wrote a letter to the late Chief Justice Charles Evans Hughes. With a twinkle in his eye, the Chief Justice would often show the letter, beautifully framed and in Spencerian script, to the many visitors to his study. The letter read: "In order to raise money for the church, our members are making aprons from the shirttails of famous men. We would be so pleased if you could send us one of your shirttails. Please have Mrs. Hughes mark them with your initials and also pin to them a short biography of the famous occasions in which they have been intimately associated with your life."[6]

Among the topics covered in the settlement agreement are those you normally include in any transactional contract:

- Description of the parties.
- Background and purpose of the agreement.
- Rights of the parties.
- Responsibilities of the parties.
- Terms of payment.
- Disposition of liens.
- Law to govern contracts.
- An ADR clause.
- Confidentiality.
- Severability clause.
- Releases.

When drafting the settlement agreement, you should keep in mind some basic rules about judicial construction and interpretation of contracts:

- A general release will void all future claims arising out of the dispute.
- Specific releases will void specified future claims but allow other unspecified (or specified) future claims.

---

6. Anecdote adapted from Braude, *Speaker's and Toastmaster's Handbook*, supra at 130.

- Courts will view the agreement as a whole, interpreting each part in light of the other parts.

- Courts favor interpretations that hold the agreement to be lawful.

- Courts favor interpretations that reflect the public interest.

- Courts interpret contracts most strongly against parties who draft them.

You should also consider whether the court needs to approve the settlement agreement. Settlement agreements involving minors and class action settlement agreements fall into this category. Whether or not the settlement occurs in a case in litigation, you and the other attorney may conclude that entry of a consent judgment would be more likely to insure the parties' compliance. If a case is not in litigation, a Complaint would have to be filed, together with the consent judgment. The consent judgment can be used to reassure third parties regarding the conclusiveness of the dispute, and it also facilitates enforceability.

6.3 ENFORCING THE SETTLEMENT AGREEMENT

As is evident to any experienced advocate, a mediated settlement agreement does not necessarily end the dispute. In one study, approximately 20 percent of the mediated disputes in a small claims court and 50 percent of the judgments experienced noncompliance.[7] Mediation tended to have a greater capacity than adjudication to achieve compliance with the settlement terms, in part because (1) mediators often encouraged defendants to make full or partial payment immediately after the settlement was reached; (2) they assisted disputants in setting up an explicit payment plan as part of their agreement; and, perhaps most important, (3) a disputant who participated in fashioning an agreement is more likely to comply with its terms than an individual who had a judgment imposed on him. Notwithstanding the higher rate of compliance in cases using mediation as opposed to adjudication, 20 percent noncompliance in mediated disputes means that you are apt to deal with enforcement issues in a significant number of settlements in which you are involved. The question then becomes, what, if anything, can be done to most efficiently enforce a mediated agreement when noncompliance becomes an issue?

The enforceability of a mediated agreement—that is, the degree to which courts apply coercion to secure compliance—is a complex issue. Some commentators view the application of pressure on a party to

---

7. C. McEwen and R. Maiman, "Small Claims Mediation in Maine: An Empirical Assessment," *Maine Law Review* 33 (1981): 262.

comply as antithetical to the nature and purpose of mediation, that being to encourage *voluntary* settlements. Others, however, take the view that a mediated agreement is no different than any other contract and should be fully enforceable to the extent of a particular jurisdiction's contract law.[8]

Like any other contract, then, the mediated agreement will generally not be enforced if any basic element of a contract is lacking or if any contract defenses, such as duress or unconscionability, are found to have validity.[9] In addition, because mediated agreements are typically agreements settling legal claims, they are subject to a number of contract doctrines applying to settlement agreements. In some states, for instance, agreements settling pending litigation are valid only if written. As a general rule, however, courts in doubt about the validity of a settlement agreement tend to uphold it to promote the public policy favoring voluntary resolution of disputed claims.

Your decision on how to enforce a mediated settlement agreement is important and should be made carefully. If you seek to enforce a settlement agreement and the court finds the agreement void for some reason, then you may be subjecting your client to the prospect of expensive litigation on the underlying dispute. Thus, in many situations, you should first consider securing compliance through the mediation process. If the parties are willing to return to the mediator who helped them reach a settlement initially, then that would seem to be the most reasonable course of action. If the parties are not willing, perhaps they should secure the services of another mediator.

If mediation is not a possible alternative, then you must resort to voluntary arbitration or to the court system. To make an informed prediction about whether a mediated agreement will be enforceable, you must examine your jurisdiction's contract law, rules pertaining to the validity of agreements deciding legal claims, rules of procedure and procedural provisions for settlement agreements, and any statutes affecting only mediated agreements.[10] Procedurally, in order to initiate the enforcement of a settlement agreement in court, you may, depending on the circumstances and the particular jurisdiction, file a motion in the instant action, file a separate action relating to the settlement agreement, or amend pleadings to include a claim or defense based on compromise.[11]

---

8. See generally Donner and Crowe, supra at sec. 22:21.
9. Rogers and Salem, supra at 156.
10. Id. at168.
11. Haydock, supra at 192–93.

Chapter Seven

DESCRIPTION OF THE HYBRID PROCESS

"To be master of any branch of knowledge,
you must master those which lie next to it."
— *Oliver Wendell Holmes*

Pure mediation or pure arbitration may not be the most appropriate alternative means for resolving some disputes. In these situations you need to exercise creativity in selecting or designing an appropriate hybrid process to satisfy your client's specific needs. Med-arb, discussed in section 1.1, is just one of many available hybrids. In binding mediation, which on its face seems to be an oxymoron, if mediation is unsuccessful, the mediator makes a binding decision at a figure within the mediated bracket. New hybrids seem to be emerging all the time. For example, if you are dissatisfied with the neutral-biasing potential of med-arb and binding mediation, you may be attracted to the clearer role distinctions for the neutral in arb-med. In that process, the parties first proceed to arbitration before an arbitrator who renders a binding decision. The decision is not shown to the parties; rather, the arbitrator places it in a sealed envelope. The parties can then negotiate a resolution on their own, or they can involve the arbitrator as a mediator to help mediate a resolution. The arbitrator's decision, having already been made, is not influenced by any confidential information of the parties. If the mediation or negotiations are unsuccessful, the parties open the sealed envelope and are bound by the award. Parties negotiating in the shadow of the sealed award tend to reach a joint decision for themselves rather than entrust their fate to an imposed solution of unknown value.

To choose the appropriate process for resolving your dispute or to have a basis for designing an appropriate process, you must have a clear understanding of the hybrid processes already in standard use. Some of the principal hybrid ADR processes are described below.

7.1 HIGH-LOW ARBITRATION

A form of arbitration that is becoming widely used in personal injury and other types of disputes is high-low arbitration, also called bracketed arbitration. It is commonly used where liability is not an issue, though that condition is not a prerequisite. In this process, the parties negotiate to impasse and then proceed to arbitration. Plaintiff's last settlement demand and defendant's last offer establish a bracket defining the limits of the arbitrator's award in the case. The arbitrator conducts the arbitration without knowledge of the endpoints of the bracket. The parties are free to make any evidence-based arguments they wish regarding damages, and if the arbitrator determines the defendant is liable, she makes a decision on damages as if it were ordinary arbitration. When the arbitrator renders an award, neither party will be liable for a figure outside the agreed-to bracket. For example, assume that in a particular case the plaintiff's last demand was $100,000 and the defendant's last offer was $50,000. The parties then proceed to an arbitration hearing at which the plaintiff argues entitlement to damages in the amount of $150,000 and the defendant argues that plaintiff is entitled to, at most, $25,000. If the arbitrator renders an award of $125,000, the defendant will pay no more than $100,000. If the arbitrator renders an award of $35,000, the plaintiff will receive $50,000. If the arbitrator renders an award of $75,000, the plaintiff will receive $75,000 because that figure falls within the bracket.

There are several advantages to high-low arbitration. First, it reduces the risk of allowing a third party to decide your fate. Going into the arbitration, both parties know the lower and upper limits on the award. Second, it encourages vigorous bargaining because the plaintiff wants to establish the highest minimum award possible and the defendant seeks to fix the lowest maximum award possible. This situation usually forces the parties to find a reasonable settlement range and, at the same time, a reasonably narrow bracket. If the bracket is too large, say, $25,000 and $1,000,000, when the parties proceed to arbitration, there is very little advantage of high-low arbitration over ordinary arbitration—unless, of course, one side or the other has thoroughly misjudged the value of the case. Finally, high-low arbitration is more economical than going to trial after an unsuccessful mediation. Typically, a skillful mediator helps the parties arrive at a reasonable settlement range, which can serve as the bracket in a subsequent high-low arbitration conducted by another neutral.

7.2 BASEBALL ARBITRATION

Baseball arbitration is a type of final-offer arbitration in which the disputing parties agree in writing to negotiate to only one position—their last and best offer—and then submit the dispute to arbitration. In baseball arbitration, the arbitrator must choose the final offer of one of the parties and may not find a different result in any circumstance.

This type of final-offer arbitration had its origin in player salary negotiations in major league baseball but now is an ADR method adaptable to practically any type of dispute involving a monetary solution. A quick decision is a valuable feature of the classic version of baseball arbitration. The arbitrator must pick one figure or the other and is encouraged to render his decision within twenty-four hours. The decision is binding, and there can be no compromise. Also, the arbitrator may give no explanation for the decision.

The rigidity of final-offer arbitration is its main selling point. It is its own deterrent. Labor experts believe that the risk involved in having your offer rejected and the other side's offer selected promotes good-faith bargaining, encourages a narrow negotiated settlement bracket, and in practice provides an incentive for parties to resolve differences without an arbitration hearing.

7.3 FACT-FINDING

Fact-finding is a dispute resolution process that provides more efficient, speedy, and sensitive resolution of claims. It is particularly helpful in resolving claims for which the traditional adversarial resolution process cannot meet all participants' needs, for example, sexual harassment claims.

In any fact-finding intervention, the court appoints a fact-finder or team of fact-finders to investigate the complaint and issue a written report of findings. Because fact-finders are generally used in cases involving sensitive issues, confidentiality is a paramount requirement. A fact-finder must be someone who is sensitive to others' concerns, a good judge of credibility using little information, able to keep absolute strict confidentiality, and a skillful interviewer. Whenever possible, fact-finders should have expertise in the field that they are investigating.

A fact-finder must also have unlimited access to relevant information, witnesses, and documentation. Parties who agree to the fact-finding process will gain little by not cooperating. The fact-finder must conduct interviews with the pertinent parties and any other persons who have relevant information. Where at all possible, this is done outside the presence of the parties' lawyers with the knowledge and permission of the parties and their lawyers.

The fact-finder's report states what the fact-finder believes happened and identifies any issues about which the fact-finder is unable to draw conclusions. Since the fact-finder is neutral and uninvolved, this report serves as a basis for resolving the conflict. The report does not reach any legal conclusions. For example, in a sexual harassment case, the report does not say whether sexual harassment has occurred.

Unless the parties have previously agreed, the report does not recommend remedies. It does, however, assess the credibility of all those interviewed.

The fact-finder's report is submitted to the court and to each party. The parties usually are given a reasonable time period to resolve the dispute on their own before the court takes its next step—which may be to commence the litigation process or to move on to a mediation or arbitration process. Generally it is not a good idea to have the fact-finder serve as either a mediator or arbitrator following the investigation. Depending on the specific circumstances and the agreement of the parties, the fact-finder's report may be provided to the mediator or arbitrator. At this stage the parties are usually represented by counsel.

In some sexual harassment claim situations, the court appoints two fact-finders, a man and a woman. This team approach allows the process to avoid the insensitivity of the usual adversary process to both the accuser and the accused in a sexual harassment claim. The more sensitive, specialized environment provided by fact-finding greatly increases the likelihood that the parties will reach mutually acceptable results on their own and avoid litigation that would be costly, both financially and emotionally, to all involved.

7.4   CO-MEDIATION

An ADR hybrid that has gained increased use over the past few years is co-mediation. Simply defined, co-mediation is a process in which more than one person serves as a mediator. It involves the concepts of team mediation and interdisciplinary problem solving, and it can be tailored to the needs of a particular dispute. Depending on the ethnic, cultural, gender, or age characteristics of the disputants, two or more mediators having characteristics matching those of the adverse parties may be able to facilitate rapport-building and communication more easily than a single mediator with whom the disputants have difficulty identifying. Multiple mediators are commonly used in complex disputes where there are multiple parties, sometimes on each side of the case, and an intricate configuration of claims, cross-claims, and counterclaims. Such complex cases routinely exist in the fields of construction, tort, and environmental law. In such situations, the mediators may be assigned specific functions, or they may be assigned to specific disputants or specific aspects of the dispute. One mediator is designated as the lead mediator. That person is the chief strategist, coordinating the mediation activities of the other mediators and serving as an advisor and clearinghouse of information for them.

The most widespread application of co-mediation is in the field of domestic law, particularly in divorce mediation. Divorce cases especially lend themselves to resolution by interdisciplinary problem solving. Usually the co-mediators in a divorce case are a lawyer and a nonlawyer, though in some situations two nonlawyers may share the mediator role. The nonlawyers are usually from disciplines other than law, for example, counseling, psychotherapy, financial or estate planning, or accounting. In a combined-neutral arrangement the lawyer usually serves as the process expert and the nonlawyer as the technical expert to help develop alternative solutions that could be part of a negotiated settlement.

7.5 SUMMARY JURY TRIAL

In 1980, Federal District Judge Thomas D. Lambros created the summary jury trial method of alternative dispute resolution as a case management option, because he found himself with a massive docket of toxic tort cases, primarily asbestos cases. Each of these cases had reached a point where the parties considered them unsettleable. In conceiving the summary jury trial, Judge Lambros had three objectives in mind. First, he wished to facilitate settlements by allowing parties who have failed to settle in traditional pretrial settlement conferencing the opportunity, at very low cost, to see the reactions of actual jurors to their case, within the courtroom environment. Second, he wished to give parties the opportunity to define their issues and learn how the presiding judge would rule on their arguments. Third, he sought to give parties the opportunity to debrief jurors following a proceeding, in order to give the lawyers and parties an idea of how a jury would react to and understand their arguments.

A summary jury trial is an actual nonbinding trial that can usually be completed in less than one day. It is designed to facilitate settlement. A party may entirely disregard the findings of the summary trial jury, but when cases that have been argued in summary proceedings go to full trial, it is quite likely that the full-trial jury will find in the same way.

To ensure that a trial with the potential to last for weeks can be completed in one day, the lawyers and the judge must work together to strip from the summary trial all unnecessary tasks. To accomplish this, the lawyers present all the evidence in a narrative fashion, based on affidavits and depositions gathered throughout discovery, which usually has already been completed. Evidentiary objections are not made at the summary trial, rather they are resolved at a comprehensive pre-summary trial conference.

At the final pre-summary trial conference, the judge rules on all pending motions and sets a date for the summary trial. Since no witnesses will be called, lengthy notice periods can be avoided, allowing a summary trial to commence within a week of the decision to have one. A few days prior to the summary trial, the judge normally directs each party to submit a short trial brief, arguing only the issues pertinent to the summary trial. These briefs also contain proposed jury instructions. The judge normally requires the parties to accompany their attorneys to the summary trial so they are able to see firsthand how a jury reacts to their arguments. The judge also sets time limits on counsel's presentations. Usually, each side is given roughly fifteen minutes for an opening statement, one hour for its case-in-chief, one-half hour to rebut, and the opportunity to carve out time in reserve for a closing statement, at the party's option.

This final pre-summary trial conference serves more than just the purpose of laying the ground rules for the hearing. It is an opportunity to provide momentum for the case to settle. Roughly one third of all summary jury cases settle between the final pre-summary trial conference and the summary trial. This happens for several reasons. Parties have had their first opportunity to see how the judge is likely to rule on motions in limine and evidentiary objections, and they begin to realize how the judge will probably rule on those motions in a full trial. For this reason, it is necessary for the judge to use all the same evidentiary standards at the summary trial that she would at a full trial and to try to rule in a similar way. Also, attorneys are made more aware of the risk of having their claims defeated, which makes settlement all the more attractive. And certainly it is true that a party who has lost a summary jury trial, whether he intended to go to full trial or not, has had his bargaining power diminished greatly.

It is vitally important that the summary jury trial mirror an actual trial. A jury is empaneled through a voir dire process, just as in a full trial. The major differences are that the jury in summary jury proceedings is usually six persons rather than ten or twelve and the judge conducts the voir dire. The judge may ask jurors to fill out profiles before the date of the summary trial. Furthermore, the judge must be careful to empanel a jury that would be just like a jury at a full trial in order for the litigants to gain the full effect of the summary trial jury's input. For this reason, the judge may allow each party's attorney two peremptory challenges. Once the jury is empaneled and sworn, the trial proceeds in much the same fashion as a full trial would, with the attorneys presenting evidence in narrative form. Some judges permit videotapes of expert witnesses and critical occurrence witnesses to be played. The attorneys may use any physical evidence, exhibits, or other devices that they would be permitted to use in a full trial. If the summary jury trial does not proceed in the same way a full trial would proceed, litigants will not have as much confidence in the jury's findings as they normally would and will have less incentive to settle.

Following the verdict, the jurors are debriefed by the judge and the lawyers, and sometimes by the litigants themselves. The debriefing is quite instructive, making the parties aware of the specific reasons supporting the jury's evaluation of the case.

Immediately following the debriefing, post-summary trial settlement conferencing begins. This conferencing may last for several weeks, as needed. If a reasonable period of time lapses without a settlement being reached, the court may set the case for full trial. A very large majority of cases that go through the summary jury trial process settle. But even in those that do not, the summary trial allows a streamlined full trial, usually shorter and usually with stronger arguments from both sides.

7.6 MINI-TRIAL

The mini-trial, as apparent from its name, is an abbreviated trial or hearing. This method of dispute resolution is a relatively new approach with two major advantages: first, mini-trials require much of the discovery process to be curtailed; and second, mini-trials involve high-level businesspersons early in the dispute resolution process. Because the discovery process is limited and because the hearing itself is in fact a miniature hearing, this method of dispute resolution can be dramatically less expensive than traditional litigation. However, compared to other methods of dispute resolution, the mini-trial is relatively more expensive.

The mini-trial method is best suited to large disputes and complex litigation such as cases involving breaches of complex contracts, particularly if there are intricate technical issues; patent cases; antitrust cases; major construction cases; and product liability cases. This is because the panel that will decide the case will include the business experts in the field—a high-level management executive of each party. The parties initiate a mini-trial by negotiating a mini-trial agreement.

Mini-trials are most successful when each party makes a genuine effort to limit discovery to only those documents and depositions that will be absolutely necessary to resolve the particular issue or issues at hand. The mini-trial agreement usually prohibits mass exchange of documents and limits the number and length of depositions. In some instances, depending on how much discovery has already taken place when the decision for a mini-trial is made, discovery may not be necessary at all. If the decision for a mini-trial is made early in the litigation process and discovery is necessary, the mini-trial agreement should always establish a discovery time limit. Sixty days seems to be standard. When possible, the agreement lists the deponents and fixes a time limit, perhaps two hours, for each deposition. If the mini-trial agreement does not appropriately limit discovery, the cost-saving purpose of the mini-trial may be defeated.

When discovery is complete, the parties to the mini-trial exchange brief position summaries, which include document and witness lists to be used at the hearing. The object of the summaries is to avoid surprise, in addition to advising the panel members of each party's position before the hearing. The number of witnesses and trial exhibits designated in the summaries is kept to a minimum. The parties make a concerted effort to keep as their objective the creation and use of a simplified process for the resolution of the dispute. Without such an effort, the mini-trial is ineffective.

The mini-trial agreement also specifies who will make up the panel for the mini-trial. This panel normally consists of three people: a business executive from each side and a third-party neutral. The third-party neutral is instrumental in insuring that the resolution process stays on course. For example, a party may be overinclusive when designating documents and witnesses in its summary. It is the responsibility of the third-party neutral to insure that only relevant witnesses and documents are listed and used. The neutral is usually an attorney with expertise in the dispute's subject matter.

The business executives appointed to the panel by the parties must have the full authority to negotiate a settlement. Without that power, the hearing may be for naught. Also, it is advisable that an executive deeply involved with the case not be designated as a panel member. No panel member should be asked to pass judgment on a superior or a person who reports directly to her in the ordinary course of the party's business. The panel members selected should also be provided with technical advisors from the respective companies if complex issues demand it. This will of course increase the cost of the hearing, but the advisors will provide the panel members with necessary assistance regarding difficult technical issues.

At the close of the hearing, negotiation commences. The success of the entire process rests on this period of negotiation. In order to insure its success, the mini-trial agreement sets up its parameters in a way most conducive to achieving settlement. The negotiation normally extends into several sessions. Ideally, the two business executives should be the only people present. The third-party neutral may be consulted for advice or clarification but should not be an active participant. This is a time for the parties to resolve their dispute. Normally the lawyers for the parties do not participate. In the event that negotiations break down completely, the mini-trial agreement normally provides for a mandatory period of time to elapse before the decision is made to resume the original litigation. A "cool-down" period often allows the parties an opportunity to rethink their reasons for entering mini-trial negotiations in the first place and often generates new settlement ideas.

Mini-trials result in settlements a high percentage of the time. They can quickly turn complex business disputes into mutual-gain settlements. As a result, the mini-trial stands as a highly effective tool for cost cutting, and it has substantial future potential for reducing the amount of complex business litigation burdening our court systems.

7.7 SIMULATED JURIES

Any party may employ a simulated or mock jury in order to evaluate a case for trial or settlement. Use of a simulated jury is very much like a "dress rehearsal." In most situations, it is a one-party endeavor. Its singular advantage as an ADR method is that the party employing it has complete control over the process. You may decide to use a mock jury simply to rehearse your case. Or you may use it to choose one of two or more case theory options.

The simulated jury experience allows you to observe how a panel of people, assembled purposefully to closely mirror potential jury makeup, will evaluate each aspect of a case. It is a useful tool in pointing out the weaknesses of the case, as well as the strengths. It may also be used to demonstrate for a client a reaction to certain trial strategies about which you and the client disagree. Watching the jury deliberate after hearing your presentation of the case, or of both sides of the case, can provide valuable insight into the hearts and minds of an average jury panel. The experience may convince you and your client to settle the case.

For these reasons, you must take great care to insure that a simulated jury mirrors, as closely as possible, an actual potential jury. If your client can afford it, you may hire a consulting firm to research and assemble a simulated jury. This is helpful, but expensive, and by no means a necessity. As an alternative, you or a paralegal can assemble a jury at minimal cost through telephone solicitation or posting with local employment agencies or college campuses.

Many attorneys assume that this process is too expensive. However, if used as a tool to facilitate settlement, the expense can be a cost saver, when considering the time and energy you avoid expending by achieving settlement prior to trial. If used as a tool to fine-tune a case during trial preparation, it may also provide long-term benefits in the form of a more favorable trial result.

7.8 SPECIAL MASTERS

Federal Rule of Civil Procedure 53 creates the special master. Special masters are judicial adjuncts created to provide judges specialized assistance in managing their dockets and facilitating settlement. In the past, special masters were viewed primarily as fact-finders with respect to discrete issues in complex cases. However, in recent years courts have begun to expand the role of the special master to include case management in preparation for trial, which can include overseeing certain aspects of the discovery process or overseeing the entire pretrial stage of the litigation. Special masters also have become more active as settlement facilitators, mediating the resolution of specified issues and conducting settlement conferences, particularly in complex cases.

Generally the intervention of a special master occurs pursuant to the agreement of the parties. However, the court may appoint a special master without such agreement. The goal in either case is usually cost reduction. Special masters may even choose to incorporate other forms of mediation or arbitration, such as early neutral evaluation or mini-trial. These forms of dispute resolution are particularly useful since they, as well as special master intervention, are well suited for cases involving technical subject matter with complex issues that could benefit from the experience of a seasoned intervenor. Usually the special master is an attorney of many years, with experience in litigation and settlement negotiation. Magistrates or retired judges are also commonly appointed to serve as special masters.

The new applications of the special master, those of case manager and mediator, are most intriguing. A judge may appoint a special master solely for the purpose of developing a case management plan expressly for settlement. Typically a judge selects a special master, directs the parties to attend a status hearing, and defines the special master's objectives in the presence of both parties and their counsel. The judge may set a deadline by which the special master must submit a plan that will include schedules of limited discovery for the purpose of settlement, not full trial, and a deposition schedule, also pared to include only what is needed for the purposes of settlement. The special master works with the parties to help them eliminate issues on which there is essential agreement. The schedules help streamline the process and keep the case moving toward settlement.

Once the special master has submitted the case management plan for settlement, depending on the desires of the parties or the orders of the court, the special master's duties may end, or he may continue in the capacity of mediator. Some judges and special masters believe that it is not appropriate to have the same person who developed the case management plan act as the settlement mediator. Some judges and masters prefer that the settlement special master ("settlement master") not have the authority to rule on discovery disputes. Each of these determinations must be made at the initial status conference with the parties, their counsel, and the first special master present. Other details may also need to be discussed there, such as whether or not ex parte communication will be allowed and how much the special master will communicate, and for what purpose, with the judge.

The settlement master hosts and conducts settlement conferences, mediating actual disputes between parties, or at least identifying them, and eliminating areas of essential agreement. Often the parties prefer to have ex parte meetings with the settlement master, although this is not generally done without each party's consent. Through such caucuses, the settlement master very often can shepherd the case to a successful settlement.

7.9 EARLY NEUTRAL EVALUATION

In 1985, the United States District Court for the Northern District of California began a judicial experiment in alternative dispute resolution that has now come to be known as early neutral evaluation. A committee had been set up to consider how the court could reduce the cost of litigation for the client. The committee determined that the greatest wasted expense was in the pretrial stage of litigation. Pretrial posturing by attorneys, vague pleading that did not allow the opposition to understand the claims against it, and poor pretrial communication, all were found to contribute to inflated expense.

The committee came up with the early neutral evaluation system as a response to these problems. In this type of ADR process, a neutral evaluator conducts a short, usually two-hour, case evaluation conference early in the litigation process. The evaluator is normally a highly respected private attorney chosen by the court. The evaluators have essentially no judicial power. They enter no binding orders.

The court usually requires the parties themselves to attend the evaluation conference with their counsel. At the evaluation conference each party presents its position within a fifteen- to thirty-minute time period. The evaluator then identifies areas of agreement or near agreement to allow trial counsel to limit the scope of the dispute. Stipulations are encouraged. The evaluator also makes an effort to discourage alternative arguments, arguments with multiple themes, or boilerplate arguments. This phase of the conference helps limit discovery to actual, rather than perceived, disputes. The evaluator has in mind at this stage of the conference that she will recommend a discovery plan, which will help keep the case moving toward settlement. This may save the court and both parties considerable time, energy, and money.

In the next phase of the evaluation conference, the evaluator assesses for each party the relative strengths and weaknesses of their case, and if possible their opponent's case. If at all possible, the evaluator attempts to predict within a certain range each party's chance for liability and the amount of damages. In doing this, the evaluator draws upon considerable trial and settlement experience, and of course to do this effectively, the evaluator must be credible and respected. The evaluator also comments on the likely cost of full discovery without settlement.

At this point the evaluator may offer to explore settlement possibilities with the parties, or if the parties wish, the process may end here. If the parties choose to explore further settlement talks, the evaluator relies on her experience to help the parties develop a plan to approach settlement. If the parties choose to explore settlement, the evaluator develops a discovery plan and shares it with the parties. The discovery plan is geared toward preparing the case to put it in the best possible posture for settlement. The evaluator may also suggest a motion plan or a deposition schedule. The evaluator must be consistent in her effort to separate information that would be necessary for settlement negotiations and that which may be necessary at full trial. Preparation for settlement, not trial, is the goal.

When early neutral evaluation works as intended, it helps parties to lower their litigation costs, to improve pretrial communication with their opponents, and to analyze their cases realistically while considering the input of a highly respected attorney in the field. Parties also avoid unnecessary discovery and normally increase their chances for early settlement.

7.10 EXPERT PANELS

A court may appoint a panel of experts to help them in any number of ways, but the most typical use of an expert panel is to instruct and educate a court on complex scientific evidence in order for the court to determine the admissibility of such evidence. More and more, however, parties are using expert panels to facilitate settlements. Generally a court issues an order that functions much like a prearbitration agreement, which defines each aspect that the panel of experts will be expected to cover. As an alternative, the parties may accomplish this by agreement.

Included in the order or agreement are the composition of the panel, or the selection method; the subject matter of the area of inquiry; any specific duties of the panel, such as conducting physical examination of evidence; time limits for accomplishing these duties; whether a report will be filed, and what is to be included in that report; how the panel members will function throughout the rest of the discovery process and trial; and how much the panel is to be compensated and by whom.

Courts can employ expert panels to manage and control discovery in cases where a judge may be wholly unqualified to do so. Scientific expert panels, therefore, can be most helpful in complex cases involving difficult scientific issues. These cases include asbestos litigation, pharmaceutical product liability cases, and tobacco industry litigation. Experts in these cases can help parties strip their cases of superfluous arguments, identify important issues of actual and significant disagreement, and guide parties in meaningful settlement negotiation. A judge may ask experts to serve as a conduit for either the parties or the judge to convey scientific issues to the court, or legal issues to the parties, respectively. A judge may accomplish this by frequent status meetings of the parties and the experts with the court.

When serving in a settlement mode, a court-appointed expert normally confers with both parties together and each party individually. This promotes candor and enables the expert or experts to freely discuss settlement in light of the party's overall case. The court-appointed experts also can consult with the judge outside the presence of the parties regarding the panel's investigation and findings. This process works most effectively when the judge appointing the experts for settlement purposes is not the judge who will be serving as the trial judge in the case. The experts typically have access to all relevant documents, deposition transcripts, and witnesses, including the parties' experts. Fully informed about the subject matter of the litigation, expert panels are able to conduct their own investigations, draw their own conclusions, and draft a report that will be used as a tool to facilitate settlement.

For this reason, the parties must agree on the expert or experts. The parties must be confident in the ability of these individuals and must respect their ability to draw intelligent conclusions from the information that they gather. The court must take great care to ensure that the experts have no ties to any party. Impartiality is vital. A court selects credible impartial experts by submitting a reasonably short list of ten to twenty experts to the parties. Each party has unlimited peremptory challenges to any potential panelist. The list then is pared down to only those experts who the parties believe are impartial and credible.

Experts must remove themselves from consideration for conflict of interest reasons.

The process of information gathering by the experts may take a few months to complete, but when considered in the light of litigation that has the potential to last five or ten years, the investment of a few months of earnest effort toward a mutually agreeable settlement may well be worth it. The expert panel's findings are provided to the court and to all parties. On the basis of this report, the parties begin settlement conferencing facilitated by the experts. By the time the settlement conferencing begins, the panel of experts may have already ascertained what each party would require in a mutually satisfactory settlement. The court, without conducting a settlement conference, may use the information and conclusions of the panel to fashion a settlement proposal on its own. It has knowledge of the parties' requirements for a settlement and may forgo further negotiations if it thinks a settlement can be accomplished solely on the basis of the work of the expert panel.

7.11 CO-MED-ARB

The ADR process called co-med-arb has emerged in recent years as an antidote to many of the ills which plague the process of med-arb, described in section 1.1 above. The basic concept of co-med-arb is to use two neutrals, one in the role of mediator and one as arbitrator, but to have them work as closely as possible together to maximize their efficiency while avoiding confusion of roles. Even though co-med-arb employs two neutrals, the design of the process seeks to avoid duplicative expenses by saving time needed to bring the arbitrator "up to speed" should the mediation prove unsuccessful.

The co-med-arb process works as follows. The parties select both the mediator and the arbitrator prior to the dispute or after the dispute arises. The two neutrals jointly tend to procedural matters such as conducting a pre-hearing conference, setting dates for meetings, and scheduling the filing of briefs. The mediator and arbitrator review all submitted documents prior to the hearing and at the initial session of the hearing, and sit as a panel to hear the parties' opening statements in what is called the open phase of the hearing. During this open phase, the arbitrator presides. Both the arbitrator and mediator may ask clarifying questions of counsel, but the mediator withholds asking "sensitive" questions regarding the parties' needs and interests until the second, or confidential, phase of the process. After the close of the open phase of the process, the rules preclude the mediator from discussing the substance of the dispute with the arbitrator, though the two neutrals may usually confer on procedural matters.

In the confidential phase, the mediator attempts to mediate the dispute to resolution. If the parties reach impasse, they proceed to the third phase of the process and present their evidence to the arbitrator. When this occurs, the mediator is usually "on call" in the event that the parties desire to resume mediation at one or more points during the arbitration. If the parties resume mediation, the mediator sets strict time limits on the mediation conference.

Although mediation efforts may not be successful initially in resolving the entire dispute, they can lead to a variety of possible beneficial results including streamlining the arbitration, achieving a stipulation of facts or agreed limitation of issues, and resolving several of the contested issues. The mediator may also be helpful after the conclusion of the arbitration hearing. If the parties desire, the arbitrator may withhold the award until after the parties have a limited-duration final session with the mediator to attempt to work out a mutually satisfactory settlement. If the mediation is successful, the parties agree that the award should not issue. If the mediation is unsuccessful, the arbitrator issues the award, and if the parties desire, they can request that the mediator conduct a post-award settlement conference.

Although the co-med-arb process is generally more expensive than pure mediation or pure arbitration, use of the process can prove to be a very wise investment. In complex, high-stakes disputes, the value of co-med-arb's collateral benefits may far outweigh its cost in dollars. Because of the continuous availability of mediation, there is opportunity for a settlement early in the co-med-arb process, or at any number of points during the process. Moreover, the process may avoid damaging continuing relationships that the parties need to maintain. In short, the two-neutral co-med-arb tandem process may allow disputants to extract the best of both the mediation and the arbitration processes while minimizing the disadvantages associated with using one or the other or with using their less-preferable sequenced amalgam, med-arb.

7.12 ARB-MED

In arb-med, a process free of the impediments of med-arb (see section 1.1) and binding mediation (see section 7.13), the parties first proceed to arbitration before an arbitrator who will render a binding decision. When the arbitrator reaches a decision and drafts the award, it is not shown to the parties. Rather the arbitrator places the award in a sealed envelope. Thereafter, the parties can negotiate a resolution on their own, or they can involve the arbitrator as a mediator to help mediate a resolution on their own, or they can involve the arbitrator as a mediator to help mediate a resolution. The arbitrator's decision, having already been made, will not be influenced by any confidential information of the parties. If the negotiations or mediation are unsuccessful, the parties open the sealed envelope, read the award and by preagreement, are bound by it. Parties negotiating in the shadow of the sealed award tend to reach a joint decision for themselves rather than to entrust their fate to an imposed solution of unknown value.

7.13 BINDING MEDIATION

Med-arb is often confused with a relative newcomer to the ADR process spectrum—"binding mediation." Insurance companies and plaintiffs' lawyers in search of finality in smaller-damage personal injury cases are turning to binding mediation routinely to avoid the disadvantages of arbitral or court adjudication—namely, the substantial delay and costs associated with discovery, trial preparation, trial, and possibly appeal. The concept of binding mediation is simple: if the parties and their counsel spend two hours in a mediation with an experienced mediator or former judge, why should the parties not have that neutral determine what the *fair settlement value* of the case is and preagree to be bound by that determination? Med-arb and binding mediation have distinctive and significant differences in their respective results. The result of a med-arb is an award—a *decision on the merits* of the parties' claims and defenses, based on evidence—which can be filed and enforced in a court of law. The result of a binding mediation is a neutral evaluation of the *fair settlement value* of a case—which may in fact have little relation to the *ultimate* merits of the case. Rather, fair settlement value is based on the risks of going forward to proof and the probabilities of success measured *at the present stage of the litigation*, sometimes without the benefit of expert evidence. This is definitely a process of speculation and "best guess" evaluation by a mediator, and the parties and counsel using it should be so informed. Binding mediation, which has no separate evidentiary phase, has been criticized for this "best guess" feature and for its susceptibility to being abused by unscrupulous counsel who exaggerate the strength of their potential evidence in caucuses. Neutrals who conduct binding mediations must be careful to detect such exaggerations and evaluate them accordingly. Counsel who participate in binding mediations must be careful to limit their risk of an unfair outcome by requiring the other side to preagree to a reasonable high-low bracket of which the mediator is unaware. This bracket safeguards each party to the binding mediation against the possibility of a "runaway" or biased evaluation. Alternatively, counsel may consider using other mediation hybrids, including arb-med and co-med-arb.

7.14 HYBRID ADR PROCESS SELECTION CHART

This section presents a tool to assist mediators, parties, and their counsel in designing the appropriate hybrid ADR process for a particular dispute. The chart takes into account the hybrid mediation, arbitration, and other processes discussed above in this chapter. The chart identifies special needs of a client or situation and simultaneously describes the hybrid process having features satisfying those special needs. An assumption underlying the use of this chart is that the general needs of the client are: (1) to accelerate resolution of the dispute as compared to the time required for resolution by traditional court adjudication, and (2) to lessen or minimize the costs of resolution.

HYBRID PROCESS	SPECIAL NEED(S) OF CLIENT OR SITUATION*	PROCESS FEATURE SATISFYING SPECIAL NEED(S) OF CLIENT OR SITUATION
HIGH-LOW ARBITRATION	• Desires binding result. • Wants to minimize risk of aberrant adverse binding award. • Does not want arbitrator(s) to be influenced by final negotiated offers and demands.	• Binding award. • Parties preagree to maximum/minimum award bracket. • Parties preagree not to disclose bracket to arbitrator(s).

BASEBALL ARBITRATION	• Wants to limit potential losses to a known tolerable level and to maximize potential gain. • Desires to maximize effectiveness of the negotiation process.	• Parties preagree to limit the arbitrator's function to choosing either the high or the low end of the parties' negotiated bracket. • Arbitrator's limited function influences parties to negotiate to a narrow bracket and cases often settle without need of arbitration.
MED-ARB **AND** **CO-MED-ARB**	• Wants to go through evidentiary hearing only if absolutely necessary. • Wants to preserve relationship with other side, if at all possible. • Desires to first attempt to find a creative solution. • Desires to use threat of arbitration to enhance opportunity for mediated result. • Desires finality. • Situation appropriate for use of two neutrals. • Wants to preserve option for mediated result throughout arbitration process.	• Evidentiary arbitration hearing conducted only if mediation unsuccessful. • Mediation can help heal and preserve relationships • Mediation can result in creative solutions. • Expense or inconvenience of arbitration can influence parties to work hard to settle case in mediation. • Arbitration yields a final, enforceable award if mediation is unsuccessful. • One neutral serves as mediator, the other, as arbitrator. • Dual neutrals preserve opportunity for settlement.

ARB-MED	• Does not want mediation process to taint evidentiary hearing in arbitration, • Wants an arbitrated result only as absolutely final alternative.	• Arbitration award withheld pending post-hearing mediation. • Arbitration award revealed only in instance where mediated result is not possible.
BINDING MEDIATION	• Does not want an evidentiary hearing (e.g., case not fully discovered; unfavorable evidence, etc.). • Wants to settle case without neutral's evaluation, if possible. • Desires neutral to evaluate case based on information disclosed in mediation. • Desires finality.	• Mediator attempts to settle dispute by facilitative caucusing; if unsuccessful, makes binding evaluation. • Mediator attempts to settle dispute, first. • Mediator gives opinion of case value if mediation is unsuccessful. • Binding case evaluation.
CO-MEDIATION	• Wants input of expert or person with special expertise or having ethnic, cultural, or gender characteristics matching those of parties. • Wants to facilitate rapport-building and communication.	• Mediator teams up with psychologist, technical expert, accountant, etc. • Mediation team relates to needs and interests of parties.

MINI-TRIAL	• Capitalize on executives' expertise in making effective business decisions.	• Corporate executives are on panel that hears the abbreviated case presentations.
	• Enhance opportunities for collaboration by executives.	• A disinterested neutral facilitates negotiation between executives after case presentations.
	• Executives need to see evidence on both or all sides.	• Presentations made to panel by the attorneys on both (or all) sides.
	• Executives need to separate themselves from dispute to get objective view of case.	• Objectivity is achieved by putting executives in a temporary "neutral" role.
	• Parties need to limit risk of adverse result.	• Process is non-binding.
SIMULATED JURIES	• Party needs private rehearsal to learn strengths and weaknesses of its strategies/tactics.	• Case is presented in an abbreviated manner to pre-selected jury.
	• Need for impartial evaluation by people closely mirroring potential jury	• Jurors deliberate and reach a verdict.
	• Party needs opportunity for feedback from one or more juries.	• Party and counsel debrief jurors.
	• Party needs to determine whether case should be settled.	• Jurors' verdict(s) and comments often lead to decision to settle.

SPECIAL MASTER	• Need for individualized case management.	• Court-appointed attorney or former judge can provide individualized case management and serve the other needs described in the adjacent column.
	• Need for overseeing certain aspects of discovery process.	
	• Need for issue framing, issue shaping, issue reduction.	
	• Need for specialized settlement skills or experience.	
	• Need for neutral to help parties and counsel design a case-appropriate dispute resolution process or case-management plan.	
	• Court needs neutral to read pleadings, hear evidence and oral argument, and report and recommend an appropriate disposition.	

EARLY NEUTRAL EVALUATION	• Need to minimize pretrial posturing by attorneys early in the life of the case. • Need to clarify vague pleadings. • Need to improve pretrial communication among counsel. • Need for early evaluation of strengths and weaknesses of claims and defenses. • Need to limit case to actual rather than merely perceived disputes.	• Highly respected, court-appointed panel attorney conducts evaluation conference early in case, minimizes pretrial posturing, and serves the other needs described in the adjacent column.
FACT-FINDING	• Facts needed before decision made on approach to resolution. • High degree of confidentiality required. • Sensitivity to parties' feelings/reputation is paramount.	• Fact-finder or team appointed to investigate and issue report. • Fact-finder/team maintains strict confidentiality. • Fact-finder is sensitive to others' concerns and is skillful interviewer.
EXPERT PANELS	• Judge or private neutral needs to be educated on one or more areas of complex scientific evidence. • Scientific specialist needed to manage or control discovery. • Parties need to explore settlement options in technically complex case.	• Experts can examine complex information and translate it into simple-to-understand concepts. • Technical experts are able to communicate on counsel's and parties' level. • Experts' report can be used as a tool by parties to settle case.

SUMMARY JURY TRIAL	• Need to see jury reaction to facts in an accelerated judicial proceeding in a courtroom environment.	• Six jurors selected by profiles; brief videotapes of expert and critical witness testimony.
	• Need to define critical legal issues and to learn how judge would rule on them.	• Comprehensive pretrial conference; evidentiary objections and jury instructions ruled on by judge.
	• Need to know why jury ruled a certain way.	• Through jury debriefing, parties learn specific reasons for jury's evaluation of case.

Chapter Eight

EFFECTIVE ADVOCACY IN CYBERMEDIATION

An invasion of armies can be resisted,
but not an idea whose time has come.
— Victor Hugo

Not since the invention of the printing press has there been such great progress in the technology of communication as the development of the Internet.[1] In less than a decade, the Internet rapidly developed from a simple network of government, military, and research computer networks to a global medium for the instantaneous exchange of ideas and information. Today, the Internet renders anyone with a computer and a connecting device the ability to communicate with and transfer documents to anyone else globally who is similarly equipped. It has been said that this Electronic Revolution, or "E-Revolution," may have an even greater impact on the world of commerce than the Industrial Revolution.[2]

It most definitely has had a faster impact. The time it took for other new technologies to be used by at least fifty million people in the twentieth century much exceeded the time the public has needed to adapt to the Internet. For example, radio required a thirty-eight-year user-acclimation period; television, thirteen years; and cable television, ten years. In contrast, it has been estimated that in the first five years of commercial Internet use, 200 million people connected to the Internet in more than 100 countries worldwide. The U.S. Commerce Department has estimated by the year 2005, there will be more than one billion commercial users worldwide, generating more than $3.2 trillion in revenue. Indeed, the growth of Internet use is unparalleled by the usage of

---

1.   Frank A. Cona, "Focus on Cyberlaw: Application of Online Systems in Alternative Dispute Resolution," 45 *Buffalo L. Rev.* 975 (1997).

2.   John W. Cooley, "New Challenges for Consumers and Businesses in the Cyber Frontier: E-Contracts, E-Torts, and E-Dispute Resolution," 13 *Loyola Consumer L. Rev.* 102 (2001); see generally Robert Hammesfahr (Ed.), *@ Risk: Internet and E-Commerce Insurance and Reinsurance Legal Issues* (Reactions Publishing Group, Ltd., London, 2000).

any other communication technology or commercial innovation in recorded history.

What does all of this mean for the twenty-first century advocate who wants to represent clients effectively not only in traditional business and personal transactions and dispute settings but also in new Internet-created cyberspace settings? It means, quite simply, that advocates have to quickly learn and adapt to new methods of communication and related technology so that they can best represent their clients in a dynamic and ever-expanding world of high-velocity information exchange, resulting in both durable deals and derisive disputes. The enormous quantity of personal interactions and commercial transactions occurring on the Internet is bound, unquestionably, to generate millions of disagreements over time and much thinking, on lawyers' parts, about how to resolve the resulting disagreements efficiently. Advocates may have to discard some traditional legal concepts and old ways of doing things in favor of more cyber-apropos methods. Newer and faster ways of conducting commerce via the Internet will continue to present a wide variety of risks and exposures for companies and consumers alike. Advocates and their clients will need to focus on some of the new legal issues that are certain to arise in electronic contract (e-contract) and electronic tort (e-tort) disputes. They will also need to consider new ways of incorporating the use of the Internet in resolving disputes which arise both in "real world" traditional ways and in cyberspace itself.[3] It is predictable that advocates, more and more, will be representing clients involved in disputes, commercial and otherwise, of an international character.[4] In doing so, advocates will need to become proficient in Electronic Dispute Resolution, which includes cyberarbitration (e-arbitration) and cybermediation (e-mediation). Dr. Petronio R. G. Muniz, President of Instituto Arbiter (arbiter@uol.com.br) in Recife, Brazil and a highly respected trailblazing leader of the ADR movement in South America, has said, "the same way e-commerce is the road ahead for conventional trade, e-arbitration and e-mediation are the beacons for solving disputes in the twenty-first century." It is the purpose of this chapter to prepare you to represent clients effectively in one of these twenty-first century "beacons for solving disputes"—the process of cybermediation.

---

3. See generally, Ethan Katsh and Janet Rifkin, *Online Dispute Resolution* (Jossey-Bass, 2001); Ethan Katsh, "Online Dispute Resolution: Some Lessons from the E-Commerce Revolution," 28 *N. Ky. L. Rev.* 810 (2001).
4. See generally, Robert C. Bordone, *Electronic Dispute Resolution: A Systems Approach—Potential, Problems, and a Proposal,* 3 *Harv. Negotiation L. Rev.* 175 (1998); Alan Wiener, *Regulations and Standards for Online Dispute Resolution: A Primer for Policymakers and Stakeholders (Part 1)* (Feb. 15, 2001), (http://www.mediate.com/articles/awiener2.cfm).

8.1 BASIC DEFINITIONS

Vocabulary is a basic ingredient in effective communication and learning. If you are not entirely convinced of that statement, consider these excerpts from actual news stories appearing in various newspapers around the United States and in Canada:[5]

> "... and now it seems that our legislature is going to fail to utilize the greatest opportunity in Arkansas history to attract people from the entire nation to visit and admire our beautiful scenery and inimical hospitality."
> *—Arkansas newspaper*

> "Correction: Our paper carried the notice last week that Mr. John Doe is a defective in the police force. This was a typographical error. Mr. Doe is really a detective in the police farce."
> *—Annapolis Log*

> "The spacious home of Judge and Mrs. Woodbury was the scene of a beautiful wedding last evening when their youngest daughter, Dorothy, was joined in holy deadlock to Mr. Wilkie."
> *—Nebraska newspaper*

> "Appointment of a master of chicanery probably will be made today by Judge K—."
> *—Corpus Christi Texas newspaper*

> "W. M. McG— lost a finger when a poisoned dog to which he was administering an anecdote bit him."
> *— El Paso newspaper*

> "[P]etty thieving ... is ... an enormous atrocity, leaving our village in a stigma. The unanswerable michery of this year alone is nefandous. These inveterate, incongruous persons with a malignant disposition, whoever they are, should immediately be dealt with by the law."
> *— Wawansa, Manitoba newspaper*

Funny? Certainly. But as advocates representing someone else's interests in a new forum for dispute resolution—cyberspace—you cannot

---

5.   These excerpts may be found in Lewis and Faye Copeland (Eds.), *10,000 Jokes, Toasts and Stories* (Doubleday, 1965), 823–25.

afford to misuse vocabulary as in the above examples. You must know the commonly accepted meaning of new terms and how to use the terms appropriately. Once you know and understand the vocabulary of cybermediation, you will feel much more comfortable engaging in this new dispute resolution process. Appropriate word selection and word usage are especially important first steps in your development of new cyberadvocacy skills. The purposes of including definitions of Internet terms here are to shorten your learning curve and to decrease your anxiety about representing clients in cybermediation.[6] The definitions presented here are not in alphabetical order, but rather are listed in an order that promotes and facilitates understanding of terms, beginning, where possible, with the broadest definitions and continuing with related or included definitions of terms.

8.1.1 Cyberspace

Cyberspace is a metaphor used to describe the non-physical, virtual terrain created by computer systems. The prefix "cyber" means anything related to computers or to the Internet. Like physical space, cyberspace contains objects (files, mail messages, graphics, etc.) and different modes of transportation and delivery. Unlike real space, exploring cyberspace does not require any physical movement other than pressing keys on a keyboard or moving a computer mouse. The following definitions are general terms related to cyberspace.

Internet. An enormous and rapidly growing system of linked computer networks, connecting millions of computers worldwide, that facilitates data communication services such as remote login, file transfer, electronic mail (e-mail), the World Wide Web, and newsgroups. Using TCP/IP, also called the Internet protocol suite, the Internet assigns every online computer a unique Internet address, also called an IP address, so that any two connected computers can locate each other on the network and exchange data. "Online" means connected to a network or, more commonly, the Internet. "Protocol" is a standard in data communications and networking that specifies the format of data as well as the rules to be followed.

World Wide Web. A global hypertext system or "Web" that uses the Internet as its transport mechanism. Communication between Web clients (browsers) and Web servers is defined by the hypertext transport protocol (HTTP). In a hypertext system, users navigate by clicking a hyperlink embedded in the current document; this action displays a second document in the same or a separate browser window. Web

---

6. The definitions contained in this section are, in part, adapted from Bryan Pfaffenberger, *Webster's New World Computer Dictionary* (9th ed.) (Hungry Minds, Inc. 2001) and Philip E. Margolis, *Random House Webster's Computer & Internet Dictionary* (3d ed.) (Random House, 2000).

documents are created using HTML, a declarative markup language. Incorporating hypermedia (graphics, sounds, animations, and video), the Web has become the ideal medium for publishing information on the Internet and serves as a platform for the emerging electronic economy.

Domain. In a computer network, a group of computers that are administered as a unit. On the Internet, this term refers to all the computers that are collectively addressable within one of the four parts of an Internet protocol (IP) address. For example, the first part of an IP address specifies the number of a computer network. All the computers within this network are part of the same domain.

Domain name. In the system of domain names used to identify individual Internet computers, a single word or abbreviation that makes up part of a computer's unique name. Consider this unique, fictitious name: cool.law.nwu.edu. "Cool" is a specific computer in the "law" school at Northwestern University (nwu). At the end of the series of domain names is the top-level domain (here, edu), which includes hundreds of colleges and universities throughout the United States.

Domain name system (DNS). In the Internet, the conceptual system, standards, and names that make up the hierarchical organization of the Internet into named domains.

IP. Abbreviation for Internet protocol. It is the standard that describes how an Internet-connected computer should break data down into packets for transmission across the network, and how those packets should be addressed so that they arrive at their destination. IP is the connectionless part of the TCP/IP protocols. The transmission control protocol (TCP) specifies how two Internet computers can establish a reliable data link.

URI. Abbreviation for uniform resource identifier. In the hypertext transfer protocol (HTTP), a string of characters that identifies and Internet resource, including the type of resource and its location. There are two types of URIs: uniform resource locators (URLs) and relative URLs (RELURLs).

URL. An acronym for uniform resource locator. On the World Wide Web, it is one of two basic kinds of URIs. It is the string of characters that precisely identifies an Internet resource's type and location. For example, consider the following fictitious URL:

http://www.wildcats.northwestern.edu/toros/refs/parking.html

This URL identifies a World Wide Web document (http://), indicates the domain name of the computer on which it is stored (www.wildcats.northwestern.edu), fully describes the document's location within the directory structure (toros/refs), and includes the document's name and extension (parking.html).

RELURL. One of two basic kinds of uniform resource identifiers (URIs). It is a string of characters that gives a resource's file name (such as parking.html) but does not specify its type or exact location.

Hot link. A method of copying information from one document (the source document) to another (the destination document) so that the destination document's information is updated automatically when the source document's information changes.

Cold link. A method of copying information from one document (the source document) to another (the target document) so that a link is created. Cold links are distinguished from hot links in that cold links are not automatically updated; one must update them manually with a command that opens the source document, reads the information, and recopies the information if it has changed.

Hyperlink. In a hypertext system, an underlined or otherwise emphasized word or phrase that displays another document when clicked with the mouse.

Hypertext. A method of preparing and publishing text, ideally suited to the computer, in which readers can choose their own paths through the material. In preparing hypertext, information is first "chunked" into small, manageable units, such as single pages of text. These units are called nodes. Then the hyperlinks (also called anchors) are embedded in the text. When a reader clicks on a hyperlink, the hypertext software displays a different node. The process of navigating among the nodes linked in this way is called browsing. A collection of nodes that are interconnected by hyperlinks is called a web.

HTML. Acronym for hypertext markup language. It is a markup language for identifying the portions of a document (called elements) so that, when accessed by a program called a Web browser, each portion appears with a distinctive format. The agency responsible for standardizing HTML is the World Wide Web Consortium (W3C).

HTTP. The Internet standard that supports the exchange of information on the World Wide Web. HTTP enables Web authors to embed hyperlinks in Web documents. HTTP defines the process by which a Web client, called a browser, originates a request for information and sends it to a Web server, a program designed to respond to HTTP requests and provide the desired information.

Web site. A site (location) on the World Wide Web. Each Web site contains a home page, which is the first document users see when they enter the site. The site might also contain additional documents and files. Each site is owned and managed by an individual, company, or organization.

Web browser. A software application used to locate and display Web pages. Most modern browsers can present multimedia information, including sound and video.

Web server. A computer that delivers (serves up) Web pages. Every Web server has an IP address and possibly a domain name. For example, if you enter the URL *http://www.advocacy.com/index.html* this sends a request to the server whose domain name is *advocacy.com*. The server then fetches the page named *index.html* and sends it to your browser. Any computer can be turned into a Web server by installing server software and connecting the machine to the Internet.

Web master. An individual who manages a Web site. Depending on the size of the site, the Web master might be responsible for any of the following: (1) making sure that the Web server hardware and software are running properly, (2) designing the Web site, (3) creating and updating Web pages, (4) replying to user feedback, (5) creating CGI scripts, and (6) monitoring traffic through the site.

8.1.2 Electronic Dispute Resolution (EDR)

Electronic dispute resolution (EDR) is an umbrella term encompassing all forms of electronic-based methods of dispute resolution (e.g., cybermediation, cyberarbitration) and their related electronic support and information-delivery technology such as telephone conferencing and voice mail, the Internet, videoconferencing technology, fax machines, and fax software. EDR should not be confused with e-dispute resolution. An "e-dispute" means a dispute arising out of online business transactions or online usage. Typical e-disputes stem from electronic contracts (e-contracts) in electronic commerce (e-commerce), or they are based on electronic torts (e-torts) which result in harm to a person or property in connection with Internet use.[7]

8.1.3 Videoconferencing

Videoconferencing means conducting a conference between two or more participants at different sites by using computer networks to transmit audio and video data. For example, a point-to-point (two person) video conferencing system works much like a video telephone. Each participant has a video camera, microphone, and speakers mounted on his or her computer. As the two participants speak to each other, their voices are carried over the network and delivered to the other's speakers, and whatever images appear in front of the video camera appear in a window on the other participant's monitor. Multipoint videoconferencing allows three or more participants to sit in a virtual

---

7. John W. Cooley, "New Challenges for Consumers and Businesses in the Cyber-Frontier: E-Contracts, E-Torts, and E-Dispute Resolution," 13 *Loyola Consumer Law Review* 102 (2001).

conference room and communicate as if they were sitting right next to one another.

8.1.4   Telephonic Dispute Resolution (TDR)

Telephone Dispute Resolution (TDR) is a term that encompasses telephone-based methods of dispute resolution, including telephone negotiation, telephone mediation, telephone arbitration, or telephone depositions. TDR can be used in conjunction with face-to-face and on-line dispute resolution processes.

8.1.5   EDR information acquisition and delivery technology

The definitions in this subsection provide meanings for electronic dispute resolution information acquisition and delivery technology. These are also called EDR "tools."

Fax machine. Abbreviation of facsimile machine, a fax machine is an electronic device that can send or receive text and pictures over a telephone line. It consists of an optical scanner for digitizing (dividing into a grid of dots) images on paper, a printer for printing incoming fax messages, and a telephone for making the connection. A related device is the fax modem. That device you can attach to a personal computer in order for you to transmit and receive electronic documents as faxes. Documents sent through a fax modem must already be in an electronic form . Documents you receive are stored in files on your disk or received as hard copy on a fax machine. To create fax documents from images on paper, you need an optical scanner.

Voice mail. A communications system in which telephone voice messages are transformed into digital form and are stored in a network. When the person to whom the message is directed logs on to the system and discovers that a message is waiting, the system plays the message. Voice mail also refers to e-mail systems that support audio. Users can leave spoken messages for one another and listen to the messages by executing the appropriate command in the e-mail system.

E-mail. Short for electronic mail, it refers to the transmission of messages over communication networks. The messages can be notes entered from the keyboard or electronic files stored on disk. Most e-mail systems include a rudimentary text editor for composing messages, but many allow you to edit your messages using any editor you want. You then send the message to the recipient by specifying the recipient's e-mail address. You can also send the same message to several users at once. This is called broadcasting. Sent messages are stored in electronic mailboxes until the recipient accesses and displays them. Many systems visually and audibly alert the recipient when mail is received. After reading your mail, you can store it in a text file, forward it to others, or delete it. Copies of memos and attachments can be printed out on a printer if you want a hard copy. Emerging standards are making it possible for users of all types of different e-mail systems to exchange messages.

WebTV. A general term for a whole category of products and technologies that enable one to surf the Web on your TV. Most WebTV products today consist of a small box that connects to a telephone line and a television. It makes a connection to the Internet via one's telephone service and then converts the downloaded Web pages to a format that can be displayed on the TV. These products also come with a remote control device so that one can navigate through the Web. In the future, WebTV products will not require telephone connections, but will instead access the Internet directly through the cable TV lines.

Chat room. Chat is real-time online communication between two or more computer users. Once an online chat has been initiated, either user can enter text in the conversation by typing on the keyboard and the entered text will appear on the other user's monitor. A chat room is a virtual space where a chat session takes place. Technically, a chat room is really a channel, but the term "room" is used to promote the chat metaphor. Web sites can be equipped with a chat room feature.

Threaded discussions. In online discussions, a thread is a series of messages that have been posted as replies to one another. A single forum or conference may contain a single topic or it may consist of many threads covering different subjects. Replies to messages are normally nested directly under the related message instead of messages being arranged in some other order, such as chronological or alphabetical order. Web sites can be equipped with a threaded discussion feature.

Instant messaging. A type of online service that enables you to create a private chat room with another individual. Typically, the instant messaging system alerts you whenever somebody on your private list is online. You can then initiate a chat session with that individual.

8.1.6 Online Dispute Resolution (ODR)

Online dispute resolution (ODR), also referred to as cyber/dispute resolution and electronic alternative dispute resolution and by their more aesthetic acronyms (C/DR) and eADR respectively,[8] encompasses processes for resolving disputes predominantly by online means. The term includes both disputes that arise off-line—in the real world—but are handled online and those disputes that arise in cyberspace (e.g., in

---

8. *See* T. Schultz, G. Kaufmann-Kohler, D. Langer, V. Bonnet, *Online Dispute Resolution: The State of the Art and the Issues,* E-Com Research Project of the University of Geneva, Geneva, 2001, http://www.online-adr.org, 3.

electronic commerce).[9] It includes recognized forms of ADR such as arbitration, mediation, and negotiation, which, in a cyberspace context are called cyberarbitration, cybermediation, and cybernegotiation. These cyberprocesses are also referred to respectively as e-arbitration, e-mediation, and e-negotiation. Cybernegotiation consists of two types: automated negotiation and assisted negotiation. Offline dispute resolution refers to traditional face-to-face negotiation, mediation, and arbitration.

8.1.7   Cyberarbitration

Arbitration that is conducted predominantly in cyberspace is referred to as cyberarbitration.

- **Cyberarbitrator.** A cyberarbitrator who is experienced and/or trained in conducting cyberarbitration.
- **Cyberparty.** A disputant in an ODR process, including cyberarbitration.
- **Cyberadvocate.** A lawyer who represents a cyberparty in an ODR process, including cyberarbitration.

8.1.8   Cybermediation

Mediation that is conducted predominantly in cyberspace is referred to as cybermediation.

- **Cybermediator.** A mediator who is experienced and/or trained in conducting cybermediation.
- **Cyberparty.** A disputant in a an ODR process, including cybermediation.
- **Cyberadvocate.** A lawyer who represents a cyberparty in an ODR process, including cybermediation.

8.1.9   Cybernegotiation

Negotiation that is conducted predominantly in cyberspace is referred to as cybernegotiation. There are two types of cybernegotiation: automated negotiation and assisted negotiation.

- **Cybernegotiator.** A person who negotiates in cyberspace.
- **Cyberparty.** A disputant in an ODR process, including cybernegotiation.

---

9.   See generally Louise Ellen Teitz, "Symposium: Providing Legal Services for the Middle Class in Cyberspace: The Promise and Challenge of On-line Dispute Resolution," 70 *Fordham L. Rev.* 985, 991 (2001).

- **Cyberadvocate.** A lawyer who represents a cyberparty in an ODR process, including cybernegotiation.

- **Automated negotiation.** Negotiation (bidding) by means of high-automation programs. These are programs that basically consist of software that match demand/settlement responses without human intervention.[10]

- **Assisted negotiation.** This process should not be confused with cybermediation. Assisted negotiation is a C/DR process in which the ODR organization provides only a secure site and possibly a storage means and other features, such as a threaded message board. No actual negotiation service (neutral third party assistance) is provided. In this process, the parties have to reach an agreement without any external entity having the capacity to decide for them, not even a computer, as in automated negotiation.[11]

8.1.10 Internet regulatory organizations and related terms[12]

ICANN. Abbreviation for Internet Corporation for Assigned Names and Numbers. It is a private, California-based, non-profit corporation managing Internet domain names and Internet protocol (IP) addresses. It administers a dispute resolution system for resolving domain name disputes.

UDRP. Abbreviation for uniform dispute resolution policy. This policy establishes a procedure for the online resolution of disputes that concern domain names. This policy has been established by ICANN. The UDRP is a non-national authority for the resolution of domain name disputes. Its purpose is to avoid the competition and conflicts that arise from a variety of national courts and rules. The UDRP is intended to be applied only to very flagrant types of cybersquatting. The four institutions designated by ICANN to resolve domain name disputes are: WIPO, eResolution, the National Arbitration Forum, and the CPR Institute for Dispute Resolution.

ICC. Abbreviation for the International Chamber of Commerce. This organization advocates for minimal government regulation of e-commerce and asserts that self-regulation by the industry is the most effective way to build confidence in e-commerce.

GBDe. Abbreviation for Global Business Dialogue on Electronic Commerce. This initiative involves seventy-two companies around the world. Its objective is to endeavor to make e-commerce reach its full

---

10. Schultz, Kaufmann-Kohler, Langer, Bonnet, supra at 4–5.
11. Id. at 5–6.
12. Adapted, in part, from id. at 84–86.

economic and social potential. It makes recommendations on ADR to Internet merchants, to ADR service providers, and to governments.

E-Commerce Group. Abbreviation for Electronic Commerce and Consumer Protection Group. It is a coalition of large companies that are involved in business-to-consumer e-commerce. The group seeks to foster consumer confidence and consumer protection by creating industry best practices and a predictable legal framework. It further promotes fair, timely, and affordable means to settle disputes and obtain redress concerning online transactions, and it encourages merchants to provide in-house procedures to resolve complaints and to provide third party dispute resolution programs, including online dispute resolution processes.

EuroCommerce. This is a lobby group that acts as the trade representation to the European Union institutions. It has published a European code of conduct for online commercial relations. It encourages online merchants to provide an in-house procedure for handling complaints.

FEDMA. Abbreviation for Federation of European Direct Marketing. It has twelve partners in national direct marketing associations in the European Union and all those of Switzerland, Hungary, Poland and the Czech and Slovak Republics. It has published a Code on e-commerce and interactive marketing.

DSA. Abbreviation for the Direct Selling Association. This is a national trade association in the United States that represents companies that market products through personal explanation and demonstration. It has established guidelines for Internet use and a code of ethics for its members. Through its educational arm, the Direct Selling Education Foundation (DSEF), it conducts international seminars and other training on online transactions and dispute resolution.

8.2   TYPES OF ALTERNATIVE ODR SERVICES— GENERAL

Dispute resolution organizations are increasingly providing mediation, arbitration, and other innovative dispute resolution services over the Internet.[13] The purpose of this section is to make you aware of the variety of types of ODR services available. A more detailed description of ODR service providers and their respective service offerings appears in section 8.6.1. A listing of online dispute resolution service providers and their Web site addresses appears in appendix L.

---

13. See generally, Alan Wiener, *Opportunities and Initiatives in Online Dispute Resolution*, SPIDR News, Vol. 24, No. 3, page 17 (Summer 2000).

8.2.1 Examples of primary ODR services

Cybermediation. Both online and traditional dispute resolution service providers (e.g., onlineresolution.com) are increasingly offering online mediation services, also called cybermediation. This form of ODR and others described in this section have come to fruition, in significant part, through the combined supportive efforts of ODR pioneers John Helie, Jim Melamed, and Colin Rule. In the pure form of cybermediation, one party initiates the process by completing a confidential form on the service provider's Internet site. The form requires a party to identify the disputants, the nature of the dispute, and the desired outcome. The service provider then contacts the other named parties, advises them of the submission, explains the online mediation process, and invites their participation. If the parties desire to participate, they typically sign an agreement to abide by the online mediation ground rules, protocols, and procedures. The parties then mutually agree to use a cybermediator from a list provided by the service provider. The selected cybermediator then conducts e-mail communication with the parties, jointly or in caucuses as appropriate, and attempts to facilitate a mutually agreeable solution. If an agreement is reached, it is commonly reduced to writing.

Another type of cybermediation (e.g., the Online Ombuds Office) has a conference room where, using technology like Internet relay chat (IRC) and chat rooms, the cyberneutral can meet with all the parties simultaneously or can put each party in a separate room and shuttle back and forth.[14]

Cyberarbitration. Several dispute resolution organizations (e.g., WEBdispute.com) currently offer online arbitration services, also called cyberarbitration. Some service providers limit their services to particular types of disputes (e.g., e-Resolution—Internet domain name disputes). Typically, parties complete and submit online an agreement to cyberarbitrate. The service provider then issues a schedule for stating and answering positions on various disputed issues. When that part of the process is completed, the provider schedules a five-day e-mail hearing. The parties select the arbitrator and he or she opens the hearing. Each party presents his or her case online. The cyberarbitrator may pose questions online to the parties as the hearing progresses. On the last day of the hearing, the parties submit final arguments to the cyberarbitrator by e-mail. The cyberarbitrator then closes the Hearing, reviews and considers the evidence, and renders a decision by U.S. mail within twenty days.

---

14. See generally M. Ethan Katsh, "Dispute Resolution in Cyberspace," 28 *Conn. L. Rev.* 953, 966–72 (1996).

Cybernegotiation: blind bidding. Also called "automated nego-tiation" and "blind negotiation," this widely offered service has proven to be a popular online method of resolving monetary disputes. At least one company (SettleSmart) permits blind negotiation of non-monetary settlement terms also. In this process, parties confidentially submit, normally by e-mail, monetary offers and demands in "rounds" to the service provider. If the offer and demand of negotiating parties match or fall within a defined range or overlap, the parties, by preagreement, set-tle the case for the matching amount, the average of the offer or demand if within a defined range, or for the demand in the event of an overlap. In most systems, parties can keep the negotiation open and confidentially e-mail their respective offers and demands at will. This allows parties to continue to engage in blind negotiation over a period of time, even as discovery ensues. If there is a settlement, the service provider immedi-ately notifies the parties by e-mail.

Cybernegotiation: private online forum. Some dispute resolu-tion service providers (e.g., SquareTrade) offer an online forum permit-ting buyers and sellers to resolve disagreements involving online purchases. Claimants can initiate a case by completing a form online describing what occurred and what relief they want. The service pro-vider then e-mails notice of the complaint to the other party and pro-vides an opportunity to respond. When there is a response, the service provider posts the complaint and response on a secure Web page and the parties are permitted, for as long as they desire, to exchange informa-tion about the disputed matter. If the matter is not resolved through this Web page discussion, the complainant may request the service pro-vider to assign a mediator to help resolve the parties' differences.

Cybernegotiation: online forum with public assessment option. At least one organization (e.g., iLevel) permits its members to submit complaints against vendors and their requested relief online. The organization sends the member's complaint to the vendor and per-mits the disputing parties a period of time to resolve the matter pri-vately. If the dispute does not resolve, the member can request the organization to post the gathered information online for public com-ment. Online public may then review the information and state their views in favor of the member or vendor. The theory is that the public will provide impartial feedback and the public pressure will ultimately as-sist the disputing parties in finding a fair or equitable solution.

Cybernegotiation: technology-assisted optimized negotiation. At least one online dispute resolution service provider (e.g., One Accord) offers disputing parties technology-assisted negotiation services at a patented neutral site.[15] The goal of this type of service provider is to integrate interest-based negotiation principles with technology that is designed to optimize settlements. As one commentator describes this service:

> A facilitator helps parties jointly model their negotiation problem and then assists each party individually input their confidential preferences from their private computer terminal. The system "elicits complex preferences by allowing parties to associate confidence in relative importance of issues and package ratings" and "accurately models negotiation cases and party satisfaction functions allowing parties to experiment with 'what if' scenarios." Finally, the system "generates fair compromises, equivalents and optimal solutions apportioning benefits according to an equity reference established by negotiating parties."[16]

Online simulated juries. Another forum for online dispute resolution (e.g., iCourthouse), offers simulated jury services called "peer jury" and "panel jury." In peer jury cases, the disputants preagree whether the jurors' verdict will be binding or advisory. The volunteer jurors then select the cases they desire to decide, review the parties' "trial books," ask any questions of the disputants, and then render their verdicts. The service provider informs the parties of the verdict, the number of votes cast, the median award, and a summary of the jurors' comments. In a variation of this process, the parties first review potential jurors' answers to voir dire questionnaires. They then choose specific jurors comprising what is called a "panel jury." A unique feature of the panel jury process permits the parties to monitor the jurors online written deliberations in real time. Besides rendering verdicts, the panel jury can also answer questionnaires from parties about the effectiveness of the evidence and arguments presented.

---

15. See generally, Ernest M. Thiessen, P. Eng, and Joseph P. McMahon, "Beyond Win-Win in Cyberspace," 15 *Ohio St. J. on Disp. Resol.* 643 (2000); Stephen J. Ware and Sarah Rudolph Cole, "Introduction: ADR in Cyberspace," 15 *Ohio St. J. on Disp. Resol.* 589, 592–93 (2000).

16. Wiener, supra at 18–19.

8.2.2   Examples of secondary ODR services[17]

Aside from their primary ADR services, some ODR organizations provide secondary or supplemental ODR services. Some of these services are described below.

Dispute prevention. Some ODR services provide background checks of potential corporate employees, advice in the use of standard business contracts and forms, and training for employees and employers.

Assistance in drafting dispute resolution clauses. Some ODR organizations provide assistance in drafting dispute resolution clauses for negotiation (e.g., NewCourtCity), mediation (e.g., Internet Neutral), and arbitration (e.g., NovaForum.com).

Training and information. Some ODR organizations simply provide general consumer information in the nature of training and dispute resolution information (e.g., WebAssured.com and Resolution Forum), or links to specific legal publications (e.g., NewCourtCity).

Complaint assistance. This is a form of technologically assisted negotiation often provided in seal or trustmark cases (see below). Some trustmark organizations serve as intermediaries, forwarding complaints to the certified merchant sites (e.g., BBBOnline and WebAssured) or requesting them to take action (e.g., iLevel). Some trustmark organizations also recommend appropriate ways for customers to deal with the allegedly offending merchant sites (Online Ombuds Office).

Portal to other ODR providers. Some ODR organizations provide links to other ODR organizations (e.g., ICANN).

Legal Assistance. Some ODR organizations post a list of attorneys on a Web site or have the personnel communicate with potential users regarding legal assistance (e.g., Online Resolution, e-Mediator, NewCourtCity, IRIS, and ClaimChoice.com). Mediation advocates with ODR advocacy experience may wish to contact such organizations to register on their lawyer referral lists.

Evaluation. This service can take the form of expert evaluation or of a procedure to test the merits of the case. It does not require the participation or cooperation of the opponent. Essentially, the first form involves a neutral expert examining the legal and technical issues and assessing the merit and value of the claim. If all parties participate in the expert evaluation, they can agree that the results will be fact-binding (e.g., Online Resolution) or entirely binding. The second form can be non-binding or binding and consists of a mock trial by a retired judge or a jury (e.g., 1-2-3 Settle.Com and clickNsettle.com).

---

17. Adapted from Schultz, Kaufman-Kohler, Langer, Bonnet, supra at 30–33.

Trustmarks or seals. These are tools whereby companies can be obligated to establish internal procedures for the handling of conflicts (e.g., Web Trader and MARS), companies' agreement to be bound by the outcome of the ODR system (e.g., WebAssured.com), or declarations by companies of their good intentions (e.g., Web Trader). These kinds of tools are often incorporated into a code of conduct governing the conduct of licensee companies and licensees are permitted to display the seal or trustmark. One ODR organization provides for a limited amount of free dispute resolution services to licensees (e.g., NovaForum.com). Trustmarks and seals may be the principal mechanism for the promotion of self-regulation and consumer confidence in e-commerce.

Publication of complaints. This is a procedure used in seal or trustmark programs. It is usually in the form of either an agreement by Internet merchants to invite their consumers to post comments on special forums about their transactional experience with the merchants (e.g., Web Trader) or the publication by the ODR organization of the results of a negotiation between a consumer and Internet merchant or of the lack of response by a merchant (e.g., iLevel and iCourthouse).

8.3 COMPARISON OF FACE-TO-FACE, TELEPHONE, AND WRITTEN COMMUNICATION IN MEDIATION

The twenty-first century advocate who represents a client in mediation is constantly confronted with the question of what mode of communication he or she should be using at various stages of the mediation process. The reason for this is that the advocate in mediation has many modes of communication from which to choose including face to face, videoconferencing, telephone, letter, e-mail, fax, or combinations of these modes. In this section we will review the relative advantages and disadvantages of the three primary modes of communication: face to face, telephonic, and written. It is hoped that the information here will assist you in choosing the appropriate mode of communication as the mediation progresses.[18]

---

18. See generally, Craver, supra at 310–16; Brunet and Craver, supra at 159–62 (LexisNexis, 2001); G. Nicholas Herman, Jean M. Cary, and Joseph E. Kennedy, *Legal Counseling and Negotiating: A Practical Approach,* (LexisNexis 2001) 251–68 ;and Leigh Thompson, *The Mind and Heart of the Negotiator,* (Simon & Schuster, 1998) 278–82 ; Ethan Katsh, Janet Rifkin, and Alan Gaitenby, "E-Commerce, E-Disputes, and E-Dispute Resolution: In the Shadow of "ebay Law," 15 *Ohio St. J. on Disp. Resol.* 705 (2000); Janice Nadler, "Electronically-Mediated Dispute Resolution and E-Commerce" 17 *Negotiation Journal No. 4* (2001); Michael Morris, Janice Nadler, Terri Kurtzberg, and Leigh Thompson, "Schmooze or Lose: Social Friction and Lubrication in E-mail Negotiations" 6 *Group Dynamics: Theory Research and Practice* 89 (March 2002).

8.3.1 Mediating face to face

When people communicate with one another, 93 percent of the meaning of their messages is contained in their facial and vocal cues, rather than in the content of the messages. Thus, generally speaking, the most communicatively efficient mode of mediation is face to face. However, there may be situations where the disputing parties are so emotionally hostile toward one another that a face-to-face mediation would do more harm than good. In such situations, a face-to-face meeting might also be counter-indicated because there is no continuing relationship to be preserved. In some situations, face-to-face mediation may be simply impossible because of geographical distance between or among the parties and their counsel. In some such situations video telephones or videoconferencing may serve as a near-equivalent substitute for a face-to-face meeting. In other mediation situations, while a face-to-face meeting may be helpful during a portion of the settlement process, an advocate might conclude for strategic, tactical, or other reasons that another mode of communication might be more appropriately used in other phases of the process. Whenever an advocate decides to engage in a face-to-face mode, usually the question arises as to where the face-to-face meeting will be held. The chart on the next page compares the advantages of holding the mediation in your own office with holding it at an opposing counsel's office or at a neutral location. When you have a choice in the matter, you may want to give some careful thought to these considerations.

MEDIATING FACE TO FACE
(LOCATION CONSIDERATIONS)

ADVANTAGES (Your Office)	ADVANTAGES (Opponent's Office or neutral location)
Ready access to documents, colleagues, needed materials	Fewer distractions from one's own office staff
Ability to control atmosphere of comfort or non-comfort	Better control over information you don't wish to disclose
Can arrange to get "called away" to relieve tension	Opponent can meet with superiors to get authority to accede to a contract term
Psychological advantage of being on your own turf and in control	
May be less expensive and less stressful in terms of travel time, etc.	Host advocate may be inclined to begin talking first, disclosing an initial proposal

8.3.2 Mediating by telephone

For some people, the telephone offers a more effective and efficient way to mediate than mediating in person. Some advocates, for example, are better skilled at sensing audible cues suggesting true meaning of a participant's telephone statement than they are at discerning nonverbal aspects of messages in a face-to-face meeting. These audible cues consist of, among others, pitch, pace, tone, volume, inflection, sighs, and pauses. Actually, nonverbal, visual cues to meaning can be distracting and overwhelming to some people in an in-person situation. Another advantage of telephonic mediations for some advocates is that they are able to give facial or hand signals to their clients if they are participating in the mediation conference together on a speakerphone. If the mediator gets into topical areas in a joint telephone session that the advocate or party does not want to discuss, it is less awkward than in a face-to-face meeting for the advocate to shift the conversation to a different topic, to think of a reason to withdraw from the teleconference, or to request that the teleconference be rescheduled to a mutually convenient time so that the advocate can become better informed about a topic. The advocate can also tell the mediator and the other parties that she is going to put everyone on hold while she caucuses with her client.

The advocate can also request a caucus with the mediator. This can be conveniently used to disrupt the communication flow of an opposing advocate when he is making an unreasonable or insulting argument, or the request to caucus may serve as an opportunity to have your client respond directly to the mediator concerning the subject matter of the opposing advocate's allegations or perspectives. Unlike negotiation by letter, advocates can ask clarifying questions immediately in a telephone mediation.

Some disadvantages of mediating over the telephone include discerning the identity of the speakers if a number of participants, including the mediator and several disputing parties, are engaged in the teleconference. Generally speaking, mediation participants are less likely to spend as much time in a telephone negotiation as they would in a face-to-face meeting. Thus, on many occasions less progress is made in a mediation teleconference than in an in-person conference. In a document-rich case, discussing documents over the telephone can often be a cumbersome task if the documents are not quickly identifiable by volume and page number. Teleconferences can also become rambling, directionless conversations if there is no agenda to guide the discussion. Teleconferences can be less personal than face-to-face conversations. Such faceless verbal exchanges sometimes facilitate competitive or even deliberately deceptive tactics. Confidentiality of communications may be a problem, particularly if participants are using cell phones or leave substantive telephone voice-mail messages that are heard by nonparticipants in the mediation. These and other advantages and disadvantages of mediating by telephone are outlined in the chart that follows.

MEDIATING BY TELEPHONE

ADVANTAGES	DISADVANTAGES
Fewer nonverbal distractions	Mediation sessions are shorter and possibly less complete
Audible cues (pitch, pace, tone, and volume) detectable	
Pause may indicate serious consideration	Less revealing in terms of reading visual nonverbal cues
Clarifying questions can be asked and answered	Lack of visual cues may cause misunderstandings
Focus can be on meaning of words	
Easier to break off mediation by withdrawing or requesting a postponement	Your opponent can easily withdraw or postpone at any time
Notes can be left open and readily available	Opposing advocate may be continuously "unavailable"
More expedient than in-person	
Easier to say "no"	Opposing advocate may use deliberately deceptive tactics
Caller has advantage of surprise; mediator can be requested to make a proposal at a particular time, which is orchestrated by you to favor your client's interests	Confidentiality may be compromised

8.3.3 Mediating in writing

Letter and fax communication. Letter writing in mediation permits the transmission of detailed information to the mediator and/or the other parties. The writer has the luxury of not being interrupted during the course of his or her written communication. Letters can also serve as a permanent record of an opposing counsel's offers and concessions. Furthermore, as an advocate, you can avoid misunderstandings by taking the time to be careful and accurate in written communications to the mediator, opposing parties, and co-counsel. Letters or faxes received by you in a mediation normally allow you as much time as necessary to review proposals and obtain input from your client, your partners, or co-counsel. Sending faxes to the mediator or opposing counsel helps you to avoid embarrassment when you cannot find time to answer their calls. Sending faxes can create a sense of urgency and maintain time pressure in settlement negotiations.

E-mail communication. There are many advantages to e-mail communication in mediation. First, you can instantaneously communicate messages, and settlement agreements or proposed provisions of settlement agreements can be modified and distributed immediately to the mediator and to all parties simultaneously as the mediation progresses. Barriers to effective communication such as perceived social status of certain mediation participants, can be easily overcome or neutralized. The informal origins of communication—even from home or from the beach—influence people to respond openly and less hesitatingly than in a face-to-face setting. Also, research has proven that although the amount of participation in an e-mail conference is quantitatively less overall than in a face-to-face context, the number of individual contributions is more equalized than in a face-to-face setting. For example studies have shown that when groups of executives meet face to face, men are five times more likely than women to make the first decision proposal. When those same groups meet in an online setting, women make first proposals as often as men do. Another advantage of e-mail mediation is that split-second tactical decisions do not have to be made. Advocates and their clients can take as much time as they need to consider and respond to proposals.

E-mail communication in mediation, however, is not without its shortcomings. The informality of e-mail communication is its strength as well as its weakness. People using e-mail can easily lapse into a mode where they are totally unconcerned about making a good appearance. In such state, they can be inappropriately informal and even offensive. One study showed that people are eight times more likely to "flame" in electronic discussion than in face-to-face discussion. Recipients of participants' messages can easily misunderstand or misinterpret them. The reason for this is that the recipient cannot always discern the emotive aspect accompanying the content of the message. Consider the e-mail statement, "You consistently have all the right answers." It is not clear whether the writer is exhibiting deference or sarcasm. Emoticons (typographical symbols indicating emotional cues) can help solve this problem if used tastefully. Also, and more problematically, insults take on permanence. Hostile exchanges can escalate rapidly. Even intended innocuous language can be perceived as deliberately inflammatory and reinforce prior preliminary impressions of recipients, causing misinterpretations to be compounded to a crisis point. In addition, behavioral research has demonstrated that it can take four times as long for a three-person group to make a decision in a real-time (chat room type) computer conference as in a face-to-face conference. It can take ten times as long for a four-person group, having no time restrictions, to come to a joint decision. Unless you exercise special care, you can also easily compromise the confidentiality of the mediation process. The split-second sending of an e-mail to an unintended addressee can be disastrous. Finally, research has shown that people are more intolerant about changing their decision on an issue when they commit their decision to write, and especially when they publish that written decision to other persons. Written positions or hard-line proposals in e-mail can be more intractable than when they are expressed in person or over the telephone.

Mediating by means of letters and faxes may have its downside. It may cause an unwanted slowdown of mediation. If you use regular mail, the mediator and opposing counsel may do likewise and thereby retard the progress of the mediation. If you send a letter proposal, you will probably receive a counterproposal which may result in your having to take a position too early in the mediation process. If you incorporate a settlement proposal in a letter or a fax, your opponent will have time to study your proposal and get input. If you make the same proposal by telephone, depending on your opposing advocate's work schedule, he or she may feel inclined to respond to your settlement proposal on the spot. In addition, sending letters or faxes rather than making a simple telephone call may cause your client to be billed extra fees unnecessarily. If not diplomatically drafted, a settlement letter may spawn antagonistic and unproductive responses from your opposing counsel. With regard to faxes, if time is of the essence, realize that there is a chance that faxes might get backlogged for transmission in your own mail room, and even if sent, they may get lost in opposing counsel's mail room or they may be misrouted.

These and other advantages and disadvantages of mediating by letter, faxes, and e-mail are outlined in the charts that follow.

MEDIATING IN WRITING
(LETTER AND FAX)

ADVANTAGES	DISADVANTAGES
Transmit detailed information	May cause unwanted slowdown of mediation
No interruptions	Inflexible; you may have to take a position too early in the mediation process
Permanent record of opponent's offers and concessions	Your opponent has time to study offer and get input
Misunderstandings more easily avoided	Time involved by lawyer may be more extensive
You have time to review proposals and got input	May spawn antagonistic responses
Faxes avoid unanswered calls	Faxes may be backlogged for transmission
Faxes maintain time pressure	Faxes may get lost in opponent's mailroom

(E-MAIL)

ADVANTAGES	DISADVANTAGES
Messages instantaneously communicated	Messages can be misunderstood and/or misinterpreted
Settlement agreements or provisions can be modified and distributed immediately	Insults take on permanence; hostile exchanges can escalate rapidly
Messages can be broadcast to any number of people simultaneously	Frustrating delays; takes up to four times longer for a group to reach consensus or a joint decision
Absence of social status cues can influence people to respond openly and less hesitatingly than in a face-to-face setting	
	Unless care is exercised, confidentiality can be easily compromised
Amount of participation in an e-mail conference is less overall than in a face-to-face context; but the number of individual contributions is more equal than in a face-to-face setting	People are less concerned about making a good appearance; they can be inappropriately informal
E-mail use breaks down gender barriers and allows freer communication	Written positions or hard-line proposals can be more intractable than when they are expressed in person or over the telephone
Split-second tactical decisions do not have to be made	True emotions are less likely to be conveyed unless emoticons are appropriately employed

8.4 BENEFITS AND LIMITATIONS OF CYBERMEDIATION

There are both benefits and limitations associated with the use of cybermediation.[19] These are discussed generally in section 8.4.1. Two

---

19. See generally Denise King, *Internet Mediation—A Summary*, 11 Australasian Dispute Resolution Journal 180–86 (August 2000); Frank A Cona, *Focus on Cyberlaw: Application of Online Systems in Alternative Dispute Resolution*, 45 *Buffalo L.Rev.* 975, 990–1000 (1997); Nadler, supra; Cheri M. Ganeles, "Cybermediation, A New Twist on an Old Concept," 12 *Alb.L.J. Sci & Tech.* 715 (2002); Llewellyn Joseph Gibbons, Robbin M. Kennedy, and Jon Michael Gibbs, "Frontiers of the Law: The Internet and Cyberspace: Cyber-mediation: Computer-mediated Communciations Medium Massaging the Message, 32 N.ML. 27 (2002).

topics that deserve special analysis under this heading are confidentiality and cost of service. These topics are discussed in sections 8.4.2 and 8.4.3, respectively.

8.4.1   Benefits and limitations—generally

Benefits. Some of the benefits of cybermediation are as follows. In cybermediation, the parties are able to choose when they want to respond or participate in the process as it proceeds through its various stages. This allows time for parties to reflect on the materials they receive from opposing parties and co-parties, get initial legal advice, strategize with counsel or co-parties, carefully craft what they want to say, and even get final input from counsel or co-parties before they finally commit to a response or to a proposed solution that their counsel will communicate to the mediator and to the other side, as appropriate. The online nature of the process eliminates the pressure to respond immediately to a received communication. Counsel and clients can craft communications in a "safe space" without the emotional pressures often present in a live setting. Cybermediation can create a collaborative learning environment and foster thoughtful discussions among all participants. Moreover, advocates can quickly consult legal and expert sources online and help their clients realistically assess the predictable outcome at trial in comparison with a consensual outcome in cybermediation.

The distance from the real world and the absence of non-verbal communication can be assets in a cybermediation. In many situations, particularly divorce cases, the couple's historic dysfunctional dynamics are often replicated when they are face to face in a conference room. These dynamics often exacerbate settlement attempts and sometimes spell doom for a negotiated solution. Cybermediation minimizes the effects of these dynamics.

It also is likely to be more cost-effective in most situations because of the absence of travel and related expenses. Another benefit of cybermediation is that there is a record of discussions at each stage of the process which can facilitate the drafting of the final settlement agreement. Often, the parties can efficiently formalize, execute, and conclude the agreement after reaching consensus.

Limitations. Cybermediation has some limitations. Varying degrees of computer literacy may affect the quality of online communication between counsel and client. Occasionally, use of online technology can create a power imbalance among the parties or counsel. This imbalance may result from varying quality of computer equipment or software, the relative competence of the cybermediation participants in using the Internet or online information resources, or the unequal experience with using the services of a cybermediator. In addition, cybermediation cannot offer the same type of spontaneity and vigor offered by face-to-face personal interaction and oral discussion. Keeping communications confidential in cybermediation is another challenge for participants. Participants can easily make mistakes and send confidential e-mail communications to participants who should not have access to them. Cybermediators sometimes are unable to gain parties' trust and confidence as quickly mediators in traditional mediation. Certain types of disputes may not be as appropriate for cybermediation as others. For example, a situation where the credibility of the parties is a crucial issue in a dispute might be more appropriate for a face-to-face meeting so that the mediator can evaluate how a jury might assess the parties' relative truthfulness. Moreover, personal injury cases where plaintiffs need to demonstrate the nature of their injuries, scars, etc. may be more appropriate for traditional mediation. Similarly, a patent or product liability case, where it is helpful to a resolution for the mediation participants to see the configuration or operation of a particular piece of equipment, may be a candidate for traditional mediation. In addition, since parties and counsel from any jurisdiction in the world can participate in a particular cybermediation, post-mediation enforcement of the agreement becomes a troublesome issue.

The above-described benefits and limitations of cybermediation and others are outlined in the chart on the next page.

BENEFITS AND LIMITATIONS OF CYBERMEDIATION

BENEFITS	LIMITATIONS
Participants can be located anywhere in the world	May take significantly more time, overall, to reach a settlement because of the asynchronous nature of the communication
Large quantities of information can be transmitted instantly to any number of recipients	Less ice-breaking schmooze occurs
Participants may communicate asynchronously—they choose when they want to respond	In certain situations where there are counsel representing multiple parties or where there are multiple co-parties, the asychronous nature of communication may cause cybermediation to be more expensive than traditional mediation
Participants may communicate synchronously through chat rooms and instant messaging	
Eliminates the problem of caucusing "wait time" of traditional mediation	Varying degrees of computer literacy may exist between counsel and their clients
Parties can get initial and final input from counsel and co-parties before submitting a response	Power imbalance may be created by unequal online expertise, experience, or equipment of parties or counsel
Eliminates the pressure to respond immediately	In contrast with traditional mediation, it may take longer for the cybermediator to gain parties' trust and confidence and to build rapport
Parties can craft communications in an emotion-free setting	
Creates collaborative learning environment	Online communication lacks the spontaneity and vigor of face-to-face interaction and oral discussion
Fosters thoughtful discussions	
Advocates have easy access to legal and expert sources to help them give realistic advice on the prospects of trial versus a settlement	Parties are more likely to distrust and suspect lying or deceit on the part of other participants
	Parties are more likely to "flame" and reach impasse

8.4.2 Confidentiality

Confidentiality has always been the soul of the mediation process. The participants' agreement to maintain the confidentiality of mediation communications is usually sufficient in face-to-face mediations to guarantee nondisclosure of sensitive information. It is the responsibility of each participant in such offline (or online) mediations not to mistakenly disclose information by e-mail or other means. ODR, however, has created a new threat to mediation confidentiality.[20] Regardless of the participants' agreement to maintain confidentiality of online mediation communications, breaches of security can originate externally from nonparticipants who intentionally invade, acquire, and perhaps even alter information the participants want to preserve as confidential and unchanged. It is generally accepted among the ODR provider community that electronic messages need to be protected by electronic means and that electronic mediation communications and access to the data must be secured before, during, and after the cybermediation. Thus, protection is needed with respect to both the transmission and the storage of confidential mediation information. These two aspects require different means of protection. The risks to be protected against are: the risk that unauthorized third parties will gain access to the information (i.e., risk of compromising the *confidentiality* of the message); and the risk that such third parties will alter it (i.e., the risk of compromising the *integrity* of the message). A current serious limitation of cybermediation is that ODR providers cannot always guarantee that mediation communications will not be disclosed.

Transmission of information. Unencrypted e-mail is considered to be about as secure as postcards. E-mail is capable, however, of being secured by several means. One means is through a software called Secure Multipurpose Internet Mail Exchange Protocol (S/MIME). If correctly used, the software provides the recipient with strong evidence of the origin of the contents of the message. It also has a feature that confirms to the sender that his or her message was delivered to a specific recipient. Another product that is free of charge but difficult to employ by non-specialists is Pretty Good Privacy (PGP). It is a message protection software with the same quality of service as S/MIME and is available from the Massachusetts Institute of Technology.

Alteration of a transmitted message can be reduced by digital signatures. These are cryptographic instruments trusted to third parties called signature- or key-holders. If a sender uses such a private key to electronically sign a message, the receiver can verify both the origin and the integrity of the message.

---

20. See generally, Schultz, Kaufmann-Kohler, Langer, Bonnet, supra at 44–50.

Other means of protection must be used to secure information that is posted on a Web site, as opposed to being sent by e-mail. The hypertext transfer protocol (HTTP) is the generally accepted protocol for on-line transactions. In addition to this Web-based security feature, secure sockets layer (SSL) provides protection of the confidentiality and integrity of Web-based communications.

Web site storage of confidential information is also a risk area. Site storage systems consist of a database and Web server. ODR providers must protect these against such risks as intrusions, viruses, and disk crashes. These storage systems can be protected by firewalls, but it is more effective to implement protection for each document instead of the system as a whole.

Because security systems are not yet widely available to satisfy high expectations of security in the ODR provider field, advocates may do well to carefully weigh the risks of using ODR for disputes in which the financial stakes are very high.

8.4.3 Cost or financing of service

Fees for use of ODR services are generally of three types: bilateral (or multilateral), unilateral, or external source.[21] In the bilateral (or multilateral) model, each party pays its proportional share of the user foo. This seems fair on its face, but one problem with this model is that the cost for the consumer may be disproportionate compared to the amount at stake. A very large majority of ODR providers charge users under this model.

In the unilateral user fee model, the business (merchant or insurance company) pays the entire fee for the ODR service. The payment can be in the form of an annual membership fee (e.g., a trustmark fee) or a fee per case. The problem with this model is the inevitable appearance of bias. It might appear to the non-business user, for example, that the business payor of the user fee is being favored in the process. The appearance of bias can be lessened by the ODR provider's implementation of strict procedural rules ensuring the availability of an adequate selection of independent neutrals, publishing clear policies of neutrality and impartiality, and establishing an independent supervisory or auditing body. Approximately 12 percent of the ODR service providers in existence as of December, 2001 have implemented the unilateral fee model.

Approximately 10 percent of ODR service providers operate under the external source fee model. In this model, a third party—university or a governmental or non-governmental organization (e.g., a consumer association) pays the entire fee for the ODR service. In general, this

---

21. Id. at 74–77.

model provides the highest guarantee of independence and impartiality. As of December, 2001, ODR service providers employing this fee model were: ECODIR, ODR.NL, IRIS, Virtual Magistrate, and Online Ombuds Office.

On the question of independence, advocates selecting ODR provider organizations may want to take into account the provider's organizational structure and outside financial support. As of December, 2001, a large majority of the ODR providers were for-profit organizations; approximately 20 percent operated on a not-for-profit basis.

8.5   ETHICS OF CYBERADVOCACY

The state codes of professional conduct for lawyers, most of which incorporate the American Bar Association's Model Rules of Professional Conduct, guide an advocate's conduct in representing clients in cybermediation.[22] (See section 5.9.2 and appendix J). The ABA maintains a Web site (http://www.elawyering.org) that provides guidance for lawyers that practice online. The site also provides ethical guidance at http://www.elawyering.org/ethics/advice.asp. The Elawyering Task Force, ABA, Legal Websites Best Practice Guidelines (2001) can be accessed at http://www.elawyering.org/tools/practices/asp.

Mediators' conduct is generally governed by Model Standards of Conduct for Mediators, published jointly by the American Arbitration Association, the American Bar Association, and the Society of Professionals in Dispute Resolution. (See section 5.9.1 and appendix I). One study reports that only one online mediation provider, Online Resolution, applies these standards.[23] Currently, some large associations of dispute resolution providers have proposed, or are considering, common policies or codes of conduct for ODR. Guidelines published by the American Arbitration Association, entitled *eCommerce Dispute Management Protocol, Principles for Managing B2B [business to business] Relationships,* acknowledges the importance of fairness, clear policies, a range of options, and resources of technology. In April, 2002 the American Bar Association Task Force on E-Commerce and ADR released a draft of its final report and concept paper. The report makes eleven recommendations, including the creation of best practices guidelines for online dispute resolution.

One critical ethical duty of advocates in cybermediation is maintaining client confidences. Online communication presents a minefield

---

22.   See generally, Louise Ellen Teitz, supra at 985, 987–91 (2001).
23.   Schultz, Kaufmann-Kohler, Langer, Bonnet, supra at 9.

of opportunities for inadvertent and harmful disclosures of client information by uncautious and unwary advocates.[24] Following the guidance presented below will help you avoid making those instant, and unintentional harmful disclosures.

Carefully manage the power of the "cc." Anyone who is or who has been a subscriber to a listserv knows how useful some of the received information is and how annoying some of it can be. Thus when communicating by e-mail or by e-mail list, make a quick check to see if all the addressees actually need to receive or would even want to receive the information you are sending. There are times when, on behalf of your client, you will want to communicate with all participants in the mediation, but there will be other times when the information sent will be merely ministerial and applicable to only one or two participants. Do not bother participants with a message that has no relevance to them just because it is convenient for you to click only once without thinking, sorting, and deciding. Also, while the "cc" option is a powerful e-mail tool, it is a horrible "accident waiting to happen." Critical, highly confidential information can be disclosed in a split, unthinking second and can doom a mediation and perhaps put a lawyer's career in jeopardy. Before commencing an online mediation, mediators normally take great pains to advise parties and counsel about the dangers of unintentional disclosures of confidentiality and to discuss procedures for preventing it from happening. This advice should be explicitly heeded.

Use caucuses judiciously. Realize that when you engage in cybermediation, you may be caucusing privately with several participants simultaneously. By that I mean you may send a confidential communication to counsel for a co-party, and while that lawyer is considering it, you may receive a confidential communication from the mediator requiring your confidential response—before you respond to counsel for the co-party. You may also receive responses out of order—which could be confusing. Consider, for example that you send one confidential e-mail message to the first participant now, and another confidential message to a second participant two hours from now. The second participant responds immediately and the first participant responds a couple hours later. If you are not careful to note which participant is e-mailing you, it is possible that your expectations about receiving a response from the first party more quickly might cause you to err by directing your confidential response to the wrong party. Thus, you must take great care not to disclose confidential information accidentally when communicating online. And, of course, when you are dealing online with four or five parties and the mediator, the pressure to guard

---

24. M. Ethan Katsh, *Dispute Resolution in Cyberspace,* 28 Conn. L. Rev. 953, 971–74 (1996).

against unintentional disclosures of confidential information is extremely intense and your ethical obligation to maintain confidentiality becomes magnified proportionately.

Take security precautions vis-a-vis other Web users. If you are engaged in the mediation of a high-profile case online, do not be too surprised if you have interlopers—related to the dispute or not—trying to acquire information on the mediation progress. If you use chat rooms, make sure they are secure and keep an eye out for new entrants whose identity you do not know.

Maintain appropriate confidentiality within your groups. It was pointed out above that the "cc" feature of e-mail is a powerful and useful tool, but that it can cause disastrous disclosures of information. Before you send any e-mail messages, you should ensure that the principal addressees and the "cc" addressees are appropriate. You may be involved in several online mediations at once. If you are simultaneously involved in several cybermediations, it is important for you to keep the e-mail addresses of participants in the various cases segregated from each other so that you don't inadvertently dispatch an e-mail to a participant in a separate mediation.

8.6 CONSIDERATIONS IN SELECTING A CYBER-MEDIATION SERVICE AND CYBERMEDIATOR

8.6.1 The cybermediation process

Before you select an ODR service provider and a cybermediator, you should decide what kind of cybermediation process you, your client, and the opposing side desire. One of the first questions you want to ask yourself is whether you want to be limited in your choice of mediators by an ODR provider's "mandatory" list of neutrals. If you and your opposing counsel have in mind a particular mediator you want to hire, you may want to consider eliminating from consideration those providers that limit your choice of mediators to their list or panel.

Also, as described more fully in section 8.6.2, all ODR providers do not provide the same type of mediation process. The nature of the mediation process provided by each ODR provider depends on the type of technology available on the Web site. For example, some provider Web sites only allow for e-mail communication and do not provide a chat room feature. Thus, if you and opposing counsel desire a traditional "joint session" of all the mediation participants, you might want to think about eliminating from consideration all those providers that do not offer the real-time chat feature. Similarly, if there are several parties on your side of the dispute you may want a Web site real-time chat feature that allows private caucusing for one or more parties and their counsel. This desired feature may further result in narrowing your search for providers. In some situations, you may need instant messaging, threaded discussion, and videoconferencing availability. You may also want a provider that offers arbitration as a back-up to mediation if the mediation is unsuccessful. In still other situations, you may desire a provider that provides only a technology platform for mediation, which the parties can use together with their independently selected mediator. Thus, in many respects, choosing the appropriate provider of online mediation is much more challenging than selecting an offline mediation service provider.

8.6.2 Selecting a cybermediation service

In addition to reasons stated in section 8.6.1, choosing a cybermediation service is much more challenging than choosing a provider of face-to-face (or offline) mediation services because there are no geographic limitations. In offline mediation, counsel normally select a mediation service that is conveniently located geographically. If several parties are located in one city and two parties are from out of state, for example, usually parties will agree to hold the mediation in the city where the most parties are located. That is not true in the case of online dispute resolution. The location of the parties is not a factor. Parties located anywhere in the United States can choose a provider of ODR services located in any state or in any foreign country. This fact greatly increases the spectrum of choice. Not limited by geography, parties can choose any ODR service provider worldwide based on, among other criteria, reputation for high-quality service, reputation for high-quality justice, Web site confidentiality features, specialty in processing specific types of disputes, competence and impartiality of neutrals, availability of binding and nonbinding process alternatives, speed of resolution process, satisfaction of foreign language needs, and effective enforcement mechanisms.

When you and your client discuss the need to select a cybermediation service, one of the first questions you should address is whether cybermediation is the only process that is appropriate to resolve your dispute. On reflection, you might conclude that a cybernegotiation service (such as blind bidding) might adequately satisfy your needs and be less costly than hiring a cybermediator. Alternatively, you might conclude that you really need cybermediation for the particular dispute, but in the event cybermediation is used and is unsuccessful in resolving the dispute, you may want to have available the option to proceed to cyberarbitration. Let's assume for a moment that you came to the second conclusion—that you need cybermediation, but if that process is unsuccessful, you want an option to go to cyberarbitration. Thus, you need to know the criteria both for selecting a service provider that offers adjudication (cyberarbitration) and consensual dispute resolution (cybermediation or online facilitated negotiation).[25]

Selection criteria for cyberarbitration service. With regard to and adjudicative hearing, in general, experts identify eleven procedural requirements that must be present to ensure due process.[26] They are as follows:

1. Unbiased neutral(s).

2. The parties' right to be represented by counsel.

3. Notice and a statement of reasons giving rise to the dispute.

4. Statement in response to the reasons giving rise to the dispute.

5. The parties' opportunity to present evidence including witnesses, in support of their positions.

6. The parties' right to know opposing evidence.

7. The right to cross-examine opposing witnesses.

8. The decision maker's duty to keep a record of the evidence presented.

9. The decision maker's duty to render a decision based on and limited to the evidence in the record and the applicable law.

10. The decision maker's duty to give reasons to the parties supporting the decision.

11. The availability of appellate review of the decision.

While most of these requirements would equally serve as due process criteria for cyberarbitration, some of them have not been due process requirements even in traditional arbitration. As to criteria 10 and 11 in the list above—the arbitrator's issuance of a reasoned decision and the parties being provided the opportunity for appellate review, while they may be "nice-to-have" court-type due-process criteria, they are not absolutely necessary requirements for adequate due process in a cyberarbitration. An important criterion for cyberarbitration not included in the list above is cost of the process. Criteria 10 and 11 could significantly and unreasonably increase the cost of any arbitration, and would certainly do so in cyberarbitration. These cost issues, however,

---

25. *See generally,* Louise Ellen Teitz, *Providing Legal Services for the Middle Class in Cyberspace: The Promise and Challenge of On-line Dispute Resolution,* 70 Fordham L. Rev. 985, 1007–09 (2001).

26. Henry H. Perritt, Jr., *Dispute Resolution in Cyberspace: Demand for New Forms of ADR,* 15 Ohio St. J. on Disp. Resol. 675, 677–84 (2000).

are really for the parties to agree upon. Even in some traditional arbitrations parties frequently opt for the arbitrator issuing reasoned findings and conclusions and, in some rare cases, parties preagree to an appellate arbitration panel to be used in the event that one or more parties desires review of the arbitration hearing panel's decision. In summary then, an arbitration service provider whose arbitration system satisfies criteria 1 through 9 above will normally satisfy at least the minimum due-process interests of your clients. If a client seeks more than minimal due process and is not opposed to paying additionally for it, you may want to explore the possibility of choosing an arbitration process that incorporates criteria 10 and 11 as well.

Selection criteria for cybermediation service. When selecting a cybermediation service, one commentator suggests that the advocate consider only the first three criteria set forth in the above eleven-point list, since the remaining eight criteria are not relevant to a consensual settlement process such as mediation.[27] Thus, you would want to ensure that a cybermediation service providor offers the parties, at a minimum: (1) a means by which they can select a neutral third party to mediate their dispute; (2) the right for the parties to be represented by counsel; and (3) an opportunity to have notice and a statement of reasons giving rise to the dispute.

Other commentators have identified what they believe to be three fundamental building blocks for a proper ODR system of any kind: convenience, trust, and expertise.[28] They believe that some measure of each factor must be present in any selected system. They also assert that the relative presence of each factor determines whether, in any particular instance, one ODR system should be used over another or whether ODR should be used (as opposed to offline ADR systems) at all. Included in the convenience factor, are "any logistical and financial factors that positively or negatively affect access to and participation in the process."

The basic question is whether an online ODR option is more convenient for a particular dispute application than, for instance, writing a letter, using the phone, a combination of these two, or even a face-to-face meeting. Would it be more convenient to drive to a nearby suburb on a sunny day for the initial joint session of a mediation conference rather than engaging in an online joint session? If so, probably the parties would opt for a face-to-face conference. If in this same scenario the mediation was in the agreement-drafting stage, it might make more sense to hold the mediation session online so that drafts of agreement

---

27. Henry H. Perritt, Jr., *Dispute Resolution in Cyberspace: Demand for New Forms of ADR,* 15 Ohio St. J. on Disp. Resol. 675, 683–84 (2000).

28. Ethan Katsh and Janet Rifkin, *Online Dispute Resolution: Resolving Conflicts in Cyberspace* 71–92 (Jossey-Bass, 2001).

provisions could be immediately exchanged and modified in writing on-line and to everyone's satisfaction. Another fundamental factor re-quired of any ODR system is trust. The parties and their counsel must be absolutely assured that when using a particular ODR system, their confidential information will not be revealed to the other side—or in fact to anyone who has no right to see or hear it. Some ODR systems have a seal or trustmark provided by an independent third party that vouches for the trustworthiness of the ODR service provider. Finally, expertise is a necessary requirement for any ODR company. Expertise involves an interactive informational process—one that satisfies the specific interactive needs of its users. Some ODR systems, blind bidding for example, can provide online dispute resolution services that cannot be done as well or efficiently offline. ODR by its very online nature has a worldwide web of online information available to its users. It is the twenty-first century challenge of the ODR providers to capitalize on its available expertise and informational resources to make the cybermediation experience as effective and rewarding online as it has proven over the years to be offline.

Several research studies have demonstrated that in most conflict situations, disputants are more concerned with issues of exoneration, with obtaining an adequate hearing, and with being treated respect-fully than they are with the actual outcome of the dispute resolution process in which they engage.[29] In effect, disputants are more concerned about the adequacy and fairness of the procedure ("procedural justice") by which the dispute is resolved than the outcome or settlement result itself. Studies show that there are three key components of procedural justice: perceived trust (did the neutral fully consider my views and needs?); standing (did the neutral treat me with politeness, dignity and respect?); neutrality (did the neutral treat me in an evenhanded, non-discriminatory way by behaving in an open, fact-based fashion?). As to perceived trust, it has been shown that the extent to which disputants are willing settle a dispute and to abide by the terms of the settlement in the future can be strongly influenced by the feeling that they have been given the opportunity to tell their side of the story. This "voice" effect stems from whether the neutral is perceived as giving adequate consid-eration to the disputant's views. Above all, disputants seem to be con-cerned with telling their story because the perception of being heard is a signal that the authority (e.g., a mediator) can be trusted to view them and treat them in a way that is benevolent and fair. In addition, the pro-cess must be dignified in itself and confer standing on the disputants to be entitled to dignity and respect. Finally, the process must be neutral

---

29. *See generally,* Janice Nadler, *Electronically-Mediated Dispute Resolution and E-Commerce,* 17 Negotiation Journal 333 (2001).

in the sense that the third party (e.g., mediator) conducts himself or herself in an unbiased way and with a concern for achieving an accurate understanding of the facts and other relevant information.

It should be noted that in a 2001 study of forty-nine ODR organizations reported by the Private International Law Department of the Geneva University Law School, the core principles of fundamental due process in online dispute resolution of consumer disputes were identified to be: (1) reasonable cost to the consumer; (2) independence and impartiality of the ODR organization and process; (3) transparency of the ODR organization (clear policies and full disclosure of statistics and corporate and/or financial support and links); (4) speed of ODR process; (5) accessibility to consumers.[30]

From this discussion, we can distill the following criteria for selecting a cybermediation service. The cybermediation service provider should, at a minimum:

1. Provide an adequate means for parties and their counsel to select a neutral third party.

2. Allow parties to be represented by counsel.

3. Provide parties an opportunity to receive notice and a statement of reasons giving rise to the dispute.

4. Make the cybermediation process as accessible and convenient as possible for the parties, at a reasonable cost.

5. Ensure that cybermediation communications are confidentially maintained.

6. Provide adequate expertise or instruction to assist the parties, technologically, in the use of the online dispute resolution services.

7. Ensure that cyberneutrals permit the parties and counsel to voice their views and needs fully.

8. Ensure that cyberneutrals accord standing to the parties and counsel by treating them with politeness, dignity, and respect.

9. Ensure that cyberneutrals act in an unbiased and impartial manner and with a concern for achieving an accurate understanding of the facts and other relevant information.

---

30. T. Schultz, G. Kaufmann-Kohler, D. Langer, V. Bonnet, *Online Dispute Resolution: The State of the Art and the Issues,* E-Com Research Project of the University of Geneva, Geneva, 2001, http://www.online-adr.org, 89–90.

and provides full disclosure of statistics and financial support and links.

ODR service providers and principal services offered. The chart below identifies organizations that provided (or have planned offerings of) ODR services as of December 2001.[31] It also states the principal type or types of dispute serviced, the principal type of ODR service or services offered, and other descriptive information. Web site addresses for each of the organizations are contained in appendix L. The letter key for each principal type of dispute serviced by the ODR organization is listed here:

A.   All disputes or unspecified Disputes.

B.   Consumer disputes.

C.   Insurance disputes.

D.   Commercial disputes.

E.   Domain-name disputes.

F.   Race discrimination and violence.

G.   Individual and public liberties.

H.   Employment.

I.   Online auction disputes.

J.   Online marketplaces.

The numerical key for each principal ODR service offered by a listed ODR organization is as follows:

1.   Automated negotiation.

2.   Assisted negotiation.

3.   Cybermediation.

4.   Cyberarbitration.

5.   Case evaluation.

6.   Trustmark or seal programs.

7.   Complaint filing for offline ADR.

T. Schultz, G. Kaufmann-Kohler, D. Langer, V. Bonnet, *Online Dispute Resolution: The State of the Art and the Issues,* E-Com Research Project of the University of Geneva, Geneva, 2001, http://www.online-adr.org, 89–90.

31. Much of the information in this table is derived from T. Schultz, G. Kaufmann-Kohler, D. Langer, V. Bonnet, *Online Dispute Resolution: The State of the Art and the Issues,* E-Com Research Project of the University of Geneva, Geneva, 2001, http://www.online-adr.org.

8. A decision-type process, with written decisions, but neither arbitration nor mediation, technically.

9. Linking cite to ADR providers.

10. Cybernegotiation.

11. Mock trial; jury verdicts.

12. Technology-assisted optimized negotiation with neutral facilitator.

13. Communication platform for cybermediation.

14. Court of law using simultaneous videoconferencing, online windows showing exhibits and instant-messenger programs with real-time written discussions of legal issues.

15. Non-binding cyberarbitration.

16. Automated complaint assistance.

ODR ORGANIZATION	PRINCIPAL TYPE OF DISPUTE	PRINCIPAL TYPE OF ODR SERVICE(S)	COMMENTS
1-2-3 Settle.com	A	1, 3, 4, 5	U.S.-based; owned and operated by attorneys
AllSettle.com	C	1	U.S.-based; private business venture
Better Business Bureau Online	B	6 (Reliability, Privacy, and Children's Privacy); 7; planned: 1, 3, 4	U.S.-based non-profit industry association to promote relationship between businesses and consumers worldwide
ClaimChoice.com	C (Accident Insurance Claims)	2	U.S.-based private business venture of eLegius, Inc.
ClaimNegotiator	A	2	Additional service of ClaimResolver.com
ClaimResolver.com	A	1	Private business venture

ClickNSettle.com	A	1	U.S.-based private business venture
CPR Institute for Dispute Resolution	E	8	U.S.-based alliance of 500 counsel of corporations and lawyers seeking to promote ADR
Cyberarbitration	A	Planned: 4	Indian-based private venture
Cybercourt	A	Planned: 3, 4	German-based program operated by Price Waterhouse Coopers
Cybersettle	A	1	North American private business venture; exclusive online settlement tool of the Association of Trial Lawyers of America
The Domain Magistrate	E	9	Assistance center to link to three or four ODR providers approved by ICANN
ECODIR	A	3, 5, 10	European Consumer Dispute Resolution; a free online dispute resolution program promoted by the European Commission
E-Mediation (also ODR.NL)	B, D	Planned: 3, 4	Netherlands-based venture created by the Dutch Electronic Commerce Platform
e-Mediator	B, D	3	Pilot project of an offline mediation institution called Consensus

eResolution	D, E	3, 4, 8	Canada-based private business venture
FordJourney	B	4	Service provided by the Chartered Institute of Arbitrators, in Ireland for online sales of Ford cars
FSM	F	6	German ODR company based in Bonn; companies agree to abide by code of conduct
iCourthouse	A	4, 5, 11	U.S.-based business venture; free for partios; oub scription basis to attorneys
iLevel	B	2	U.S.-based consumer service
IntelliCOURT	A	3, 4	California-based private business venture providing offline ADR
Internet Neutral	A	3	U.S.-based private business venture
Intersettle	A	1	Scotland-based private business venture
IRIS	G	3	France-based organization
Judicial Dispute Resolution, Inc.	A	3, 4, 5	Chicago-based private business venture of former judges providing offline ADR for domestic and international commercial disputes

Mediation Arbitration Resolution Services (MARS)	A	1, 3, 4	U.S.-based private business ventures
National Arbitration Forum	A	4	U.S.-based arbitration institution providing DR services under UDRP; accredited by ICANN
New Court City	B, D	1, 3	U.S.-based private business venture
NovaForum.com	D, H	3, 4	Canada-based private business venture, providing ADR services after exhaustion of internal corporate procedures
One Accord	A	12	ODR provider with goal of integrating interest-based negotiation principles with technology that is designed to optimize settlements
Online Disputes	A	Planned: 1	U.S.-based private business venture
Online Ombuds Office	I	3	U.S.-based nonprofit research project created by University of Massachusetts
Online Resolution	A	2, 3, 4	U.S.-based organization created by the Mediation Information and Research Center (MIRC)
ResolveitNow.com	A	1	Private business venture
Resolution Forum	A	2, 3, 4	U.S.-based nonprofit program to make ODR more accessible and affordable to the general public

SettleOnline	A	1, 13	Private business venture
SettleOnline	A	1	U.S.-based private business venture created by Resolution Systems, Inc., a provider of offline ADR
SettleSmart	A	1	Private business venture
SettleTheCase	A	3, 4	Private business venture
SquareTrade	J	2, 3, 4	U.S.-based private business venture
State of Michigan	D	Planned: 14	Michigan court of law for claims greater than $25,000
The Claim Room	A	1, 2, 13	UK-based private business venture
TRUSTe	D	2	Non-profit initiative operated by private business venture
U. S. Settle	A	1	Private business venture
Virtual Magistrate	A	15	U.S.-based academic and non-profit institution, operated by the Chicago-Kent College of Law
WebAssured.com	A	3, 4, 16	U.S.-based private business venture
WEBDispute	A	4, Planned: 3	U.S.-based private business venture
Web Dispute Resolution	A	3, 4	U.S.-based private business venture
WebMediate	A	1, 3, 4	U.S.-based private business venture

WeCanSettle	A	1	UK-based private business venture
Web Trader	A	6	UK-based private business venture
World Intellectual Property Organization (WIPO)	E	3, 4	Dispute resolution provider approved by ICANN, applying the UDRP and its own supplemental rules
Word&Bond	A	6, 4	UK-based private business venture

8.6.3 Selecting a cybermediator

If you are selecting a cybermediator, apart from all the criteria discussed in section 2.7, two obvious attributes you would be looking for are a candidate's degree of computer literacy and his or her training or experience in resolving disputes online. Until cybermediation is used more widely, you may have to be content with finding a candidate that is simply computer literate. Don't be afraid to interview a cybermediator candidate and ask him or her direct questions about his or her online resolution experience. Also talk to other counsel that you know who have participated in cybermediation and obtain their suggestions as to effective cybermediators. Dispute resolution organizations that provide online dispute resolution services exclusively would be a good source for identifying and locating experienced cybermediators. (See appendix L). The American Bar Association operates a Web site (http://www.elawyering.org) that provides guidance for lawyers who practice online. That Web site eventually may be a resource for lawyers to network in order to facilitate selection of cybermediators.

8.6.4 Scenario for cybermediation "walk through"

In order to have a realistic feel for what it is like to engage in a cybermediation, we will "walk through" the next four sections concerning preparing the case and client for cybermediation and in-session and post-session advocacy by means of a four-party dispute scenario. To take full advantage of the walk through experience, you are encouraged to put yourself in the role of counsel for each of these parties at various times as you proceed through the cybermediation process.

The time of year is early June. The dispute concerns the just completed construction of a new building in the Chicago area that tenant doctors complain has a faulty air conditioning system. The owner of the building is withholding a final $100,000 payment to the general contractor until the problem is corrected. The four parties to the dispute are the general contractor, Best Contracting Co., ("BEST") (a national company headquartered in New York with local office in Chicago); the heating and cooling subcontractor, Perfectemp Co., ("PERFECTEMP") (Milwaukee), with outside counsel in Milwaukee, the Project Engineer; Imagineering, Inc. ("IMAGINEERING") (national engineering firm headquartered in San Diego, California); and Aircon Fabricators Ltd., ("AIRCON"), the manufacturer of the cooling system, a company in Frankfurt, Germany with international counsel in London, England. PERFECTEMP had purchased the cooling system from AIRCON through a business-to-business Internet transaction. Because of the urgency of solving the problem, the relatively modest dollar amount of the corrective measures that might need to be taken, the geographic distances separating the parties and counsel to parties, the prohibitive costs of a face to face meeting, the parties and their lawyers have agreed to engage in cybermediation for a ten-day period to see if a resolution can be reached without costly litigation or arbitration. They have secured the services of a cybermediator on the panel of CYBERSOLUTIONS, a full service ODR provider located in Sydney Australia. The chart on the next page identifies the participants in the cybermediation and their geographic locations. The parties have chosen as their neutral the world famous construction dispute mediator, Michael Fairman ("FAIRMAN") who is located in Melbourne, Australia.

PARTY	PARTY'S REP	LOCATION OF PARTY'S REP	PARTY'S COUNSEL	LOCATION OF PARTY'S COUNSEL
BEST	District Manager of General Contractor	Chicago, Illinois	BEST's in-house general counsel	New York, New York
PERFECTEMP	CEO of heating and cooling installation subcontractor	Milwaukee, Wisconsin	Outside litigation counsel	Milwaukee, Wisconsin
IMAGINEERING	President of engineering firm	San Diego, California	Retained local litigation counsel	Chicago, Illinois
AIRCON	Technical supervisor and sales manager of air conditioner manufacturer; bilingual	Frankfurt, Germany	International bilingual counsel; mega law firm	London, England

GENERAL INFORMATION CONCERNING
CONSTRUCTION DISPUTE

About two months ago, BEST completed construction of a two-story (98,000 square feet) medical office building in the Chicago, Illinois area. Within a week after its completion, the tenants—who are all doctors practicing in various medical specialties—moved in. The doctors have been complaining to the building's OWNER that the building's air conditioning system was not operating properly. Four doctors reported having to send their office staff home early on four occasions because their office temperatures approached 90 degrees. These four doctors wrote letters to the OWNER documenting their complaints.

After faxing the four letters of complaint to BEST's district manager in Chicago, the OWNER called the district manager and told him to get the air conditioning matter corrected. The OWNER told BEST that the medical building's director of maintenance had carefully followed the procedures detailed in AIRCON's air conditioner manual in an effort to correct the problem, but to no avail. The director of maintenance e-mailed AIRCON's technical supervisor and sales manager in Frankfurt, Germany who informed the director of maintenance that the procedures he followed were correct and that the problem was "definitely not with the air conditioning equipment." AIRCON suggested that the problem was with the ductwork, and that if anyone was at fault, it was either the heating and cooling subcontractor (PERFECTEMP), or the project engineer (IMAGINEERING). The director of maintenance e-mailed each of these companies, and they both denied responsibility, claiming the problem was caused by the other or by the air conditioner manufacturer, AIRCON.

BEST's district manager e-mailed his company's in-house general counsel in New York, who contacted the lawyers for the other three parties to discuss the possibility of cybermediation. After e-mail back and forth for a few days, they all agreed to use CYBERSOLUTIONS in Australia as the ODR provider, and specifically, FAIRMAN, a broadly experienced and highly skilled construction cybermediator.

CONFIDENTIAL INFORMATION FOR BEST,
THE GENERAL CONTRACTOR

You are BEST's in-house general counsel in New York. You have interviewed BEST's Chicago district manager by telephone and he has told you the general information appearing immediately above and the following information.

He said that when the OWNER called him, the OWNER was irate. Many doctors had called the OWNER "raising Cain" about the air conditioning problem. The OWNER said he wanted the situation corrected *immediately*. The doctors were demanding 50 percent discounts on their monthly rent payments and the OWNER told your district manager that he would have to recoup the value of such discounts from BEST. The OWNER further told your district manager that he was withholding paying BEST the final $100,000 owed on the project "until the doctors are happy as larks" with the temperatures of their offices. The OWNER said he wanted to stay out of it—he didn't want any more expense like hiring a lawyer or paying for a mediator. He said it was BEST's responsibility to "straighten out this mess."

BEST's Chicago district manager further told you that after he talked to the OWNER, he immediately telephoned PERFECTEMP's CEO and advised him of the situation. The Chicago district manger also reminded PERFECTEMP's CEO that, under his contract with BEST, he was subject to liquidated damages in the amount of $1,000 a day if it was determined that his installation of the cooling system was faulty. PERFECTEMP's CEO got angry. He vigorously asserted that his crews installed the equipment and ductwork according to IMAGINEERING's and AIRCON's specifications. He further said that any problems with the air conditioning were not his fault. He said either IMAGINEERING or AIRCON or both were to blame.

Also, BEST's Chicago district manager told you that he had no idea whether the equipment, the installation, or the engineering was to blame, but he was convinced that this problem had to be solved quickly so as to minimize any costs to BEST. Finally BEST tells you that it still owes AIRCON $48,500 for the medical building cooling system and that it has initiated the purchase of ten other cooling systems for buildings it is constructing around the United States. The cash flow of the Chicago district office is currently in dire straits pending receipt of final payment from the OWNER of the Chicago medical building and due to other substantial unpaid receivables.

CONFIDENTIAL INFORMATION FOR PERFECTEMP, THE INSTALLER

You are PERFECTEMP'S outside litigation counsel in Milwaukee, Wisconsin. You have interviewed president of PERFECTEMP in person. Since the president's office is in Milwaukee, you see him quite often and know him well. In the interview, he told you the general information appearing above and the following information.

He said that BEST's district manager told him in a phone call that under PERFECTEMP's contract with BEST, PERFECTEMP is subject to liquidated damages in the amount of $1,000 per day if PERFECTEMP is found to be responsible for the faulty cooling condition of the building. PERFECTEMP's president further told you that he vigorously asserted in the phone conversation that PERFECTEMP was not at fault here, but that either IMAGINEERING or AIRCON were to blame.

PERFECTEMP's president also admitted to you that despite what he told BEST's district manager on the phone, he in fact did not know whether PERFECTEMP may be responsible or partially responsible here. He said that when the building was completed, he himself tested and balanced the air conditioning system. It was a relatively cool day—about 70 degrees. He said that he noted in his internal report that even under those mild temperatures, the building took an inordinate amount of time to cool down and that the temperatures fluctuated from floor to floor. In examining some of the exposed ductwork, he noticed that several sections had much smaller dimensions than IMAGINEERING's specifications in the engineering drawings. At the time he believed this to be inconsequential, and so he did nothing about it. He, however, took pictures of the undersized ductwork.

Finally, PERFECTEMP's President told you that BEST still owes PERFECTEMP $20,000 for the installation work on the medical building complex.

CONFIDENTIAL INFORMATION FOR IMAGINEERING, PROJECT ENGINEER

You are IMAGINEERING'S locally retained litigation counsel in Chicago, Illinois. IMAGINEERING is headquartered in San Diego, California. You have done some minor litigation work for IMAGINEERING in Chicago in the past, but you have never worked with the president of the company directly. You have interviewed IMAGINEERING'S president by telephone recently. In the interview, he told you the general information appearing above and the following information.

IMAGINEERING's president told you that he is taking this complaint very seriously because his company is in the process of doing engineering drawings for approximately ten similar medical buildings around the United States. He also has several engineering contracts in process and about to be executed. He did not want any bad publicity over this Chicago medical building because it might adversely affect his relationships with his present clients and the development of relationships with new clients. He was very happy that this dispute was being kept out of court through cybermediation conducted by someone in Australia.

IMAGINEERING's president further told you that the IMAGINEERING engineer that worked on the project originally had since left the company. He said that when he first got word about the air conditioning problem in the Chicago medical building, he pulled the file on the project and reviewed it.

He said that he noticed something startling. He said that because of a typographical error in an early analysis of the project, an error was made in specifying the appropriate tonnage of the cooling system for the project. This error was carried through to all documents and specifications related to the project. The final specifications called for a 250 ton cooling system, whereas the tonnage specification based on the building size and floor area should have been 280 tons. Luckily, the error was smaller than it could have been, but it certainly does carry with it some professional malpractice implications.

Finally, he told you that luckily, all the other engineering specifications, including the size of the ductwork, were appropriate for the higher tonnage (280 ton) cooling system.

CONFIDENTIAL INFORMATION FOR AIRCON, THE MANUFACTURER

You are AIRCON'S international counsel in London, England. You speak German and English fluently. AIRCON is headquartered in Frankfurt, Germany. You have interviewed AIRCON's technical supervisor and sales representative by telephone. She also speaks both German and English fluently. You know her well since you have represented AIRCON on many occasions in the last few years in major international sales transactions and in business disputes arising out of AIRCON's new venture into Internet product sales. In the interview, she told you the general information appearing above and the following information.

She told you that the medical building's director of maintenance had e-mailed her recently complaining that there might be a defect in the air conditioning system because the building was experiencing unusually high temperatures at the beginning of the summer. In a reply e-mail she said that she told him there was no problem with the equipment. It had been pre-tested and it was working fine before shipment. She further told him that if it had been damaged during shipment or during its transportation to the building site, it was not AIRCON's responsibility. Additionally she told him that the problem could have been caused either by the installer's ductwork or by the project engineer's specifications.

She also told you that there had been some new developments since she had e-mailed the building's director of maintenance. She said that she had received similar e-mail complaints from two other building owners, one in Brazil and one in Italy, regarding the particular model of cooling system that had been installed in the Chicago medical building. In the Brazil situation, it had been a voltage problem; in the Italy situation, the cause of the problem had not yet been determined. She further said that the large majority of owners of this particular air conditioner model, internationally, had nothing but high praise for it.

Finally, she told you that BEST has not yet fully paid AIRCON for the air conditioning system installed in the Chicago medical building. The unpaid balance of the air conditioning unit is $48,500. BEST has initiated purchase orders for ten other air conditioner units for buildings it is constructing in various areas of the United States.

Now we are ready to analyze how this dispute might be processed in a cybermediation. Apart from the advocacy suggestions presented below in the next four sections, you are encouraged to imagine other ways you might handle each situation as counsel for one of the four parties. By agreement of the participants, the manager of CYBERSOLUTIONS has e-mailed the contact information to all participants, including e-mail addresses; regular addresses, telephone numbers, fax numbers, and company Web site addresses.

8.7 PREPARING THE CASE FOR CYBERMEDIATION

Much of the advice given in chapter 3 regarding preparing the case for mediation also applies to cybermediation. There are some differences, however, that are explained below. The scenario and cybermediation participants described in subsection 8.6.4 will be used as vehicles to consider preparation strategies in this section 8.7.

8.7.1 Selecting case-specific documents and gathering relevant Internet information

Selecting Case-specific documents.

- **All counsel.** The basic differences between selecting case-specific documents for an online mediation, as compared with an offline mediation, revolve around issues of time, expense, technology, and convenience. First, you have to consider whether there is enough time to get the documents to the addressee if you have to send hard copies (multiple transcripts of proceedings; pleadings). Overnight mail or other delivery service is no problem in the United States, but if you have to send documents internationally, they might not be received for three to five days, even under the speediest of circumstances. Late receipt of documents may make it difficult for recipients to review them in advance of the beginning of the online mediation. Also, for some clients, sending voluminous documents to all mediation participants might be cost-prohibitive. If many documents need to be provided to the mediator, often counsel can collaboratively compile a set of documents to send the cybermediator, and perhaps share the cost of doing so.

  If just a few documents need to be provided to the cybermediator and/or other participants at certain points during the cybermediation process, e-transmission of them is no problem if they are in digital form. If they are not, you would need to scan them into your computer hard drive or floppy disk so that you could attach them to an e-mail. If you do not have scanning equipment available, you could use a colleague's scanner or visit a storefront offering office technology services.

Faxing may also be an alternate transmission possibility. But if you fax something, you should determine whether the addressees will be able to retrieve the information from the machine, depending where they are going to be located at any particular point during the cybermediation, which may spread across a period of days or even weeks.

Convenience of the recipients is also a factor. Reading one-hundred pages of material on a computer screen can be very tiring. And it may be a burden for cybermediation participants to print out that size document from their computer. You should also realize that, depending on where they are located during a cybermediation, a printer may not be available to them. Thus, it may be more convenient for everyone to send hard copies of large documents commercially.

- **As counsel for BEST.** In some respects BEST, besides representing its own interests in this dispute, is also the surrogate for the OWNER. After securing the OWNER's permission, you should consider providing all the participants with copies of the complaint letters of the four doctors prior to the beginning of the cybermediation. Such documents would set an urgent tone for the cybermediation and perhaps help speed the process to resolution. You should also have available to e-mail or fax to mediator FAIRMAN in caucus, the portion of BEST's contract with PERFECTEMP that states that PERFECTEMP is subject to $1,000 dollar per day liquidated damages. You should also have available the construction contract between BEST and the OWNER, and the engineering drawings. Finally, you want to see the purchase order relative to BEST's purchase of the AIRCON cooling system for the Chicago medical building and the documents related to BEST's initiation of the purchase of ten more cooling systems from AIRCON.

- **As counsel for PERFECTEMP.** Aside from the engineering drawings, you should have available during the cybermediation the same contracts available to BEST's counsel (see above). You should also have available for your use PERFECTEMP's president's internal test and balance report and the pictures of the undersized ductwork. At some point in the cybermediation, you may want to share some of this information with the cybermediator by e-mail attachment. Disclosure will depend on how the information in the cybermediation unfolds.

- **As counsel for IMAGINEERING.** Aside from the engineering drawings, you want to have available a copy of the contract between your client and the OWNER. Your client tells you that the contract provides for arbitration of any dispute arising out of the OWNER-IMAGINEERING relationship. You may want to use this fact as leverage to hasten a settlement in the cybermediation. You also want your client to provide you with documents specifying the appropriate air conditioner tonnage requirements for the building. You also need information, in addition to that on IMAGINEERING's Web site, describing the credentials of the firm including any professional awards received over the years.

- **As counsel for AIRCON.** You want to see all correspondence, e-mail, and otherwise between AIRCON and any of the parties to the cybermediation. You also want to review similar correspondence between the Brazilian and Italian complainants and AIRCON. You also want available for the cybermediation all correspondence from purchasers praising AIRCON's air conditioner systems. Finally, you want a copy of the Internet purchase contract between BEST and AIRCON for the medical building cooling system and copies of any documents related to BEST's initiating the purchase of ten more AIRCON cooling systems for other U.S. construction projects.

This analysis of the advocates' document needs is intentionally incomplete. It would be a useful exercise for you assume the role of each lawyer and think about other documents you might need—either case-specific documents or relevant information from the Internet, as discussed next.

Gathering relevant Internet information.

Apart from selecting documents relevant to your case, you should realize in your preparation that you have at your fingertips a virtual wealth of Internet information useful to your cybermediation presentation. Remember that in cybermediation, your presentation is not restricted by the rules of evidence, the rule against hearsay, or other measures barring information helpful to problem solving. Sometimes in court proceedings, highly relevant and reliable information is precluded by evidentiary rules conservatively crafted to protect the integrity of the judicial process. Not so in mediation or cybermediation. Through Web research in advance of the cybermediation, advocates can gather information highly relevant to the problem to be addressed in the session with the mediator. Such research might yield these types of information, to name just a few: (1) applicable cases decided by relevant courts in the last few days (or hours)(LEXIS, WestLaw, etc.); (2) newspaper articles concerning statements made by various mediation parties publicly (NEXIS); (3) background information on the parties and their counsel contained in Web professional directories or on corporate Web sites (this might be appropriate research in the medical building scenario); (4) prospecti or annual reports of corporate parties; (5) information showing structures of corporations, identifying subsidiaries, interlocking directorates, or other linkages; (6) articles or book synopses written by various parties, and/or their counsel or other experts taking positions opposite those being taken in the cybermediation; (7) items of information in the judicial notice category: day of week on a particular date, weather conditions on a particular date in a particular city, date and time of day that a particular historical or catastrophic event occurred, etc.; (8) jury verdicts in cases similar to the one in cybermediation; (9) published settlement figures in similar cases; (10) creative settlement remedies crafted in similar cases; (11) state government information; (12) federal government information. To gather this information, you must be able to use not only computer-aided legal research techniques (in which lawyers are by now reasonably skilled) but also general Web research techniques. Some tips on using the latter techniques follow.

- **Search Engines.** A search engine is a program that searches one or more documents for specified key words and returns a list of locations where those keywords were found. Some search engines are capable of doing Boolean searches; others are not. A Boolean search involves using Boolean operators (i.e., AND, OR, and NOT) that are used to refine or broaden a search (see below in this subsection). You may find the following legal search engines useful in preparing for cybermediation (first type http://www):

  > abanet.org
  > American Law Sources Online
  > Catalaw (meta search engine)
  > CyberAttorney
  > Findlaw
  > GSU Law (meta search engine)
  > Hieros Gamos
  > InternetLegalResourceGuide
  > Law.com
  > LawCrawler
  > LawGuru

The chart below identifies the leading general search engines and describes relevant attributes.

SEARCH ENGINES	RELEVANT ATTRIBUTES
Alta Vista	Searches in any language using Boolean operators and date limitation
Excite	Uses Boolean operators and offers extensive retrieval options
Fast/All the Web	Allows Boolean queries and content limitors
GO	Good coverage of Web, newsgroup information, and news and company sites
Google.com Google/ Uncle Sam	No Boolean operators; very accurate searching; specialized search engine for searching for government information
Hot Bot	"Super Search" feature offers the user word filters, page, location, and media type limitation; drop-down menus give user straightforward limiting options
Lycos	Full Boolean search available; indexing of fifty million Web pages
Northern Light	Great degree of precision searching; limits include dates, subjects, sources, and document types
Yahoo!	Considered more of a search directory than a traditional search engine

Other search engines and meta search engines include (first type http://www):

> About.com
> Ask Jeeves
> Looksmart
> Search.com
> Cyber 411
> Inference
> Metacrawler
> ProFusion
> SavvySearch

Other Internet reference tools. Other reference tools that you can use to find information to aid problem solving are listed in the chart below with comments as appropriate (first type http://www.):

RFERENCE TOOL	COMMENTS
clearinghouse.net	Argus Clearinghouse. Reviews and rates top Web sites
www.ipl.org	Internet Public Library. General information
lli.org	Librarian's Index to the Internet. General information index
vlib.stanford.edu/ overview.html	The WWW Virtual Library. General information
anywho.com	Phone and address lookup site from AT&T locates people when you have only partial information; includes a reverse telephone number lookup feature
switchboard.com	Phone and address lookup site
whowhere.com	Phone and address lookup site
infospace.com	E-mail, business, and residential address lookup site
zip2.com	Business address and phone number lookup site
companysleuth.com	Background on businesses, including information on litigation and patent applications
mapquest.com	Detailed street maps for any place in the U.S.
nypl.org	New York Public Library. A library card is required; library bar code number is used as a password; has several excellent electronic databases available to the public including Proquest, which provides full-text articles from many newspapers and periodicals
iTools.com	All-in-one reference desk: dictionary, quotes, translators, and more

onelook.com	400 dictionaries; specialized and general
britannica.com	Encyclopedia Brittanica; free of charge
thesaurus.com	Roget's Internet Thesaurus
infoplease.com/	Information Please Almanac; dictionary and full Columbia Encyclopedia
biography.com	Brief cross-referenced biographies of more that 15,000 notable people, some adapted from Cambridge Biographical Encyclopedia
nolo.com/lawcenter/ dictionary/ wordindex.cfm	Nolo's legal dictionary
odci.gov/cia/ publications/pubs.html	C.I.A. World Factbook; brief profiles of countries around the world
usps.com	U.S. Postal Service's Zip Code finder and express mail tracker
ups.com	Track UPS packages
fedex.com	Track Fedex packages

Tips for using search engines. When conducting a search, break down the topic into key concepts. For example, to find out what the Federal Aviation Administration (FAA) has said about making handicapped seating available on commercial airliners, the keywords might be:

> FAA handicapped seating

- **Boolean AND.** If you connect search terms with AND, you tell the search engine to retrieve Web pages containing all the keywords. Consider the following search command:

   > FAA and handicapped and seating

   In this example, the search engine will not return pages with just the word FAA; nor will it return pages with the word FAA and the word handicapped. Rather the search engine will only return pages where the words FAA, handicapped, and seating all appear somewhere on the page. Thus, the word AND helps to narrow your search results to pages where all keywords appear.

- **Boolean OR.** If you connect search terms with OR, you tell the search engine to return pages with a single keyword, several keywords, and all keywords. Thus, OR expands your search results. Use OR when you have synonyms for a keyword. It is best to surround OR statements with parentheses. Combine OR statements with AND statements if you wish to narrow your results as much as possible. For example, the following search statement locates information on buying an insolvent company:

> (company or corporation or business) and (buy or purchase) and insolvent

- **Boolean AND NOT.** If you connect search terms with AND NOT, you tell the search engine to retrieve Web pages containing one keyword but not the other. Consider this example:

> insurance and not life

This search statement tells the search engine to return Web pages about insurance, but not Web pages concerning life insurance. Essentially, you should use AND NOT when you have a keyword that has multiple meanings.

- **Implied Boolean: plus and minus.** In some search engines, plus and minus symbols can be used as alternatives to full Boolean AND and AND NOT. The plus sign is the equivalent of AND, and the minus sign is the equivalent of AND NOT. No space is placed between the plus or minus sign and the keyword.

- **Phrase searching.** Placing a group of words in double quotes tells the search engine to only retrieve documents in which those words appear side by side. Phrase searching is a powerful tool for narrowing searches. Examples are: "mediation advocacy training"; "evaluative mediator"; "online dispute resolution service."

- **Combining phrase searching with implied Boolean or full Boolean.** Consider the following examples:

> +"deep vein thrombosis" +cause
>
> "deep vein thrombosis" and cause

These search statements tell the search engine to retrieve pages where the words "deep vein thrombosis" appear side by side and the word *cause* appears somewhere on the page.

- **Plural forms, capital letters, and alternate spellings.** Most search engines interpret singular keywords as singular or plural. If you desire plural forms only, type your keywords that way. If you want both upper and lowercase occurrences returned, type your keywords in all lowercase letters. On the other hand, if you want to limit your results to initial capital letters (e.g., Abraham Lincoln) or all uppercase letters (TOP SECRET), you should type your keywords accordingly. A few search engines allow variations in spelling or word forms by use of the asterisk (*) symbol. For example, capital* returns Web pages with capital, capitals, capitalize, and capitalization.

- **Title search.** A Web page is composed of a number of fields such as title, domain, host, URL, and link. If you combine field searches with phrase searches and Boolean logic, you increase your search effectiveness. Consider these examples:

    +title:"Abraham Lincoln" +President +"Mary Todd"

    title:"Abraham Lincoln" and President and "Mary Todd"

    The above title search tells the search engine to return Web pages where the phrase Abraham Lincoln appears in the title and the words President and Mary Todd appear somewhere on the page. Like plus and minus, there is no space between the colon after title and the keyword.

- **Domain search.** The domain search allows you to limit your results to certain domains such as Web sites from educational institutions, other countries, or the government. The current U.S. domains include the following:

    .com = commercial business

    .edu = educational institution

    .gov = governmental institution

    .org = a non-profit organization

    .mil = a military site

    .net = a network site

Consider these examples:

    domain:edu and "cloning" and animal*

    domain:uk and title: "Winston Churchill"

    domain:gov and "freedom of information" and bribe*

- **Host search.** This type of search allows you to search all the pages at a Web site for keywords or phrases of interest. An example is shown below.

    +host:www.abanet.org +cyber*

    host:www.abanet.org and cyber*

- **URL search.** If you do a URL search, you tell the search engine to return the Web pages where the keyword appears in the URL or Web site address. A URL search narrows results to Web pages devoted to the keyword topic.

Consider these examples:

    +url:mediation +title:articles

    url:mediation and title:articles

- **Link search.** If you want to know what Web sites are linked to a particular site of interest, use a link search. For example, you would use this type of search if you have a home page and you want to know if anyone has put a link to your page on their Web site. Typically, researchers use link searches for conducting backward citations. Consider these examples:

  link:www.nita.org

  link:www.mediate.com

  link:www.onlineresolution.com

8.7.2   Deciding the format of the presentation

Winston Churchill once mused that:

> The human story does not always unfold like a mathematical calculation on the principle that two and two make four. Sometimes in life they make five or minus three; and sometimes the blackboard topples down in the middle of the sum and leaves the class in disorder and the pedagogue with a black eye.[32]

Although Churchill, in the above quote, is referring to presentations made in a world of physical objects, his poignant message is equally applicable to presentations made in the world of cyberspace. The format of your presentation in cybermediation can set the stage for the success or failure of the process from your client's point of view.

- **All counsel.** Much of the information contained in section 3.7 is relevant to cybermediation. There are some differences, however. Some ODR providers, for example, dictate how a particular mediation should be formatted, processwise. Some providers leave the format decision completely in the hands of the cybermediator, and still others leave such a decision up to the parties and the cybermediator to work out collaboratively. Some providers do not have technology support for a chat-room discussion, where all participants are online simultaneously in real-time. In such a real-time chat, the cybermediator normally determines the order of initial statements of the parties. The real-time chat format is useful in certain circumstances and not in others. It is useful to parties in uncomplicated cases to briefly state their opening remarks. It is also useful, after the cybermediator has caucused with each of the parties, to have a joint real-time chat to answer

---

32. Churchill as quoted by Bill Adler, *The Churchill Wit* (Coward-McCann, Inc. 1965), 50.

the cybermediator's clarifying questions and to determine the priority of issues and to structure the evolving process.

In cases that are complex, real-time chat may be effective in the design of the structure of the process, but not so for allowing multiple parties to make lengthy opening statements. For the most part, this can be a waste of time for all participants because the same goal can be accomplished by each party separately preparing an opening statement, at leisure, and sending it to the other participants, including the cybermediator, by e-mail. The mediator can ask clarifying questions of all participants by e-mail and the parties can decide individually if they want to copy everyone with their response, to certain participants, or to the cybermediator only. Real-time chat has the major drawback of counsel being asked a question without sufficient time to discuss the question with his client prior to responding. If this occurs, counsel should politely decline to respond to the question until after he or she has had an opportunity to consult with the client.

Threaded discussions of all participants or of certain participants on particular issues may be more efficacious than real-time chat. In threaded discussions, participants have time to think about their responses or their comments on other responses before making them. Threaded discussions can also occur in caucuses among aligned parties as other e-mail communications are occurring jointly among all the parties or while the cybermediator is conducting e-mail caucuses with the parties.

- **As counsel for BEST.** Because of the urgency of the situation for your client and the OWNER, you are inclined to favor opening statements in a real-time chat format. You are concerned that if the cybermediator waits for each party's counsel to submit opening statements to all participants by e-mail, it may take a couple weeks or more for that to happen. The doctors could file a lawsuit in that period of time. Everyday BEST is losing money because the OWNER is withholding a $100,000 final payment. BEST's unpaid subcontractors may file for arbitration if BEST doesn't pay them for their already completed work, soon. That would mean more legal bills for your client. You would favor opening statements by separate e-mails to all participants only if the cybermediator set a three-day submission deadline on such e-mail opening statement. You really don't have that much to say, except to emphasize the urgency of the situation.

- **As counsel for PERFECTEMP.** You feel the same as BEST. You favor real-time chat and abbreviated opening statements. Your client is risking payment of $1,000 per day liquidated damages if BEST holds it fully responsible for the cooling system problem. However, you would go along with a three-day filing deadline for separate e-mail opening statements if the parties and cybermediator prefer to go this route.

- **As counsel for IMAGINEERING.** You prefer a short real-time chat session, just to hear what the other participants have to say and to determine whether any of them is alleging that the engineering drawings have errors or that the tonnage requirements were misspecified. There is very little you want to say in the opening statement.

- **As counsel for AIRCON.** You also prefer a short, real-time chat session. You want to emphasize the worldwide praise that this particular model of cooling system has received and you want to express your indignation that someone would allege that there is a defect in this finely tooled and expertly crafted German product. You also want to mildly scold BEST for delay in paying the amount remaining on the invoice ($48,500).

The cybermediator and the parties jointly decide to use CYBERSOLUTIONS' real-time chat feature for an opening format. This analysis of the advocates' preference for an opening format for the cybermediation is only one of many possibilities. It would be a useful exercise for you assume the role of each lawyer and think about the reasons why some other format may be more proper or more useful.

8.7.3 Determining what information should be kept confidential

- **All counsel.** The information contained in section 3.8 provides relevant guidance in determining what information should be kept confidential in cybermediation. One thing you should keep in mind, however, is that in cybermediation, what you do decide to disclose in confidence to the cybermediator or to an aligned party may not be as secure or protectible as information so disclosed in an offline mediation.

- **As counsel for BEST.** You want to refrain from affirmatively disclosing that you have not yet paid AIRCON the outstanding balance of $48,500 for the medical building cooling system. Also, you do not want it known that you still owe PERFECTEMP $20,000 for installation work. You are hoping that AIRCON and PERFECTEMP will not make this side issue a matter of bargaining leverage in the cybermediation. On the other hand, you may share these facts with the cybermediator in an e-mail caucus as a measure the cybermediator can use as leverage in your favor when he caucuses with those two parties. You certainly don't want to reveal to anyone BEST's current overall cash flow problems. This might give other parties unfair bargaining leverage.

- **As counsel for PERFECTEMP.** You definitely want to keep confidential from the other parties that PERFECTEMP's test and balance report reveals that the installed ductwork was undersized in relation to IMAGINEERING's engineering specifications.

- **As counsel for IMAGINEERING.** You definitely want to keep confidential from the other parties that IMAGINEERING's drawings had a typographical error that caused the wrong tonnage air conditioning system to be installed.

- **As counsel for AIRCON.** You definitely want to keep confidential from the other parties that AIRCON has recently received two other complaints regarding possible defects in the same model air conditioning system as was installed in the Chicago medical building.

This analysis of the advocates' preferences for confidentiality of certain information is only one possibility. It would be a useful exercise for you to assume the role of each lawyer and think about the reasons why other information should also be kept confidential.

8.7.4 Determining whether a premediation caucus would be helpful

- **All counsel.** The suggestions contained in section 3.9 are equally applicable to cybermediation.

- **As counsel for BEST.** Even though the parties have agreed to a real-time chat opening format, you believe it is necessary to have a pre-mediation e-mail caucus with the mediator. You want to emphasize the urgency of the situation and your willingness to cooperate fully in crafting a fair, and perhaps creative, solution to the dispute. You also want to offer the cybermediator the option of corresponding with the OWNER directly as the cybermediation proceeds. The OWNER is willing to participate in the wings in this manner.

- **As counsel for PERFECTEMP.** You have nothing to say to the cybermediator in a premediation caucus, except that he can expect your full cooperation in the cybermediation process. You can just as easily say this in a real-time chat opening format.

- **As counsel for IMAGINEERING.** You feel the same as PERFECTEMP's counsel in this regard.

- **As counsel for AIRCON.** You feel the same as PERFECTEMP's counsel in this regard.

This analysis of the advocates' preferences for a premediation caucus is only one possibility. It would be a useful exercise for you assume the role of each lawyer and think about other reasons why a premediation caucus may be beneficial.

8.7.5 Determining your negotiation strategy and related tactics

- **All counsel.** The suggestions contained in section 3.14 are equally applicable to cybermediation. One caution, however. In cybermediation, your strategies and tactics will be recorded *in writing*. If you initially take a highly competitive or a highly cooperative approach and you later want to reverse the respective approaches, you run the risk of not being taken seriously or of being trustworthy (competitive to cooperative) or of having already made concessions (cooperative to competitive). In either case, earlier e-mail impeaching comments may come back to haunt you as the cybermediation proceeds.

- **As counsel for BEST.** You wish to take a very collaborative approach. Although BEST's district manager has threatened PERFECTEMP with $1,000 per day liquidated damages, you would rather not make a further issue of that in the cybermediation unless you determine that a compromise or win-win solution is impossible. You want the cybermediator to determine whether IMAGINEERING believes that the cooling system was installed by PERFECTEMP according to IMAGINEERING's specifications. You also want the cybermediator to directly confront PERFECTEMP with the question of the results of its "test and balance" inspection and of whether it believes PERFECTEMP's workers correctly installed the ductwork.

- **As counsel for PERFECTEMP.** Initially you want to take a competitive approach, denying any responsibility or liability but willing to work toward a solution.

- **As counsel for IMAGINEERING.** You want to take a professional, accommodating approach. Essentially, you want to come across as being very professional and above the fray, so to speak, but willing to help the others come to a solution to *their* dispute.

- **As counsel for AIRCON.** Initially you want to take a highly competitive, indignant approach. The reputation of German manufacturing craftsmanship is at stake here. In your initial statements in real-time chat you intend to let it be known that BEST has not yet paid the outstanding balance for the Chicago medical building cooling system. You also intend to threaten BEST that

AIRCON will not ship any cooling systems to any of BEST's construction sites until AIRCON receives payment for the system installed in the Chicago medical building. This represents a lot of leverage for AIRCON because preventing shipment of cooling systems could delay completion of construction on ten of BEST's construction projects. You are willing later on to become more cooperative, if the process becomes more problem solving in nature.

This analysis of the advocates' preferences for negotiation strategies is only one possibility. It would be a useful exercise for you assume the role of each lawyer and think about how other cybermediation approaches, strategies, or tactics may be beneficial.

8.7.6 Deciding who should be online or available during the cybermediation session

- **All counsel.** Some of the considerations of section 3.15 are applicable here, but the nature of the cybermediation process must take many other considerations into account. In real-time chat, for example, even if your client is not present, he or she can be apprised later—word for word—of what transpired in the chat session, assuming that the ODR provider has the technology and capability to save and store this information. Threaded discussions can also be available for client review and providing input to counsel at the convenience of the client. Normally, clients will receive all the e-mail from participants and therefore will be "present" for joint e-mailings and for e-mail caucuses at the client's convenience. Although the nature of cybermediation is more relaxed for clients, it puts, at the same time, more pressure on their lawyers. Lawyers may feel frustrated when a response is required quickly to an e-mail, for example from the cybermediator, and the lawyer's client is unavailable for e-mail consultation. The asynchronous nature of the cybermediation process also puts a lawyer's written comments and replies in e-mails to other participants "under a microscope" so to speak.

    Clients who are not consulted prior to their lawyers' sending an e-mail reply may take issue, after the fact, with the precise words the lawyers used or the implication that the words were left with the other participants about the clients' specific positions or interest. Clients may even take issue with the tone of their lawyers' e-mail messages sent to other participants. Aside from this "lawyer-in-a-fishbowl" problem, lawyers also face the problem that their clients may decide that they want to "forward" an e-mail to a person outside the circle of parties to the mediation. To head off any breach of confidentiality problems, advocates representing clients in cybermediaiton should specifically agree up front as to the persons outside of the actual participants in the cybermediation can have access to e-mail communications—and specifically as to what types of e-mail communication and other cybermediation-generated information. Persons that advocates may suggest to be listed and approved for access to cybermediation-generated information are, to name a few, persons who have co-settlement authority, the parties' experts, peripheral co-counsel in the dispute, corporate general counsel, insurance companies holding liens on any settlement, and in the appropriate situation, structured settlement consultants. Such persons would have to agree to be subject to and to sign the confidentiality agreement covering the cybermediaiton.

- **As counsel for BEST.** BEST has requested and all parties and the mediator have agreed that the OWNER can be copied on all cybermediation-generated information and that the OWNER can caucus privately with the mediator. The parties agree that BEST's district manager can be contacted by mediator FAIRMAN if necessary.

- **As counsel for PERFECTEMP.** PERFECTEMP has sought and has been granted permission by the parties to allow the company president to consult with the company's CEO during the course of the cybermediation and to share cybermediation-generated information with her.

- **As counsel for IMAGINEERING.** IMAGINEERING has requested permission to consult during the course of the cybermediation with the engineer that actually produced the medical building drawings. The parties agreed.

- **As counsel for AIRCON.** AIRCON has requested permission to allow London counsel to consult with AIRCON's outside counsel in Frankfurt, Germany during the course of the cybermediation. He has also noted that while the technical supervisor has the most knowledge regarding the model air conditioning system in question, he would need to obtain the approval of the president of AIRCON before any settlement agreement could be executed. The parties agreed that these two people could be on the disclosure listing.

This analysis of the advocates' preferences as to who should have access to cybermediation-generated information is only one of many possibilities. It would be a useful exercise for you assume the role of each lawyer and think about other persons who might be candidates for access to such information, subject to the agreement of the parties.

8.8   PREPARING THE CLIENT FOR CYBERMEDIATION

Some of the advice given in chapter 4 regarding preparing the client for mediation also applies to cybermediation. There many differences, however, that are explained below.

8.8.1   Advising the client about the nature of the cybermediation process

If your client has never been a party in a private mediation before, you will have to explain the basic mediation process, as described in section 4.1, before you advise him or her about the nature of the cybermediation process. With regard to cybermediation, you might consider providing your client with the description of cybermediation contained in subsection 8.6.1. You should also explain the benefits and limitations of cybermediation (subsection 8.4.1) and emphasize concerns about confidentiality.

You may want to use the figure below to help explain to your client the relationship between real-world (offline) and virtual-world (online) mediation.[33]

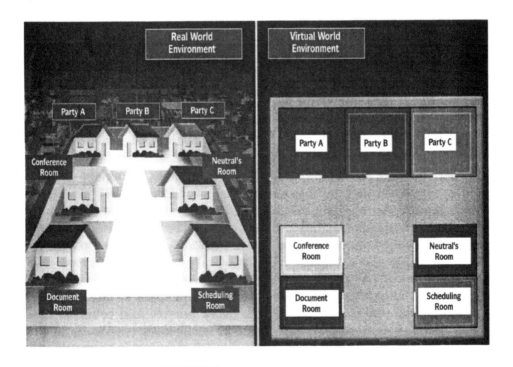

---

33.   This figure was included as part of a presentation by Dr. Mauricio Chabaneix Belling (www.servilex.com.pe/arbitraje), from Arequipa, Peru, at the International Congress of the Private Resolution of Disputes, held in Recife Brazil in November, 2001. It is reproduced here with Dr. Belling's permission.

The left-hand portion of the figure above illustrates features of the real-world mediation environment. Parties (A, B, and C) occupy separate physical spaces—small conference rooms (here depicted as separate houses) in an ADR center. At the ADR center, there are also other rooms (also depicted as houses), including a large conference room (where parties and counsel can caucus with or without the mediator), a room for the neutral or neutrals to meet privately with a party or to develop settlement proposals based on the parties' suggestions, and physical spaces for document storage and retrieval and for scheduling or calendaring of mediation events.

The right-hand portion of the figure illustrates that virtual spaces can similarly be created for use in a virtual-world mediation. The three cyberparties (and their cyberadvocates) can be viewed as occupying three separate virtual conference rooms. A large virtual conference room can be viewed as available to allow aligned cyberparties and cyberadvocates to caucus privately; to allow the cybermediator to meet with all the parties, or a couple of them, in real-time chat or by means of "reply to all" e-mail. Another virtual room can be viewed as being used by a cybermediator (or co-cybermediators) to meet privately with a party or to privately develop settlement proposals that he or she can later share with the parties, either in real-time chat in the large virtual conference room or by "reply to all" e-mail. Like the real-world mediation model, the cybermediator and the cyberparties have virtual spaces available to them for storage and retrieval of digital and Internet documents and for scheduling and calendaring of cybermediation events.

8.8.2   Advising the client about the role of the cybermediator

You should explain to your client that the facilitative cybermediator's role is to manage the online communication process, to remain neutral and impartial throughout the cybermediation, and to assist the parties, predominantly through online communication, to come to a resolution. The facilitative cybermediator may use real-time chat, "reply to all" e-mails, threaded discussions, or e-mail caucuses, and other technological options to achieve that end. The facilitative cybermediator may also use e-mail to advise the parties of the caucus schedule and to assign "homework" questions for the parties and their counsel to discuss when the cybermediator is caucusing with other parties and counsel. The cybermediator may consolidate drafts of settlement proposals of the parties, sometimes include his or her own suggestions, and distribute the drafts to the parties by e-mail for e-mail feedback.

If you have opted for an evaluative cybermediation, then the cybermediator's role will be different. He or she may or may not conduct e-mail caucuses. But the primary difference is that near the end of the evaluative cybermediation, the cybermediator will give his opinion in writing as to the fair settlement value or an appropriate settlement structure for the case. Depending on the parties' preagreement, the cybermediator may or may not give reasons for arriving at his or her suggested solution.

8.8.3 Advising the client about the role of the cyberadvocate

You should also advise your client that in your role as cyberadvocate, you will need to be in frequent contact with him or her. You should stress that you will not always know in advance when you will be receiving and needing to quickly respond to e-mail or other communication from the cybermediator, counsel for aligned parties, or from counsel for opposing parties. You should emphasize the need for the client to respond to you as soon as possible so that the settlement process will not be unnecessarily delayed. You should also emphasize the fact that since nearly every communication in the cybermediation will be in writing, special care must be taken in word selection. Semantics is a key consideration. The extent to which written words can be interpreted or misinterpreted by another party or by opposing counsel can have a great influence on the success or failure of the cybermediation process. Thus, in your role as cyberadvocate, you will have to be constantly focused on crafting sentences in simple, direct, and unoffensive ways. This is particularly true when engaged in a cybermediation with international parties who speak English as their second language.

8.8.4 Advising the client about the role of the client

The importance of preparing a client for speaking (or not speaking) in any dispute resolution process is no better illustrated than in the story of the novice lawyer in central Illinois who was presenting his first case in court. He spent two hours preparing his plaintiff client for direct examination in a damage suit that charged a railroad company whose train had killed twenty-four of his prized hogs. Early in the jury trial, the young lawyer asked his client on direct examination, "How many dead hogs did you find on and around the tracks?" His client testified—precisely as he had been coached—"Twenty-four dead hogs, sir—twenty-four big, fat, dead hogs." But then, to dramatize his testimony, the client added gratuitously, "That's twice the number that are on the jury!" The plaintiff lost his case and you can be assured that the young lawyer learned an important lesson about client preparation.[34]

All counsel. While in offline mediation it is often appropriate to allow your client to speak in a joint session, it is almost never

---

34. Adapted from Herbert V. Prochnow, *The Speaker's Treasure of Stories for All Occasions,* (Prentice Hall, Inc. 1953), 30.

appropriate to allow a client to communicate to an opposing party or to opposing counsel in an online mediation. This is because in online mediation, communicating means making a written record. A client's unintentional admission against interest in a hastily drafted response can be devastating. The role of the lawyer-represented client in most cybermediations is to communicate with his or her lawyer only. There may be a few narrow exceptions to this rule. One exception might be for the lawyer to allow a client to directly communicate with the cybermediator by e-mail. However, this should be permitted only after the lawyer has had the opportunity to review the exact e-mail message the client intends to send to the cybermediator. Another exception might be to allow the client to communicate with other mediation participants only with regard to administrative matters—real-time chat availability, scheduling, and the like. In no event should a client be allowed to communicate substantively with other participants without first clearing the content of the communication with his or her counsel.

- **As counsel for BEST.** You decide that the district manager can communicate with the cybermediator, so long as each communication is screened by you, first. He can also respond to administrative (scheduling) inquiries without clearance from you.

- **As counsel for PERFECTEMP.** You and the president of PERFECTEMP have discussed the matter and have concluded that the President need not communicate directly with any participant, including the mediator. You and he are both located in the same city. It will be easy for you to consult with each other on schedules, and only you will need to communicate with the other participants regarding you and your client's scheduling information.

- **As counsel for IMAGINEERING.** Because of the sensitive nature of the professional liability aspect of your client's situation, you prefer to not risk allowing your client to directly communicate with any participants, including the mediator. You do not want her to directly communicate about administrative matters, either.

- **As counsel for AIRCON.** Because of the potential for misunderstandings based on semantical issues of German and English connotations, you have asked your client not to communicate directly with any participant either on substantive or administrative matters.

The analysis above, of course, is only one possibility of the type of advice you may want to give these respective clients about their role in this cybermediation. You should feel free to think about other advice you might want to give these clients concerning their role in this cybermediation.

8.8.5   Reviewing the case, settlement goals, strategies and tactics with the client

The suggestions given in section 4.5 regarding reviewing the case, settlement goals, and strategies and tactics with your client prior to a mediation are equally applicable in your preparation for a cybermediation. However, as you probably realize, because of the asynchronous nature of cybermediation and the fact that it will extend over a period of days or weeks, you will have ample opportunities during the course of the process to reexamine with your client his or her settlement goals and the appropriate strategies and tactics for achieving those goals.

8.9   EFFECTIVE ADVOCACY IN THE CYBERMEDIATION SESSIONS

8.9.1   Cybermediation protocols

Several ODR service providers publish protocols on their Web sites. These protocols establish the ground rules governing the participants' conduct in the particular ODR process selected. Online Resolution (www.onlineresolution.com) has one of the most sophisticated, elegant, and complete set of ground rules among the ODR service providers. Some of its protocols are produced here, with permission, as examples of ground rules that you might expect to see on a professionally operated Web site. Protocols developed by the Mediation Information & Resource Center (MIRC) (www.mediate.com) are also discussed below.

Online Resolution protocols.

PROTOCOL

Responsibilities of Participants

Working toward resolution online can be much more convenient than arranging face-to-face meetings. Nonetheless, it can pose its own challenges. We found electronically assisted information exchange and online meetings to be most productive when participants agree to a process-specific protocol such as the following:

- Check and respond to Online Resolution e-mail daily during the workweek (or as agreed at the outset).

- Notify all participants if you are not able to e-mail daily during the workweek.

- Exert your best effort to reach agreement.

- A mediator can't give you legal advice during the course of mediation. It's your responsibility to speak to a lawyer if you are unsure about your rights in a dispute. . . .

- Understand that any and all participation in dispute mediation is voluntary and that all decision-making power resides with the participants. The Mediator will not make any decisions for participants.

- In the event that you are dissatisfied with the impartiality or neutrality of the mediator, you will ask that the mediator withdraw and you will seek agreement with the other parties to accept another mediator.

- Following the completion of the online mediation process, you will complete a short evaluation form. This form will include evaluation of the online mediator with regard to responsiveness, courtesy and effectiveness. This form will also include evaluation of the online mediation program itself.

PROTOCOL

Confidentiality and Security

. . . Online Resolution requires our neutrals to operate within the boundaries of the Model Standards of Practice of the ABA, SPIDR [now ACR], and AAA.

Under these standards, confidentiality is taken very seriously.

Neutrals will not share information designated as confidential with the other party/parties unless there is an explicit agreement to do so. Unless waived, no negotiation, mediation, arbitration, or evaluation communications may be utilized in any contested action between participants. Participant Settlement Agreement will be presumed not confidential, but may be made confidential by agreement of participants.

Communications are between the neutral and participants. Online Resolution does not review nor retain these communications. Online Resolution does maintain case files indicating the fact that parties entered into a dispute resolution process, who the neutral was, who the parties were and whether the session is reported to have resulted in agreement or not. Online Resolution also retains, analyzes and displays information regarding participant satisfaction with the Online Neutral and with the Online Resolution program as a whole.

Online Resolution disagreement information forms will be viewed only by the individual participant, the case manager who assigns the neutral, and the neutral. Unless required by law, this information will not be released to any party not explicitly authorized to see it.

Under no circumstances will the Online Resolution Neutral be asked to testify in any contested hearing nor provide materials from the Online Resolution.

Our Web site utilizes secure Web technologies and a firewall to protect all of the data we collect. Our full-time network coordinator is constantly monitoring our system and protecting it from outside threats.

That being said, the Internet is not a perfectly secure environment. We commit to work to the best of our abilities to keep the Online Resolution site secure and to keep information visible only to those authorized to view it, but we cannot give any absolute assurance, nor can any Internet site, that our system will remain secure at all times.

MIRC Protocols for Online Mediation.

The Mediation Information & Resource Center (MIRC) has developed the following protocols for online mediation:[35]

Special Note: These Protocols are in addition to online mediation practice consistent with the ABA/SPIDR [now ACR]/AAA Model Standards of Practice to which all MIRC [mediators] subscribe.

I. Description of the Process

The process of Online Mediation typically involves a series of email messages between the mediator and each participant. In his or her professional discretion, the mediator may utilize joint email communication, Web forum (more highly secure) discussion, textual or audio chat, instant messaging, fax, and phone communications.

MIRC ... encourages mediators to structure their facilitation in the following manner:

A.   Each participant should be encouraged to present one or more confidential statements to the mediator setting forth the issue(s) they believe are in dispute, their interests for any settlement, and the various options the participant sees as possible.

B.   The mediator should summarize the issues and seek to gain agreement that the full range of presented issues will be addressed.

C. The mediator is then encouraged to engage in a series of private electronic conversations with each participant and jointly with participants in the mediator's professional discretion. These conversations are to include questions to fully understand each participant's perspective, interests, and perceived options as well as any comments and suggestions that may further settlement by the mediator.

---

35.   James C. Melamed, *Mediating on the Internet Today and Tomorrow*, 1 Pepp. Disp. Resol. L.J. 11, 24–27 (2000).

D.   Upon conclusion of the electronic conversations, there should either be a confirmed settlement, including means of implementation, or the mediator's declaration that no agreement has been reached.

E.   If there is a settlement, the mediator should prepare a summary of the terms of settlement and ask each side to confirm that they will abide by the terms.

II. Suggested Ground Rules

A.   Pre-mediation Responsibilities

1.   The participants are asked to notify the mediator of any travel plans or other circumstances that may prevent them from participating for more than 24 hours in the mediation.

2.   The participants are asked to notify the mediator of any acceptable alternative email addresses in the event of technical difficulty.

B.   Sending/Receiving E-mail

1.   In the event the mediator sends a message to both parties at one time, be aware that REPLY TO ALL will have you sharing information with all listed participants. If you want to only contact the mediator, be sure that you simply REPLY. You can never be too careful in ensuring that only those whom you want to get your message are in fact sent your message.

2.   The mediator should respond within 24 hours of receipt of any participant email message or other communication.

3.   It is the responsibility of all participants to check their email at least once per 24 hours and to be responsive to mediator communications.

C.   Delay in Sending/Receiving Email

In the event there is a delay in receiving a response online, the mediator shall be empowered to telephone, fax, or use whatever other means are available to contact a participant. The parties should assume that if there has been no contact for 3 days, they should make every effort to contact the mediator to determine what the problem is.

D.   Attachments

It is possible that the mediator will be transmitting attachments to certain messages. If this occurs, it is important that all participants are able to read the attachment(s). The mediator is therefore to seek to obtain agreement on an acceptable format (i.e., Word, WordPerfect, Rich Text Format or ascii) at the beginning of the mediation.

E.   Distribution of Messages

All electronic communications generated from the mediation shall not be permitted to be distributed to a non-participant at any time without the express permission of all parties and the mediator. In the event of an inadvertent distribution, all effected participants shall be promptly notified.

F.   Management and Disclosure of Information Online

The mediator shall only disclose specific offers and ideas from one participant to another as the mediator is expressly authorized to share. If it is unclear whether a mediator is authorized to share information, the mediator shall request this permission from a participant and only share information with the other participant as is authorized.

G.   Privacy Protected

1. The participants agree to not use any of the information presented or received during the mediation in any future legal, administrative, or other contested proceeding nor in the media. This includes all communications between the participants and the mediator, and ... [the mediation] program from the earliest contact regarding possible mediation to the completion of the mediation.

2. The participants further agree to not disclose any information presented or received to other people who are not participants to the mediation, with the exception of participant professional advisors (attorneys, financial advisors, union representatives, and the like). In all such events, the fact that a participant consults with a professional advisor does not in any way lessen the confidentiality of the online mediation process. The confidentiality of Online Mediation is intended to protect all participants with the expectation of such confidentiality (non-admissibility and no contacts with media) and also to protect the mediator and ... [the mediation] program.

8.9.2   Cyberspace Netiquette

Communication on the Internet involves different dynamics and rules than does communication through other media.[36] Thus, when you are communicating messages or conducting a mediation online, you will have to take into account the benefits and limitations of this medium in order to capitalize on the experience. One principal difference between online communication and ordinary verbal communication is that in e-mail or threaded discussions you have the opportunity to compose,

---

36. *See generally*, Jeffrey G. Kichaven, *Virtual Mediation* 7–8 (Business Law Today, ABA, May/June 1996).

read, reflect, and modify the content of your message before you send or convey it. Thus, you can catch errors or unintentional misstatements of facts before you actually communicate them. In a chat-room mode, this advantage is not present and you must take care to carefully and tactfully craft your message as your fingers fly.

When you are mediating online, you may find this set of communication guidelines—or "netiquette"—helpful.[37]

Communicate only with permission. You must take special precautions to ensure that you know who is "in the loop" for communicating online. You should clarify with other counsel whether they prefer to have all of your e-mail sent solely to them, or whether they want copies sent to their clients also. You should also, of course, specify whether or not you want your client to be a recipient of participants' e-mail. In some situations you may want your client to receive the mediator's e-mail, but not the e-mail of other lawyers. There may be other people outside of the circle of actual participants in the cybermediation who need to be kept abreast of various happenings during the course of the mediation. Make sure you know whom you are authorized to contact and whom you are not to contact. Sending an e-mail message to a person not authorized to receive it could doom a mediation in some situations.

Don't take time for granted. When you are communicating sequentially in cyberspace, you may find that people behave as though there are no time constraints—as if they have "all the time in the world." Because this phenomenon is widespread, accomplishing simple tasks, such as getting a response from the mediator as to other parties' views on certain issues, may seem to take forever. To minimize this problem, you will have to be pleasantly assertive and possibly suggest time limits in which you expect the mediator or a party to respond by e-mail.

Be conscious of time zones. While you may need to set time limits for replies, be conscious that the mediator's or a party's ability to reply may be hampered by the timing of your request. On the Web, you may be communicating with people who live and work in various parts of the United States and even in various countries in the world who are in different time zones. Some of these people may even be traveling through various time zones during the course of an extended cybermediation. Thus, if you send an e-mail to someone in the early morning from New York to San Francisco, don't expect even the earliest response to be before about mid-afternoon. You must factor in not only the time-zone differential, but also the time it will take the party to communicate with

---

37. *See generally*, Jeffrey Krivis, *Mediating in Cyberspace* 128–31 (CPR Institute for Dispute Resolution, Alternatives to the High Cost of Litigation, Vol. 14, No. 10, November 1996); John R. Helie and James C. Melamed, *Email Management and Etiquette,* (http://www.mediate.com/articles/email.cfm).

others—perhaps even by e-mail—before the party will be able to respond to you. Also, if an attorney, for example, had to be in court early in the morning, he or she may not even have a chance to check e-mail until later in the day, which will additionally delay the response. Thus, be mindful of these delaying factors and take care to avoid setting unrealistic reply deadlines for your mediation or cybercourse participants.

Respect people's space. Avoid overwhelming the mediator, the parties, and their counsel with e-mail messages. It is disconcerting for someone to open his or her mailbox to find a whole list of e-mails from the same person. People have lives; and counsel not only have personal lives, but they also have other clients to represent. Mediators may have several cases they are cybermediating simultaneously. While cybermediation that you are engaged in may be the only one you are currently working on, do not convey that impression to the participants, and do not let the mediation overtake your life. Sometimes people mediate online because they like the leisurely pace and opportunity for considered decision making. Be cognizant of that possibility and avoid being obsessive. Also, realize that your unrelenting e-mail involvement may unnecessarily increase the costs for all parties in the case, including your own client. Realize that every e-mail you send not only documents time you've spent on the case, but also takes up the time of the mediator and of other counsel who must communicate with their clients and get back to the mediator. High aggregate fees can mount up quickly.

Request and provide confirmations. Breakdown in communication may occur simply because the mediator and other counsel never received your e-mail communication. This may occur because of an address error, misdirection, or even an inadvertent failure to "send" the prepared message. Thus, if you are dispatching an important e-mail message, it is a good idea to request the addressees to acknowledge receipt of the message even before they review and consider its content. If you do not receive confirmation from each addressee, then you will be able to investigate right away to determine whether you will need to resend the message or relay it to him or her via another mode of communication. Similarly, if the mediator or other counsel request that you acknowledge receipt of an e-mail, you should confirm receipt immediately and respond to the substance of the message later.

Check and answer e-mail regularly. As an advocate in a cybermediation, you will need to develop the discipline of checking and answering e-mail periodically during each day. Because e-mail is not as intrusive as telephone contact, you will find that some counsel, or parties, or the mediator, as the case may be, may send you e-mail on the weekend. The policy you adopt for handling e-mail communication on the weekends will conform to your individual preferences or lifestyle.

Some cybermediation participants prefer not to respond to such communications until the next business day; others prefer to respond in order to sustain the momentum of dialogue or to keep their mailboxes cleared out.

Give notice of extended absences. If you are involved in a cybermediation, it is important that you let your participants know when you are going to be unavailable for e-mail communication for a day or more. They will appreciate your courtesy, and by mutual agreement may be able to arrange some alternate mode of communication to substitute for e-mail, in case of an emergency for example.

Forward e-mails with an explanation. You have probably received forwarded e-mails from senders who provide no accompanying explanation. This can be disconcerting and annoying. Often, when you receive such an unadorned forwarded message, you are not sure why you have received it and what you are expected to do with it now that you have it. Thus, when you are forwarding messages, you should get into the habit of inserting a short explanatory note prior to any message you forward so that the receiving party will understand why you are sending it and whether he or she needs to respond to you in some way.

Attach only necessary documents. Be respectful of people's time. If you attach a document to an e-mail, make sure that each addressee needs to review it. Before you attach a document, review your list of addressees and segregate those out who do not need to receive it. Then send a separate e-mail to those people without the document attached.

Police hostile or hurtful language. E-mail is a type of communication that can quickly degenerate into an abusive exchange. It can create a faceless "bunker" mentality among users that is regrettably conducive to sniping and taking "potshots" at others in an insulting way. Insults can be exchanged privately—one-on-one—or in the open for all to see. Such exchanges can quickly escalate into situations that are difficult to bring back into balance. As a professional matter, you must be vigilant to halt even the slightest signs of hostile or hurtful language. Left unattended, such offensive remarks can disrupt the cybermediation at the very least, and at worst they can cause the process to disintegrate.

Be polite and diplomatic in your own language. As a cyberadvocate, you can provide a model for the type of written communication that you expect the others to use in an online mediation. You will find, generally speaking, that if you make an effort to use polite, respectful, and diplomatic language, the other participants will do likewise.

Keep communications crisp, pithy, and relevant. Most of us have experienced online communication where a participant goes well outside the relevant topic and writes interminably about matters that fail to move the discussion to a common goal. In an online mediation, counsel may engage in this type of communication to divert the process from an issue where his position is weak, to issues where he can speak from a position of strength. This kind of communication may also indicate a desire on counsel's part to control the agenda. Normally the mediator will nip this kind of communication in the bud and encourage the participants to keep communications crisp, pithy, and relevant. But if the mediator does not control this behavior, you may want to cybercaucus with the mediator and suggest that he or she send an e-mail to all participants requesting more abbreviated communications.

Mind your grammar, spelling, and punctuation. Your e-mail communications need not be perfect, but you should pay respect to common rules of grammar, spelling, and punctuation. Consider this sentence from a hypothetical e-mail message between co-counsel in a cybermediation:

> "i think your principle goal here, mary, is far out. don't go there. you'll be disappointed and hack-off the our oponents."

This sentence communicates much about its writer. Failure to use capital letters and to spell properly says that the writer is in a hurry and may be invested only superficially in the communication process. Use of slang and failure to capitalize names can be degrading to receivers of e-mail. A good rule of thumb is to take the type of drafting care with your e-mail communications that you expect others to take when they are sending e-mails to you.

Use emoticons and abbreviations minimally. Emoticons are groups of punctuation and other symbols used to convey emotions. Do not assume that everyone knows what emoticons mean. You may do harm in an e-mail communication if you intend one meaning by your use of an emoticon and your addressee infers another meaning. Here is a list of common emoticons so that you will be able to understand them if you receive them in online communication:

｜-)	happy, humorous
｜-(	unhappy
｜-0	shocked
｜-}	wry, ironic
<g>	grin
<s>	sigh
<VBG>	very big grin

Abbreviations can save time and space, but if your addressees do not understand what they mean, they can be aggravating to them. It is a wise practice to use abbreviations minimally or not at all, or when you first use them to put their meanings in parentheses. Here are a few common abbreviations that you may receive or even use in your online communications:

BTW	by the way
F2F	face to face
FYI	for your information
imo	in my opinion
imho	in my humble opinion
LOL	laughing out loud
TIA	thanks in advance
BR	best regards
BPR	best personal regards

Use telephone backup. When mediating online, sometimes there is no equal substitute for picking up the telephone and talking directly to someone. Some people communicate better verbally than in writing. Also, people can often relay communications more effectively and meaningfully by voice. For example, in a speaking context you can give support, provide detailed explanations, and answer questions more quickly and sensitively. Thus, while written online communication can be very effective in mediations, telephone backup will also be quite useful from time to time.

Save your e-mail correspondence. It is a wise practice to save all your e-mail correspondence relating to a particular mediation, at least until the mediation has concluded, and sometimes well beyond the conclusion. You will find it helpful to refer back to certain e-mail communications from time to time—especially near the end of the mediation when you are drafting the settlement agreement. You may also find it useful during the course of the mediation to print out hard copies of critical communications for your reference in your final, wrap-up sessions. The e-mail correspondence may also be helpful to you long after the mediation if an issue arises as to whether a party is in compliance with the agreement reached in the cybermediation. Exactly how long you retain your e-mail correspondence after the conclusion of the mediation will be dictated by your firm's own retention policies or, perhaps, the rules of your particular jurisdiction.

8.9.3 Preparing the premediation submission

In many cybermediations, particularly those involving non-complex disputes, there may be no need for a premediation submission, unless the cybermediator requests parties to submit confidential statements regarding settlement prospects in advance. In complex cases, you may want to transmit an extensive premediation submission to the mediator. In this regard, section 5.1 provides helpful suggestions as to which material you may want to provide the cybermediator in advance. You may want to provide some information digitally; other information may not be in digital form or available on the Web, in which case you may have to provide it in hard copy form. To avoid sending duplicate materials to the mediator, it is always a good idea to consult with other counsel in the case and agree on what nonconfidential materials will be sent and who will be sending them.

8.9.4   The opening statement in cybermediation

All counsel. Section 5.2, concerning opening statements in offline mediation, may be of some help to you with respect to opening statements in online mediation. However, in cybermediation, unlike most face-to-face mediations, if the parties have jointly transmitted an extensive premediation statement to the cybermediator, it is unusual for the parties to engage in extensive real-time chat in their opening statements. More often in such situations, the mediator sends to all parties and counsel the mediator's opening statement which describes the process and sets out or suggests some ground rules that will be applicable to the cybermediation. In less complex cases, particularly where there have been no premediation submissions to the cybermediator, the parties may present their opening statements in real-time chat format or in a send-to-all e-mail format. But customarily, these opening statements are much more truncated than in face-to-face mediations. Normally, the bulk of time in cybermediation is spent in caucus e-mail sessions with the cybermediator. One obvious advantage with online mediation is that an advocate can present his or her opening statement, word-for-word, to the client first for any input prior to sending it simultaneously to the other counsel, parties, and the cybermediator.

With regard to the Chicago medical building scenario, the topics of the parties' use of documents and points of emphasis in the opening statements are covered in subsection 8.7.1.

8.9.5   Applied negotiation tactics—knowing what to do and when to do it

All of the advice presented in section 5.3 regarding applied negotiation tactics in face-to-face mediation is equally applicable to online mediation. You will have an initial strategic approach in mind when you begin the cybermediation, but you should be flexible in your choice of strategies and tactics as you move through the process. Your change in strategies and tactics will depend in large part on information supplied to you by your client, by the mediator, or perhaps directly by the opposing parties and their counsel.

As counsel for BEST. After reading AIRCON's threat in the real-time chat opening statement, the Chicago district manager tells you that "this thing's gotta be resolved as soon as possible." He says that if AIRCON delays shipping the air conditioning systems to ten other of BEST's construction sites, AIRCON could subject BEST to business losses in the range of $75,000 to $100,000. The Chicago district manager tells you that if the air conditioning system and the ductwork are not found to be defective but rather out-of-specification, he would be willing to use the removed equipment and materials in other projects under construction. He authorizes you to e-mail mediator FAIRMAN to advise him of this concession. He also permits FAIRMAN to advise the other parties and their counsel of this concession. FAIRMAN should tell them that the reason BEST is making this concession is to "get the ball rolling" toward a win-win settlement.

As counsel for PERFECTEMP. FAIRMAN advises you by e-mail of BEST's concession. You remind your client that PERFECTEMP may be subject to a $1,000 a day liquidated damages penalty if he doesn't cooperate to resolve this. Your client tells you that as a last resort, he could replace the ductwork, if necessary, with correct-sized ductwork left over from another project. He would rather not pay the laborers' wages for the ductwork replacement, however. He estimates that it would take thirty man hours at $20 per hour ($600) to replace the ductwork. He authorizes you to e-mail FAIRMAN with this information, but to tell him not to advise the other parties of this concession yet.

As counsel for IMAGINEERING. Because of innuendos in the real-time chat opening statement of BEST's counsel regarding his client's knowledge of tonnage requirements in his other ongoing construction projects, your client is scared to death that professional malpractice might be alleged here if another engineering firm is called in to examine the drawings. Thus, he tells you that he is willing to revisit the tonnage requirement (which he already knows is thirty tons underspecified) and, if necessary, pay for an add-on cooling unit and the labor required to install it. He estimates an AIRCON add-on unit would probably be in the range of $7,500 and the labor to install it would cost $200. He authorizes you to e-mail FAIRMAN and advise him of this concession. He does not want FAIRMAN to disclose this information to the other parties yet.

As counsel for AIRCON. Your client does not believe that AIRCON's product is defective. She would like to get this matter resolved, however, so AIRCON can get its money from BEST for the Chicago medical building system and close the deals on systems for BEST's ten other projects. Your client e-mails you that as a last resort, you can offer this proposal. AIRCON, she says, has in stock, three air conditioning systems (40, 250, 280 tons) which were installed but repossessed from bankrupt and uncompleted building projects in Europe. Any one of these could be substituted for (or added onto) the one currently installed in the Chicago medical building at a substantial discount. AIRCON, however, would not want to pay for the installation labor. She estimates that the discounted price for the three systems would be, respectively, $5,500, $60,000, and $80,000. AIRCON would take care of the shipping, which would be absorbed as part of a larger expedited shipment of several systems scheduled to be sent to the U.S. in the next couple of days.

8.9.6 Deriving the most tactical advantage from caucuses

All counsel. All of the suggestions contained in section 5.4 for getting the most tactical advantage from caucuses also apply to cybermediation. Four of those suggestions are particularly important to focus on when you are communicating with the mediator in writing, as in using e-mail. The first of these suggestions is that when stating your settlement proposal or when moving from one settlement demand or offer to another, provide the cybermediator with reasons why you are making the change. Since your reasons will be in writing, it is more likely that the cybermediator will be able to convey to the intended party the precise substance of your proposal and the precise reasons supporting it. Second, when preparing to send your final e-mail to the cybermediator in an e-mail caucus, always review your correspondence (which may have occurred over days) and determine what is confidential and undisclosable, and so advise the cybermediator in your final e-mail. Third, do not make or accept a settlement proposal by means of e-mail that you have no authority to make or accept.

Written communication is unforgiving. If you put an offer in writing, your opposing counsel will be in a much better position to keep you committed to it—even if your client is not enamored with it. Fourth, avoid making e-mail threats in cybermediation, either for delivery by the cybermediator to the other parties or directly to them. Written threats often escalate into a fusillade of intimidating e-mails that are totally counterproductive to the settlement mission.

As counsel for BEST. FAIRMAN e-mailed you that he told the other parties that if the air conditioning system and the ductwork are not found to be defective but rather out-of-specification, BEST would be willing to use the removed equipment and materials in other projects under construction.

FAIRMAN told them BEST made this concession to "get the ball rolling" toward a win-win settlement. FAIRMAN further said in his e-mail that the other parties were conducting separate e-mail caucuses with their separate counsel to come up with a response to BEST's movement in the direction of settlement.

As counsel for PERFECTEMP. PERFECTEMP e-mails FAIRMAN to say that PERFECTEMP, as part of a settlement, in which each party would contribute something, would be willing to supply replacement ductwork with correct-sized ductwork left over from another project if the present ductwork is deemed to be undersized. FAIRMAN is instructed to say nothing about the cost of the labor required to install the ductwork.

As counsel for IMAGINEERING. IMAGINEERING e-mails FAIRMAN that he can inform the other parties that it is willing to revisit the tonnage requirement and, if necessary, pay for an add-on cooling unit. FAIRMAN is to say nothing regarding the cost of the labor required to install it.

As counsel for AIRCON. AIRCON e-mails FAIRMAN that he can inform the other parties as follows. AIRCON has in stock, three air conditioning systems (40, 250, 280 tons) which were installed but repossessed from bankrupt and uncompleted building projects in Europe. Any one of these could be substituted for (or added onto) the one currently installed in the Chicago medical building at a substantial discount. AIRCON, however, would not want to pay for the installation labor. The discounted price for the three systems would be, respectively, $5,500, $60,000, and $80,000. AIRCON would take care of the shipping, which would be absorbed as part of a larger expedited shipment of several systems scheduled to be sent to the U.S. in the next couple of days. You instruct FAIRMAN to NOT tell the other parties about these possibilities yet.

8.9.7 Persuasion through effective communication

There's more to persuasion than mere logic. A purely logical solution, reached without sufficient information, may produce thoroughly odd results. For instance, there once was a lawyer who was defending a man accused of housebreaking. The lawyer said to the judge in court: "Your Honor, I submit that my client did not break into the house at all. He found the living-room window open and merely inserted his right arm and removed a few trifling articles. Now, my client's arm is not himself, and I fail to see how you can punish the whole individual for an offense committed by only one of his limbs." The judge considered the lawyer's argument for several moments, and then replied, "That argument is very well put. Following it logically, I sentence the defendant's arm to one year's imprisonment. He can accompany it or not, as he chooses." The defendant beamed a smile, and with his lawyer's assistance unscrewed his cork arm and, leaving it on the dock, walked out a free man.[38]

All counsel. As pointed out in section 5.5, studies have shown that at least 55 percent of the meaning of messages expressed in face-to-face communication has its source in nonverbal cues including posture, stride, gestures, eye contact, facial expressions, mannerisms, and movement. The source of 38 percent of such meaning derives from voice and vocal qualities including rate, pitch, tone, volume, and intensity. Only a meager 7 percent of such meaning derives from the actual words, the dictionary meaning of vocabulary. These facts produce at least two consequences for advocates engaged in cybermediation—currently, a mediation process that occurs largely through written communication. The first consequence is that much of section 5.5, concerning effective communication in face-to-face communication does not apply to cybermediation. Important aspects of section 5.5 do apply, however. For example, the five objectives of persuasive messages and the three artistic means of persuasion (ethos, pathos, and logos) still should guide your written communication in cybermediation and you should consistently measure your e-mail communications against those standards. Not only should your e-mail communications be logical, but they should also have appropriate levels of truthful and emotional content.

The second consequence for cyberadvocates is that because only 7 percent of the intended meaning of your e-mail communications is being expressed through the dictionary meaning of the words you use, you must compensate for this deficit by consciously and appropriately embellishing your e-mail communication with words that collectively incorporate the "packaging" techniques discussed in section 5.5. Thus, your e-mail language should be concrete, pithy, and to the point; demonstrate your knowledge of the situation; and, at appropriate times, convey enthusiasm, alignment, emphasis, optimism, humor, and apologetic comments.

As counsel for BEST. FAIRMAN has e-mailed you what the other counsel are proposing to "contribute" toward achieving a fair resolution of the matter. With your client's permission and notice to the cybermediator, you send an e-mail to all the participants expressing your optimism that a settlement is possible here and your commitment to expedite the matter to a fair resolution.

As counsel for PERFECTEMP. After receiving BEST's e-mail and giving notice to FAIRMAN of your intention to e-mail all the participants, with your client's permission you e-mail all participants to say that you have reviewed the test and balance report and would now have

---

38. Adapted from Lewis and Faye Copeland, *10,000 Jokes, Toasts, and Stories,* (Doubleday 1965), 460.

to acknowledge that some of the ductwork was undersized and not in conformity with IMAGINEERING's specifications. You restate your willingness to supply replacement ductwork.

As counsel for IMAGINEERING. After receiving BEST's and PERFECTEMP's e-mails and giving notice to FAIRMAN of your intention to e-mail all the participants, with your client's permission you e-mail all participants to say that you and your client have revisited the engineering specifications and have concluded that the tonnage requirements appear to be understated by thirty tons. You attribute this to a typographical (clerical) error rather than an engineering error. Your engineer had calculated the correct tonnage, but the typist inserted the wrong figure. You restate your willingness to pay for an add-on cooling system.

As counsel for AIRCON. After receiving the above e-mails and consulting with your client, you e-mail FAIRMAN that from your perspective the parties have resolved "their" dispute. There is no evidence whatsoever that the AIRCON product is defective in any way. It's merely a matter of clerical errors caused by IMAGINEERING and bad ductwork installation on PERFECTEMP's part. If IMAGINEERING wants to pay for an add-on cooling system, it can pay the retail price for a new one—not a repossessed one. FAIRMAN requests permission to inform BEST of the availability of the three repossessed cooling systems at discounted prices. AIRCON has no objection, so long as BEST agrees not to tell the other two parties about the availability of the discounted systems.

8.9.8 Applying creative problem-solving techniques

Whistler, the famous artist, once undertook to get a fellow artist's work into a famous art exhibition. He succeeded and the picture was hung. When Whistler took him to the gallery for the first time to see his artwork displayed, the fellow artist gasped in dismay. "Good Heavens!" he cried, "You've hung my picture upside down!" "Be happy," said Whistler. "The committee refused it the other way."[39] This story underscores the basic human condition that people see things in very different ways. It is one's willingness to see what other people see that leads, on many occasions, to creative solutions in mediation and, with no less frequency, in cybermediation.

All counsel. All of the creative problem-solving techniques discussed in section 5.6 and subsection 3.13 apply to cybermediation. To produce win-win, optimal, and super-optimal solutions in cybermediation, the parties must be willing to try to see what the other

---

39. Adapted from Lewis and Faye Copeland, *10,000 Jokes Toasts & Stories,* (Doubleday 1965), 41.

participants see. With the help of the cybermediator, the integration of the parties different perceptions often yields solutions that no one party acting independently could perceive.

As counsel for BEST. With your assurance to keep the information confidential, FAIRMAN informs you of AIRCON's three repossessed cooling systems that it has for sale at discounted prices. He also tells you that AIRCON does not want to sell one of these to AIRCON at a discounted price. AIRCON would rather have IMAGINEERING pay for a new add-on or replacement system at retail prices. BEST immediately says that BEST would buy all three repossessed systems, assuming they are not defective. IMAGINEERING could buy the forty ton add-on from BEST at the discounted price and BEST could use the other two systems in other projects. Even though only a thirty ton add-on is needed the ten extra tons will help to ensure that there will be no further cooling problems in the medical building.

As counsel for AIRCON. FAIRMAN e-mails you and tells you that BEST is willing to purchase all three discounted systems from you. AIRCON is very pleased because it was having difficulty selling the two larger systems to its customers. AIRCON understands that IMAGINEERING will pay BEST for the discounted forty ton cooling system. AIRCON gives FAIRMAN permission to disclose this new development involving BEST's agreement to purchase the repossessed systems to the other two parties.

As counsel for IMAGINEERING. FAIRMAN e-mails you about the availability of the discounted forty ton system that IMAGINEERING will be able to purchase from BEST. Your client is ecstatic to be able to get out of this mess for a little over $5,000 plus attorney and cybermediator fees.

As counsel for PERFECTEMP. FAIRMAN e-mails you to bring you up-to-date on the above described developments. You tell FAIRMAN that your client is happy with the progress toward settlement. However, although PERFECTEMP is willing to provide the replacement ductwork, it is not willing to pay the cost of reinstallation. PERFECTEMP thinks that AIRCON should pay for it because it is contributing nothing to this settlement. AIRCON is getting off scot-free—even though it should have caught the error in the tonnage requirement. It had access to the building specs and it deals day to day with the issue of tonnage requirements for all size buildings and systems.

8.9.9 Assisting the mediator to achieve closure

To solve a problem, or to help someone else solve one, you often must give something up—maybe even temporarily—to get the result you want. For example, long ago in Missouri a farmer died leaving seventeen horses and three sons. In his will, he disposed of his horses as follows: one-half to the eldest son, one-third to the next, and one-ninth to the youngest. The administrator of the estate, a lawyer, rode a horse to the farm, and when he went to divide the seventeen horses into halves, thirds and ninths, he found it impossible. So he thought a minute, and directly, he dismounted and put his horse with the seventeen horses—making eighteen horses. He then proceeded to divide the horses as follows: one-half, or nine horses to the eldest; one-third, or six to the next son; and one-ninth, or two, to the youngest. Adding up nine, six, and two, he got seventeen. Having quickly solved the problem, he mounted his steed and rode away rejoicing.[40] In cybermediation, just as in this story, parties often must, temporarily or in the end, be willing to give up something in order to assist the mediator to solve the problem. Sometimes in cybermediation, what a party proposes to give up or contribute to the settlement is not needed to achieve the resolution the parties eventually want. Also, it is frequently the ultimately unneeded concession that "gets the ball rolling" toward settlement. (See BEST's situation, below).

All counsel. All of the suggestions contained in section 5.8 on how to assist the mediator to achieve closure apply to cybermediation. In the Chicago medical building cybermediation, the parties are very close to a solution. The cybermediator sends an e-mail and suggests that they have a real-time chat session to bring the matter to closure. All agree to participate. FAIRMAN sends the e-mail shown below in advance of the real-time chat session, outlining his view of the terms of the tentative settlement agreement and noting that from his perspective, the only open matter is who is going to pay the costs of labor.

Mediator FAIRMAN. The settlement agreement seems to be developing along the following lines. If I have misstated what your tentative agreement is, please let me know. The only items that seem to be unresolved are the labor costs for installing the add-on cooling system and removing the nonconforming ductwork and installing the new ductwork.

BEST agrees to pay AIRCON the balance due on the current cooling system within two weeks. BEST also agrees to purchase the three repossessed cooling systems from AIRCON. (Since the resolution involves an add-on cooling system, BEST will not have to remove the current system and move it to another construction project as BEST had offered to do).

---

40. Adapted from Lewis and Faye Copeland, *10,000 Jokes, Toasts, and Stories,* (Doubleday 1965), 150.

PERFECTEMP is willing to supply replacement ductwork with correct-sized ductwork left over from another project. PERFECTEMP will also keep the ductwork removed from the Chicago medical building.

IMAGINEERING is willing to pay BEST the discounted price for the forty ton add-on cooling unit to be installed in the Chicago medical building.

AIRCON is willing to receive the balance due on the current cooling system within two weeks and to sell and ship all three repossessed cooling systems to BEST in the next few days.

As counsel for BEST. In the real-time chat session, you point out that the costs of installation of the add-on cooling system and the removal and installation of the ductwork will be approximately $800. You suggest that each party contribute $200 for labor costs.

As counsel for PERFECTEMP. You say that you believe that AIRCON should pay these labor costs because it is contributing nothing and gaining a lot, in terms of sales of cooling systems, from the settlement.

As counsel for IMAGINEERING. You say that you are willing to pay half of the installation costs if AIRCON will pay the other half.

As counsel for AIRCON. AIRCON agrees to discount the sales of the three repossessed systems to BEST by an additional $400. Then BEST and IMAGINEERING would share equally the $800 installation cost. All parties agree to this solution.

As a cyberadvocate, you may see many other possible resolutions of this scenario, and you are definitely encouraged to do so.

8.10 POST-CYBERMEDATION ADVOCACY

8.10.1 Continuing the negotiations

The material contained in section 6.1 concerning continuing negotiations after a mediation is equally applicable to cybermediation. Actually, it is more likely that negotiations will continue after online mediation as compared to after offline mediation. The reason for this is that, with respect to online mediation, the parties and their counsel are already in a written-communication mode. Almost all, if not all, the information developed during the course of a cybermediation is recorded in digital form and is available to counsel and their clients at their fingertips. This availability of information facilitates reconsideration and redrafting of cybermediation proposals, and subsequent circulation to other parties for their consideration. Also, if the dispute is only about money, the parties may continue to engage in automated negotiation or blind bidding and eventually reach a settlement through that process.

8.10.2 Drafting the settlement agreement

The material contained in section 6.2 concerning drafting the settlement agreement is equally applicable to cybermediation. However, you should be aware that in online mediation, the cybermediator often plays a more active role in agreement drafting than in offline mediation. Many cybermediators use a "one-text procedure" whereby the settlement agreement is developed through the course of the cybermediation process by the cybermediator who combines the parties' settlement proposals and adds his or her own suggestions. Unlike offline mediation, where the agreement is drafted at the end of or after completion of the mediation session, in cybermediation, frequently the process ends with a finalized agreement, subject to fine-tuning.

8.10.3 Considering other online or offline ADR processes

Of course if cybermediation is unsuccessful, you should consider the possibility of using other online or offline ADR processes to resolve the dispute. A variety of offline hybrid ADR processes are described in chapter 7 and some of the other online ADR processes are described in section 8.2.

8.10.4 Enforcing the settlement agreement

The material contained in section 6.3 concerning enforcing the settlement agreement is equally applicable to cybermediation. Because cybermediation often involves the participation of disputants who reside in different states or different countries, it is sometimes wise practice to include an arbitration clause in a settlement agreement by which the parties agree to cyberarbitrate any dispute over whether a party is in compliance with a settlement agreement achieved through cybermediation. Another approach would be for the parties to enter into a mutual confession of judgment clause by which they preagree that a judgment could be filed and enforced against them in any jurisdiction in which the noncompliant party resides. An alternative confession of judgment mechanism might consist of a cybermediation agreement clause that would identify a few elements that would need to be required to be proved up, ex parte if necessary, in the jurisdiction of the noncompliant party's residence. These, and similar mechanisms that you could creatively design, would have the effect of ensuring greater durability of settlement reached in cybermediation.

EPILOGUE

In the preface we began our journey through mediation advocacy with some wise advice of Abraham Lincoln regarding anecdotes, and it seems only fitting that we end with an anecdote that he liked to tell about his sons.

According to Abe, one day a dispute broke out between his two young boys on his front lawn in Springfield, Illinois, and they were flinging their arms wildly and arguing at the top of their lungs. A neighbor approached Abe, who, sitting in his rocker on his front porch, was in a contemplative mood, seemingly oblivious to the commotion. Gesturing toward the boys, the neighbor asked Abe, "What's wrong?" Continuing to rock as if nothing were happening, Abe droned, "Same thing that's wrong with the whole world. . . . I've got three walnuts and each boy wants two."

In truth, the world has not changed much since the days of Abe Lincoln. Conflict is still pervasive, as it was then. What is different, however, is that we now have new processes, new methods, and new techniques to deal with it, such as those described in this book. It is hoped that the advocacy skills addressed here will help you get both walnuts—or their equivalent—every time.

CONTENTS OF APPENDICES

Appendix A

MEDIATOR SELECTION CHECKLIST

1. **What is the nature of the dispute?**

   ___ Area of law requiring special mediator knowledge, experience, or ability to modify process

   ___ Mostly factual issues

   ___ Mostly legal issues

   ___ Mixed factual and legal issues

2. **What is the nature of the parties?**

   ___ Two parties

   ___ More than two parties

   ___ All parties represented by counsel

   ___ One or more parties not represented by counsel

   ___ Engaged in a friendly disagreement

   ___ Stubborn, but rational

   ___ Extremely hostile and irate

       ___ Hostility developed over a long period

       ___ Hostility developed in a brief encounter

       ___ Have acted in bad faith in the past

   ___ Substantially differing interests and positions

   ___ Overlapping, identical interests and positions

   ___ Will have a continuing relationship after the mediation

   ___ Will not have a continuing relationship after the mediation

3. **Considering the nature of dispute and the nature of the parties, what status of mediator would be appropriate?**

   ___ Former judge

   ___ Attorney

   ___ Nonattorney

   ___ Psychologist

   ___ Other professional

   ___ Combination (cross-trained or co-mediators)

4. **Considering the nature of dispute and the nature of the parties, what style of mediation would be appropriate?**

    ___ Facilitative

    ___ Evaluative

    ___ With caucuses

    ___ Without caucuses

5. **Does the mediator you are considering possess the most important basic qualities of a good mediator?**

    ___ Impartiality/neutrality/confidentiality

    ___ Patience

    ___ Flexibility

    ___ Open-mindedness

          Creativity, if helpful to the particular dispute

    ___ Good listening and communication skills

    ___ Appropriate sense of humor

    ___ Optimism

    ___ Respect for lawyers and clients

    ___ Motivation without coercion

    ___ Good judgment

6. **Does the mediator you are considering have training and/or experience?**

    ___ Has training in mediation or conflict resolution

    ___ Is certified as a mediator by a court system or dispute resolution organization

    ___ Conducts training in mediation, negotiation, or conflict resolution

    ___ Has substantial mediation experience as a facilitative or evaluative mediator, or both, as appropriate to the present dispute

    ___ Has been appointed by the court as a mediator or special master in the past

    ___ Has sufficient litigation experience, if required

    ___ Will provide lawyer references from prior mediations the candidate has conducted

___ Is listed on the panels of one or more dispute resolution organizations

___ Has a reputation for professional excellence among dispute resolution practitioners

___ Is a member or officer in local or national professional associations

7. **Can the mediator satisfy the practical needs of the parties?**

___ Affordable fees: hourly, daily, by sessions

___ Policy on fees if session cancelled or postponed

___ Willing to conduct premediation caucuses if parties believe it necessary

___ Willing to travel to provide mediation services

___ Fees charged for travel time

___ Types of expenses

___ Able to provide, schedule, or suggest facilities where the mediation can be held

___ Available to serve as mediator for the number of sessions and at the times the parties and their counsel are available

Appendix B
MEDIATION PREPARATION CHECKLIST

1. **Reviewing the Case File**

    ___ Review Pleadings Chronologically

        ___ Claims of parties and relief requested

        ___ Counterclaims and relief requested

        ___ Motions and related orders and opinions

        ___ Nature and status of pending undecided motions

        ___ Status of discovery

        ___ Order setting trial date, if any

    ___ Review Important Documents and Deposition Transcripts

        ___ Note pages strongly supportive of your position

        ___ Note pages strongly unsupportive of your position

    ___ Review Correspondence File

        ___ Read history of demands and offers to settle

        ___ Note last demand and last offer figures

        ___ Read correspondence regarding any limitations on settlement authority

    ___ Review Important Case Law

        ___ Cases foreclosing opponent's claim or defense

        ___ Cases foreclosing opponent's theory of damages

2. **Ensuring You Have All Pertinent Information**

    ___ Hospital records, bills

    ___ Doctors' reports, bills

    ___ Police reports

    ___ Photographs

    ___ Deposition transcripts

    ___ Contracts

    ___ Leases

    ___ Waivers

    ___ Releases

___ Bills

___ Work orders

___ Liens

___ Verification of lost wages

___ Other

3. **Considering Any Time Constraints**

___ Opponent's business or personal deadlines

___ My own business or personal deadlines

___ Discovery cutoff date

___ Trial date

___ Time constraints that I can create or impose

4. **Identifying the Parties' Underlying Needs and Interests**

___ Identify the legal positions of the parties.

   ___ What are the claims of the parties?

   ___ Identify the defenses of the parties.

   ___ What are the parties' claims for relief?

   ___ What are the true legal issues?

___ Identify the present and potential negotiating positions of the parties.

   ___ What are the respective parties' needs?

      ___ Economic

      ___ Emotional

      ___ Psychological

      ___ Physical

      ___ Social

   ___ What are the respective parties' interests?

      ___ Ask myself why the opponent may be taking a particular negotiating position

      ___ Ask myself why the opponent may not want to embrace my negotiating position

      ___ Use the Interest-Resource Table to generate other potential interests of the parties

    ___ What are the available resources to satisfy the parties' respective interests?

    ___ What resources does my client have available to satisfy his own interests?

    ___ What resources does my client have available to satisfy the other parties' interests?

    ___ What resources do other parties have to satisfy their own interests?

    ___ What resources do other parties have to satisfy my client's interests?

    ___ What resources are available outside the circle of disputants to satisfy the other parties' interests?

    ___ What resources are available outside the circle of disputants to satisfy my client's interests?

    ___ Use Interest-Resource Table to generate other possible interest-satisfying resources

5. Determining the Overall Goal, Plan, and Theme

___ Determine the overall goal

    ___ Description of overall strategic goal

        ___ Aggressive

        ___ Competitive

        ___ Cooperative

        ___ Self-centered

        ___ Defensive

        ___ Combination

    ___ Monetary goals

    ___ Acceptable settlement range

        ___ Reasoned basis for the range

        ___ Nonmonetary goals

        ___ Integrated monetary and nonmonetary goals

___ Determine the overall plan

    ___ Succinct opening statement

    ___ Summary of damages (plaintiff)

    ___ Summary of contested damages (defendant)

   ___ Booklet of documentary evidence, organized and tabbed, with a table of contents

   ___ Demonstrative evidence

   ___ Analysis of opponent's legal and negotiating positions and my responses to them

   ___ Consideration of the nature and amount of client's participation in the mediation

___ Determine the overall theme

   ___ Focus of parties' disagreement

   ___ Replies to opponent's potential counterthemes

6.   Selecting Documents for Presentation to the Mediator

___ Documents defining the rights and duties of the parties

   ___ Business contract

   ___ Commercial lease

   ___ Residential lease

   ___ Warranty

   ___ Release

   ___ Will

   ___ Trust

   ___ Operator's manual

   ___ Ordinance

   ___ Court rule

   ___ Statute

   ___ Court opinion

___ Documents confirming the occurrence or nonoccurrence of certain events

   ___ Police or security guard report

   ___ Receipts

   ___ Telephone records

   ___ Hospital reports

   ___ Sign-in registers

   ___ Construction change orders

___ Documents confirming the type of conduct engaged in or not engaged in by the parties

     ___ Eyewitness statements

     ___ Excerpts from deposition transcripts

     ___ Monthly securities account statement

     ___ Monthly bank account statement

     ___ Videotape

     ___ Letter

     ___ Notes

     ___ Other correspondence

___ Documents containing admissions of wrongdoing, knowledge, or lack of knowledge

     ___ Correspondence between the parties

     ___ Deposition transcripts

     ___ Statements given to the police

     ___ Completed application forms

     ___ Performance evaluations

     ___ Releases

___ Documents verifying the nature and extent of damage, loss, or injury

     ___ Photographs

     ___ X-rays

     ___ Doctors' reports

     ___ Estimates

     ___ Time sheets

     ___ Attendance records

     ___ Accountants' reports

     ___ Billing statements

     ___ Work logs

___ Documents suggesting or explaining the potential for trade-offs and win-win or integrative solutions

     ___ Sketch

     ___ Blueprints

    ___ Organizational diagram

    ___ Modified work schedule

    ___ Flow chart

    ___ Model

    ___ Benefits manual

    ___ Annuity schedule

    ___ Catalog

7. Deciding the Format of the Presentation

___ Separately consider the format needs related to the substance of the dispute and the relationship between the parties

___ Need for premediation in person or telephone conference with mediator

___ Format at mediation conference

    ___ Sequence of document presentation

    ___ Documents to be initially withheld

    ___ Need for break-out rooms

    ___ Need for adequate telephone access

    ___ Equipment for visual aids

8. Determining What Information Should Be Kept Confidential

___ Identity of confidential information

___ Documents not to be disclosed

___ Timing of disclosure of certain confidential documents

9. Determining Whether a Premediation Meeting or Caucus Would Be Helpful

___ Meeting with opposing counsel only

___ Meeting with opposing counsel and clients

___ Meeting with opposing counsel and the mediator

    ___ Explore areas of emphasis in mediation

    ___ Determine what other parties should be present at mediation

    ___ Determine what premediation materials the mediator needs

___ Determine the agenda, format, and logistics for the mediation

___ Caucus with mediator without client

___ Caucus with mediator and client(s)

    ___ Save mediation conference time

    ___ Calm angry party

    ___ Apprise mediator of legal, technical, or highly confidential information

    ___ Get mediator's reaction to unusual proposals for settlement

    ___ Have mediator meet and talk to persons who have information relevant to the dispute but will not be present at the mediation conference

10. Knowing the Status of the Litigation and Negotiations

___ Status of litigation

    ___ Parties' depositions

    ___ Witnesses' depositions

    ___ Experts' depositions

    ___ Document production

    ___ Discovery cutoff date

    ___ Trial date

___ Status of negotiations

    ___ Read correspondence to determine last demand and last offer

    ___ Confirm with opposing counsel by telephone

11. Knowing the Limits of Settlement Authority

___ Confirm limits of settlement authority with client in writing

___ If multiple clients, meet with them to confirm limits orally and afterwards in writing

12. Determining Reasonable Settlement Value, Opening Positions, and Bottom Lines

___ Rules of thumb

___ Calculate fair settlement value

___ Determine reasonable settlement range

___ Set opening position

___ Set bottom line

___ Estimate opponent's opening position

___ Estimate opponent's bottom line

13. Considering Potential for Creative Solutions

___ Generation of alternatives

___ Challenging assumptions

___ Suspending judgment

___ Fractionation

___ Thought reversal

___ Brainstorming

___ Using analogies

___ Random stimulation

14. Determining Negotiating Strategy and Related Tactics

___ Determine strategy

___ Review and determine tactics

   ___ Competitive tactics

      ___ Alternative opportunities

      ___ Belly up

      ___ Bluffing

      ___ Brer Rabbit

      ___ Creating deadlock

      ___ Fait accompli

      ___ Feigning

      ___ Good cop/bad cop

      ___ Limited authority

      ___ Media pressure

      ___ Preconditions

      ___ Reversal

      ___ Threat or show of power

      ___ Time pressure

  ___   Cooperative tactics

    ___   Association

    ___   Conditional proposals

    ___   Creating movement

    ___   Cutting the salami

    ___   Face-saving

    ___   Focusing on process

    ___   Flexibility

    ___   Logrolling

    ___   Participation

    ___   Psychological commitment

    ___   Reasonable deadlines

    ___   Reciprocity

    ___   Romancing

    ___   Splitting the difference

 ___   Avoidance tactics

    ___   Demand to negotiate monetary issues first

    ___   Demand to negotiate nonmonetary issues first

    ___   Decline to negotiate a related matter

    ___   Withdraw issue(s) from consideration

    ___   Walk out of mediation session

15. Deciding Who Should Attend the Mediation Session

 ___   Party plaintiff(s)

 ___   Party defendant(s)

 ___   Witnesses

 ___   Expert(s)

    ___   Corporate in-house

    ___   Independent

    ___   Structured settlement expert

MEDIATION PREPARATION FORM

YOUR OWN CLIENT—NAME: _____
(Use separate form for each client)

STRENGTHS	WEAKNESSES
1.	1.
2.	2.
3.	3.
4.	4.
NEEDS AND INTERESTS	SATISFACTION RESOURCES
1.	1.
2.	2.
3.	3.
4.	4.
AUTHORITY OR MINIMUM GOALS	POSSIBLE CREATIVE SOLUTIONS
1.	1.
2.	2.
3.	3.
4.	4.
STRATEGY AND TACTICS	SETTING THE AGENDA
1.	1.
2.	2.
3.	3.
4.	4.
CONCESSIONS/TRADE-OFFS	BATNA
1.	1.
2.	2.
3.	3.
OPENING POSITION	BOTTOM LINE
1.	1.
2.	2.

Appendix B-2

MEDIATION PREPARATION FORM

OTHER PARTY—NAME: _____

(Use separate form for each party)

STRENGTHS	INFORMATION NEEDED
1.	1.
2.	2.
3.	3.
4.	4.
WEAKNESSES	INFORMATION NEEDED
1.	1.
2.	2.
3.	3.
4.	4.
NEEDS AND INTERESTS	INFORMATION NEEDED
1.	1.
2.	2.
3.	3.
4.	4.
YOUR SATISFACTION RESOURCES	OTHER SATISFACTION RESOURCES
1.	1.
2.	2.
3.	3.
4.	4.
POSSIBLE STRATEGY AND TACTICS	POSSIBLE BATNA
1.	1.
2.	2.
3.	3.
PREDICTED OPENING POSITION	PREDICTED BOTTOM LINE
1.	1.
2.	2.

Appendix C
CLIENT PREPARATION CHECKLIST

1. **Advising the Client About the Nature of the Mediation Process**

   ___ Voluntary or court-mandated mediation

   ___ Stages of mediation process

   ___ Mediation participants

   ___ Caucusing

   ___ Confidentiality

   ___ Mediation is not a trial

   ___ Client may discontinue mediation at any time

   ___ Primary and secondary purposes of mediation

   ___ Difference between facilitative and evaluative mediation

   ___ Type of mediation selected

   ___ Premediation agreement: purpose, content

       ___ Confidentiality

       ___ Immunity of mediator from lawsuit/subpoena

       ___ Manner and timing of payment for mediator's services

   ___ Informal atmosphere of mediations

   ___ Possible alternative discussion formats

       ___ Parties and counsel negotiating directly without mediator present

       ___ Counsel meeting with opposing counsel without the parties being present

       ___ With the agreement of counsel, the mediator meeting privately with the parties without counsel being present

2. **Advising the Client About the Role of the Mediator**

   ___ Describe mediator's qualifications, background, practice experience, style

   ___ Mediator's duty is to be neutral and impartial with respect to the parties and the subject matter of the dispute.

345

___ Mediator gives no legal advice

___ Mediator does not determine who is right or wrong

___ Mediator assists the parties by

    ___ Identifying issues, needs, and interests

    ___ Exploring alternative solutions

    ___ Focusing the discussion

    ___ Controlliing any emotional outbursts

___ Mediator lends structure to the conference by

    ___ Clarifying communications

    ___ Educating the parties

    ___ Translating proposals into nonpolarizing terms

    ___ Expanding the resources available for settlement

    ___ Testing tho reality of proposed solutions

    ___ Insuring the parties can comply with the proposed settlement terms

    ___ Serving as a scapegoat for the parties' vehemence and/or frustration

    ___ Protecting the integrity of the mediation process

___ Mediator is ethically bound not to disclose not to disclose information received in confidence

___ Mediator is most effective when parties share suggestions for creative settlement solutions

___ Mediator may play devil's advocate in caucuses to help parties reality test their claims, defenses, and settlement proposals

___ Client may have long waiting periods while the mediator is caucusing with the other side

    ___ Not an indication of mediator bias

    ___ Consider bringing reading material or work to do during waiting periods

___ Mediator will do a lot of listening

___ Mediator may ask many types of questions

    ___ Probing

    ___ Clarifying

    ___ Hypothetical

    ___ Open-ended

3. **Advising the Client About the Role of the Advocate**

___ If facilitative mediation:

    ___ Goal is to obtain best possible resolution for client

    ___ Respectful conversation in a problem-solving atmosphere

    ___ Discussion of weaknesses as well as strengths of case

    ___ Listening as well as speaking

    ___ May express empathy toward opposing party or counsel

    ___ Case law normally will not be discussed

    ___ Creative solutions will be explored

___ If evaluative mediation:

    ___ Goal is to obtain best possible resolution for client

    ___ Relative strengths or weaknesses of the parties' legal positions will be emphasized

    ___ Pertinent case law may be discussed

    ___ Approach to problem is more legalistic

    ___ More traditional courtroom persuasion skills are used

___ Advocate will speak privately with client during course of mediation

    ___ Seeking client's impressions, feelings, input

    ___ Jointly determining what move to make next

    ___ Flexibility is key to strategic and tactical success

___ Ultimate decision as to whether to accept a settlement proposal is the client's

___ Advocate will work with opposing counsel in drafting an agreement if a settlement is reached

4. **Advising the Client About the Client's Role**

___ Delineate extent of client's verbal participation

    ___ Tests for allowing client's verbal participation

        ___ Credible

        ___ Likable

        ___ Persuasive

___ Tests for not allowing client's verbal participation

    ___ Easily confused

    ___ Unsure

    ___ Less than credible

    ___ Case is too complex, technically

    ___ Case is too complex, legally

    ___ Case has too many emotional/sentimental aspects

    ___ Opponents are too aggressive; client is too meek

    ___ Opponents are too aggressive; client is too reactive

___ Difficulty of staying quiet during mediation

___ Possible negative impact of nonverbal communication

___ Client, if silent, should appear interested, objective, and reasonable

___ If client is to participate verbally in personal injury mediation, specify division of responsibility between lawyer and client on:

    ___ Facts of the accident

    ___ Conversations with the opposing party at accident scene or afterwards

    ___ Initial injuries and treatment

    ___ Doctor visits and treatment

    ___ Effect of injuries on employment

    ___ Effect of injuries on family life

    ___ Residual and long-term pain and health problems, future treatment, future surgery, etc.

    ___ Preexisting medical conditions

    ___ Depression, fear, anxiety, embarrassment over injuries

    ___ Financial concerns caused by the accident

___ Discuss which documents to use and how

___ Advise client on participation ground rules

   ___ Rehearse client on potential routine questions from mediator or opposing party

   ___ Client should face the mediator when speaking

      ___ Otherwise, opponents may interpret your client's words as accusatory and demeaning

      ___ Client's message is more persuasive

      ___ Helps begin to build trust and rapport with mediator

      ___ Conveys forthrightness of purpose, desire, and motivation to achieve a joint goal

      ___ Opponents can actually listen to your client without being threatened

      ___ Gives advocate opportunity to watch body language of opponents while client is speaking

   ___ Client should speak to be understood

      ___ Rehearse factual presentation with client

         ___ Is it organized?

         ___ Does it begin at the beginning and touch on all necessary points?

         ___ Is it a fair, honest statement of what occurred?

         ___ Does the client use terms whose meanings are not commonly known?

   ___ Client should state only facts

      ___ Point out difference between facts and exaggeration

      ___ If client finds it necessary to use speculation or hearsay, client should identify it as such

      ___ Stretching the truth may cause opponents and mediators to lose confidence in the reliability of client's message

   ___ Client should never argue

      ___ Explain difference between two types of arguing

      ___ Advise client against making arguments that are combative and offensive and detract from achieving settlement goal

___ Client should display no reaction to settlement offers

   ___ Advise client not to react verbally or nonverbally to settlement offers

   ___ Elation reaction may preclude an even better settlement result

   ___ Berating reaction may end mediation

___ Client should behave as if before a jury

   ___ The client should tell the story straightforwardly and sincerely

   ___ When speaking, the client should not pretend to be someone he is not

___ Client should neither answer nor ask difficult questions

   ___ Difficult questions are ones that

      ___ Require some knowledge of the law to answer

      ___ Seek information beyond the expertise of the client

      ___ Require the client to make or imply an admission against interest without the availability of explanatory information

___ Client should defer to advocate when a difficult question is posed

___ Client should always pause slightly when asked any question to give advocate an opportunity to interject

___ Client should not ask difficult questions of the other side or of the mediator. Such questions can:

   ___ Undermine a negotiation strategy

   ___ Expose a negotiation tactic

   ___ Reveal your client's gullibility

   ___ Threaten the other side

   ___ Reveal clues to your bottom line

   ___ Demonstrate client's lack of knowledge, skill, ability, or competence

___ Client should listen carefully to the statements of the opposing party and should not interrupt

 ___ Client should not interrupt opposing party or counsel

 ___ Client should take notes while opponents are speaking

 ___ Client should listen to opponents in order to

  ___ Refresh memory about certain details

  ___ Alert advocate to inaccurate or false statements of opponents

  ___ Ensure that client and advocate clearly understand opponents' positions, needs, and interests

5. **Review of the Case, Settlement Goals, Strategies and Tactics**

 ___ Treat initial planning decisions as tentative

 ___ Be flexible about changing them after speaking with client

 ___ Be alert to changed circumstances

  ___ Client has redefined needs or interests

  ___ Client has discovered new evidence, favorable or unfavorable

  ___ Client has thought of some creative solution

  ___ Client has identified other persons who should be brought into the mediation process

 ___ Consider whether mediation conference needs to be rescheduled

 ___ Reconsider whether premediation meetings with opponents or caucusing with mediator would be helpful

 ___ Consider whether changed circumstances would require accelerating the mediation process

 ___ Review the probabilities of succeeding in litigation and related costs as compared with those in mediation

6. **Advising the Client on Miscellaneous Matters**

 ___ Date of mediation

 ___ Time of mediation

    ___ Change of time zones

    ___ Effect of daylight savings time

    ___ Effect of jet lag on travel schedule

___ Place of mediation

    ___ Provide client written directions

    ___ Provide client a map

    ___ Explain any peculiarities of building

      ___ Elevators

      ___ Location of reception area

    ___ Telephone number to call, if lost

___ Effect of rush hour traffic on timely arrival

___ Effect of weather conditions on timely arrival

___ Prearranged meeting place

___ Special instructions for disabled clients

    ___ Accessible entrances to building

    ___ Location of elevators

___ Dress for mediation

___ Expected duration of the mediation conference

___ Identity of person(s) client may need to contact prior to agreeing to a settlement

___ Identity of any person who will be accompanying client to mediation conference

___ Ask client to provide limits of your settlement authority in writing

Appendix D
MEDIATION SESSION CHECKLIST

1. **Preparing the Premediation Submission**

   ___ Pre-lawsuit mediation

       ___ A summary of the events precipitating the dispute

       ___ Plaintiff's contemplated legal claims and the relief to be requested if a lawsuit is filed

       ___ Documents defining the heart of the conflict

       ___ Short legal memorandum and copies of any critical appellate court opinions

   ___ Mid-litigation mediation

       ___ Overview of the history of the dispute and the litigation, together with a description of the status of the litigation

       ___ Complaint, Answer, Counterclaim, etc.

       ___ Motion for summary judgment, responsive memorandum, ruling

       ___ Court-filed legal briefs or excerpts of them on aspects of law important to discussions during the mediation

       ___ Legal memorandum, if any, regarding lack of plaintiff's entitlement to damages

   ___ Appellate mediation

       ___ Judgment being appealed (with any Memorandum Opinion)

       ___ Jury instructions

       ___ General and special verdicts

       ___ Motion for new trial, response, ruling

       ___ Appellate briefs

2. **The Opening Statement**

   ___ The Mediator's Opening Statement

       ___ Introduces the mediator and other participants

       ___ Describes the mediator's background and experience

353

___ Disclaims any bias, prejudice, or conflict of interest on the mediator's part or discloses possible conflicts of interest that the parties may consider in deciding whether to proceed with the mediation or not

___ Estimates length of the mediation session

___ Discusses "housekeeping" matters

   ___ Rules about smoking

   ___ Rules about interruptions

   ___ Rules regarding outside observers or witnesses

   ___ Understandings regarding talking to the media

   ___ Understandings regarding when breaks will be taken for meals, etc.

   ___ Asks parties to review and sign premediation agreement (if they have not already done so)

___ Educates parties on the mediation process, the mediator's role, and what to expect during the course of the mediation

___ Sets tone for the mediation session

___ Establishes rapport and credibility with the parties

___ Obtains commitment from the parties to negotiate in good faith

___ Establishes initial pattern of agreement

___ Outlines procedural considerations, including those related to caucusing and confidentiality

___ Suggests an agenda for the mediation session

___ Party's Opening Statement

   ___ Introduction of advocate and client

   ___ Advocate's Opening Remarks

     ___ Speak as if you are making a trial opening statement and a trial closing argument combined into one presentation

     ___ Make apologetic comments or acknowlege other party's injury, pain, or distress, if appropriate

     ___ Discuss pertinent facts

     ___ Note which facts are disputed and which are undisputed

___ Outline claims (if representing plaintiff) and defenses (if representing defendant)

___ State nature of relief sought in court re claim (if representing a plaintiff) or re counterclaim or crossclaim (if representing a defendant)

___ Present pertinent documentary evidence as appropriate

___ Discuss applicable law, as appropriate

___ Describe how damages to be sought in court were computed

___ Describe prior negotiation history and current status of negotiations

___ Using client to tell story

___ Client uses narrative style

___ Listen to client

___ Make notes of omissions

___ When client finishes, ask pertinent follow-up questions

___ Make concluding remarks

___ Ask the mediator if he has any questions

___ Using documents

___ Before beginning your presentation provide mediator and other side with a set of the documents to be referred to in the opening statement

___ Allow client to refer to documents you have preorganized; or

___ Feed documents to client or provide a tabbed binder

___ You discuss pertinent documents following your client's presentation

___ Using audiovisual aids

___ Test audio and visual equipment before mediation session

___ Make sure visual aids are situated so that all participants can view them

   ___ Decide who will activate screen changes

   ___ Ensure client understands how the audiovisual aids are going to be used during the opening statement

3. **Applied Negotiation Tactics**

___ Five principal conflict behaviors

   ___ Competing

   ___ Accommodating

   ___ Compromising

   ___ Collaborating

   ___ Avoiding

___ Circumstances prompting use of behaviors

   ___ Competing

      ___ Need quick solution

      ___ You have power

      ___ Issue vital to client

      ___ Client protection

   ___ Accommodating

      ___ You are wrong

      ___ Avoid disruptions

      ___ Issue more important to other side

      ___ Build credits for later

      ___ Avoid damaging cause

   ___ Compromising

      ___ Moderately important goals

      ___ Temporary settlement

      ___ Time pressures

      ___ Back-up mode

   ___ Collaborating

      ___ Integrative solution

      ___ Merge insights

      ___ Gain commitment

___ Work through hard feelings

___ Avoiding

    ___ Trivial issue

    ___ Low power

    ___ Risk of damage outweighs gain from a negotiated result

    ___ Gain time to cool down

    ___ Gain time to gather information

___ Choose appropriate negotiation tactic (See Tactic Selection Chart)

4. Deriving the Most Tactical Advantage from Caucuses

___ Identifying mediator tactics

    ___ Communication tactics

        ___ Conduit

        ___ Surrogate

        ___ Reshaping

        ___ Clarification

    ___ Substantive tactics

        ___ Translation

        ___ Norm-deviating

        ___ Opinion

        ___ Recommendation

    ___ Procedural tactics

        ___ Controlling meeting times or places

        ___ Prescribing extramediation activities

        ___ Threatening to withdraw

    ___ Best use of mediator and caucusing process

        ___ Take charge of the initial caucus

        ___ Make a reasonable first offer/demand through the mediator

        ___ Do not disclose your bottom line to the mediator up front

        ___ Listen to the mediator

___ Watch for clues about the other side's strategy and bottom line

___ Make your messages effectuate your tactics

___ Do not try to make extramediation threats through the mediator

___ Hold back some good information until the final caucuses

___ Take the time necessary to caucus with your client

___ Support new proposals with sound reasons

___ At end of each caucus, advise mediator concerning what information is confidential

___ Make sure you have authority to make or accept a settlement proposal

___ Leave your fees and mediator's fees out of caucus discussions with the mediator

5. Persuasion Refresher

___ Persuasion in general

___ Five objectives of persuasive messages

___ To command the attention of the receiver

___ To be understood by the receiver as intended by the sender

___ To warrant the receiver's belief that the information presented is credible or accurate

___ To present information that conforms to the receiver's values of what is right and wrong

___ To motivate the receiver to act

___ Three artistic means of persuasion

___ *Ethos* (character of speaker) (behavioral)

___ *Pathos* (emotions aroused in audience) (affective)

___ *Logos* (true or probable argument) (cognitive)

___ Persuasion through effective speaking

___ Voice

___ Concrete language

___ Knowledge

___ Enthusiasm

___ Emphasis

___ Alignment

___ Optimism

___ Engage listening styles

   ___ Leisure

   ___ Inclusive

   ___ Stylistic

   ___ Technical

   ___ Empathetic

   ___ Nonconforming

___ Power of example

___ Persuasion through effective use of body language

   ___ Dress and demeanor

   ___ Eye contact

   ___ Facial expressions

   ___ Other body language to enhance message

___ Persuasion through effective listening

   ___ Know your own listening style

   ___ Use critical listening

   ___ Use active listening

___ Persuasion through effective processing of sensed body language

   ___ Know the attitudes being expressed by particular body language

   ___ Respond appropriately

6. Applying Creative Problem-Solving Techniques

___ Designing (finding or defining) the problem

   ___ List specific and general needs of the parties

   ___ List resources available to each party to satisfy own needs

   ___ List resources available to each party to satisfy the other party's needs

___ List resources beyond the control of the parties that could be made available to satisfy the parties' specific and general needs

___ Designing the process for solving the problem

   ___ Caucus with client

   ___ Caucus with mediator

   ___ Call for joint session

   ___ Make telephone calls to determine availability of outside resources

   ___ Caucus privately with opposing counsel

___ Designing the solution

   ___ Sketch out potential solution patterns

   ___ Experiment with repatternings

   ___ Select optimal solution pattern

7. **Structured Settlement**

___ Is this a personal injury or wrongful death case?

___ Is the plaintiff a minor, spendthrift, or a person otherwise incapable of managing a substantial cash settlement?

___ Is the settlement large enough to convince defendant that it is advantageous to pay the settlement over time?

___ Is there some other reason for suggesting a structured settlement?

___ If a structure is chosen, what will be the design?

   ___ Cash paid at time of settlement

     ___ How much?

     ___ When?

     ___ Terms?

   ___ Future periodic lump sums

     ___ Amount?

     ___ For what purposes?

     ___ Future medical expenses

     ___ Schooling

     ___ Wedding

___ Educational travel

___ Purchase of home

___ Start of new business

___ Retirement

___ When?

___ Spouse protection needed?

___ Annuities

___ Amount?

___ When?

___ Escalator amount needed?

___ What is the value of the structured settlement?

___ Interest rate

___ Mortality data

___ Value of uniform periodic payments

___ Value of future lump sum payments

___ Growth of future payments

___ Present value of lost income

8. **Assisting the Mediator to Achieve Closure**

___ Suggest mediator present proposal as own idea

___ Suggest mediator make proposal conditional without communicating a commitment on your part

___ Suggest parties split the difference

___ Suggest a structured settlement or payment in installments

___ Suggest a future business arrangement

___ Suggest a portion of the settlement be paid to a mutually acceptable charity

___ Suggest payment in kind instead of in dollars

___ Suggest substitution of goods

___ Suggest an apology

___ Suggest a change in title, label, or description

___ Suggest extradispute resources for satisfying a party's extradispute interests

___ Suggest confidentiality agreement

___ Suggest a change in language or in the interpretation of language

9. **Ethical Considerations**

___ Mediator ethics

    ___ Must recognize self-determination of parties

    ___ Must be impartial

    ___ Must disclose conflicts of interest

    ___ Must have necessary qualifications

    ___ Must maintain confidentiality

    ___ Must conduct mediation fairly, diligently, and in a manner consistent with the principle of parties' self-determination

    ___ Must be truthful in advertising and solicitations for mediation

    ___ Must fully disclose and explain the basis for compensation, fees, and charges

    ___ Must make an effort to improve the practice of mediation

    ___ Duty to process

    ___ Duty to nonparties

    ___ Duty to other professionals

___ Lawyer-negotiator ethics

    ___ Advising the client

        ___ Keep client reasonably informed of status of matter

        ___ Promptly comply with client's reasonable requests for information

        ___ Explain a matter to extent necessary to permit client to make informed decisions regarding the representation

    ___ Advocacy

        ___ Exercise independent judgment on behalf of client

___ Advocate client's interests and positions so long as positions can be argued in good faith and are supported by law

___ Duty of advocacy qualified by expectations of community and court

___ Limitations on advocacy

___ No contact with other side directly if that party is represented by counsel, unless properly authorized

___ May not request persons other than a client (or relatives or agents) refrain from voluntarily giving relevant information to another party

___ Must make reasonable efforts to expedite litigation consistent with the needs of the client

___ Truthfulness

___ May not knowingly make a false statement of material fact or law to a third person

___ May not fail to disclose a material fact to a third person when disclosure is necessary to avoid assisting a criminal or fraudulent act by a client

___ Certain statements normally are not taken as material facts:

___ Estimates of price or value

___ Party's intention as to an acceptable settlement of a claim

___ Existence of an undisclosed principal except where nondisclosure of principal would constitute fraud

___ Confidentiality

___ May not reveal information relating to representation of a client unless the client consents after consultation, except for disclosures that are impliedly authorized in order to carry out the representation

___ Impliedly authorized disclosures include

___ In litigation, lawyer may disclose information by admitting a fact that cannot properly be disputed

___ In negotiation, a lawyer may make a disclosure that facilitates a satisfactory conclusion

___ Drafting agreements

___ May not prepare a settlement agreement giving the lawyer or person related to the lawyer any substantial gift from a client, including a testamentary gift, except where the client is related to the donee

___ May not make or negotiate an agreement giving the lawyer literary or media rights to a portrayal or account based in substantial part on information relating to the representation

___ May not participate in the making of a partnership or employment agreement that restricts the rights of a lawyer to practice after termination of the relationship (except an agreement concerning benefits upon retirement)

___ May not participate in the making of an agreement in which a restriction on lawyer's right to practice is part of the settlement of a controversy between private parties

Appendix E

POSTMEDIATION ADVOCACY CHECKLIST

1. **Continuing the Negotiations**

   ___ General techniques for dealing with the parties' emotions

       ___ Focus on the process

           ___ To acknowledge the legitimacy of feelings

           ___ To enhance understanding

           ___ To depersonalize the situation

       ___ Use selective information disclosure and information bargaining, instead of making accusations

       ___ Create an environment for a "fresh start"

       ___ Redefine the issues

       ___ Emphasize the problem solving approach

       ___ Jointly develop win-win proposals

   ___ Specific focusing tactics to allow parties to deal more effectively with problem solving

       ___ Modifying the payment terms

       ___ Altering the allocation of risk

       ___ Modifying the time of performance

       ___ Adding guarantees of satisfaction

       ___ Adding a grievance mechanism

       ___ Changing the specifications

       ___ Adjusting the terms

       ___ Recognizing inaccurate information

       ___ Obtaining correct information

2. **Drafting the Settlement Agreement**

   ___ Reasons to have opposing counsel draft agreement

       ___ Client cannot afford it

       ___ Let other side explore alternatives; you refine

       ___ Courts interpret contract against drafter

___ Reasons for you to draft agreement

    ___ Choice of terms is critical to your client's interests

    ___ You will be able to include provisions not specifically negotiated

___ Use commonsense writing techniques

    ___ Organize the document logically

    ___ Use simple and direct language

    ___ Provide a definitions section

    ___ Use the same word to describe the same idea or concept throughout

    ___ Use short paragraphs with boldface topic headings

    ___ Use the active voice

    ___ Say what you mean

    ___ Be careful of possible dual interpretations

___ Topics covered in the settlement agreement

    ___ Description of the parties

    ___ Background and purpose of the agreement

    ___ Rights of the parties

    ___ Responsibilities of the parties

    ___ Terms of payment

    ___ Disposition of liens

    ___ Law to govern contracts

    ___ An ADR clause

    ___ Confidentiality

    ___ Severability clause

    ___ Releases

___ Basic rules of contract construction

    ___ A general release will void all future claims arising out of the dispute

    ___ Specific releases will void specified future claims but allow other unspecified (or specified) future claims

    ___ Courts will view the agreement as a whole, interpreting each part in light of the other parts

___ Courts favor interpretations that hold the agreement to be lawful

___ Courts favor interpretations that reflect the public interest

___ Courts interpret contracts most strongly against parties who draft them

___ Does the settlement agreement need to be approved by the court?

___ Should a consent judgment be entered?

3. **Enforcing the Settlement Agreement**

___ Try mediating compliance with the agreement

___ Arbitration?

___ Court proceeding?

___ File motion in pending action

___ File separate new action regarding enforcement of agreement

___ Amend pleadings to include claim or defense on compromise

Appendix F

SAMPLE MEDIATION CLAUSES

AMERICAN ARBITRATION ASSOCIATION

AND

J.A.M.S./ENDISPUTE
(Now, "JAMS")

MEDIATION

The parties may wish to attempt mediation before submitting their dispute to arbitration. This can be accomplished by making reference to mediation in the arbitration clause. To be most effective, the mediation clause can specify the AAA's Commercial or Construction Industry Mediation Rules. Examples of such language follows:

> If a dispute arises out of or relates to this contract, or the breach thereof, and if said dispute cannot be settled through negotiation, the parties agree first to try in good faith to settle the dispute by mediation administered by the American Arbitration Association under its Commercial Mediation Rules, before resorting to arbitration, litigation, or some other dispute resolution procedure.

> The parties hereby submit the following dispute to mediation under the Commercial Mediation Rules of the American Arbitration Association. [The clause may also provide for the qualifications of the mediator(s), method of payment, locale of meetings, and any other item of concern to the parties.]

MEDIATION/ARBITRATION

A clause can be inserted into a contract that first provides for mediation under the AAA's mediation rules. If the mediation is unsuccessful, the dispute would then go to arbitration under the AAA's arbitration rules. This process is sometimes referred to as "Med-Arb." A sample of a med-arb clause follows:

> If a dispute arises out of or relates to this contract, or the breach thereof, and if said dispute cannot be settled through direct discussions, the parties agree to first endeavor to settle the dispute in an amicable manner by mediation administered by the American Arbitration Association under its Commercial Mediation Rules, before resorting to arbitration. Thereafter, any unresolved controversy or claim arising out of or relating to

this contract, or breach thereof, shall be settled by arbitration administered by the American Arbitration Association in accordance with its Commercial Arbitration Rules, and judgment upon the Award rendered by the arbitrator(s) may be entered in any court having jurisdiction thereof.

J.A.M.S./ENDISPUTE [Now, "JAMS"]

Dispute Resolution Clauses

The following are simple dispute resolution provisions that can be inserted into any contract governing a business relationship. For example, these clauses are used in contracts for the provision of goods and services and for contracts establishing joint business ventures. A variation on these clauses makes them appropriate for employment or professional service contracts

The provisions can be made for details or tailored if the parties, at the time of the drafting of the contract, can anticipate the types of disputes that will arise and the most effective means of resolving them. For example, many users of these basic clauses have supplemented them with language mandating a good faith negotiation period and a procedure for such negotiations, establishing requirements for the exchange of relevant information, specifying a mediator or arbitrator or type of person that the parties would like as mediator or arbitrator and setting limits on the length of time that either the mediation or arbitration can take.

Option 1-Mediation

Any dispute arising out of or relating to this contract that cannot be settled by good faith negotiation between the parties will be submitted to J.A.M.S./ENDISPUTE [Now, "JAMS"] for non-binding mediation.

Option 2-Arbitration

Any dispute arising out of or relating to this contract that cannot be settled by good faith negotiation between the parties will be submitted to J.A.M.S./ENDISPUTE [Now, "JAMS"]for final and binding arbitration pursuant to J.A.M.S./ENDISPUTE's [Now, "JAMS"] [specify set] Arbitration Rules.

Option 3-Mediation/Arbitration

Any dispute arising out of or relating to this contract that cannot be settled by good faith negotiation between the parties will be submitted to J.A.M.S./ENDISPUTE [Now, "JAMS"] for non-binding mediation. If complete agreement cannot be reached within __ days of submission to mediation, any remaining issues will be submitted to J.A.M.S./ENDISPUTE [Now, "JAMS"] for final and binding arbitration pursuant to J.A.M.S./ENDISPUTE's [Now, "JAMS"] [specify set] Arbitration Rules.

Appendix G

SAMPLE PREMEDIATION AGREEMENT

(J.A.M.S./ENDISPUTE)
(Now, "JAMS")

J.A.M.S./ENDISPUTE [Now, "JAMS"] MEDIATION AGREEMENT

XXX vs. XXX

1. Role of the Mediator. The undersigned parties agree voluntarily to submit the above captioned dispute to J.A.M.S./ENDISPUTE, Incorporated [Now, "JAMS"] for a non-binding Mediation. The parties understand that the role of the Mediator is not to render a decision but to assist the parties in reaching agreement. The parties accept responsibility for any agreement they reach.

2. Disclosure. The parties have chosen the Mediator. The Mediator and each party confirm that they have disclosed, in the space provided, any past or present relationship that a reasonable person would believe would influence the Mediator's impartiality (use back if necessary):

_____

_____

3. Exchange of Information, Participant Lists, and Use of Documents. In order to avoid surprise, at least one week prior to the mediation, each party shall (if mutually agreed) exchange all memoranda, documents, and mediation participants lists, relating to this matter, including any documents known to the parties herein to be within the possession or control of others, that are intended to be referenced in the mediation. If requested, counsel shall provide the Mediator with copies of key cases and statutes cited in the memorandum submitted to the Mediator. Documents or participants not previously exchanged or described shall not be considered in the mediation unless by mutual agreement or if deemed necessary by the Mediator. The Mediator will have complete authority over all mediation procedures.

4. Limited Questions to be Asked of Participants. The mediation is not a discovery deposition. However, decision makers often need to have issues or positions clarified. Therefore, the Mediator shall encourage clarifying questions, particularly by participants who are decision makers.

5. Settlement Authority. All parties agree to have an individual present at the mediation who has settlement authority consistent with the demand in this case. When such an individual is not available, other parties shall be notified.

6. Confidentiality. All parties deem the mediation to be a settlement discussion. Therefore, all statements by the parties, Mediator, or J.A.M.S./ENDISPUTE [Now, "JAMS"], relating to the mediation process, and any documents created for or during these proceedings, are inadmissible and not discoverable for any purpose, including

impeachment, in any pending or subsequent judicial, quasi-judicial, arbitration, or any other proceeding, absent consent of all parties. Neither the Mediator nor anyone else associated with J.A.M.S./ENDISPUTE [Now, "JAMS"] will be subpoenaed or requested to testify by any party for any reason.

No notes or any other materials generated during the conference by the mediator or the parties will be subpoenaed by any party. However, evidence that is otherwise admissible or discoverable shall not be rendered inadmissible or non-discoverable as a result of its use in the mediation.

7. Caucus. When a party meets alone with the Mediator, he or she will clearly inform the Mediator what statements or documents shall remain confidential, and what may be shared with the other party(ies).

8. Limited Immunity. Given the very limited time and nature of this professional retention, the Mediator and J.A.M.S./ENDISPUTE [Now, "JAMS"] shall have the same limited immunity as judges and court employees would have under federal law, and the parties agree to defend the Mediator and J.A.M.S./ENDISPUTE [Now, "JAMS"] in connection with any subpoena arising out of this mediation. Neither J.A.M.S./ENDISPUTE [Now, "JAMS"] nor the Mediator are a necessary party in any judicial or arbitration proceeding relating to the mediation.

9. Legal Advice. There is no attorney/client relationship between the Mediator and any party herein and the Mediator does not provide legal advice. The parties recognize that in the process of reaching agreement they may choose to waive or forego a claim or defense, and will consult an attorney if they have any questions about their legal rights.

10. Mediation is Voluntary. Any party may withdraw from the mediation on written notice to all other parties and the Mediator. In the event of such withdrawal, such party shall remain responsible for its share of the fees and expenses incurred by the mediator and J.A.M.S./ENDISPUTE [Now, "JAMS"] up to the date of withdrawal, and remain subject to the other provisions, particularly paragraphs 6, 8, 9 and 11 of this agreement.

11. Fees. The parties agree to pay the estimated fees and expenses described in the preliminary invoice. Additional time for review, follow-up telephone conferences or meetings with any party to attempt to reach settlement of this matter, or any subsequent related judicial or other proceeding, will be billed at $XXX an hour. The mediation will not begin unless the preliminary invoice has been paid.

By the signatures below each party, either directly or through its counsel, certifies that it agrees with everything stated. This agreement may be signed in counterparts.

by: _____   by: _____

by: _____   by: _____

Date: _____   Mediator _____

Appendix H

Commercial Mediation Rules

American Arbitration Association

Introduction

In some situations, the involvement of an impartial mediator can assist parties in reaching a settlement of a commercial dispute. Mediation is a process under which the parties submit their dispute to an impartial person—the mediator. The mediator may suggest ways of resolving the dispute, but may not impose a settlement on the parties.

If the parties want to use a mediator to resolve an existing dispute under these rules, they can enter into the following submission.

The parties hereby submit the following dispute to mediation administered by the American Arbitration Association under its Commercial Mediation Rules (the clause may also provide for the qualifications of the mediator, the method of payment, the locale of meetings, and any other item of concern to the parties).

If the parties want to adapt mediation as an integral part of their contractual dispute-settlement procedure, they can insert the following mediation clause into their contract in conjunction with a standard arbitration provision

If a dispute arises out of or relates to this contract or the breach thereof and if the dispute cannot be settled through negotiation, the parties agree first to try in good faith to settle the dispute by mediation administered by the American Arbitration Association under its Commercial Mediation Rules before resorting to arbitration, litigation, or some other dispute-resolution procedure.

These rules were prepared by the staff of the American Arbitration Association with the assistance of the Harry de Jar Commercial Mediation Center's Advisory Committee. The committee, chaired by David A Botwinik, included Robert F. Borg, Ralph Katz, Robert McLucas, Roland Plottel, Frank J. Scardilli, Janet M. Spencer, and Robert B. Underhill.

The American Arbitration Association is a public-service, not-for-profit organization offering a broad range of dispute-resolution services to business executives, attorneys, individuals, trade associations, unions, management, consumers, families, communities, and all levels of government. Services are available through AAA headquarters in New York and through offices located in major cities throughout the United States. Mediation conferences may be held at locations convenient for the parties and are not limited to cities with AAA offices. In addition, the AAA serves as a center for education and training, issues specialized publications, and conducts research on all forms of out-of-court dispute settlement.

Resolving Business Disputes

Business disputes may now be submitted to a special program of alternatives to litigation.

How the Program Works

Any party to an existing business dispute may ask the AAA to ascertain whether the other party or parties are willing to submit the dispute to alternative dispute resolution (ADR). Cases that are new or pending litigation are eligible.

An AAA representative will explain the various dispute-resolution techniques and assist the parties in choosing one that meets their needs. Once the AAA has the parties' agreement to submit a dispute to alternative resolution, it will administer the case under its applicable rules or procedures.

Beyond mediation, ADR might take the form of arbitration, minitrial, or any variation of these procedures on which the parties agree.

Arbitration is a process in which each side presents its case at a hearing to a neutral for a final and binding decision.

Minitrial is a structures settlement procedure in which attorneys present their best case in an abbreviated form with experts, if appropriate, before senior executives of the companies involved and a neutral who chaired the presentation. After the presentation, the senior executives meet for a settlement discussion. In the event that the senior executives are unable to settle the dispute, the neutral may be empowered to mediate and/or provide a non-binding advisory opinion regarding the likely outcome if the case were litigated.

Advisory arbitration in most respects mirrors traditional arbitration. It differs, however, in focusing on specific issues in a dispute and deciding them in an award that is not binding on the parties.

Other ADR methods include factfinding, investigation of a dispute by a neutral who issues findings and a non-binding report, and med-arb, which combines the two primary processes.

The Neutrals

Mediators and arbitrators selected for this program are qualified, experienced neutrals with an understanding of current legal and business practices. The parties select the neutral best qualified to hear their controversy.

Cost

The administrative fees of the AAA and the compensation arrangements for the neutral are set forth in the particular dispute resolution agreed on. Pamphlets containing the various procedures are available through any AAA regional office.

Filing

A party may list a case with the AAA and request that the AAA invite the other party to join in a submission to arbitration, mediation, or other form of dispute resolution. The AAA will, upon request, provide a form to do so. It is sufficient, however, to provide the information outlined below in a letter or by telephone. Upon receipt of this information, the AAA will contact the other party or parties to the dispute.

A party listing a case under the program must provide the AAA with the following—

names of the parties to the case, including any court docket number;

the ADR procedure requested—e.g., arbitration, mediation, or factfinding;

the nature and the amount of the claim (a brief statement of the claim and the response of the other party or parties);

desired qualifications of the neutral, if any;

the preferred place of hearing; and

addresses and telephone numbers of all parties, including counsel, if any.

If there is no agreement among the parties to submit the dispute to an ADR procedure, there is no charge to the filing party. If the matter settles as a result of AAA contact with the parties, the filing party will pay a $150 fee. If there is a submission to an ADR procedure, the fee schedule in the appropriate AAA rules or procedures will apply.

Further Information

For further information, contact the nearest AAA office.

Contents

Commercial Mediation Rules

1. Agreement of Parties

Whenever, by stipulation or in their contract, the parties have provided for mediation or conciliation of existing or future disputes under the auspices of the American Arbitration Association (AAA) or under these rules, they shall be deemed to have made these rules, as amended and in effect as of the date of the submission of the dispute, a part of their agreement.

2. Initiation of Mediation

Any party or parties to a dispute may initiate mediation by filing with the AAA a submission to mediation or a written request for mediation pursuant to these rules, together with the appropriate Filing Fee (page 12). Where there is no submission to mediation or contract providing for mediation, a party may request the AAA to invite another party to join in a submission to mediation. Upon receipt of such a request, the AAA will contact the other parties involved in the dispute and attempt to obtain a submission to mediation.

3. Requests for Mediation

A request for mediation shall contain a brief statement of the nature of the dispute and the names, addresses, and telephone numbers of all parties to the dispute and those who will represent them, if any, in the mediation. The initiating party shall simultaneously file two copies of the request with the AAA and one copy with every other party to the dispute.

4. Appointment of the Mediator

Upon receipt of a request for mediation, the AAA will appoint a qualified mediator to serve. Normally, a single mediator will be appointed unless the parties agree otherwise or the AAA determines otherwise. If the agreement of the parties names a mediator or specifies a method of appointing a mediator, that designation or method shall be followed.

5. Qualifications of the Mediator

No person shall serve as a mediator in any dispute in which that person has any financial or personal interest in the result of the mediation, except by the written consent of all parties. Prior to accepting an appointment, the prospective mediator shall disclose any circumstance likely to create a presumption of bias or prevent a prompt meeting with the parties. Upon receipt of such information, the AAA shall either replace the mediator or immediately communicate the information to the parties for their comments. In the event that the parties disagree as to whether the mediator shall serve, the AAA will appoint another. The AAA is authorized to appoint another mediator if the appointed mediator is unable to serve promptly.

6. Vacancies

If any mediator shall become unwilling or unable to serve, the AAA will appoint another mediator, unless the parties agree otherwise.

7. Representation

Any party may be represented by persons of the party's choice. The names and addresses of such persons shall be communicated in writing to all parties and to the AAA.

8. Date, Time, and Place of Mediation

The mediator shall fix the date and the time of each mediation session. The Mediation shall be held at the appropriate regional office of the AAA, or at any other convenient location agreeable to the mediator and the parties, as the mediator shall determine.

9. Identification of Matters in Dispute

At least ten days prior to the first scheduled mediation session, each party shall provide the mediator with a brief memorandum setting forth its position with regard to the issues that need to be resolved. At the discretion of the mediator, such memoranda may be mutually exchanged by the parties.

At the first session, the parties will be expected to produce all information reasonably required for the mediator to understand the issues presented.

The mediator may require any party to supplement such information.

10. Authority of the Mediator

The mediator does not have the authority to impose a settlement on the parties but will attempt to help them reach a satisfactory resolution of their dispute. The mediator is authorized to conduct joint and separate meetings with the parties and to make oral and written recommendations for settlement. Whenever necessary, the mediator may also obtain expert advice concerning technical aspects of the dispute, provided that the parties agree and assume the expenses of obtaining such advice. Arrangements for obtaining such advice shall be made by the mediator or the parties, as the mediator shall determine.

The mediator is authorized to end the mediation whenever, in the judgement of the mediator, further efforts at mediation would not contribute to a resolution of the dispute between the parties.

11. Privacy

Mediation sessions are private. The parties and their representatives may attend mediation sessions. Other persons may attend only with the permission of the parties and with the consent of the mediator.

12.   Confidentiality

Confidential information disclosed to a mediator by the parties or by witnesses in the course or the mediation shall not be divulged by the mediator. All records, reports, or other documents received by a mediator while serving in that capacity shall be confidential. The mediator shall not be compelled to divulge such records or to testify in regard to the mediation in any adversary proceeding or judicial forum.

The parties shall maintain the confidentiality of the mediation and shall not rely on, or introduce as evidence in any arbitral, judicial, or other proceeding:

(a) views expressed or suggestions made by another party with respect to a possible settlement of the dispute;

(b) admissions made by another party in the course of the mediation proceedings;

(c) proposals made or views expresses by the mediator; or

(d) the fact that another party had or had not indicated willingness to accept a proposal for settlement made by the mediator.

13. No Stenographic Record

There shall be no stenographic records of the mediation process.

14. Termination of Mediation

The mediation shall be terminated:

(a) by the execution of a settlement agreement by the parties;

(b) by a written declaration of the mediator to the effect that further efforts at mediation are no longer worthwhile; or

(c) by a written declaration of a party or parties to the effect that the mediation proceedings are terminated.

15. Exclusion of Liability

Neither the AAA nor any mediator is a necessary part in judicial proceedings relating to the mediation.

Neither the AAA nor any mediator shall be liable to any party for any act or omission in connection with any mediation conducted under these rules.

16. Interpretation and Application of Rules

The mediator shall interpret and apply these rules insofar as they relate to the mediator's duties and responsibilities. All other rules shall be interpreted and applied by the AAA.

17. Expenses

The expenses of witnesses for either side shall be paid by the party producing such witnesses. All other expenses of the mediation, including required traveling and other expenses of the mediator and representatives of the AAA, and the expenses of any witness and the cost of any proofs or expert advice produced at the direct request of the mediator, shall be borne equally by the parties unless they agree otherwise.

Administrative Fees

The Filing Fee

The case filing or set-up fee is $300. This fee is to be borne equally or as otherwise agreed by the parties.

Additionally, the parties are charged a fee based on the number of hours of mediator time. The hourly fee is for the compensation of both the mediator and the AAA and varies according to region. Check with your local office for specific availability and rates.

There is no charge to the filing party where the AAA is requested to invite other parties to join in a submission to mediation. However, if a case settles after AAA involvement but prior to dispute resolution, the filing party will be charged a $150 filing fee.

The expenses of the AAA and the mediator, if any, are generally borne equally by the parties. The parties may vary this arrangement by agreement.

Where the parties have attempted mediation under these rules but have failed to reach a settlement, the AAA will apply the administrative fee on the mediation toward subsequent AAA arbitration, which is filed with the AAA within ninety days of the termination of mediation.

Deposits

Before the commencement of mediation, the parties shall each deposit such portion of the fee covering the cost of mediation as the AAA shall direct and all appropriate additional sums that the AAA deems necessary to defray the expenses of the proceeding. When the mediation had terminated, the AAA shall render an accounting and return any unexpected balance to the parties.

Refunds

Once the parties agree to mediate, no refund of the administrative fee will be made.

Appendix I

MODEL STANDARDS OF CONDUCT FOR MEDIATORS

(AAA, ABA, SPIDR)

Reproduced with permission from the
Society of Professionals in
Dispute Resolution

The Model Standards of Conduct for Mediators were prepared from 1992 through 1994 by a joint committee composed of two delegates from the American Arbitration Association, John D. Feerick, Chair, and David Botwinik, two from the American Bar Association, James Alfini and Nancy Rogers, and two from the Society of Professionals in Dispute Resolution, Susan Dearborn and Lemoine Pierce.

The Model Standards have been approved by the American Arbitration Association, the Litigation Section and the Dispute Resolution Section of the American Bar Association, and the Society of Professionals in Dispute Resolution.

Reporters: Bryant Garth and Kimberlee K. Kovach

Staff Project Director: Frederick E. Woods

The views set out in this publication have not been considered by the American Bar Association House of Delegates and do not constitute the policy of the American Bar Association.

MODEL STANDARDS OF CONDUCT
FOR MEDIATORS

Introductory Note

The initiative for these standards came from three professional groups: The American Arbitration Association, the American Bar Association, and the Society of Professionals in Dispute Resolution.

The purpose of this initiative was to develop a set of standards to serve as a general framework for the practice of mediation. The effort is a step in the development of the field and a tool to assist practitioners in it—a beginning, not an end. The model standards are intended to apply to all types of mediation. It is recognized, however, that in some cases the application of these standards may be affected by laws or contractual agreements.

Preface

The model standards of conduct for mediators are intended to perform three major functions: to serve as a guide for the conduct of mediators; to inform the mediating parties; and to promote public confidence in mediation as a process for resolving disputes. The standards draw on existing codes of conduct for mediators and take into account issues and problems that have surfaced in mediation practice. They are offered in the hope that they will serve an educational function and provide assistance to individuals, organizations, and institutes involved in mediation.

Mediation is a process in which an impartial third party—a mediator—facilitates the resolution of a dispute by promoting voluntary agreement (or "self-determination") by the parties to the dispute. A mediator facilitates communications, promotes understanding, focuses the parties on their interests, and seeks creative problem solving to enable the parties to reach their own agreement. These standards give meaning to this definition of mediation.

I. Self-Determination: A Mediator Shall Recognize that Mediation is Based on the Principle of Self-Determination by the Parties.

Self-determination is the fundamental principle of mediation. It requires that the mediation process rely upon the ability of the parties to reach a voluntary, uncoerced agreement. Any party may withdraw from mediation at any time.

Comments:

The mediator may provide information about the process, raise issues, and help parties explore options. The primary role of the mediator is to facilitate a voluntary resolution of a dispute. Parties shall be given the opportunity to consider all proposed options.

A mediator cannot personally ensure that each party had made a fully informed choice to reach a particular agreement, but it is a good practice for the mediator to make the parties aware of the importance of consulting other professionals, where appropriate, to help them make informed decisions.

II. Impartiality: A Mediator Shall Conduct the Mediation in an Impartial Manner

The concept of mediator impartiality is central to the mediation process. A mediator shall mediate only those matters in which she or he can remain impartial and evenhanded. If at any time the mediator is unable to conduct the process in an impartial manner, the mediator is obligated to withdraw.

Comments:

A mediator shall avoid conduct that gives the appearance of partiality toward one of the parties. The quality of the mediation process is enhanced when the parties have confidence in the impartiality of the modiator.

When mediators are appointed by a court or institution, the appointing agency shall make reasonable efforts to ensure that mediators serve impartially.

A mediator should guard against partiality or prejudice based on the parties' personal characteristics, background or performance at the mediation.

III. Conflicts of Interest: A Mediator Shall Disclose all Actual and Potential Conflicts of Interest Reasonably Known to the Mediator. After Disclosure, the Mediator Shall Decline to Mediate unless all Parties Choose to Retain the Mediator. The Need to Protect Against Conflicts of Interest also Governs Conduct that occurs During and After the Mediation.

A conflict of interest is a dealing or relationship that might create an impression of possible bias. The basic approach to questions for conflict of interest is consistent with the concept of self-determination. The mediator has a responsibility to disclose all actual and potential conflicts that are reasonably known to the mediator and could reasonably be seen as raising a question about impartiality. If all parties agree to mediate after being informed of conflicts, the mediator may proceed with the mediation. If, however, the conflict of interest casts serious doubt on the integrity of the process, the mediator shall decline to proceed.

A mediator must avoid the appearance of conflict of interest both during and after the mediation. Without the consent of all parties, a mediator shall not subsequently establish a professional relationship on an unrelated matter under circumstances which would raise legitimate questions about the integrity of the mediation process.

Comments:

A mediator shall avoid conflicts of interest in recommending the services of other professionals. A mediator may make reference to professional services or associates which maintain rosters of qualified professionals.

Potential conflicts of interest may arise between administrators of mediation programs and mediators and there may be strong pressures on the mediator to settle a particular case or cases. The mediator's commitment must be to the parties and the process. Pressure from outside of the mediation process should never influence the mediator to coerce parties to settle.

IV. Competence: A Mediator Shall Mediate Only When the Mediator Has the Necessary Qualifications to Satisfy the Reasonable Expectation of the Parties.

Any person may be selected as a mediator, provided that the parties are satisfied with the mediator's qualifications. Training and experience in mediation, however, are often necessary for effective mediation. A person who offers herself or himself as available to serve as a mediator gives parties and the public the expectation that she or he has the competency to mediate effectively. In court-connected or other forms of mandated mediation, it is essential that mediators assigned to the parties have the requisite training and experience.

Comments:

Mediators should have information available for the parties regarding their relevant training, education, and experience.

The requirements for appearing on a list of mediators must be made public and available to interested persons.

When mediators are appointed by a court or institution, the appointing agency shall make reasonable efforts to ensure that each mediator is qualified for the particular mediation.

V. Confidentiality: A Mediator Shall Maintain the Reasonable Expectation of the Parties with Regard to Confidentiality.

The reasonable expectations of the parties with regard to confidentiality shall be met by the mediator. The parties' expectations of confidentiality depend on the circumstance of the mediation and any agreements they may make. The mediator shall not disclose any matter that a party expects to be confidential unless given permission by all parties or unless required by law or other public policy.

Comments:

The parties may make their own rules with respect to confidentiality, or the accepted practice of an individual mediator or institution may dictate a particular set of expectations. Since the parties' expectations regarding confidentiality are important, the mediator should discuss these expectations with the parties.

If the mediator holds private sessions with a party, the nature of these sessions with regard to confidentiality should be discussed prior to undertaking such sessions. In order to protect the integrity of the mediation, a mediator should avoid communicating information about how the parties acted in the mediation process, the merits of the case, or settlement offers. The mediator may report, if required, whether parties appeared at a scheduled mediation.

Where the parties have agreed that all or a portion of the information disclosed during a mediation is confidential, the parties' agreement should be respected by the mediator.

Confidentiality should not be construed to limit or prohibit the effective monitoring, research, or evaluation of mediation programs by responsible persons. Under appropriate circumstances, researchers may be permitted to obtain access to statistical data and, with the permission of the parties, to individual case files, observations of live mediation, and interviews with participants.

VI. Quality of the Process: A Mediator Shall Conduct the Mediation Fairly, Diligently, and in a Manner Consistent with the Principle of Self-Determination by the Parties.

A mediator shall work to ensure a quality process and to encourage mutual respect among the parties. A quality process requires a commitment by the mediator to diligence and procedural fairness. There should be adequate opportunity for each party in the mediation to participate in the discussions. The parties decide when and under what conditions they will reach an agreement or terminate a mediation.

Comments:

A mediator may agree to mediate only when he or she is prepared to commit the attention essential to an effective mediation.

Mediators should only accept cases when they can satisfy the reasonable expectations of the parties concerning the timing of the process. A mediator should not allow a mediation to be unduly delayed by the parties or their representatives.

The presence or absence of persons at a mediation depends on the agreement of the parties and mediator. The parties and mediator may agree that others may be excluded from particular sessions or from the entire mediation process.

The primary purpose of a mediator is to facilitate the parties' voluntary agreement. This role differs substantially from other professional-client relationships. Mixing the role of a mediator and the role of a professional advising a client is problematic, and mediators must strive to distinguish between the roles. A mediator should, therefore, refrain from providing professional advice. Where appropriate, a mediator should recommend that parties seek outside professional advice, or consider resolving their dispute through arbitration, counseling, neutral evaluation, or other processes. A mediator who undertakes, at the request of the parties, an additional dispute resolution role in the same matter assumes increased responsibilities and obligations that may be governed by the standards of other professions.

A mediator shall withdraw from a mediation or postpone a session if the mediation is being used to further illegal conduct, or if a party is unable to participate due to drug, alcohol, or other physical or mental incapacity.

Mediators should not permit their behavior in the mediation process to be guided by a desire for a high settlement rate.

VII. Advertising and Solicitation: A Mediator Shall Be Truthful in Advertising and Solicitation for Mediation

Advertising or any other communication with the public concerning services offered or regarding the education, training, and expertise of the mediator shall be truthful. A mediator shall refrain from promises and guarantees of results.

Comments:

It is imperative that communication with the public educate and instill confidence in the process.

In an advertisement or other communication to the public, a mediator may make reference to meeting state, national, or private organization qualifications only if the entity referred to has a procedure for qualifying mediators and the mediator has been duly granted the requisite status.

VIII. Fees: A Mediator Shall Fully Disclose and Explain the Basis of Compensation, Fees, and Charges to the Parties.

The parties should be provided sufficient information about fees at the outset of a mediation to determine if they wish to retain the services of a mediator. If a mediator charges fees, the fees shall be reasonable, considering, among other things, the mediation service, the type and complexity of the matter, the expertise of the mediator, the time required, and the rates customary in the community. The better practice in reaching an understanding about fees is to set down the arrangements in a written agreement.

Comments:

A mediator should not enter into a fee agreement which is contingent upon the result of the mediation or amount of the settlement.

Co-mediators who share a fee should hold to standards of reasonableness in determining the allocation of fees.

A mediator should not accept a fee for referral of a matter to another mediator or to any other person.

IX. Obligations to the Mediation Process: Mediators Have a Duty to Improve the Practice of Mediation.

Comments:

Mediators are regarded as knowledgeable in the process of mediation. They have an obligation to use their knowledge to help educate the public about mediation; to make mediation accessible to those who would like to use it; to correct abuses; and to improve their professional skills and abilities.

Copies of the Model Standards of Conduct for Mediators are available from the offices of the participating organizations.

We wish to express our appreciation for a grant from the Harry De Jur Foundation.

Appendix J

Selected ABA Model Rules of Professional Conduct

Copies of the ABA Model Rules of Professional Conduct, 2002 Edition are available from Member Services, American Bar Association, 750 North Lake Shore Drive, Chicago, IIL 60611, (800) 285-2221.

SELECTED ABA MODEL RULES OF
PROFESSIONAL CONDUCT
(Effective February, 2002)

RULE 1.4: COMMUNICATION

(a) A lawyer shall:

(1) promptly inform the client of any decision or circumstance with respect to which the client's informed consent, as defined in Rule 1.0(e), is required by these Rules;

(2) reasonably consult with the client about the means by which the client's objectives are to be accomplished;

(3) keep the client reasonably informed about the status of the matter;

(4) promptly comply with reasonable requests for information; and

(5) consult with the client about any relevant limitation on the lawyer's conduct when the lawyer knows that the client expects assistance not permitted by the Rules of Professional Conduct or other law.

(b) A lawyer shall explain a matter to the extent reasonably necessary to permit the client to make informed decisions regarding the representation.

RULE 1.6: CONFIDENTIALITY OF INFORMATION

(a) A lawyer shall not reveal information relating to the representation of a client unless the client gives informed consent, the disclosure is impliedly authorized in order to carry out the representation or the disclosure is permitted by paragraph (b).

(b) A lawyer may reveal information relating to the representation of a client to the extent the lawyer reasonably believes necessary:

(1) to prevent reasonably certain death or substantial bodily harm;

(2) to secure legal advice about the lawyer's compliance with these Rules;

(3) to establish a claim or defense on behalf of the lawyer in a controversy between the lawyer and the client, to establish a defense to a criminal charge or civil claim against the lawyer based upon conduct in which the client was involved, or to respond to

allegations in any proceeding converning the lawyer's representation of the client; or

(4) to comply with other law or a court order.

RULE 1.7: CONFLICT OF INTEREST: CURRENT CLIENTS

(a) Except as provided in paragraph (b), a lawyer shall not represent a client if the representation involves a concurrent conflict of interest. A concurrent conflict of interest exists if:

(1) the representation of one client will be directly adverse to another client; or

(2) there is a significant risk that the representation of one or more clients will be materially limited by the lawyer's responsibilities to another client, a former client or a third person or by a personal interest of the lawyer.

(b) Notwithstanding the existence of a concurrent conflict of interest under paragraph (a), a lawyer may represent a client if:

(1) the lawyer reasonably believes that the lawyer will be able to provide competent and diligent representation to each affected client;

(2) the representation is not prohibited by law;

(3) the representation does not involve the assertion of a claim by one client against another client representated by the lawyer in the same litigation or other proceeding before a tribunal; and

(4) each affected client gives informed consent, confirmed in writing.

RULE 4.1: TRUTHFULNESS IN STATEMENTS TO OTHERS

In the course of representing a client a lawyer shall not knowingly:

(a) make a false statement of material fact or law to a third person; or

(b) fail to disclose a materials fact when disclosure is necessary to avoid assisting a criminal or fraudulent act by a client, unless disclosure is prohibited by Rule 1.6.

RULE 4.2: COMMUNICATION WITH PERSON REPRESENTED BY COUNSEL

In representing a client, a lawyer shall not communicate about the subject of the representation with a person the lawyer knows to be represented by another lawyer in the matter, unless the lawyer has the consent of the other lawyer or is authorized to do so by law of a court order.

RULE 4.3: DEALING WITH UNREPRESENTED PERSON

In dealing on behalf of a client with a person who is not represented by counsel, a lawyer shall not state or imply that the lawyer is disinterested. When the lawyer knows or reasonably should know that the unrepresented person misunderstand the lawyer's role in the matter, the lawyer shall make reasonable efforts to correct the misunderstanding. The lawyer shall not give legal advice to an unrepresented person, other than the advice to secure counsel, if the lawyer knows or reasonably should know that the interests of such a person are or have a reasonable possibility of being in conflict with the interest of the client.

RULE 8.4: MISCONDUCT

It is professional misconduct for a lawyer to:

(a) violate or attempt to violate the Rule of Professional Conduct, knowingly assist or induce another to do so, or do so through the acts of another;

(b) commit a criminal act that reflects adversely on the lawyer's honesty, trustworthiness or fitness as a lawyer in other respects;

(c) engage in conduct involving dishonesty, fraud, deceit or misrepresentation;

(d) engage in conduct that is prejudicial to the administration of justice;

(e) state or imply an ability to influence improperly a government agency or official or to achieve results by means that violate the Rules of Professional Conduct or other law; or

(f) knowingly assist a judge or judicial officer in conduct that is a violation of applicable rules of judicial conduct or other law.

Appendix K

Organizations Offering ADR Services

Organizations Offering ADR Services

EASTERN UNITED STATES

Organization	Contract Info.	Type of Disputes
American Arbitration Association	New York, NY (212) 716-5800 www.adr.org	General civil
	Boston, MA (617) 451-6600 www.adr.org	
	Atlanta, GA (404) 325-0101 www.adr.org	
	Miami, FL (305) 358-7777 www.adr.org	
Arbitration Forums, Inc.	Tampa, FL (813) 931-4004 www.arb.file.org	Insurance claims
Clean Sites	Alexandria, VA (703) 838-0710	Environmental
JAMS	Boston, MA (617) 228-0200 www.jamsadr.com	General civil
	New York, NY (212) 751-2700 www.jamsadr.com	
	Washington, DC (202) 942-9180 www.jamsadr.com	
	Atlanta, GA (404) 588-0900 www.jamsadr.com	

International Centre for Settlement of Investment Disputes (Pub. Internat. Org.)	Washington, DC (202) 477-1234 www.worldbank.org	International investment
Resolution Resources, Inc.	Atlanta, GA (404) 215-9800 www.clrp.com	General civil
World Wildlife Fund	Washington, DC (202) 293-4800 www.worldwildlife.org	Environmental; natural resources

CENTRAL UNITED STATES

ADR Systems of America, LLC	Chicago, IL (312) 960-2264 www.adrsystems.com adrsystems@aol.com	
American Arbitration Association	Chicago, IL (312) 616-6560 www.adr.org	General civil
	Denver, CO (303) 831-0823 www.adr.org	
	Cincinnati, OH (513) 241-8434 www.adr.org	
	Minneapolis, MN (612) 332-6545 www.adr.org	
	St. Louis, MO (314) 621-7175 www.adr.org	
Center for Reso- lution of Disputes	Cincinnati, OH (513) 721-4466 www.cfrdmediation.com	Private and public policy disputes

Chicago International Dispute Resolution Association (CIDRA)	Chicago, IL (312) 782-8477 www.cidra.org	International
Global Solutions	Inverness, IL (847) 358-8856 globalbohn@msn.com	Commercial and international
JAMS	Chicago, IL (312) 739-0200 www.jams.com	General civil
	Indianapolis, IN (317) 231-6320 www.vbradr.com	
	Denver, CO (303) 534-1254 www.jamsadr.com	
	Dallas, TX (214) 744-5267 www.jamsadr.com	
	Houston, TX (713) 651-1400 www.jamsadr.com	
Judicial Dispute Resolution, Inc.	Chicago, IL (312) 917-8828 jdrinc@jdrinc.com	General civil
Mediation Research and Education Project, Inc.	Chicago, IL (312) 503-8426 www.mrep.org	Coal industry, manufacturing, communications, education

WESTERN UNITED STATES

American Arbitration Association	San Franciso, CA (415) 981-3901 www.adr.org	General civil
	Los Angeles, CA (213) 383-6516 www.adr.org	

	Salt Lake City, UT (801) 531-9748 www.adr.org	
	Seattle, WA (206) 622-6435 www.adr.org	
CDR Associates	Boulder, CO (303) 442-7367 www.mediate.org	Commercial, government
JAMS	San Francisco, CA (415) 982-5267 www.jamsadr.org	
	Los Angeles, CA (213) 620-1133 www.jamsadr.org	
	Portland, OR (800) 626-5267 www.jamsadr.org	
	Seattle, WA (206) 622-5267 www.jamsadr.org	
Judicial Arbiter Group, Inc.	Colorado Springs, CO (719) 473-8282 www.jaginc.com	General civil
	Denver, CO (303) 572-1919 www.jaginc.com	
Keystone Center	Keystone, CO (303) 513-5800/7220 www.keystone.org	Environmental
United States Arbitration & Mediation, Inc.	Seattle, WA (206) 467-0794 www.usamwa.com	Commercial, tort

NONPROFIT ORGANIZATIONS THAT STUDY
AND PROMOTE ADR

ABA Section of Dispute Resolution 740 15th Street, N.W Washington, DC 20005	(202) 662-1680 www.abanet.org/ dispute dispute@abanet.org	ADR services to ABA members and general public
Association for Conflict Resolution 1527 New Hampshire Ave, N.W. Washington, DC 20005	(202) 667-9700 www.acresolution.org info@acresolution.org	Association of ADR professional and supporters
CPR Institute for Dispute Resolution 366 Madison Avenue New York, NY 10017	(212) 949-6490 www.cpradr.org	Promotes ADR through corporate policy statements
American Arbitration Association 140 W. 51st Street New York, NY 10020	(212) 716-5800 www.adr.org usadrpub@arb.com	ADR publications, training, meetings, and seminars
Center for Analysis of Alternative Dispute Resolution Systems 11 E. Adams St. Suite 500 Chicago, IL 60603	(312) 922-6475 ext. 924 www.caadrs.org caadrs@caadrs.org	Conducts studies of the effectiveness of court sponsored ADR programs
Center for Conflict Resolution 11 E. Adams St. Suite 500 Chicago, IL 60603	(312) 922-6464 www.caadrs.org	ADR training and mediation center

413

Appendix L

Online Dispute Resolution Organizations

ONLINE DISPUTE RESOLUTION ORGANIZATIONS

Unless otherwise indicated, the listed websites of ODR service providers were active as of December 2001.

1-2-3-Settle (http://www.123Settle.com)

AllSettle.Com (also called SettlementNOW)(http://www.allsettle.com)

Better Business Bureau Online (http://www.bbbonline.org)

ClaimChoice.com (http://claimchoice.com/Public/PublicHomepage.jsp)

ClaimNegotiator (http://www.claimnegotiator.com/cnhome.nsf/ frameset)

ClaimResolver.com (http://www.claimresolver.com/ecAbout.nsf/ mainpage?OpenPage)

ClickNSettle.com (http://www.clicknsettle.com)

CPR Institute for Dispute Resolution (http://www.cpradr.org/ ICANNmenu.htm)

Cyberarbitration (planned) (http//www.cyberarbitration.com)

Cybercourt (planned) (http://www.cybercourt.com)

Cybersettle (http://www.cybersettle.com)

The Domain Magistrate (http://www.domainmagistrate.com)

ECODIR (http://www.ecodir.org)

E-Mediation (also ODR.NL)(planned) (http://www.e-mediation.nl/ english.shtml)

e-Mediator (http//www.consensus.uk.com/e-mediator.html)

eResolution (htp://www.eresolution.ca)

FordJourney (http://www.arbitrators.org/fordjourney/INDEX.HTM)

FSM (http://www.fsm.de/ueb/index.html)

iCourthouse (http://www.icourthouse.com)

iLevel (http://www.ilevel.com/)

IntelliCOURT (http://www.intellicourt.com)

Internet Neutral (http://www.internetneutral.com)

Intersettle (http://www.intersettle.co.uk)

IRIS (http://www.iris.sgdg.org/mediation)

Judicial Dispute Resolution, Inc. (http://www.jdrinc.com)

Mediation Arbitration Resolution Services (MARS)
    (http://www.resolvemydispute.com)

National Arbitration Forum (http://www.arb-forum.com/domains)

New Court City (http://www.newcourtcity.com)

NovaForum.com (http://www.novaforum.com)

One Accord (http://www.oneaccordinc.com/)

Online Disputes (planned) (http://www.onlinedisputes.org)

Online Ombuds Office (http://www.ombuds.org)

Online Resolution (http://www.onlineresolution.com);
    (http://www.onlinearb.com); (http://www.onlinemediators.com); and
    (http://www.onlinenegotiation.com)

ResolveitNow.com (http://www.resolveitnow.com)

Resolution Forum (http://www.resolutionforum.org)

SettlementOnline (http://www.settlementonline.com/Index.html)

SettleOnline (http://www.settleonline.com)

SettleSmart (http://www.settlesmart.com)

SettleTheCase (http://www.settlethecase.com/main.html)

SquareTrade (http://www.squaretrade.com) and
    (http://www.transecure.org)

State of Michigan (planned) (http://www.michigancybercourt.net)

The Claim Room (http://www.theclaimroom.com)

TRUSTe (http://www.truste.org)

U.S. Settle (http://www.ussettle.com)

Virtual Magistrate (http://www.vmag.org)

WebAssured.com (http://www.webassured.com)

WEBDispute.com (mediation planned) (http://www.webdispute.com)

Web Dispute Resolution (http://www.webdisputeresolutions.com)

WebMediate (http://www.webmediate.com)

WeCanSettle (http:www.wecansettle.com)

Web Trader (http://www.which.net/webtrader)

World Intellectual Property Organization (WIPO)
    (http://www.arbiter.wipo.int/domains)

Word&Bond (http://www.wordandbond.com)

Appendix M

Uniform Mediation Act
(Without Comments)

The Uniform Mediation Act is reprinted here without comments by permission of the National Conference of Commissioners on Uniform State Laws

UNIFORM MEDIATION ACT

Drated by the

NATIONAL CONFERENCE OF COMMISSIONERS
ON UNIFORM STATE LAWS

and by it

APPROVED AND RECOMMENDED FOR ENACTMENT
IN ALL THE STATES

at its

ANNUAL CONFERENCE
MEETING IN ITS ONE-HUNDRED-AND-TENTH YEAR
WHITE SULPHUR SPRINGS, WEST VIRGINIA
AUGUST 10–17, 2001

WITHOUT COMMENTS

NATIONAL CONFERENCE OF COMMISSIONERS ON UNIFORM STATE LAWS DRAFTING COMMITTEE ON UNIFORM MEDIATION ACT:

MICHAEL B. GETTY, 1560 Sandburg Terrace, Suite 1104, Chicago, IL 60610, *Chair*

PHILLIP CARROLL, 120 E. Fourth Street, Little Rock, AR 72201

JOSE FELICIANO, 3200 National City Center, 1900 E. 9th Street, Cleveland, OH 44114-3485, *American Bar Association Member*

STANLEY M. FISHER, 1100 Huntington Building, 925 Euclid Avenue, Cleveland, OH 44115-1475, *Enactment Coordinator*

ROGER C. HENDERSON, University of Arizona, James E. Rogers College of Law, Mountain and Speedway Streets, Tucson, AZ 85721, *Committee on Style Liaison*

ELIZABETH KENT, P.O. Box 2560, Honolulu, HI 96804

RICHARD C. REUBEN, University of Missouri Columbia School of Law, Hulston Hall, Columbia, MO 65211, *Associate Reporter*

NANCY H. ROGERS, Ohio State University, Michael E. Moritz College of Law, 55 W. 12th Avenue, Columbus, OH 43210, *National Conference Reporter*

FRANK E.A. SANDER, Harvard University Law School, Cambridge, MA 02138, *American Bar Association Member*

BYRON D. SHER, State Capitol, Suite 2082, Sacramento, CA 95814

MARTHA LEE WALTERS, Suite 220, 975 Oak Street, Eugene, OR 97401

JOAN ZELDON, D.C. Superior Court, 500 Indiana Ave., Washington, DC 20001

EX OFFICIO

JOHN L. McCLAUGHERTY, P.O. Box 553, Charleston, WV, 25322, *President*

LEON M. McCORKLE, JR., P.O. Box 387, Dublin, OH 43017-0387, *Division Chair*

AMERICAN BAR ASSOCIATION ADVISOR

ROBERTA COOPER RAMO, Sunwest Building, Suite 1000, 500 W. 4th Street, NW, Albuquerque, NM 87102

EXECUTIVE DIRECTOR

FRED H. MILLER, University of Oklahoma, College of Law, 300 Timberdell Road, Norman, OK 73019, *Executive Director*

WILLIAM J. PIERCE, 1505 Roxbury Road, Ann Arbor, MI 48104, *Executive Director Emeritus*

Copies of this Act may be obtained from:

NATIONAL CONFERENCE OF COMMISSIONERS
ON UNIFORM STATE LAWS
211 E. Ontario Street, Suite 1300
Chicago, Illinois 60611
312/915-0195
www.nccusl.org

ABA SECTION ON DISPUTE RESOLUTION DRAFTING
COMMITTEE ON UNIFORM MEDIATION ACT

THOMAS J. MOYER, *Co-Chair*, Supreme Court of Ohio, 30 E. Broad Street, Columbus, OH 43266

ROBERTA COOPER RAMO, *Co-Chair*, Modrall, Sperling, Roehl, Harris & Sisk, P.A., Sunwest Building, Suite 1000, albuquerque, NM 87102

JAMES DIGGS, PPG Industries, 1 PPG Place, Pittsburgh, PA 15272

JOSE FELICIANO, Baker & Hostetler, 3200 National City Center, 1900 East 9th St., Cleveland, OH 44114

MICHAEL B. GETTY, 1560 Sandburg Terrace, Suite 1104, Chicago, IL 60610, *NCCUSL Representative*

EMILY STEWART HAYNES, Supreme Court of Ohio, 30 E. Broad Street, Columbus, OH 43266, *Reporting Coordinator*

RICHARD C. REUBEN, University of Missouri-Columbia School of Law, Hulston Hall, Columbia, MO 65211, *Reporter*

NANCY H. ROGERS, Ohio State University, College of Law and Office of Academic Affairs, 203 Bricker Hall, 190 N. Oval Mall, Columbus, OH 43210, Coordinator, *Faculty Advisory Committee*

FRANK E.A. SANDER, Harvard Law School, Cambridge, MA 01238

JUDITH SAUL, Community Dispute Resolution Center, 120 W. State Street, Ithaca, NY 14850

ANNICE M. WAGNER, Court of Appeals of the District of Columbia, 500 Indiana Ave., NW, Washington, DC 20001

UNIFORM MEDIATION ACT

SECTION 1. TITLE. This [Act] may be cited as the Uniform Mediation Act.

SECTION 2. DEFINITIONS. In this [Act]:

(1) "Mediation" means a process in which a mediator facilitates communication and negotiation between parties to assist them in reaching a voluntary agreement regarding their dispute.

(2) "Mediation communication" means a statement, whether oral or in a record or verbal or nonverbal, that occurs during a mediation or is made for purposes of considering, conducting, participating in, initiating, continuing, or reconvening a mediation or retaining a mediator.

(3) "Mediator" means an individual who conducts a mediation.

(4) "Nonparty participant" means a person, other than a party or mediator, that participates in a mediation.

(5) "Mediation party" means a person that participates in a mediation and whose agreement is necessary to resolve the dispute.

(6) "Person" means an individual, corporation, business trust, estate, trust, partnership, limited liability company, association, joint venture, government; governmental subdivision, agency, or instrumentality; public corporation, or any other legal or commercial entity.

(7) "Proceeding" means:

(A) a judicial, administrative, arbitral, or other adjudicative process, including related pre-hearing and post-hearing motions, conferences, and discovery; or

(B) a legislative hearing or similar process.

(8) "Record" means information that is inscribed on a tangible medium or that is stored in an electronic or other medium and is retrievable in perceivable form.

(9) "Sign" means:

(A) to execute or adopt a tangible symbol with the present intent to authenticate a record; or

(B) to attach or logically associate an electronic symbol, sound, or process to or with a record with the present intent to authenticate a record.

SECTION 3. SCOPE.

(a) Except as otherwise provided in subsection (b) or (c), this [Act] applies to a mediation in which:

(1) the mediation parties are required to mediate by statute or court or administrative agency rule or referred to mediation by a court, administrative agency, or arbitrator;

(2) the mediation parties and the mediator agree to mediate in a record that demonstrates an expectation that mediation communications will be privileged against disclosure; or

(3) the mediation parties use as a mediator an individual who holds himself or herself out as a mediator or the mediation is provided by a person that holds itself out as providing mediation.

(b) The [Act] does not apply to a mediation:

(1) relating to the establishment, negotiation, administration, or termination of a collective bargaining relationship;

(2) relating to a dispute that is pending under or is part of the processes established by a collective bargaining agreement, except that the [Act] applies to a mediation arising out of a dispute that has been filed with an administrative agency or court;

(3) conducted by a judge who might make a ruling on the case; or

(4) conducted under the auspices of;

(A) a primary or secondary school if all the parties are students or

(B) a correctional institution for youths if all the parties are residents of that institution.

(c) If the parties agree in advance in a signed record, or a record of proceeding reflects agreements by the parties, that all or part of a mediation is not privileged, the privileges under Sections 4 through 6 do not apply to the mediation or part agreed upon. However, Sections 4 through 6 apply to a mediation communication made by a person that has not received actual notice of the agreement before the communication is made.

Legislative Note: To the extent that the Act applies to mediations conducted under the authority of a State's courts, State judiciaries should consider enacting conforming court rules.

SECTION 4. PRIVILEGE AGAINST DISCLOSURE; ADMISSIBILITY; DISCOVERY.

(a) Except as otherwise provided in Section 6, a mediation communication is privileged as provided in subsection (b) and is not subject to discovery or admissible in evidence in a proceeding unless waived or precluded as providod by Section 5.

(b) In a proceeding, the following privileges apply:

(1) A mediation party may refuse to disclose, and may prevent any other person from disclosing, a mediation communication.

(2) A mediator may refuse to disclose a mediation communication, and may prevent any other person from disclosing a mediation communication of the mediator.

(3) A nonparty participant may refuse to disclose, and may prevent any other person from disclosing, a mediation communication of the nonparty participant.

(c) Evidence or information that is otherwise admissible or subject to discovery does not become inadmissible or protected from discovery solely by reason of its disclosure or use in a mediation.

Legislative Note: The Act does not supersede existing state statutes that make mediators incompetent to testify, or that provide for costs and attorney fees to mediators who are wrongfully subpoenaed. See, e.g., Cal. Evid. Code Section 703.5 (West 1994).

SECTION 5. WAIVER AND PRECLUSION OF PRIVILEGE.

(a) A privilege under Section 4 may be waived in a record or orally during a proceeding if it is expressly waived by all parties to the mediation and:

(1) in the case of the privilege of a mediator, it is expressly waived by the mediator; and

(2) in the case of the privilege of a nonparty participant, it is expressly waived by the nonparty participant.

(b) A person that discloses or makes a representation about a mediation communication which prejudices another person in a proceeding is precluded from asserting a privilege under Section 4, but only to the extent necessary for the person prejudiced to respond to the representation or disclosure.

(c) A person that intentionally uses a mediation to plan, attempt to commit or commit a crime, or to conceal an ongoing crime or ongoing criminal activity is precluded from asserting a privilege under Section 4.

SECTION 6. EXCEPTIONS TO PRIVILEGE.

(a) There is no privilege under Section 4 for a mediation communication that is:

(1) in an agreement evidenced by a record signed by all parties to the agreement;

(2) available to the public under [insert statutory reference to open records act] or made during a session of a mediation which is open, or is required by law to be open, to the public;

(3) a threat or statement of a plan to inflict bodily injury or commit a crime of violence;

(4) intentionally used to plan a crime, attempt to commit or commit a crime, or to conceal an ongoing crime or ongoing criminal activity;

(5) sought or offered to prove or disprove a claim or complaint of professional misconduct or malpractice filed against a mediator;

(6) except as otherwise provided in subsection (c), sought or offered to prove or disprove a claim or complaint of professional misconduct or malpractice filed against a mediation party, nonparty participant, or representative of a party based on conduct occurring during a mediation; or

(7) sought or offered to prove or disprove abuse, neglect, abandonment, or exploitation in a proceeding in which a child or adult protective services agency is a party, unless the

[Alternative A: [State to insert, for example, child or adult protection] case is referred by a court to mediation and a public agency particpates.]

[Alternative B: public agency particpates in the [State to insert, for example, child or adult protection] mediation].

(b) There is no privilege under Section 4 if a court, administrative agency, or arbitrator finds, after a hearing in camera, that the party seeking discovery or the proponent of the evidence has shown that the evidence is not otherwise available, that there is a need for the evidence that substantially outweighs the interest in protecting confidentiality, and that the mediation communication is sought or offered in:

(1) a court proceeding involving a felony [or misdemeanor]; or

(2) except as otherwise provided in subsection (c), a proceeding to prove a claim to rescind or reform or a defense to avoid liability on a contract arising out of the mediation.

(c) A mediator may not be compelled to provide evidence of a mediation communication referred to in subsection (a)(6) or (b)(2).

(d) If a mediation communication is not privileged under subsection (a) or (b), only the portion of the communication necessary for the application of the exception from nondisclosure may be admitted. Admission of evidence under subsection (a) or (b) does not render the evidence, or any other mediation communication, discoverable or admissible for any other purpose.

Legislative Note: If the enacting state does not have an open records act, the following language in paragraph (2) of subsection (a) needs to be deleted: "available to the public under [insert statutory reference to open records act] or".

SECTION 7. PROHIBITED MEDIATOR REPORTS

(a) Except as required in subsection (b), a mediator may not make a report, assessment, evaluation, recommendation, finding, or other communication regarding a mediation to a court, administrative agency, or other authority that may make a ruling on the dispute that is the subject of the mediation.

(b) A mediator may disclose:

(1) whether the mediation occurred or has terminated, whether a settlement was reached, and attendance;

(2) a mediation communication as permitted under Section 6; or

(3) a mediation communication evidencing abuse, neglect, abandonment, or exploitation of an individual to a public agency responsible for protecting individuals against such mistreatment.

(c) A communication made in violation of subsection (a) may not be considered by a court, administrative agency, or arbitrator.

SECTION 8. CONFIDENTIALITY. Unless subject to the [insert statutory references to open meetings act and open records act], mediation communications are confidential to the extent agreed by the parties or provided by other law or rule of this State.

SECTION 9. MEDIATOR'S DISCLOSURE OF CONFLICTS OF INTEREST; BACKGROUND.

(a) Before accepting a mediation, an individual who is requested to serve as a mediator shall:

(1) make an inquiry that is reasonable under the circumstances to determine whether there are any known facts that a reasonable individual would consider likely to affect the impartiality of the mediator, including a financial or personal interest in the outcome of the mediation and an existing or past relationship with a mediation party or foreseeable participant in the mediation; and

(2) disclose any such known fact to the mediation parties as soon as is practical before accepting a mediation.

434

(b) If a mediator learns any fact described in subsection (a)(1) after accepting a mediation, the mediator shall disclose it as soon as is practicable.

(c) At the request of a mediation party, an individual who is requested to serve as a mediator shall disclose the mediator's qualifications to mediate a dispute.

(d) A person that violates subsection [(a) or (b)] [(a), (b), or (g)] is precluded by the violation from asserting a privilege under Section 4.

(e) Subsections (a), (b), [and] (c), [and] [(g)] is precluded by the violation from asserting a privilege under Section 4.

(f) This [Act] does not require that a mediator have a special qualification by background or profession.

[(g) A mediator must be impartial, unless after disclosure of the facts required in subsections (a) and (b) to be disclosed, the parties agree otherwise.]

SECTION 10. PARTICIPATION IN MEDIATION. An attorney or other individual designated by a party may accompany the party to and participate in a mediation. A waiver of participation given before the mediation may be rescinded. The right to accompaniment does not operate to excuse any participation requirements for the parties themselves.

SECTION 11. RELATION TO ELECTRONIC SIGNATURES IN GLOBAL AND NATIONAL COMMERCE ACT. This [Act] modifies, limits, or supersedes the federal Electronic Signatures in Global and National Commerce Act, 15 U.S.C. Section 7001 et seq., but this [Act] does not modify, limit, or supersede Section 101(c) of that Act or authorize electronic delivery of any of the notices described in Section 103(b) of that Act.

SECTION 12. UNIFORMITY OF APPLICATION AND CONSTRUCTION. In applying and construing this [Act], consideration should be given to the need to promote uniformity of the law with respect to its subject matter among States that enact it.

SECTION 13. SEVERABILITY CLAUSE. If any provision of this [Act] or its application to any person or circumstance is held invalid, the invalidity does not affect other provisions or applications of this [Act] which can be given effect without the invalid provision or application, and to this end the provisions of this [Act] are severable.

SECTION 14. EFFECTIVE DATE. This [Act] takes effect............... .

SECTION 15. REPEALS. The following acts and parts of acts are hereby repealed:

(1)

(2)

(3)

SECTION 16. APPLICATION TO EXISTING AGREEMENTS OR REFERRALS.

(a) This [Act] governs a mediation pursuant to a referral or an agreement to mediate made on or after [the effective date of this [Act]].

(b) On or after [a delayed date], this [Act] governs an agreement to mediate whenever made.

INDEX

The Arbitrator's Handbook

John W. Cooley

"Being concise—whether it be in describing each stage of the arbitration process or boiling down the arbitration's hearing functions into a single checklist—is one of Cooley's strengths. No wonder the book's publisher is promoting the book as a quick reference tool that can be brought to hearing sessions. A handy reference tool for arbitrators and advocates—this book definitely is."—Dispute Resolution Journal

The Arbitrator's Handbook offers a full range of features geared to assist the arbitrator in performing his or her basic duties. Chapter One provides basic information on the nature of arbitration, including a description of its stages and types, and its benefits and limitations. Cooley defines the role, authority, and ethics requirements of the arbitrator. Chapter Two describes the pre-hearing functions and duties of the arbitrator, focusing on the time of initiation of the arbitration as well as the preparation stage. Chapter Three focuses on the arbitrator's hearing functions and duties. It covers such topics as the arbitrator's opening statement, handling preliminary matters, a review of basic rules of evidence, and making rulings on motions and objections. Chapter Four, on the arbitrator's post-hearing functions and duties, addresses such topics as ruling on post-hearing motions, deciding the merits of the case, and drafting the award and the opinion supporting the award.

In addition, tables and checklists are included in the appendices for key actions at critical stages of the arbitration process. The appendices also contain sample arbitration forms and rules of leading arbitration organizations, making this the most comprehensive text available for "hands-on" arbitration instruction.

464 pp., © 1998, ISBN 1-55681-616-2

To order: 800.225.6482 or www.nita.org